# THE ASHGATE RESEARCH COMPANION TO BLACK SOCIOLOGY

*As we deepen into the twenty-first century, there is abundant evidence that Black Sociology is the original American sociology, despite the dominant narratives of the discipline. The contents of Wright II and Wallace's Ashgate Research Companion to Black Sociology show that not only has Black Sociology continued since its late nineteenth century beginnings, but, that it is thriving and continuously pushing a rigorous and impactful sociology across every substantive area of the discipline.*

David L. Brunsma, Virginia Tech, USA

*In this necessary and expansive volume, Earl Wright II and Edward V. Wallace build upon the great work and legacy of W.E.B. Du Bois. Drawing on Du Bois's sociological scholarship and agenda as the leader of the Atlanta Sociological Laboratory, this impressive book successfully brings together a wonderful array of scholars to deepen our understanding and appreciation for Black Sociology.*

Marcus Anthony Hunter, UCLA, USA and author of *Black Citymakers: How the Philadelphia Negro Changed Urban America*

*The Ashgate Research Companion to Black Sociology is a must-read for anyone teaching introductory sociology, race relations or any related subject. The editors have done a wonderful job of finding young creative scholars to cover contemporary topics such as parental incarceration and its effects on children, stand-your-ground laws, and the effects of job stratification on the working class to name a few. The clustering of the topics along with the origins of Black or Du Boisian Sociology is extremely relevant to the societal changes currently taking place around the world.*

Obie Clayton, Clark Atlanta University, USA

ASHGATE
**RESEARCH**
COMPANION

The *Ashgate Research Companions* are designed to offer scholars and graduate students a comprehensive and authoritative state-of-the-art review of current research in a particular area. The companions' editors bring together a team of respected and experienced experts to write chapters on the key issues in their speciality, providing a comprehensive reference to the field.

# The Ashgate Research Companion to Black Sociology

*Edited by*

EARL WRIGHT II
*University of Cincinnati, USA*

EDWARD V. WALLACE
*University of Cincinnati, USA*

ASHGATE

Published by
Ashgate Publishing Limited
Wey Court East
Union Road
Farnham
Surrey, GU9 7PT
England

Ashgate Publishing Company
110 Cherry Street
Suite 3–1
Burlington, VT 05401–3818
USA

www.ashgate.com

**British Library Cataloguing in Publication Data**
A catalogue record for this book is available from the British Library.


**Library of Congress Cataloging-in-Publication Data**
Wright, Earl, II.
    The Ashgate research companion to Black sociology / by Earl Wright II and
    Edward V. Wallace.
        pages cm
    Includes bibliographical references and index.
    ISBN 978–1–4724–5676–2 (hardback : alk. paper) – ISBN 978–1–4724–5677–9 (ebook) –
    ISBN 978–1–4724–5678–6 (epub) 1. African Americans – Social conditions. 2. African
    Americans – Race identity. 3. Sociology – United States.
    I. Wallace, Edward V. II. Title.
    E185.86.W952 2015
    305.896'073–dc23                                                    2015004380


ISBN: 9781472456762 (hbk)
ISBN: 9781472456779 (ebk – PDF)
ISBN: 9781472456786 (ebk – ePUB)

Printed in the United Kingdom by Henry Ling Limited,
at the Dorset Press, Dorchester, DT1 1HD

# Contents

# List of Figures and Tables

## Figures

## Tables

# List of Contributors

**Omotayo O. Banjo** is an Assistant Professor in the Department of Communication at the University of Cincinnati. Her research focuses on racial representations in the media, with a particular interest in race-oriented entertainment. Dr. Banjo also examines the impact of media messages on individuals' perceptions of self and others.

**Littisha Bates** is an Assistant Professor of Sociology and faculty affiliate of the Department of Africana Studies at the University of Cincinnati. Her current research examines racial/ethnic differences in educational outcomes, with added focus on moving beyond customary white/ Black comparisons to include a number of racial/ethnic groups. Her work also examines specific ethnic groups as opposed to broad pan-ethnic categories. She is also examining within-group differences across socioeconomic strata as well as within-socioeconomic strata differences across racial/ethnic groups.

**Marye Bernard** holds a doctorate of nursing practice and is a family nurse practitioner at the Regional Medical Center in Memphis, Tennessee. She is an AECT-certified HIV/AIDS educator and one of the leading public speakers on the topic.

**Teresa A. Booker** is a political scientist and tenured Assistant Professor of Africana Studies at John Jay College of Criminal Justice (CUNY) in New York. Her research interests include peacekeeping, peacemaking, restorative justice and the implementation of public policy. In addition to authoring numerous peer-reviewed publications, her edited book *Race and Urban Communities* was published in 2014.

**Derrick R. Brooms** is Assistant Professor of Sociology at the University of Louisville. He also is a Task Force Member to the African American Male Initiative Program. His research interests include a focus on museums and contemporary exhibits on African American history and culture. His research also focuses on African American males by examining their educational experiences in both secondary and post-secondary institutions, along with their relationships and identity development.

**Timothy Broughton, D.A.** is the Director of Teaching and Learning and Instructor of History at Bishop State Community College in Mobile, Alabama. His research interests include the economic impact of unions in the African American community, cultural competency in health care, the treatment of African Americans in the Alabama Criminal Justice System, and the New Civil Rights Movement in the United States.

**Edith Burns, M.D.** is Professor of Medicine, Division of Geriatrics at the Medical College of Wisconsin and she holds adjunct appointments as Professor of Population Health-Epidemiology (MCW) and clinical Professor of Medicine at Marquette University. Her research expertise is in the area of geriatrics and internal medicine, with a focus on health behaviors, and beliefs and perceptions about disease as these relate to chronic illness and self-management. Her most recent work has addressed self-management of diabetes, joint dysfunction and use of agile technology to enhance self–management.

**Farrah Gafford Cambrice** is, currently, a non-institutionally affiliated independent scholar. Her research interests include race, class and disaster, with a specific focus on Hurricane Katrina that has resulted in peer-reviewed publications in the *Journal of Black Studies, Journal of Global Policy and Resilience* and *Journal of Urban History.*

**Malinda R. Conrad** is nationally certified (ANCC) Family Nurse Practitioner licensed in the states of Tennessee and Georgia. She provides chronic disease management and treatment to persons with metabolic and hypertensive disorders. In pursuance to her Doctorate in Nursing Practice degree, Malinda's current clinical focus is in grief and depression in persons living with the diagnosis of HIV/AIDS. Malinda completed requirements for the doctorate in May 2014, and is now Dr. Conrad.

**Katrinell M. Davis** is Assistant Professor of Sociology at the University of Vermont, where she teaches Race and Ethnic Relations courses, as well as courses exploring the intersections between race, gender and work trends within the American labor market. Her research interests concentrate on links between social stratification, the actions of state and labor-market institutions and the changing expressions of racialization within American society.

**Tomeka Davis** is Assistant Professor in the Department of Sociology at Georgia State University. Her areas of interests include the sociology of education, education policy and racial inequality. She has published research which examines the impact of race and class on school quality, the relationship between gentrification and charter school emergence, the association between charter school competition and achievement in traditional public schools and racial equity in school choice.

**Darwin Fishman** is Visiting Assistant Professor in Sociology and Criminology at California State University San Marcos. He has numerous publications including books including *Tarred and Feathered, Again: Racial Attacks on President Obama That Provoke, Disappear, and Fester; From Misunderstood Apathy to Radical Engagement: How Race, Gender, and Sexuality Influence Contemporary Youth Politics* and *Political Activities of African American Teenagers: A Case Study of High School Students in the Washington DC Metropolitan Area.* He has been a professor at Western Illinois University, Temple University and Stony Brook University and holds a Ph.D. in American Studies from the University of Maryland, College Park.

**Natalie M. Fountain, B.A.** is president of Fountain Consulting Services, a broad-based firm specializing in organizational development, communications and project management for non-profit organizations and small to medium-sized businesses. Prior to forming her consulting company, she followed her passion (and in the footsteps of three generations of educators within her family) to embark on a second career as a teacher in both Title 1 and National Blue Ribbon schools in the Florida state school system. She earned her B.A. in Business, graduating cum laude from Eckerd College in Saint Petersburg, Florida.

**Nathaniel Frederick II** is Assistant Professor in Department of Mass Communication at Winthrop University. His research focuses on representations of masculinity and race in television and film. He earned his Ph.D. in mass communication from Pennsylvania State University.

**Angelique Harris, Ph.D.** is Assistant Professor of Sociology in the Department of Social and Cultural Sciences at Marquette University. Her research and teaching interests include the sociology of health and illness, race and ethnicity, gender and sexuality, sociology of religion, urban studies, media studies and social movements. Her research program examines how women, people of color and LGBTQ people understand and construct social problems, and in particular, health issues and how their marginalization impacts their access to health care. Along with articles and other publications, she has authored the book *AIDS, Sexuality, and the Black Church: Making the Wounded Whole* and co-authored the writing reference book *Writing for Emerging Sociologists*.

**Kimberly Salas Harris, M.A.** serves as the Projector Director and Community Engagement Liaison for a health and wellness promotion program targeting African American women that is housed at the Bread of Healing Clinic in the Lindsay Heights neighborhood of Milwaukee. Her research interests include community health, urban populations, race and ethnicity, and gender and sexuality.

**Barbara A. Horner-Ibler, M.D., M.Div., M.S.W.** is the medical director of the Bread of Healing Clinic, a free clinic serving uninsured patients with chronic illness on Milwaukee's north side. The clinic is a teaching site for medical students and internal medicine residents from the University of Wisconsin School of Medicine and Public Health. Her research interest in medicine focuses on underserved care and outpatient medicine. In addition to the M.D., she has earned a master's degree in divinity and a master's in social work, both of which are used on a daily basis in her work at the medical director of a free clinic located in three Milwaukee churches.

**Hayward Derrick Horton** is Professor of Sociology in the School of Public Health at the State University of New York at Albany. His areas of specialty are demography, race/ethnicity and public sociology. Recognized internationally as the "Father of Critical Demography," he has published extensively in the area of the demography of racial inequality, entrepreneurship and the impact of race on wealth, status and power.

**Shewanee Howard-Baptiste** is currently Assistant Professor in the Department of Health and Human Performance at the University of Tennessee at Chattanooga. She teaches courses related to health behavior change, sociology of sport, and community and environmental health. She has also taught and studied abroad in Denmark, Switzerland, France, the Dominican Republic and Haiti, and has been teaching at the secondary and collegiate level for over 12 years.

**Sachin Karnik, Ph.D., L.C.S.W., C.P.S.,** is currently the Director of Prevention and Criminal Justice for the Delaware Council on Gambling Problems (DCGP), Inc. He worked with adolescents and their families for over eight years in outpatient counseling before joining DCGP. He uses a multi-systemic approach to tackle gambling addiction and related problems. Additionally, he gives workshops on linking gambling addiction with other addictions and mental health problems.

**Taralyn Keese** is a graduate student in the Department of Sociology at Georgia State University. Her dissertation explores the connections between gendered socialization, mental health and male-female relationships among Black women.

**Sheridan Quarless Kingsberry, M.S.W., Ph.D.**, is Associate Professor in the Department of Social Work at Delaware State University. She served as Principal Investigator/Project Director for the Pilot HOPE Project: A Community Partnership. Prior to joining DSU, she served as Executive Director of the Division of Programs for the New Jersey Department of State and held various administrative positions in higher education and non-profit organizations. She received the B.A. degree from Douglass College, M.S.W. from Rutgers University School of Social Work and Ph.D. from the Graduate School, Rutgers, the State University of New Jersey.

**Jerod D. Lindsey** is an undergraduate student majoring in Africana Studies. Jerod plans to attend graduate school.

**Marci Bounds Littlefield** received her Ph.D. from the University of Texas at Austin and the Master's of Public Affairs from the Lyndon B. Johnson Graduate School of Public Affairs. She has published in the areas of religion, race and gender and currently teaches sociology and African American studies at the Borough of Manhattan Community College in New York City.

**Lori Latrice Martin, Ph.D.**, is Associate Professor of Sociology and African and African American Studies at Louisiana State University. Martin is the author of numerous books and articles. Her book, *Black Asset Poverty and the Enduring Racial Award (First Forum Press)*, was named a *CHOICE* 2013 Outstanding Academic Title *and her* most recent book is the edited volume, *Out of Bounds: Racism and the Black Athlete (Praeger Publishers, 2014)*.

**Ervin (Maliq) Matthew** is Assistant Professor of Sociology at the University of Cincinnati. He earned his B.A. in sociology and political science from Herbert H. Lehman College of the City University of New York, and his M.A. and Ph.D. from Ohio State University. His research interests are social stratification, education and urbanicity. His current research assesses the uneven relationship between assumed measures of academic merit—in particular, school grades and standardized exam scores—and racial inequalities in educational and occupational attainment processes. He also follows a line of research that examines host-neighborhood effects on racial variance in school-level measures of academic success.

**Krista D. Mincey** is Assistant Professor in the Department of Public Health Sciences at Xavier University of Louisiana. Her research focuses on Black men's health, particularly the elements (masculinity, relationships, education, etc.) that impact the health and health behaviors of Black men. She is particularly interested in the health of Black male college students.

**Komanduri S. Murty, Ph.D.**, Professor and Coordinator of Sociology Program at Fort Valley State University, is the author or co-author of five books including *Historical Black Colleges and Universities: Their Place in American Higher Education* (Praeger, 1993), and more than 60 book chapters and articles which have appeared in numerous books and journals, including the *Encyclopedia of American Prisons, Encyclopedia of Anthropology, Encyclopedia of Great Black Migration, Intimate Violence, Criminal Justice Review, The Status of Black Atlanta, Studies in Symbolic Interactionism, Deviant Behavior, International Journal of Comparative and Applied Criminal Justice, Journal of Police Science Administration, Journal of Social and Behavioral Sciences,* and *Victimology*. He served as Professor and Chairman of Criminal Justice and Sociology for 25 years at Clark Atlanta University, where he received the 2005 Aldridge McMillan award for Outstanding Overall Achievement. His research interests include African American issues, race and racism, quantitative criminology and applied demography.

**David Nelson, Ph.D., M.S.** is Assistant Professor of Family and Community Medicine, Medical College of Wisconsin, Department of Family and Community Medicine and Center for Healthy Communities. He possesses years of experience working with communities in Maine and Wisconsin on a number of projects through federal, state and local funding. During his time in Milwaukee, he completed an assessment of three neighborhoods concerning physical activity and nutrition, worked on a team that developed a diabetes education curriculum for Spanish-speaking individuals taught by community health workers and led an effort that resulted in funding from the Robert Wood Johnson Foundation to develop and implement policy and environmental change strategies to decrease childhood obesity in Milwaukee.

**Claire M. Norris** is Assistant Professor in the Department of Sociology at Xavier University of Louisiana. Her research interests primarily focus on variations in stress, social support and social networks on mental health outcomes, specifically for black women.

**Makeda Roberts** is a research assistant in the Department of Sociology at Xavier University of Louisiana. Her research interests include the social, political and economical interrelations of health disparities within urban and minority populations.

**Meagan Sylvester** is a doctoral student in the Sociology of Music at the University of the West Indies, St. Augustine campus in her native Trinidad and Tobago. Her academic interests include analysis of the indigenous musics of Trinidad and Tobago and the related and attendant pluri-lingualism, pluri-culturalism and pluri-identifiers that are inclusive in the sounds, beats and lyrics.

**Brian L. Turner** is Assistant Professor of Psychology at Xavier University of Louisiana in New Orleans, LA. He received his doctoral degree in Clinical Psychology from Jackson State University. His research interests include the interaction of culture and psychology, coping styles and gender issues.

**Edward V. Wallace, Ph.D., M.P.H.** is a graduate of the State University of New York College at Cortland, the University of Massachusetts, Amherst School of Public Health and the University of Alabama. He is Associate Professor, College of Arts and Sciences at the University of Cincinnati. His academic interest and research expertise are in the area of health disparities among African Americans, with a primary focus on obesity, poor nutrition, access to healthy foods and mental health.

**Clare Walsh** is Visiting Assistant Professor at Texas Tech University. Her research focus is on intersectionality, especially as it relates to individuals who navigate the social world at the intersection of race and sexuality. She received her Ph.D. from the University of Florida. Her dissertation explored the everyday lived experiences of individuals who negotiate their social world at the intersection of racism and heterosexism/homophobia.

**Yvonne Wesley, R.N., Ph.D., F.A.A.N.** is the Director of the Leadership Institute for Black Nurses in the College of Nursing at New York University. With more than 15 years of executive leadership experience, she has specialized in health equity and overseeing highly successful community-based social responsibility projects that produce successful interdisciplinary teams. Her deep-rooted commitment to producing effective partnerships that increase financial support and improve the quality of life for all community members has yielded numerous publications in peer-review journals documenting the value of wellness initiatives in a continually changing health-care environment.

**Kelly Wetzel, B.A.**, attended the University of Scranton from 1999 to 2003 and graduated with a Bachelor's Degree in Counseling and Human Services. She has been working with the "at-risk youth and families" population for ten years. Currently, she is an Intensive Outpatient Therapist at Aquila of Delaware, Inc. She is attending Delaware State University and should attain her Master's Degree in Social Work in May, 2015.

**Guy-Lucien S. Whembolua** is a behavioral scientist with general areas of expertise in health disparities, global health and substance abuse. His research agenda is divided into three areas: minority health, African/Afro-Caribbean immigrant health and public health in the African continent and the Caribbean region. He is the director of the Africana Health Research Laboratory (AFROLAB) and is currently Assistant Professor of Health Policy and Management in the Department of Africana Studies at the University of Cincinnati and the Program Chair of the American Public Health Association Caucus on Refugee and Immigrant Health.

**Earl Wright II** is Professor of Africana Studies and affiliate faculty member of Sociology at the University of Cincinnati. His primary research interests are W.E.B. Du Bois and the contributions of early Black sociologists to the discipline of sociology. He recently co-authored an edited volume titled *Repositioning Race: Prophetic Research in a Postracial Obama Age* (2015), with Sandra L. Barnes and Zandria F. Robinson.

**Jennifer Padilla Wyse** is Assistant Professor of Sociology at Armstrong State University in Savannah, Georgia. Her areas of specialization are race, gender and class; social inequality, Africana studies, sociology of knowledge, race and ethnicity, and race and social policy.

# PART I
# Black Sociology: Yesterday, Today and Tomorrow

# Black Sociology: Continuing the Agenda

## Earl Wright II and Edward V. Wallace

The primary objective of this edited volume is to present to the reader some of the most up-to-date research in the substantive area known as "Black sociology." However, it is anticipated that some may have misconceptions about what Black sociology actually is. While some believe it is simply the ghettoization into a collective *all* research conducted by *all* Blacks, others suggest it is simply *regular* sociology in blackface. Neither of these characterizations is accurate. In addition to these misconstructions, some have questions about what Black sociology is. Some of the questions include "what is Black sociology," "where did it come from," "isn't Black sociology just mainstream (White) sociology in Blackface" and "do we need Black sociology in the twenty-first century?' In this chapter, we address these topics and questions and briefly outline how the essays in this volume contribute to the Black sociology tradition.

## The Origin of Black Sociology

The most commonly accepted narrative on the origin of Black sociology is that it was birthed during the Civil Rights and Black Power eras of the mid-twentieth century by young African American college students seeking greater representations of themselves in institutions of higher education, largely predominately White, throughout the United States (Ladner [1973] 1998). While it is true that academic courses, programs (e.g., Black Studies) and an increase in Black faculty at predominately White institutions were byproducts of the direct activities of those involved in the movements cited above, it is also true that the intellectual foundation for Black sociology was established more than fifty years earlier in response to biased and unscientific studies on Blacks in America after emancipation.

Prior to the twentieth century, the existing scholarly literature in medicine and the social sciences largely excluded objective scientific inquiries into the status and condition of Blacks in America. When the medical community did conduct research on Blacks, the findings largely supported the preexisting belief that biological differences existed between Blacks and Whites. These biological differences were believed to be so extreme that a superior/inferior dichotomy emerged to validate the differential treatment between, for example, free Whites and enslaved Blacks and, post-emancipation, White American citizens and America's second-class Black citizens. Belief in the biological differences between Blacks and Whites led the medical community to engage in one of the most infamous research studies conducted in the United States, the Tuskegee syphilis study. Grounded in an existing literature supportive of the idea of biological difference between the races, this study was conceptualized to objectively test the theory on racial difference and was guided by the question, "Does syphilis affect Blacks and Whites similarly?" This question was apropos since the medical community was advancing the notion that some diseases were less harmful to Blacks than Whites. It only took six months of investigation for the medical community to ascertain that syphilis impacted both races the same. It was at this point that the medical community possessed data challenging its preconceived notions on racial difference(s). Unfortunately, the Tuskegee syphilis study on Black men did not end after the research question guiding the study was answered. Instead, at this point, the study was altered from its emphasis on assessing whether or not the disease impacted Blacks and Whites similarly to an open-ended investigation on the long-term implications of untreated syphilis in Black males, who were unknowing and unwitting subjects in a program that lasted from 1932 to 1972 (Jones 1981). While support for the idea of biological difference by race was beginning to crumble in the medical community in the early 1900s, the social sciences remained firmly entrenched in its belief of racial difference.

Many founding and prominent early sociologists promoted theories of *Negro* inferiority and biological difference between the races in their scholarly works. Pioneering early Black sociologist E. Franklin Frazier, via contextualization by Elliott Rudwick, offers an overview of sociology's scientific analysis of the status and condition of Blacks in America at the turn of the twentieth century:

> … the general "point of view" of the first sociologists to study the Black man was that "the Negro is an inferior race because of either biological or social hereditary or both" … These conclusions were generally supported by the marshalling of a vast amount of statistical data on the pathological aspects of Negro life. In short, "The sociological theories which were implicit in the writings on the Negro problem were merely rationalizations of the existing racial situation." (Rudwick 1974: 48)

Elliott Rudwick (1974: 48) offers an equally profound assessment of the profession's scientific posture concerning the status and condition of Blacks in America and the type of scholarship contained in the discipline's leading journal, the *American Journal of Sociology*:

> It is true that the Journal did carry articles by a man like W. I. Thomas, who criticized racist theories, but other items displayed the racial biases of their authors. The September 1903 issue included an article by H. E. Berlin entitled "The Civil War as Seen through Southern Glasses," in which the author described slavery as "the humane and the most practical method ever devised for bearing the White man's burden." (Ibid., emphasis added)

Commenting on the thoughts and writings of the American Sociological Association's "Big 5" presidents from 1905 to 1914, Green and Driver (1976: 331) state:

> [R. Charles] Key's analysis of the writings of Sumner, Giddings, Small, Ward and Ross leads him to conclude [that] … The racism of the pioneering sociologists and the incidents of racism found in their works seems to range from unashamed bigotry to tacit acceptance. Their racism can be understood in the same manner by which their theories and prophecies can be understood; with reference to the socio-culture in which they took meaning and shape; their opportunity structures; "styles of life;" and world views.

Scientific theories on the biological and intellectual inferiority of Blacks was evidence to many that not only were *ordinary* Black and White citizens different, but that Black and

White sociologists were *different* also, and the two could not be considered professional equals or employed as colleagues even if both were credentialed from the same highly prestigious White institutions. Even attempting to *meet* as equals at Black institutions also proved problematic. W.E.B. Du Bois's recounting of the difficulty a White colleague from Mississippi had simply trying to meet with him as an equal on the campus of Atlanta University is insightful. Du Bois (1980: 163) said:

> We had absolutely no social contact with white Atlanta. Once in a while a white person would call on me—I remember one professor of sociology from Mississippi, who slipped up on the campus at dusk and came to my office. He said, "You're the first person I've visited in Atlanta, and I wouldn't want people to know it." He didn't dare come up to call on me in broad daylight.

Prodded by the interviewer to comment further on this experience, Du Bois replied:

> I had no simple response. I mean, the way he said it, you knew he was perfectly honest. Here was a situation which I understood as well as he did: a professor from a white Mississippi college couldn't come and visit as a social equal with a Negro professor. He simply couldn't do it. I knew it as well as he did, of course. Of course, on the other hand he knew perfectly well that I wasn't going to call on him no matter where he was; that the next time we meet, on the street or anything of that sort, I was going to fail to see him. I always had difficulties of that sort. (Ibid.: 163–4)

It is within the problem of the color line that Du Bois successfully spearheaded a program of sociological research that surpassed any similar institutional effort, before or since. But for race, the accomplishments of this group would be as revered and canonized as the vaunted Chicago School. It is, perhaps, this racial quandary that inspired Du Bois (1968: 228) to write: "So far as the American world of science and letters as concerned, we never 'belonged'; we remained unrecognized in learned societies and academic groups. We rated merely as Negroes studying Negroes, and after all, what had Negroes to do with America or science."

This is the sociological and societal environment that Du Bois faced as he began his quest to objectively and scientifically study "the Negro problem" in the United States. In a milieu where, taken as a collective, it was believed that Blacks were inferior and did not possess the intellectual acuity or biological sameness of Whites, the study of Blacks, at least by many White sociologists, was of little to no concern since the science was clear: Blacks were unequal. The time, energy and attention of White sociologists, they believed, was better expended on studying social problems more directly connected with the condition and well-being of Whites, particularly those arriving as immigrants from Europe. When some White sociologists did engage in research on Blacks, the product was often biased and unscientific. Du Bois notes this concern in his classic book, *The Souls of Black Folk*. Here Du Bois identifies a void in the existing literature on race caused by the preconceived notions of his group's biological and intellectual inferiority. Instead of engaging in objective and scientific inquiries into Black life, Du Bois charges that some White sociologists haphazardly conduct research in a manner that validates their existing belief in the inferiority of Blacks. This position is captured in his description of the "car window sociologist." According to Du Bois ([1903] 1969: 94) the car window sociologist is "the man who seeks to understand and know the South by devoting the few leisure hours of a holiday trip to unraveling the snarl of centuries." Whether through benign ignorance or malicious intent, early White car window sociologists contributed to the existing literature many inaccurate and false accounts of the status and condition of Blacks in the United States. It is this void that necessitated a program of scholarly inquiry that would objectively and scientifically analyze the social, economic and physical condition of Blacks. The seeds of Black sociology were now planted, as it was at this time that Du Bois desired to develop a research program on Blacks in the United States and at a location where this new perspective would thrive.

## Toward a Definition and Principles of Black Sociology

After Du Bois completed the first urban sociological study conducted in the United States, *The Philadelphia Negro*, he wanted to establish a research program on Blacks to counter that of mainstream (White) (car window) sociologists. He initially wanted to establish this program within a consortium of Ivy League schools that possessed the physical resources and financial backing for him to successfully accomplish his ambitious idea. In a recorded 1961 interview, Du Bois says "What we needed was an academic study of the Negro. I wanted the universities of Pennsylvania and Harvard and Yale and so forth to go into a sort of partnership by which this kind of study could be forwarded" (Asch 1961: 3). Despite his impressive scholarly record, being the first African American to take the Ph.D. at Harvard and his peripheral status as a faculty member at the University of Pennsylvania while collecting data for *The Philadelphia Negro*, Du Bois's idea was not acted upon; in his own words, "But of course they didn't do anything at all" (ibid.). It is provident that Atlanta University was simultaneously initiating a program of research on Blacks and was seeking a qualified researcher to lead their effort. According to Du Bois, "Atlanta University … asked me to come down there and teach and take charge of some such study" (ibid.).

The Atlanta University Study of the Negro Problems was established at Atlanta University in 1895 by trustee George Bradford and President Horace Bumstead. This program of research into the social, economic and physical condition of Blacks in the United States emanated from correspondence from school graduates to their former teachers and administrators. Atlanta University graduates asked that investigations into the transitions of Blacks moving from slavery to freedom and from rural to urban life be investigated as the peculiar institution of slavery had only been eliminated a mere thirty years prior and because they had identified many social problems that needed social science answers. The Atlanta University Studies were loosely modeled after existing research programs and conferences at Hampton University, which centered on Blacks in the industrial profession, and the Tuskegee Institute, which emphasized Blacks in agriculture. Atlanta University's primary, but not exclusive, emphasis on urban issues not only served as a point of departure from the existing programs, it set the stage for this school to make substantive contributions to sociology and the social sciences.

W.E.B. Du Bois was not the founder of the Atlanta Sociological Laboratory. As indicated earlier, George Bradford and Horace Bumstead are responsible for establishing the research program in 1895. However, it was Du Bois's groundbreaking scientific rigor that provided a blueprint for how research is conducted today. It is coincidental that the establishment of the Atlanta University Studies and Du Bois's desire to spearhead a program of research into the social, economic and physical condition of Blacks were nearly simultaneous. Upon his arrival in 1897, Du Bois provided the leadership, vision and academic training in the social sciences that was badly needed and sought by Atlanta University officials. One of his first goals upon assuming leadership of the program was to make the annual investigations more scientific. Du Bois (1968: 214) criticized the two studies published prior to his arrival as not being important since they "followed the Hampton and Tuskegee model of being primarily meetings of inspiration, directed toward specific efforts at social reform and aimed at propaganda for social uplift in certain preconceived lines." With his rigorous standard for scientific investigations in place, Du Bois carried out a 13-year objective and scientific research program on Blacks in the United States. Some of the results of Du Bois's efforts include conducting the first American sociological study on the family and the first American sociological study on religion, the institutionalization of method triangulation, the institutionalization of the insider researcher, and the institutionalization of the acknowledgement of the limitations of one's research (Wright 2002a, 2002b, 2002c, 2006, 2009, 2012). In addition to these accomplishments, Du Bois's research program countered much of the existing and biased scholarship of many White sociologists and now serves as the foundation for the substantive area called "Black sociology."

In 2006, the lead author of this chapter and Thomas C. Calhoun published an article titled "Jim Crow Sociology," that examined the nearly thirty-year life span of the Du Bois-led Atlanta University Study of the Negro Problems. In this effort, Thomas and I were interested in identifying the unique way(s) the sociological investigations conducted at Atlanta University compared and contrasted with those conducted by mainstream (White) sociologists. We discovered that, while mainstream (White) sociology largely focused on positivism and attempts to validate the discipline's very existence, Du Bois and the emerging Black sociology agenda at Atlanta University placed its efforts on engaging in scientific and objective investigations on Blacks that should, when applicable, result in social policy directives. Mainstream (White) sociology, again attempting to legitimate itself as a *real* science, largely resisted this and similar agendas (e.g., the social gospel movement). It was quite apparent to us that, because of 1) the lack of attention/desire by Whites to conduct research on Blacks, 2) the biased and un-objective research on Blacks when conducted, and 3) the discipline's lack of an emphasis on impacting social/public policy, the type of sociology practiced by Du Bois at Atlanta differed from that of most mainstream (White) sociologists. Consequently, we identified the parallel area as Black sociology. We defined Black sociology as

> ... *an area of research, which may be performed by Black or White scholars, that is focused on eliminating Blacks from social oppression through objective scientific investigations into their social, economic and physical condition for the express purpose of obtaining data aimed at understanding, explaining and ameliorating the problems discovered in the Black American community in a manner that could have social policy implications. (Wright and Calhoun 2006: 16)*

In addition to offering a definition of Black sociology, we identify five principles. The principles of Black sociology are that

> ... *1) the research be conducted primarily by Black American scholars; 2) the focus of research center on the experiences of Black Americans; 3) the research efforts of Black sociology be interdisciplinary; 4) the findings, whenever possible, be generalizable beyond Black Americans; and 5) the findings, whenever possible, produce data that could have social policy implications. (Ibid.: 16)*

All of the principles of Black sociology were gleaned through the nearly thirty-year sociological research program at Atlanta University. While we remain committed to our original conception of Black sociology, there is one part that requires additional explanation, since we did not clearly or fully articulate our true meaning.

In our original articulation we argued "This conceptualization of Black sociology is important insomuch as it does not suggest a difference in ... theoretical assumptions between Black sociology and mainstream sociology" (ibid.: 16). This statement is incorrect and was poorly worded. We do believe there is a difference in the theoretical assumptions between Black sociology and mainstream sociology. Black sociology operates within a theoretical frame that is objective and does not prejudge its subjects as deficient actors with pathological tendencies. Some early sociology and social science theories were, and some remain, influenced by their authors' belief in the biological and intellectual inferiority of non-White actors, and their theories reflect as much. Black sociological analysis does not begin or end with the position that Blacks, or any other group for that matter, suffer from pathologies that are immutable, unchangeable and engrained by heredity. Nor does Black sociology support race-based macro-level theories that support the idea that groups of people, whether by race, class gender, etc., share common biological and/or intellectual traits that render them inferior. The argument that we failed to make in the original article is that some early sociological theories were developed with the deficiency model in mind and used to explain the condition of Blacks in America through that lens. It is that body of sociological theory that we argue departs from Black sociology.

We also assert that Black sociology is not a means of self-ghettoizing Black scholars or their work. Nor is Black sociology a more "respectable" shelter from the perceived negative stigma of being assigned to a Black Studies or Africana Studies department. Simply because one conducts research on a particular topic and the subject(s) in said project happens to be Black does not make that work Black sociology. Just because a researcher may be Black and conduct research on a topic whereby the subject happens to be Black, or not, does not make that work Black sociology. Just because one may be Black and conduct research on any topic, their race does not automatically render their work Black sociology. Black sociology, as a perspective, is guided by the subject matter and implications of one's research. It is a given that the research will adhere to the basic tenets of science (e.g., objective, ethical, etc.). The essence of Black sociology is what the ultimate purpose and impact of one's research will be. Will the research impact social/public policy? Does the research place Blacks at the center of analysis? Does the research reject the deficit model? Is the research project interdisciplinary? A positive answer to these simple questions, combined with the definition and principles outlined earlier, delineates Black sociology from the simple substantive area and study of race and ethnicity and similar false comparisons. At its core, Black sociology is the objective and scientific study of Blacks that offers the possibility of proposing public and social policy outcomes to improve or ameliorate the conditions discovered in the study. It is this perspective that guides the authors of the chapters in this volume as they, and we, continue using the Atlanta Sociological Laboratory model as a guide for implementing a twenty-first-century agenda to investigate the social conditions Blacks experience in America and around the world.

## Black Sociology in the Twenty-first Century

It should be stated here that this volume is not intended to be a replication of the Du Bois-led Atlanta University Studies. If this were a replication or continuation of Du Bois's Atlanta University Studies, then the process and product would be much different. First, one substantive area of inquiry would be selected (e.g., deviance, education, health, poverty, etc.). Second, a 6–9-month-long study would be conducted by our research team on that specific topical area. Third, findings from that study would be presented at a conference held at our institution. Fourth, findings from that study would be packaged for publication consideration. Our objective in this project is not to accomplish that end. Instead of viewing this project as a continuation of the Du Bois-led research program, one would be more accurate if they view this project as an examination of contemporary issues and future directions in Black sociology that highlights some of the best and most recent research in the United States on issues impacting Blacks. Toward that end, we held an open call for voluntary paper submissions in the broad area of Black Sociology as articulated by Wright and Calhoun (2006). Accordingly, since this volume centers on contemporary issues and future directions in Black sociology, multiple substantive areas of study (e.g., deviance, education, health, poverty, etc.) are included—not the singular emphasis on one substantive area like Du Bois's Atlanta University Studies. Our call for papers elicited numerous submissions and twenty were selected for this volume. The accepted papers are organized into six parts that provide a substantive and holistic perspective on the condition of Blacks in the United States.

In Part I, we have already offered a definition and principles of Black sociology. Additionally, a brief overview of the origin of the research unit that provided the foundation for Black sociology, the Atlanta Sociological Laboratory, is presented. In Chapter 2, Jennifer Wyse offers a new paradigm for future examinations of Black Sociology. She suggests that studies be conducted through a lens that de-emphasizes the Eurocentric scientific model. Wyse ultimately concludes that if Black Sociology is to remain relevant in the twenty-first century, it is critical that scholars continue to deracialize and decolonize the ways that we obtain and assess our knowledge of "others."

In Part II, emphasis is placed on the contemporary condition of Black youth, emerging adults and family. Darwin Fishman opens this section with a nuanced theoretical analysis of the problematic nature of race and physical space in the murder of Trayvon Martin. In his conclusion, he surmises that the "Stand Your Ground" death of the African American youth was predictable given America's problematic legacy of racial strife. Focusing on the experiences of African Americans who experienced Hurricane Katrina in New Orleans, Louisiana, Farrah Gafford Cambrice reports on the past and current survival strategies employed by emerging adults in a city that, even prior to the storm, experienced high levels of crime and poverty. Continuing the focus on Blacks in cities, Sheridan Kingsberry and colleagues, in response to the disproportionate number of incarcerated Blacks in America, particularly males, offer proactive strategies and techniques for increasing the levels of educational attainment for children with one or more currently incarcerated parents. If the solutions offered herein are implemented, then the African American family may again become, according to the authors, the backbone of the Black community. In the concluding chapter of Part II, Clare Walsh examines the co-parenting experiences of African American lesbian families. Walsh offers an intersectional analysis on the different forms and manifestations of oppression. Her interviewees underscore the difficulty and importance of teasing out differences and degrees of oppression since "it's really not just about being gay but Africana American and gay." For many of the participants in this investigation, they conclude that issues surrounding sexuality often have more impact on their everyday lives than racism. As a collective, Part II intertwines multiple social issues impacting the African American family with solutions to address often overwhelming and negative data on that familial unit. If the strategies and techniques suggested herein are employed, the impact on the Black family could be significant.

Again, while this volume is not intended to serve as a replication of the Atlanta University Studies, we do acknowledge a connection with various components of the school and its research agenda. The Atlanta University Studies often focused on education and economic issues, as Du Bois and his peers viewed these institutions as vital to the survival and progress of the race. The chapters in Part III have a similar focus, beginning with Tomeka Davis's examination of the significance of family structure on educational attainment for African

American adolescents. Davis provokes some intriguing dialog by asking the question, "if both Black men and Black women are doing poorly, to whom should policy makers direct their attention and resources?" Since we understand that education and economic success are vital for upward social mobility in any community, policy makers have a responsibility to address and, when possible, ameliorate the structural challenges leading to high incarceration rates among Black men that contribute to reduced parental expectation and mobility. Maliq Ervin and Littisha Bates extend the emphasis on education by offering several explanations for the gap in educational attainment between Blacks and Whites. They ultimately conclude that proactive strategies to reduce the gap between the races should be developed and implemented such that economic opportunities for Blacks could be increased, even in the face of failing public school systems across the nation. Katrinell M. Davis then offers an examination of the impact of educational attainment on the wage gap between African American women and other workers. Ultimately, if the wage gap between African American women and other workers is not due to educational attainment then proactive corrective measures must be offered to remedy this problem. Relatedly, Lori Martin and colleagues conclude this section with an examination of the educational attainment of Blacks over a thirty-year period and its impact on class mobility. If there is a correlation between educational attainment and class mobility, then the prescriptions offered in the previous chapter could be used to improve future economic opportunities for Blacks.

In 1906, Du Bois conducted one of the earliest, if not *the* earliest, scientific repudiations of the biological inferiority of Blacks vis-à-vis Whites. Not only does Du Bois provide a counter-narrative to the accepted physical inferiority of Blacks, he equally challenged members of his race to engage in effective hygiene and sanitation practices such that the likelihood they would become susceptible to the primary diseases and illnesses of the era would be greatly reduced. That Du Bois and his Atlanta University researchers were unafraid to challenge accepted mainstream medical thought concerning Black inferiority, while simultaneously challenging Blacks to improve their sanitation practices, captures the essence of Part IV, which covers health and health disparity issues that disproportionately impact African Americans. Claire Norris and colleagues offer an examination of the negative health implications for poverty-level African American women, who have high levels of stress caused by a number of factors. Most importantly, this chapter serves as a platform for the development and implementation of age-appropriate interventions geared toward empowering black women to manage stress and, in turn, improve their mental health outcomes and quality of life. In the next chapter, Angelique Harris and colleagues examine the ways that Black women's bodies are often demonized as not fitting the ideal type and disparaged as not healthy. The authors offer a new paradigm which suggests that interventions to reduce obesity should not only focus on sociocultural constructions of obesity and overweight, but should also take into consideration community resources and assets such as sharing knowledge via "word of mouth" and the influence of religion and spirituality. In the concluding chapter of Part IV, it is indicated that, although they comprise roughly 13 percent of the total US population, Blacks account for roughly 50 percent of all HIV/AIDS cases in the United States. Marye Bernard and Malinda R. Conrad offer an overview of the origin of HIV/AIDS, its impact in the United States and its specific implications for African American women. Bernard and Conrad also challenge us to overcome the HIV pandemic through continued education, testing and honest conversations about HIV.

For twenty years, Atlanta University released the published findings of its annual investigations. The report always concluded with a section outlining the resolutions, or theories, adopted to solve the problems identified therein. Although this school was deeply committed to objective scientific inquiry, a tangential objective was the promotion of solutions to address the myriad problems facing Blacks in America. Part V of this volume follows that tradition as the emphasis here is on solutions to health disparities experienced by African Americans. Without question, the number of baby boomers now in need of medical and hospice care is increasing. Given this demographic fact, Yvonne Wesley offers a new paradigm in the execution of nursing practices whereby the focus is principally directed at wellness intervention, not illness care. Such an emphasis could possible extend and/or improve the lives of all Americans, but Blacks specifically. Relatedly, Ed Wallace offers proactive strategies and techniques to increase community engagement with specific attention on cultural competency and how organizations build community relationships within the African American community to address mental health disparities. While a historical overview of HIV/AIDS is presented in Part IV, Omotayo Banjo and colleagues extend that focus in this section to include sexually transmitted diseases in their examination of the benefits of using hip hop artists, videos and popular culture to address (and hopefully ameliorate) health problems within the African American community. They conclude that the high rate of sexually transmitted diseases in the Black community could be decreased with assistance from the hip hop community.

From its inception, the Atlanta University Studies was an interdisciplinary endeavor. Topics including, but not limited to, economics, education, crime and health were the central focus of multiple year-long investigations. Part VI is reflective of the interdisciplinary and eclectic research interests included in Black sociology. This section begins with Meagan Sylvester's examination of the influence of music on the Caribbean nationalist movements on the islands of Trinidad and Tobago. Similar to the freedom songs that inspired American Blacks during the civil rights movement, it is proposed here that music is a transformative tool in the fight to address and challenge governmental oppression and overreach. Understanding the significant role of the Black church in the lives of many American Blacks in areas, historically speaking, such as voting rights, Marci Littlefield examines the role of African American churches in creating economic opportunities for its members and those in their local community. It is suggested that if the Black church is as ambitious in this area as it is in protecting the voting rights of its constituents, the economic realities of many African Americans would be improved within a relatively short period of time. Timothy Broughton and Komanduri S. Murty next offer a case study of one state's classic attempt at limiting voting opportunities for southern Blacks and the ways the example they highlight bears a similarity to contemporary attempts to limit voter participation of African Americans and Hispanic Americans throughout this nation. This chapter is significant as it demonstrates that recent attempts to limit voting opportunities for minorities in the United States are not new and that earlier generations effectively protected their right to the ballot. A fitting culmination of this section and volume is Derrick Brooms's chapter on the significance and role of museums in preserving artifacts from the Black Power era, specifically, and African American history, in general. Without institutions such as these, it is very possible that the accurate representation of events such as disenfranchisement, role of the Black Church, and the significance of music for a people could be lost or, worse, retold in a manner that provides a completely false and inaccurate narrative.

## Toward a Twenty-first-century Agenda

When the Atlanta Sociological Laboratory was established in 1895, Blacks in America were thirty years removed from the "peculiar institution" of slavery, forced to live by de facto and de jure Jim Crow rule and were subject to death by lynching at the slightest whim of any White man they encountered. As we continue through the twenty-first century, 150 years after the passage of the 13th Amendment to the United States Constitution, Blacks in America are disproportionately the victims of police killings and (female) victims of intimate partner violence, and continue to suffer from both subtle and overt acts of racism. It is without question that the social problems before us today must be scientifically analyzed through a Black sociology lens that seeks solutions to the problems studied, not simply appear in yet another book to place on one's shelf or in a peer-reviewed publication to cite on one's curriculum vitae. Accordingly, the chapters in this volume should be viewed, at a minimum, as attempts to provide some context or solutions to the numerous challenges faced by Blacks in America and the diaspora in the areas of family, health and popular culture. In an ideal world, this effort will serve as the spark to renew the spirit of the W.E.B. Du Bois-inspired research agenda at Atlanta University. Namely, that car window sociology and attempts to achieve acceptance from the mainstream sociology community be replaced with a new agenda that puts a premium on how science can be used to alter and/or improve lives. This is what Black sociology is all about: how science can be used to positively impact one's life. Such a research agenda can help in the efforts to make America a more perfect union—a union that is perfected through objective and scientific research guided by a Black sociology perspective.

# References

Asch, Moses. 1961. *W.E.B. Du Bois: A Recorded Autobiography*. New York: Folkways Records.

Dodoo, F. Nii-Amoo and Nicola Kay Beisel. 2005. "Africa in American Sociology: Invisibility, Opportunity, and Obligation." *Social Forces* 84(1): 595–600.

Du Bois. W.E.B. 1968. *The Autobiography of W.E.B. Du Bois: A Soliloquy on Viewing My Life from the Last Decade of Its First Century*. New York: International Publishers.

———. ([1903] 1969. *The Souls of Black Folk*. New York: Signet Classic.

———. 1980. W.E.B. Du Bois Papers. Special Collections and University Archives, W.E.B. Du Bois Library, University of Massachusetts at Amherst.

Green, Dan S. and Edwin Driver. 1976. "W.E.B. Du Bois: A Case in the Sociology of Sociological Negation." *Phylon* 37: 308–33.

Jones, James H. 1981. *Bad Blood: The Tuskegee Syphilis Experiment*. New York: The Free Press.

Ladner, Joyce. [1973] 1998. *The Death of White Sociology: Essays on Race and Culture*. Baltimore, MD: Black Classic Press.

Pascale, Celine-Marie. 2010. "Epistemology and the Politics of Knowledge." *The Sociological Review* 58: 154–65.

Rudwick, Elliott. 1974. "W.E.B. Du Bois as Sociologist." in *Black Sociologists: Historical and Perspectives*, eds. James Blackwell and Morris Janowitz. Chicago, IL: University of Chicago Press, pp. 25–55.

Wright II, Earl. 2002a. "The Atlanta Sociological Laboratory, 1896–1924: A Historical Account of the First American School of Sociology." *Western Journal of Black Studies* 26(3):165–174.

———. 2002b. "Using the Master's Tools: Atlanta University and American Sociology, 1896–1924." *Sociological Spectrum* 22(1): 15–39.

———. 2002c. "Why Black People Tend To Shout!: An Earnest Attempt To Explain the Sociological Negation of the Atlanta Sociological Laboratory despite Its Possible Unpleasantness." *Sociological Spectrum* 22(3): 325–61.

———. 2006. "W.E.B. Du Bois and the Atlanta University Studies on the Negro, Revisited." *Journal of African American Studies* 9(4): 3–17.

————. 2009. "Beyond W.E.B. Du Bois: A Note on Some of the Lesser Known Members of the Atlanta Sociological Laboratory." *Sociological Spectrum* 29(6): 700–717.

————. 2012. "Why, Where and How to Infuse the Atlanta Sociological Laboratory into the Sociology Curriculum." *Teaching Sociology* 40: 257–70.

———— and Thomas C. Calhoun. 2006. "Jim Crow Sociology: Toward an Understanding Of the Origin and Principles of Black Sociology via the Atlanta Sociological Laboratory." *Sociological Focus* 39(1): 1–18.

# Black Sociology: The Sociology of Knowledge, Racialized Power Relations of Knowledge and Humanistic Liberation

Jennifer Padilla Wyse

Theories of knowledge creation, or epistemology, are socio-historical, political and cultural processes of meaning-making (Bourdieu 1977; Du Bois 1935; Sprague 2005; Collins 2000). Within the tradition of Black sociology, the sociology of knowledge is an important area of study that seeks to understand social and racialized forces shaping knowledge production and reproduction (Collins 2000: 270; Du Bois 1935; Woodson 1933). Feminist scholars identify three essential elements of epistemology: the knower, the known, and the process of knowing (Sprague 2005: 31). Together the triad of epistemology allows for an analysis of the ways "power-relations shape who is believed and why" (Collins 2000: 270).

The creation of knowledge is socio-historically and culturally grounded in communities and societies to "facilitate 'seeing' and 'knowing'" the social world and social reality (Stanfield 2011a). Stanfield conceptualizes this as "cognitive style" (ibid.: 20). Cognitive style is the superstructure of knowledge. Contemporarily, the superstructure of humanity's knowledge is reflexive of the political-economic capitalist colonial and Imperial world-system (de Sousa Santos et al. 2007; Stanfield 2011a). The capitalist colonial and imperial world-system is such that core nation-states exploit periphery nations' productive forces economically, socially and ideologically through forces of racism and nationalism (Nkrumah 1965; Robinson 1983; Rodney 1972). Capitalistic colonialism and imperialism violently oppress, dehumanize and alienate for the purpose of economic and political exploitation (Césaire 1972; Fanon 1965; Memmi 1965).

To be sure, capitalistic colonialism and imperialism serve as a *total* world-system such that the political-economic structure is reflected in the superstructure of knowledge (Marx [1972] 2008; Rodney 1972; Stanfield 2011a). The total capitalist world-system monopolizes knowledge that enforces a colonality of knowledge reflexive of the political-economic colonality of power (de Sousa Santos et. al. 2007; Rodney 1972). Colonality of knowledge reproduces a globalized localism of Eurocentric and ethnocentric knowledge that is normalized as the status quo and seen as *the* only path of valid knowledge production (Collins 2000; de Sousa Santos et. al. 2007; Smith 2012; Stanfield 2011a). The colonality of knowledge reproduces monocultural, Eurocentric knowledge that denies the validity of racially Othered knowers and knowledges in order to reproduce oppressive, dehumanizing, alienating and exploitive culture and action (Mills 1999; Smith 2012; de Sousa Santos et. al. 2007; Stanfield 2011a). This is exampled most furiously in the representations of Indigenous African knowledge(s) and western education. Indigenous African knowledge(s) frames education from a circular world-view where knowledge is (re)produced as concrete understandings of natural and social environments in which "no separation of education[,] ... productive activity" and social responsibility exists (Abdi and Cleghorn 2005: 5). In contrast, western knowledge is compartmentalized into formal (i.e., schooling), informal (i.e., deliberate occasions) and non-formal (i.e., lived experiences) education (Abdi and Cleghorn 2005; Rodney 1972). Knowledge compartmentalized into western formal education is classified and institutionalized and requires funding (Camic 2010; Douglas 1986; Fuller 1993; Sica 2007; Stanfield 2011a: 39). Institutionalized knowledge is consequently disciplined into *disciplinary boundaries* that legitimize the validity of knowledge through a set of ideas and assumptions. For example, the western formal education institution of natural science has a set of ideas (the scientific method) that determine the validity of scientific knowledge and is disciplined apart from social humanistic knowledges (Fuller 1993). As such, disciplinary boundaries enclose what is considered to be valid thought and reinforce preferred paths of knowledge creation (Douglas 1986; Fuller 1993). Reinforcing disciplinary boundaries of institutionalized knowledge requires a disciplining process whereby boundaries are created, maintained and revolutionized (Fuller 1993). Disciplining institutionalized knowledge requires power, where gatekeepers act as disciplinarians and knowledge dissemination is a critical aspect of disciplining knowledge (Collins 2007; Rabaka 2010). To be sure, it is the colonaity of knowledge that denies the validity of Indigenous African knowledge(s) and misrepresents said knowledge as mythical and ideological, overdevelops western formal education as *the* way to create knowledge and perpetuates dehumanizing relations born out of the capitalistic colonial and imperial world-system (Rodney 1972; Smith 2012).

However, the purpose of the reproduction of disciplinary boundaries and western formal education depends on the theoretical frame of one's sociological imagination. Critical theorists, utilizing various approaches, argue that education is a tentacle of the dominant power that reinforces hegemonic ideology and structured power-relations (Bourdieu 1977; Collins 2000; Friere 1970; Rodney 1972; Stanfield 2011a; Woodson [1933]1977). Disciplined boundaries of institutionalized knowledge reflect structured power-relations that reproduce hegemonic, elite knowledge to perpetuate societal power-relations (Collins 2007; Friere 1970; Rabaka 2010; Stanfield 2011a). Analytically, Bourdieu (1977) critically emphasized that educational institutions produce socialized persons that embody the hegemonic power's "system of predispositions," or habitus, such that socialized persons accept and take part in the reproduction of structured power-relations, whereby these relations are taken for granted and made invisible (Collins 2007). Western formal education then, in its organization, content and implementation, reflects and reproduces hegemonic economic, political, ideological and social power-relations (Bourdieu 1977; Collins 2000; Collins 2007; Oakes 1985).

Africana critical social theorists, whose epistemology is centered in a Black sociological paradigm, criticize the role of western formal education in perpetuating oppressive, dehumanizing and alienating culture and action (Collins 2000; Du Bois 1935; Fanon 1965; Memmi 1965; Woodson [1933]1977). They believe that education has been used as a tool to mis-educate and colonize minds, and perpetuate political-economic exploitation (Fanon 1965; Stanfield 2011a; Woodson [1933] 1977). For example, the imposition of western formal education in colonized African nations meant, for those colonies where formal education was implemented, the colonizer's language was required and *only* the colonizer's history was taught (Fanon 1965; Ngũgĩ 1986). Forcing colonized peoples to use only the colonizer's language is a "means of spiritual subjugation" (Ngũgĩ 1986: 9). Further, to ignore, distort and mis-represent the history of colonized peoples enacts historical violence that dehumanizes cultural groups for the purpose of reducing human groups into economic things and suppressing cultures of resistance and liberatory action (Césaire 1972; Fanon 1965). Utilizing the colonizer's language and distorting the history of colonized peoples, as western formal education attempts, shapes the way people see and know, or don't see or don't know, their social world and social reality—or our cognitive style (Asante 2003; Fanon 1965; Ngũgĩ 1986; Stanfield 2011a). However, while education is a tool to oppress, dialectically education is also a tool for liberation.

In the end, the process of reproducing social power-relations in education is multifaceted, as education legitimizes the social order structured by the dominant power and, while illusively remaining neutral to the very structures it reinforces, silently perpetuates a culture of ignorance (Bourdieu 1977; Friere 1970). The essential element in hegemonic institutionalized knowledge reproduction is its invisibility, where the ability to render invisibility is a manifestation of power (Collins 2007; Douglas 1986; Trouillot 1995). The reproduction of hegemonic power-relations of knowledge is particularly important because, in the words of Carter G. Woodson ([1933] 1977: xix), "when you control a man's thinking you [don't] have to worry about his actions." Ultimately, the process of knowing is not objective, ahistorical, or with no value, but rather producing and reproducing knowledge is a political act that is also action (Collins 2000; Friere 1970; Pascale 2010; Sprague 2005).

The capitalist colonial and imperial world-system is an explicitly racialized project. The historical development and social construction of race as a social structure of white supremacy was made real through enslavement and colonization—essential elements to the development of the capitalistic colonial and imperial world-system. As illustrated above, the superstructure of knowledge reflects the political-economic capitalist colonial and imperial world-system and, as such, is also structured by racialized power-relations of knowledge. Therefore, the next section defines race as white supremacy and illustrates how race structures western formal education's institutionalized knowledge by historically contextualizing both the hegemonic white(ness)[1] and Black sociological paradigms.

## Black Sociology and Hegemonic White(ness) Sociology: White Supremacy and Institutionalized Knowledge

Race is a socially constructed, fluid meaning-system applied to human bodies, places, spaces and knowledges that structures people's lived experiences and dictates social meanings, as well as social processes, social institutions, social systems, socio-psyches and social outcomes (Bell 1992; Blauner 1972; Better 2008; Feagin 2006; Higginbothom 1995; Fanon 1965; Mills 1999; Omi and Winant 1994; Stanfield 2011a). Analytically, race is a social structure that is relational and reads as scripts of cultural representations (Glenn 1999; Bonilla-Silva 1997). The meaning of race is a globally enforced *political structure* that reads as a racial contract of white supremacy that is centered in economic exploitation, whereby whiteness is privileged (white privilege) and non-whiteness is exploited and oppressed (racism) (Memmi 1965; Mills 1997). Fanon (1965: 44, 45) conceptualized that capitalistic colonialism enforces a 'Manichean Structure' whereby the social world is dichotomized into perpetual conflict of being and having. The white supremacist racial structure privileges being and having whiteness and exploits and oppresses being and having non-whiteness; that is, where "whiteness isn't a color but a set of power-relations" (Mills 1999: 127). Power, the essential element of white supremacy, is determined by those who control the political-economic

---

1    The idea of hegemonic White(ness) sociology uses Hughey's (2010) conceptual framework of "hegemonic whiteness" and applies it to knowledge (re)production.

forces of society (Higginbothom 1995; Kaba 2007). The racialized power-relations of white supremacy that are read in the superstructure of institutionalized knowledge, and western formal education, is magnificently exampled by the invisibility of hegemonic white(ness) sociology and the materialization of Black sociology.

Early American sociologist W.E.B. Du Bois ([1903] 1973) theorized that white supremacy powerfully fragments consciousnesses, thus, gifting Black Americans with double-sight of our social world. Just as Du Bois theorized white supremacy's power to fragment human consciousnesses, so too does white supremacy fragment the epistemological consciousness of American sociology into privileged hegemonic white(ness) sociology and Black sociology (Rabaka 2010). During the 1950s and 1960s, social movements across the US and around the globe called for civil rights, human rights and political decolonization. In academia, students of color and sympathetic white students, most notably the Students for a Democratic Society, fought to institutionalize various Othered knowledges into academic disciplines including, but not limited to, Black Studies, Women Studies, Chicano Studies, and American Indian Studies (Bailey [1973] 2007; Wallerstein 2007).

During this same time, American sociology's disciplinary boundary of institutionalized knowledge experienced a racialized paradigmatic revolution (Fuller 1993; Staples 1973). Scientific revolutions come in the form of paradigm shifts that concern the validity of knowledge production (Kuhn 1970). When a science can no longer explain, or allow for quality research to the satisfaction of the knower, the reproduced knowledge is rendered invalid and a new set of ideas and basic assumptions are validated (Kuhn 1970). Paradigms are boundaries that define the set process and practice guided by assumptions that "encompass interpretive frameworks … that are used to explain social phenomena" (Collins 2000: 270). In consequence, paradigms affect every aspect of the scientific process including, but not limited to, epistemology, methodology, methods, theory and data interpretation (Collins 2000; Kuhn 1970; Zuberi and Bonilla-Silva 2008). Paradigmatic revolutions are "political just as they are intellectual conflicts" (Stanfield 2011a: 40). In American sociology, the inability of hegemonic white(ness) sociology to explain and provide centered empirical research with communities of color for social justice and liberation required a paradigmatic shift (Blauner 1972; Ladner 1973). Hence in the 1960s and 1970s, racially Othered knowers affirmed American sociology's paradigmatic revolution by operationalizing Black sociology vis-à-vis hegemonic white(ness) sociology (Ladner 1973; Staples 1973, 1976). Certainly, American sociology's scientific revolution must be rooted in its historical context, where the paradigmatic materialization of Black sociology is a qualitative leap in American sociology's history, per the quantitative accumulation of knowledge (ideas) and knowers (researchers) dating back to the influential scholarship and practices of W.E.B. Du Bois, Ida B. Wells-Barnett, Anna J. Cooper, as well as Black sociologists influenced by, but thinking independently of, the Chicago School, including Franklin E. Frazier, St. Clair Drake, Horace Clayton, Oliver C. Cox and Richard Wright (Ladner 1973).

Racially Othered knowledges, centered in historical and cultural communities, share the commonality of knowledge production being centered in a humanistic understanding of the social world. Just as Fanon (1965: 43) argued "the realization of humanity sharpens the tools" of decolonization, Black sociology is a humanistic understanding of our social world that serves to decolonize and deracialize knowledge production and action (Zuberi and Bonilla-Silva 2008). Hegemonic white(ness) sociology, often uncritically referred to as "mainstream American sociology," is the discipline's hegemonic thought style (Collins 2007; Sica 2007). The basic paradigmatic assumptions of hegemonic white(ness) sociology include the notion that social science is value-free and objective. Hegemonic white(ness) sociology produces knowledge centered in Eurocentric experiences that privileges those experiences and ethnocentrically utilizes them to understand the social world; where ethnocentrism does not "account for the cultural imbeddedness of the knower" (Sprague 2005: 36). As such, hegemonic white(ness) sociology is Eurocentric and internalizes white supremacy such that racialized power-relations are normalized as the status quo (Stanfield 2011a). In practice, the white supremacist racial structure normalizes whiteness such that objectivity is never in favor of the racialized "Other." Instead, only whiteness is afforded objectivity (Memmi 1965). These paradigmatic assumptions elide the relationship between the knower and the known, making multiple realities, per standpoint theory, invisible, as well as the racialized power-relations of knowledge (Stanfield 2011).

Stanfield (2011a: 19) posits that "the objectification of knowledge is a matter of power and privilege" which grounds hegemonic white(ness) sociology in ethnocentricism and Eurocentricism. Eurocentric and ethnocentric assumptions create a hegemonic white(ness) sociology paradigm deeply entrenched in racism and discrimination that affect the practice of social inquiry into communities of color. The result is that racially Othered communities become the object of study (Bailey [1973] 2007; Staples 1976; Steinberg 2007; Zuberi and Bonilla-Silva 2008).

Furthermore, the hegemonic white(ness) sociological practice that transforms racialized Others into objects of study is ahistorical and atheoretical (Steinberg 2007; Zuberi and Bonilla-Silva 2008). Rather, hegemonic white(ness) sociology distorts, de-centers and makes invisible social histories and ahistoricizes race (e.g., pulling it from its meaning as a social structure). The hegemonic white(ness) sociological practice of objectifying racially Othered human groups into an ahistorical and atheoretical vacuum is poignantly illustrated by the framing of Black communities as the "Negro Problem." To this framing, Du Bois ([1903] 1973:44) asserted, "To the real question, how does it feel to be a problem? I answer seldom a word."

The hegemonic white(ness) sociological practice of being objective is really the practice of moral detachment where social inquiry is not *what is* and *what ought to be*, but rather what is and how it came to be (Steinberg 2007). This paradigmatic assumption refutes the connection between social thought and action, where social inquiry, theory and action are not meant to be means for social change. Instead, social action is surveilled and disciplined as antithetical to science (Collins 2007; Feagin and Vera 2008). Robert Park, the *father* of the race relations model, was a strong proponent of moral detachment (Steinberg 2007). Thus, while studying "race relations," Park, as a hegemonic white(ness) sociology paradigmatic path maker, made objective and value-free observations of Chicago's Race Riot of 1919 from the ivory towers of the University of Chicago (ibid.). The view from the ivory towers, in a metaphorical sense, allows for "evasion through silence" (ibid.: 43). Speaking through silence, hegemonic white(ness) sociology reinforces the status quo by rendering it invisible (ibid.). When sociologists paradigmatically centered in hegemonic white(ness) sociology historicize sociological inquiry, it is often grand theorizing which presents contemporary society as but a bystander of history (ibid.). Therefore, as hegemonic white(ness) sociology assumes race and racism are devoid of socio-historical contexts, race and racism are rendered ahistorical or just as a cycle of race-relations (ibid.). As such, Ida B. Wells-Barnett's social inquiry into lynching is rendered invisible by a hegemonic white(ness) sociology that maintained silence on the racialized social phenomena of lynching, although it was regarded as a regrettable instance of the cycle of race-relations.

In total, hegemonic white(ness) sociology, in its paradigmatic assumptions and practices, perpetuates white supremacy by reproducing misguided, non-centered ahistorical and atheoretical research of communities of color. This paradigm promotes what Steinberg (ibid.: 11) describes as an "epistemology of ignorance" (Kershaw 1992; Staples 1976). The reproduction of the white supremacist status quo in American sociology led Staples to aggressively critique hegemonic white(ness) sociology as the "science of oppression" (Staples 1973: 168). While hegemonic white(ness) sociology, in its privileged position within American sociology's disciplinary boundary of institutionalized knowledge, illusively reinforces social science as a tool of oppression, dialectically Black sociology paradigmatically assumes social science is a tool for liberation (Staples 1976). Therefore, just as white supremacy engages in a dialectic of oppression and liberation, so too does hegemonic white(ness) sociology and Black sociology engage in a dialectic of oppression and liberation.

Paradigmatically, Black sociology assumes history is central to understanding the social world and as such all social inquiry should be historically centered. As Fanon (1965: 13) asserted, there are no "timeless truths ... every human problem must be considered from the standpoint of time." History matters to the development of the sociological imagination, as articulated by C. Wright Mills (1959) whom Staples (1973: 169) acknowledged "provided a theoretical framework for Black sociology." Black sociology requires a global perspective that investigates exploitation and privilege of the capitalistic colonial and imperial world-system as well as how white supremacy structures power-relations therein. Accordingly, theory building is integral to Black sociology's paradigm, whereby contemporary social forces in the United States and globally are understood as grounded in the socio-historical foundations of institutions and structures. Thus, the study of contemporary social problems requires historical contextualization and theoretical conceptualizations centered within the community of study (Kershaw 1992; Robinson 1983; Zuberi and Bonilla-Silva 2008). For example, from a Black sociological paradigmatic center, the comparison of middle-class Black and white families requires differing norms of wealth accumulation and thus class situation (Oliver and Shapiro 1995). As such, historically centered research illustrates how white privilege and racism materializes in racial sedimentation of wealth disparities in the US as well as how colonialism and imperialism underdevelops Indigenous communities and nations while overdeveloping western communities and nation-states (Oliver and Shapiro 1995; Rodney 1972).

Centered within a historical global context, Black sociology is an Africana-centered paradigm whereby race, color, culture and racism are central in shaping and affecting peoples' socially lived experiences as well as social meanings, processes, institutions, systems and outcomes (Bell 1992; Better 2008; Ladner 1973). Importantly, race matters. However, while Black sociology assumes race underwrites socially lived experiences, social processes, structures and institutions, race is not solely understood as a means of oppression (Mills 1999). Rather, race serves to make meaning for lived experiences and develops a double-voiced discourse of both oppression and liberation (Higginbothom 1995).

Undeniably, Black sociology asserts that scientific objectivity is a fallacy. Instead, hegemonic white(ness) sociology's objectivity makes valid the status quo whereby anything else is biased or ideological (Bonilla-Silva 2014; Kershaw 1992; Steinberg 2007). Since knowledge is socially created and reproduced, dependent upon one's social location within the matrices of race, gender, class and nation, knowledge, itself is not objective (Collins 2000; Jones 1973; Sprague 2005). In an attempt to claim objectivity, sociological scholars must be forthright about their paradigm and the methodological components of their research. Making invisible one's paradigm, while rendering any subjectivity vacant, furthers racializes power-relations of knowledge. To refute concepts of ethnocentricism and Eurocentricism in hegemonic white(ness) sociology, Black sociology recognizes difference but not deference. This paradigmatic assumption is known as "cultural relativism" and it frames the notion that no one culture is superior rather all are relative (Staples 1976).

Specifically, Black sociology seeks to challenge racism, injustice and oppression in all its forms in addition to finding solutions for needs within the Black community for the express purpose of empowerment towards racial and social justice (Kershaw 1992; Ladner 1973; Staples 1976). Consequently, Black sociology seeks to determine the process of what is and what ought to be, for and by the community. Sociological knowledge is not meant for the ivory towers, but for grass-roots activism directed at social action, social justice and liberation. This idea is codified most notably in the scholar-activist approach (see Kershaw 1992; Collins 2000; Staples 1973). Consequently, Staples (1973: 168) identified Black sociology as the "science of liberation."

In total, white supremacy structures American sociology's disciplinary boundary of institutionalized knowledge that reinforces the racialized power-relations of the capitalistic colonial and imperial world-system superstructure of knowledge. American sociology's paradigmatic revolution and the qualitative materialization of Black sociology make visible white supremacist power-relations of knowledge and the real consequences for sociological inquiry. Black sociology's paradigmatic assumptions include the notion that social inquiry, theory and research are meant to challenge racism, injustice and oppression for the purpose of empowerment, social justice and social action for humanistic liberation. Centered within Black sociology's promotion of humanistic liberation, the sociology of knowledge has historically been and contemporarily is a central area of inquiry for Black sociology. The next section sojourns the history and contemporary issues of Black sociology's inquiry into the sociology of knowledge.

## Black Sociology: The Sociology of Knowledge and Contemporary Issues of Racialized Power-Relations of Knowledge

The sociology of knowledge is, at most, a humanistic and revolutionary endeavor, as the common denominator of every human group is the ability to create history and knowledge. As such, the sociology of knowledge has been, is and will be an important aspect of Black sociology as well as an integral part of the interdisciplinary Black Studies (Bonilla-Silva 2008; Du Bois 1935; Jones 1973; Turner [1984] 2007). The following section explores Black sociology's historical and contemporary utilization of the sociology of knowledge that makes visible racialized power-relations and the colonization of knowledge in order to promote deracialized and decolonized knowledge for social change and humanistic liberation.

As part of Black sociology, Africana social theorists interrogate the capitalist colonial and imperial world-system as a *total* system that includes the superstructure of knowledge and the "ideological aspect" (Rodney 1972: 99; Stanfield 2011a). Within this framework, a critical sociology of knowledge explores the "development of ideas in the [European] superstructure" and the monopoly of knowledge that allows for European and American domination (Rodney 1972: 99). Education and religion are two tentacles of capitalistic colonialism and imperialism that reinforce a Eurocentric monopolization of knowledge which Fanon (1965: 224) stated is an "intellectual endeavor [of] European culture [that enacts] intellectual alienation" (Rodney 1972). The problem with western formal education and its monopoly of knowledge is that it promotes a mis-education that enslaves the mind to ignorance and as a result enslaves actions whereby the educated are not taught to apply their knowledge for social change (Woodson [1933] 1977; Steinberg 2007). W.E.B. Du Bois, in *Black Reconstruction* (1935), illustrated how the US educational system used textbooks and university research to produce a *propaganda of history* that concealed the historical truth of reconstruction in order to promote white supremacist ideology. Du Bois ([1935]1995: 213) stated: "We shall never have a science of history until we have in our colleges men who regard the truth as more important than the defense of the white race, and who will not deliberately encourage students to gather thesis material in order to support a prejudice or buttress a lie."

Almost forty years later, Rhett Jones (1973: 134), in *The Death of White Sociology*, reiterated Du Bois's statement by suggesting that "[in the sciences a] vicious cycle operated [where]

21

whites believed Blacks to be inferior. Therefore white scientists believed them inferior and their experiments 'proved' them to be." As such, historically and contemporarily, an important issue in Black sociology is the use of the sociology of knowledge to illuminate racialized power-relations of knowledge, including research methods, methodology, theory and epistemology in order to deracialize and decolonize knowledge.

Historically atheoretical and acontextual data validated racism and the dehumanization of Africana and Indigenous peoples. Unfortunately, this practice continues today. Research centered in the Black sociological paradigm and the sociology of knowledge has produced knowledge that illustrates the ways in which white supremacy is deeply entrenched in sociological knowledge production including, but not limited to, research methods, methodology, theoretical application and production, and thus conclusions and outcomes (Bailey 2007; Bonilla-Silva and Biaocchi 2008; Holland 2008). Bonilla-Silva and Zuberi (2008: 17) identify how white supremacy underwrites hegemonic white(ness) sociology's epistemological practices and processes within social science as "white logic, [whereby] white supremacy define[s] the techniques and processes of reasoning about social facts." With "white logic, white methods [are employed] to manufacture empirical data and analysis [to sustain and perpetuate] racial stratification of society" (ibid.: 18). Sociological researchers paradigmatically centered within hegemonic white(ness) sociology are often atheoretical and acontextual in their study of contemporary social problems, particularly promoted by the positivist methodology (Dodoo and Beisel 2005; Khalfani et al. 2008; Sprague 2005). For instance, Khalfani and colleagues (2008: 80) illustrate how the use of acontextual demographic statistics "reinforce, legally, discrimination and privilege" as was the case in South Africa. Even further, the use of race as an independent, demographic and/or control variable is particularly problematic because "it flattens out the meanings of racial differences and replaces it with a generic notion of difference, [unless the race variable is] assessed and grounded in the set of historical and social circumstances that give [it] meaning" (James 2008: 43, 45; Holland 2008; Marks 2008). For that reason, scholars have argued race should be conceptualized as "'racialized group,' which stands for structures, ideologies, and attitudes historically instilled with 'racial meaning' [that is] also contingent and contested" (Bonilla-Silva 1997; Marks 2008:59; Zuberi and Bonilla-Silva 2008).

Aside from quantitative methods, scholars have also explored the role of qualitative methods in reproducing racialized knowledge. Bonilla-Silva, in his work *Racism without Racists* (2014), utilized both survey data on racial attitudes and interviews to explain contemporary racist ideology that he categorized as colorblind racism. Interviews were integral to interpreting the data on colorblind ideology because it allowed for an examination of how "racial ideology, and ideology, racial or not, is produced and reproduced in communicative action" (Bonilla-Silva 2014: 11). Due to this contemporary era of colorblind ideology, Eileen O'Brien (2011: 88) argues that in order to deracialize knowledge produced from interviews, and not reproduce "the default of colorblind racism," interviewers should "consciously activate race." Hence, while matching interviewers and interviewees based on shared racial identification is important, race alone does not create a sense of rapport when delving into topics about race. Instead, interviewers should engage ways in which the interviewer and interviewee share "racialized content of views and experiences" (ibid.).

Furthermore, scholars centered in the Black sociological paradigm who explore the sociology of knowledge find the interrogation of discourse to be critical (Fanon 1965; Rodney 1972). A critical, racialized lens frames language, spoken word and written text as cultural knowledge of meaning-making that, when institutionalized, reveals racialized power-relations. Africana social theorists illustrate how colonialism utilizes language as a tool to enact cultural violence where utilizing the colonizer's language means one sees and knows the world around them through the colonizer's socio-historical, cultural center (Asante 2003;

Fanon 1967; Memmi 1965; Ngũgĩ 1986; Rodney 1972). Discourse "plays a central role in the reproduction of racist attitudes and ideologies that are the socio-cognitive basis of the social system of racism [and as such the discipline of discourse studies] provides methodologies and theories to understanding how discourse reproduces racist ideology" (Dijk 2011: 43). Discourse analysis is a qualitative form of data analysis that reveals racist ideology.

Utilizing the Black sociological paradigm and the sociology of knowledge to critically explore American sociology's institutionalized knowledge, Rabaka (2010) makes visible how the white supremacist racialized structure of institutionalized knowledge enacts epistemic violence and epistemic apartheid of sociological knowledge (Steinberg 2007). Rabaka (2010) conceptualizes epistemic apartheid as "the processes of institutional racism or rather academic racial colonization and conceptual quarantining of knowledge, anti-imperial thought, and/or radical political praxis produced and presented by non-white—especially Black—intellectual activists."

Epistemic violence creates, maintains and revolutionizes racialized boundaries of valid knowledge whereby racially Othered knowledges are segregated, subjugated and seen as invalid while hegemonic white(ness) sociology is privileged. The segregation, exclusion, marginalization and subjugation of racially Othered knowers and knowledges enacts epistemic violence that affects American sociology's institutionalized knowledge reproduction and memory (Rabaka 2010; Wright II 2002a). For example, scholars have utilized the sociology of knowledge to illustrate the ways in which racialized power-relations of knowledge make the work of W.E.B. Du Bois, a foundational American sociologist, and the sociological knowledge produced at the Atlanta Sociological Laboratory, forgotten, academically ghettoized and marginalized, both historically and contemporarily, within American sociology (Rabaka 2010: 22; Wright II 2002a, 2002b, 2009, 2012a, 2012b). To combat this exclusion, or put into practice deracialized knowledge and social justice educational practices, Wright II (2012b) and Rabaka (2010) illustrate ways in which the Atlanta Sociological Laboratory and Du Bois's scholarship should be incorporated into the sociological curriculum (Wright II 2002a).

Lastly, epistemology is a central issue in Black sociology's exploration of the sociology of knowledge. Questions such as "what counts as knowledge," "whose knowledge counts as knowledge," and "how is deracialized knowledge created that refutes the monopoly of knowledge?" are especially important. Patricia Hill Collins (2000: 275), in *Black Feminist Thought*, outlines a "Black feminist epistemology [that is] consistent with Black women's criteria for substantiated knowledge and … criteria for methodological adequacy." First, Black feminist epistemology validates that Black women's lived experiences provide wisdom about matrices of domination (race, gender and class). This is an important aspect of "assessing knowledge, [where] knowledge without wisdom is adequate for the powerful, but wisdom is essential to the survival of the subordinate" (ibid.: 275, 276). Within the Black sociological paradigm, Black feminist epistemology and Black women's wisdom of race, gender and class as a matrix of domination produced the concept of intersectionality as an interpretive frame to produce knowledge for social action (ibid.). Second, Black feminist epistemology emphasizes the importance of dialogue. Collins centers dialogue as a "criteria for methodological adequacy [in African roots illustrated in] call-and-response discourse" (ibid.: 282). A third aspect of Black feminist epistemology is the "ethic of caring [that includes] the value placed on individual expressiveness, the appropriateness of emotions, and the capacity for empathy … [as] central to the knowledge validation process" (ibid.: 282). Lastly, the ethic of personal accountability is another central aspect of Black feminist epistemology. Knowledge produced, "views expressed[,] and actions taken are thought to derive from a central set of core beliefs that cannot be other than personal[, as such] assessments of an individual's knowledge claims simultaneously evaluate an individual's character, values, and ethics" (ibid.: 284). In total, Black feminist epistemology refutes "Eurocentric knowledge validation processes [and, based on its tenets, assesses that] values lie at the heart of the knowledge validation process such that [social] inquiry always has an ethical aim[,]" [meaning the prospects for social justice action are endless] (ibid.: 285).


## Discussion and Directions for Future Research

In total, the capitalist colonial and imperial world-system reinforces a superstructure of knowledge that reflects political-economic power (de Sousa Santos et. al. 2007; Stanfield 2011a). The colonaity of knowledge reproduces a Eurocentric, monocultural monopoly of knowledge that invalidates racially Othered knowledges and thus too dehumanizes human groups (Rodney 1972; de Sousa Santos et. al. 2007; Stanfield 2011a). The reproduction of racialized power-relations of knowledge, and especially within institutionalized knowledge, is such that racially Othered knowledge is colonized and made invisible while at the same time privileged hegemonic white(ness) knowledge is also made invisible as common-sense knowledge (Collins 2007; Rabaka 2010; Wright II 2002a). The reproduction of racialized power-relations and structural inequalities of knowledge is illustrated in American sociology's disciplinary boundary of institutionalized knowledge that materializes both hegemonic white(ness) sociology and Black sociology. Scholars centered in a Black sociological paradigm have utilized the sociology of knowledge as a tool to make visible racialized power-relations of knowledge, including but not limited to, in research methods, methodology, theory and epistemology, in order to promote social inquiry for the purpose of social justice and humanistic liberation.

Future directions of Black sociology's exploration of the sociology of knowledge are unlimited. Walter Rodney's (1972: 42) exploration of Africa's social and economic process of development "before the coming of Europeans [in] the 15th century [illustrated that religion was an important] part of [the African Indigenous] superstructure." Similarly, Collins (2000) stated that every tenet of Black feminist epistemology could be explored within the institution of the Black Church. Therefore, future directions of Black sociology's utilization of the sociology of knowledge could include an exploration of epistemological aspects of the Black Church, the role of religion as part of the Africana superstructure, as well as an exploration of spirituality as a means for creating and assessing knowledge (Collins 2000; Stanfield 2011a).

Being that history is a form of knowledge, scholars centered in a Black sociological paradigm should direct future research toward the ways in which educational socialization processes reproduce racialized structural inequalities of knowledge, where socialization within institutions includes repeating history. For example, Rabaka (2010:24) argues that "intellectual historical amnesia [is] undeniably a consequence of epistemic apartheid." To better understand the collective history of disciplines that are structured by racialized power-relations of knowledge requires the use of historical archival methods to make visible subjugated and excluded knowledges. Future research in this area is much needed (Deegan 2011; Stanfield 2011b).

Future research may also lie in the role of racialized power-relations of knowledge structuring the (in)visibility of the sociology of knowledge as a subfield in American sociology that ties directly to the racialized paradigmatic revolution of the 1970s. Interestingly, the year that Joyce Ladner's *The Death of White Sociology* was published (1973) is the same year that Black sociological paradigmatic scholars argued for the importance of the sociology of knowledge. Curtis and Petras (1973: 187) illustrated that although the sociology of knowledge was historically a central subfield of American sociology, it was "now nearly dead, especially in America." Therefore, future research should explore the subjugation of the sociology of knowledge within American sociology as a racial project born out of the racialized paradigmatic revolution of the 1960s and 1970s.

Lastly, critical race theory is an important area of Black sociological paradigm's future directions in the exploration of the sociology of knowledge. Critical race theory and methodology make visible the intellectual property of whiteness and the privileging of whiteness propertied knowledge (Dei and Calliste 2000; Harris 1993; Ladson-Billings and Tate IV 1998). It is "race-based methodologies [that] offer an epistemological shift in how we know what we know, how we come to believe such knowledge, and how we use it in our daily lives [and as such] contributes to a decentralization of Eurocentric thought" (Pillow 2003: 183, 189). In line with Black feminist epistemology, critical race theory assumes "personal storytelling and narratives ... shape ways of knowing" that "function as a counter-discourse ... that [allows an] analysis ... [of] epistemologies of racially oppressed peoples" (Carter 2003: 30; Tyson 2003: 20). Utilizing critical race theory and methodology directs future researchers to engage in research that explores how socialization practices "maintain an implicit hierarchy of knowledge," makes visible whiteness and non-whiteness epistemologies, the "ways of white folks—mores and practices—that have been institutionalized" in knowledge, and to challenge "Eurocentricism and racism in existing frameworks and epistemologies" (Margolis and Romero [1998] 2000: 19; Pillow 2003: 196; Tyson 2003: 23).

Regardless of the specific directions of future research, Black paradigmatic sociologists must continue to be

> ... willing to sacrifice white (mainstream) validation in exchange for research that is heavily self-directed and unapologetically critical of mainstream research [and] decolonize ... sociological imagination[s] ... to unlearn received truths about race, race relations, race research, and even ourselves and our own potential. (Hordge-Freeman et al. 2011: 114–15).

Black Sociology's exploration of the sociology of knowledge with the goal of deracializing and decolonizing knowledge is absolutely critical for social justice and humanistic liberation, because when you deracialize and decolonize "a man's [or a discipline's] thinking you [don't] have to worry about his [or the discipline's] actions" (Woodson [1933] 1977: xix).

# References

Abdi, Ali A. and Ailie Cleghorn. 2005. "Sociology of Education: Theoretical and Conceptual Perspectives." in *Issues in African Education: Sociological Perspectives*, eds. Ali A. Abdi and Ailie Cleghorn. New York: Palgrave MacMillan, pp. 3–23.

Asante, Molefi K. 2003. *Afrocentricity: The Theory of Social Change*. Chicago, IL: African American Images.

Bailey, Ronald. [1973] 2007. "Black Studies in Historical Perspective." in *The African American Studies Reader*, 2nd edn., ed. Nathaniel Norment, Jr. Durham, NC: Carolina Academic Press, pp. 302–10.

Bell, Derrick. 1992. *Faces at the Bottom of the Well: The Permanence of Racism*. New York: Basic Books Academic Press.

Better, Shirley. 2008. *Institutional Racism: A Primer on Theory and Strategies for Social Change*, 2nd edn. New York: Rowman and Littlefield Publishers, Inc.

Blauner, Robert. 1972. *Racial Oppression in America*. New York: Harper and Row Publishers.

Bonilla-Silva, Eduardo. 1997. "Rethinking Racism: Towards a Structural Interpretation." *American Sociological Review* 62: 465–80.

———. 2014. *Racism without Racists: Color-blind Racism and the Persistence of Racial Inequality in the United States*, 3rd edn. Lanham, M.D.: Rowman and Littlefield Publishers, Inc.

——— and Gianpaolo Biaocchi. 2008. "Anything but Racism: How Sociologists Limit the Significance of Racism." in *White Logic, White Methods: Racism and Methodology*, eds. Tukufu Zuberi and Eduardo Bonilla-Silva. Lanham, MD: Rowman and Littlefield Publishers, Inc., pp. 137–52.

——— and Tukufu Zuberi. 2008. "Toward a Definition of White Logic and White Methods." in *White Logic, White Methods: Racism and Methodology*, eds. Tukufu Zuberi and Eduardo Bonilla-Silva. Lanham, MD: Rowman and Littlefield Publishers, Inc., pp. 3–30.

Bourdieu, Pierre. 1977. "Cultural Reproduction and Social Reproduction." in *Power and Ideology in Education*, eds. J. Karabel and A.H. Halsey. New York: Oxford University Press, pp. 487–511.

Camic, Charles. 2010. "How Merton Sociologizes the History of Ideas." in *Robert K Merton: Sociology of Science and Sociology as Science*, ed. Craig Calhoun. New York: Columbia University Press, pp. 273–95.

Carter, Melanie. 2003. "Telling Tales Out of School: What's the Fate of a Black Story in a White World of Stones." in *Interrogating Racism in Qualitative Research Methodology*, eds. Gerardo R. Lopez and Laurence Parker. New York: Peter Lang, pp. 29–48.

Césaire, Aimé. 1972. *Discourse on Colonialism*. New York: MR.

Collins, Patricia Hill. 2000. *Black Feminist Thought: Knowledge, Consciousness, and the Politics of Empowerment*. Boston, MA: Unwin Hyman.

———. 2007. "Pushing the Boundaries or Business as Usual? Race, Class, and Gender Studies and Sociological Inquiry." in *Sociology in America A History*, ed. Craig Calhoun. Chicago, IL: University of Chicago Press, pp. 572–604.

Curtis, James E. and John W. Petras. 1972. "The Sociology of Knowledge in American Sociology: Origins, Development, and Future." *Kansas Journal of Sociology* 8(2): 181–204.

Deegan, Mary Jo. 2011. "Archival Methods and the Veil of Sociology." in *Rethinking Race and Ethnicity in Research Methods*, ed. John Stanfield II. Walnut Creek, CA: Left Coast Press, pp. 123–40.

Dei, George J. Sefa and Agnes Calliste. 2000. "Introduction: Mapping the Terrain: Power, Knowledge and Anti-Racism Education." in *Power, Knowledge, and Anti-Racism Education*, eds. Margarida Aguiar, Agnes Calliste and George Dei. Halifax: Fernwood Publishing, pp. 1–12.

van Dijk, Teun A. 2011. "Discourse Analysis of Racism." in *Rethinking Race and Ethnicity in Research Methods*, ed. John Stanfield II. Walnut Creek, CA: Left Coast Press, pp. 43–66.

Douglas, Mary. 1986. *How Institutions Think*. Syracuse, NY: Syracuse University Press.

Du Bois, W.E.B. [1903] 1973. *The Souls of Black Folk*. Millwood, NY: Kraus-Thomson Organization Ltd.

———. 1935. *Black Reconstruction in America 1860–1880*. New York: Free Press

Fanon, Frantz. 1965. *The Wretched of the Earth*. New York: Grove Press.

Feagin, Joe. 2006. *Systemic Racism: A Theory of Oppression*. New York: Routledge.

——— and Hernan Vera. 2008. *Liberation Sociology*, 2nd edn. London: Paradigm Publishers.

Friere, Paulo. 1970. *Pedagogy of the Oppressed*. New York: Seabury Press.

Fuller, Steve. 1993. "Disciplinary Boundaries and the Rhetoric of the Social Sciences." in *Knowledges: Historical and Critical Studies in Disciplinarity*, eds. Ellen Messer-Davidow,

David R. Shumway, and David J Sylvan. Charlottesville, VA: University of Virginia Press, pp. 125–49.

Glenn, Evelyn Nakano. 1999. "The Social Construction and Institutionalization of Gender and Race." in *Revisioning Gender*, eds. Mara Marx Ferree, Judith Lorber, and Beth B. Hess. Thousand Oaks, CA: Sage, pp. 3–43.

Harris, Cheryl I. 1993. "Whiteness as Property." *Harvard Law Review* 106(8): 1709–95.

Higginbothom, Evelyn Brooks. 1995. "African-American Women's History and the Metalanguage of Race." *We Specialize in the Wholly Impossible: A Reader in Black Women's History*, eds. Darlene Clark Hine, Wilma King, and Linda Reed. Brooklyn, NY: Carlson Publishing, Inc., pp. 3–24.

Holland, Paul W. 2008. "Causation and Race." in *White Logic, White Methods: Racism and Methodology*, eds. Tukufu Zuberi and Eduardo Bonilla-Silva. Lanham, MD: Rowman and Littlefield Publishers, Inc., pp. 93–110.

Hordge-Freeman, Elizabeth, Sarah Mayorga, and Eduardo Bonilla-Silva. 2011. "Exposing Whiteness Because We Are Free: Emancipation Methodological Practice in Identifying and Challenging Racial Practices in Sociology Departments." in *Rethinking Race and Ethnicity Research Methods*, ed. John Stanfield II. Walnut Creek, CA: Left Coast Press, pp. 95–122.

Hughey, Matthew W. 2010. "The (dis)similarities of white racial identities: the conceptual framework of 'hegemonic whiteness.'" *Ethnic and Racial Studies* 33(8): 1289–1309.

James, Angela. 2008. "Making Sense of Race and Racial Classification." in *White Logic, White Methods: Racism and Methodology*, eds. Tukufu Zuberi and Eduardo Bonilla-Silva. Lanham, MD: Rowman and Littlefield Publishers, Inc., pp. 31–45.

Jones, Rhett S. 1973. "Proving Blacks Inferior: The Sociology of Knowledge." in *The Death of White Sociology*, ed. Joyce Ladner. New York: Vintage Books, pp. 114–35.

Kaba, Lansine. 2007. "Historical Consciousness and Politics of Africa." in *Africana Studies: Philosophical Perspectives and Theoretical Paradigms*, eds. Delores P. Aldridge and E. Lincoln James. Pullman, WA: Washington State University Press, pp. 58–69.

Kershaw, Terry. 1992. "Toward a Black Studies Paradigm: An Assessment and Some Directions." *Journal of Black Studies* 22(4): 477–93.

Khalfani, Akil Koyaki, Tukufu Zuberi, Sulaiman Bah and Pali J. Lehohla. 2008. "Race and Population Statistics in South Africa." in *White Logic, White Methods: Racism and Methodology*, eds. Tukufu Zuberi and Eduardo Bonilla-Silva. Lanham, MD: Rowman and Littlefield Publishers, Inc., pp. 63–92.

Kuhn, Thomas S. 1970. *The Structure of Scientific Revolutions*. Chicago, IL: University of Chicago Press.

Ladner, Joyce. 1973. *The Death of White Sociology*. New York: Vintage Books.

Ladson-Billings, Gloria J. and William F. Tate IV. 1994. "Toward a Theory of Critical Race Theory in Education." *Teachers College Record* 97: 47–68.

Margolis, Eric and Mary Romero. [1998] 2000. "The Department is Very Male, Very White, Very Old, and Very Conservative: The Functioning of the Hidden Curriculum in Graduate Sociology Departments." in *The Sociology of Education* Vol. III, ed. Stephen Ball. London: Routledge, pp. 1276–311.

Marks, Carole. 2008. "Methodologically Eliminating Race and Racism." in *White Logic, White Methods: Racism and Methodology*, eds. Tukufu Zuberi and Eduardo Bonilla-Silva. Lanham, MD: Rowman and Littlefield Publishers, Inc., pp. 47–62

Marx, Karl. [1972] 2008. "Ideology and Class." in *Social Stratification: Class, Race, and Gender in Sociological Perspective*, ed. D.B. Grusky. Philadelphia, PA: Westview Press, pp. 89–90.

Memmi, Albert. 1965. *The Colonizer and the Colonized*. New York: Orion Press.

Mills, Charles. 1999. *The Racial Contract*. Ithaca, NY: Cornell University Press.

Mills, C. Wright. 1959. *The Sociological Imagination*. New York: Oxford University Press.

Ngũgĩ wa Thiang'o. 1986. *Decolonizing the Mind: The Politics of Language in African Literature*. London: J. Currey.

Oakes, Jeannie. 1985. *Keeping Track: How Schools Structure Inequality*. New Haven, CT: Yale University Press.

O'Brien, Eileen. 2011. "The Transformation of the Role of 'Race' in the Qualitative Interview: Not If Race Matters, But How?" in *Rethinking Race and Ethnicity in Research Methods*, ed. John Stanfield II. Walnut Creek, CA: Left Coast Press, pp. 67–94.

Oliver, Melvin L. and Thomas M. Shapiro. 1995. *Black Wealth/White Wealth: A New Perspective on Racial Inequality*. New York: Routledge.

Omi, Michael and Howard Winant. 1994. *Racial Formation in the United States: From the 1960s to the 1980s*, 2nd edn. New York: Routledge.

Pillow, Wanda. 2003. "Race-Based Methodologies: Multicultural Methods or Epistemological Shifts." in *Interrogating Racism in Qualitative Research Methodology*, eds. Gerardo R. Lopez and Laurence Parker. New York: Peter Lang, pp. 181–202.

Rabaka, Reiland. 2010. *Against Epistemic Apartheid: W.E.B. Du Bois and the Disciplinary Decadence of Sociology*. New York: Rowman and Littlefield Publishers, Inc.

Robinson, Cedric J. 1983. *Black Marxism: The Making of the Black Radical Tradition*. London: Zed.

Rodney, Walter. 1972. *How Europe Underdeveloped Africa*. London: Bogle-L'Ouverture Publications.

Sica, Alan. 2007. "Defining Disciplinary Identity: The Historiography of U.S. Sociology." in *Sociology in America A History*, ed. Craig Calhoun. Chicago, IL: University of Chicago Press, pp. 713–31.

Smith, Linda Tuhiwai. 2012. *Decolonizing Methodologies: Research and Indigenous Peoples*, 2nd edn. New York: Zed Books.

de Sousa Santos, Boaventura, João Arriscado Nunes, and Maria Paula Meneses. 2007. "Introduction: Opening Up the Canon of Knowledge and Recognition of Difference." in *Another Knowledge is Possible: Beyond Northern Epistemologies*, ed. Boaventura de Sousa Santos. New York: Verso, pp. xvivx–lxii.

Sprague, Joey. 2005. *Feminist Methodologies for Critical Researchers: Bridging Differences*. New York: AltaMira Press.

Stanfield II, John H. 2011a. *Black Reflective Sociology: Epistemology, Theory, and Methodology*. Walnut Creek, CA: Left Coast Press.

———. 2011b. *Rethinking Race and Ethnicity in Research Methods*, ed. John H. Stanfield. Walnut Creek, C.A.: Left Coast Press.

Staples, Robert. 1973. "What is Black Sociology?" in *The Death of White Sociology*, ed. Joyce Ladner. New York: Vintage Books, pp. 161–72.

———. 1976. *Introduction to Black Sociology*. New York: McGraw-Hill.

Steinberg, Stephen. 2007. *Race Relations: A Critique*. Stanford, CA: Stanford Social Sciences

Trouillot, Michel-Rolph. 1995. *Silencing the Past: Power and the Production of History*. Boston, MA: Beacon Press.

Turner, James E. [1984] 2007. "Africana Studies and Epistemology: A Discourse in the Sociology of Knowledge." in *The African American Studies Reader*, ed. Nathaniel Norment, Jr. Durham, NC: Carolina Academic Press, pp. 74–87.

Tyson, Cynthia. 2003. "Research, Race, and an Epistemology of Emancipation." in *Interrogating Racism in Qualitative Research Methodology*, eds. Gerardo R. Lopez and Laurence Parker. New York: Peter Lang, pp. 19–28.

Wallerstein, Immanuel. 2007. "The Culture of Sociology in Disarray: The Impact of 1968 on U.S. Sociologists." in *Sociology in America A History*, ed. Craig Calhoun. Chicago, IL: University of Chicago Press, pp. 427–37.

Woodson, Carter G. [1933] 1977. *The Mis-Education of the Negro*. New York: AMS Press.

Wright II, Earl. 2002a. "The Atlanta Sociological Laboratory 1896–1924: A Historical Account of the First American School of Sociology." *The Western Journal of Black Studies* 26(3): 165–74.

———. 2002b. "Why Black People Tend To Shout!: An Earnest Attempt To Explain the Sociological Negation of the Atlanta Sociological Laboratory Despite Its Possible Unpleasantness." *Sociological Spectrum* 22(3): 325–61.

———. 2009. "Beyond W.E.B. Du Bois: A Note on Some of the Little Known Members of the Atlanta Sociological Laboratory." *Sociological Spectrum* 29:6:700–717.

———. 2012a. "Using the Master's Tools: The Atlanta Sociological Laboratory and American Sociology, 1896–1924." *Sociological Spectrum* 22(1):15–39.

———. 2012b. "Why, Where, and How to Infuse the Atlanta Sociological Laboratory into the Sociology Curriculum." *Teaching Sociology* 40(3): 257–70.

Zuberi, Tukufu and Eduardo Bonilla-Silva (eds.). 2008. *White Logic, White Methods: Racism and Methodology*. Lanham, MD: Rowman and Littlefield Publishers, Inc.

# PART II
# Black Youth, Emerging Adults and the Family

# The Death of Trayvon Martin and Public Space: Why the Racial Contract Still Matters

## Darwin Fishman

*Thus in effect, on matters related to race, the racial contract prescribes for its signatories an inverted epistemology, an epistemology of ignorance, a particular pattern of localized and global cognitive dysfunctions (which are psychologically and socially functional), producing the ironic outcome that whites will in general be unable to understand the world they themselves have made.*

*– Charles W. Mills (1997: 18)*

## Introduction

In the current debates about whether or not we are in a post-racial moment one can see the outline of a perpetual debate that can never be satisfied. On one side of this debate, the loud clamor for racial success can be seen and the endless examples, usually starting with our first African American President Barack Obama, of racial success will and can be articulated quite clearly. On the other side of this debate is the much less vocal and visible group that can point out racial inequities and structural deficits. What can be less noticed in this debate is how predictable and obvious future conversations on this topic will (d)evolve in future generations. Charles Mills's work, *The Racial Contract* (1997), provides insight into this debate by allowing one to safely reach this conclusion. At first blush it appears that Mills's work is deeply entrenched in western philosophical traditions and that his scholarship has little utility beyond the narrow confines of these broader philosophical debates. Closer scrutiny of his writings help highlight the way that Mills's work confronts some of the most sacrosanct underpinnings of western philosophy while providing an exceptional lens through which one can examine current racial trends. Specifically, Mills's work on a racial contract can be used to examine what happened to Trayvon Martin when he was confronted by George Zimmerman on February 26th, 2012 in Sanford, Florida. This fatal meeting between a man and an adolescent can be understood as not just another retort in the perpetual debate on whether or not we have reached a post-racial moment; but it can be persuasively presented that this fateful meeting was very much anticipated in Mills's works from 15 years prior. Mills provides the groundwork for a theoretical foundation that successfully challenges the most critical building blocks of western philosophy. However, his theoretical framework also provides a potent lens to observe and evaluate why our current race relations continue to be tied to so many lethal and tragic racial encounters, especially for young African American males.

Finding the proper place for race and racism within the western philosophical tradition appears to be a never-ending struggle. There have been attempts to both refute and embrace

race and racism as essential components of the western philosophical tradition. A prime example of this battle is discourse centered on and around social contract theories and its history. Social contract theory is typically presented as not just the basis of modern nation-states, it is also presented as a masterful race-less, class-less, gender-less, sex-less and timeless narrative. This narrative represents the cornerstone of western political and philosophical thought. Charles Mills re-centers the debate about our understanding of the social contract as an organizing principle in our society in his book, *The Racial Contract*. Here he introduces the theoretical and conceptual framework for a racial contract as a critique of social contract theories. Examining traditional social contract discourse, as developed by Thomas Hobbes, John Locke, Jean-Jacques Rousseau and Immanuel Kant, through a race and racism lens forces difficult epistemological and ontological questions to be raised. These questions do not center exclusively on social contract discourse, but the ways that western politics and philosophies have been traditionally presented and understood. Establishing race as a foundational concept in our modern world, Mills provides a way to contest, reform and displace our familiar and comfortable understanding and use of social contract theories and narratives. Mills's work is a particularly noteworthy effort for a variety of substantive reasons and it is these areas that will be the focus of this work.

There have been many attempts to challenge the dominant western paradigm and provide alternative accounts and theoretical frameworks for this western political and philosophical tradition. In one camp are those that use deconstructive tools to shed light on the weaknesses and failings of the western philosophical tradition. These critical review strategies can be typically mapped along the lines of identity politics (gender, race and sexuality) or liberal and radical politics (reform and revolutionary). These camps can be divided further into those that are willing not only to critique certain aspects of western discourse or western politics and thought in and of itself, but those that dare to posit a solution or a new overarching paradigm. These divisions also provide insights into postmodern and post-structuralist positions that call into question the viability and value of attempting to replace certain aspects, or all, of western thought and politics. Mills firmly wades into these dangerous waters by not only providing a scathing critique of social contract theory and narrative, but also by advocating for a distinctly new, race-based approach.

To the extent it is possible that Mills's development of a counter-theory can successfully challenge the larger western philosophical discourse, or simply be dismissed as irrelevant, the next phase of advancing this perspective includes examining his theory within contemporary examples and frames. That is what this inquiry attempts to accomplish. Fifteen years after the publication of *The Racial Contract*, combined with landmark racial events in the US, including civilian and police shootings of unarmed African American men, a fertile milieu within which Mills's work can now be re-evaluated and re-assessed exists. First, the way in which the racial contract fits into contemporary political, social and economic debates is addressed.

Mills's vision of a racial contract and how it fits into larger philosophical and theoretical debates can be seen in the context of other debates about the nature, scope and significance of the social contract, as well as the larger debates about western discourse itself. How well Mills navigates these debates and the strength of his arguments can be evaluated from various political and moral standpoints. In introducing Mills's work, most attention is devoted to larger meta-theoretical divisions and the implications of what is being contested and defended. Less attention is devoted to Mills's specific use of the social contract and how faithfully he follows the schematic established by previous scholars. It is critical that the merits of Mills's work are not analyzed through the narrow lens of what the accuracy (or inaccuracy) of a particular use of the social contract means. Instead it should be examined through alternative arguments, including whose voice is involved in the presentation(s) of social contract theory and how that history will be examined. The potential benefits of utilizing a racial contract as a way to address and correct the weaknesses that any use of a social contract theory or narrative might have for our understanding of the world is also addressed.

From this larger frame of analysis, it will be possible to move into the more specific terrain of race and racism. In this section of the analysis, a case can be made that this work connects to and supports that of previous African American scholars and activists. These scholars' works help to highlight the strength Mills's work can have in the realm of analyzing current issues and events and, specifically, what explanatory power a racial contract approach can hold for all of us. While examining Mills's racial contract through the specific filter of African American experience, it is important to draw attention to the way that the meaning and significance of our history is supplemented and supported by his work. With this guiding principle in mind, the shooting death of Trayvon Martin serves as an example of how Mills's understanding of a racial contract might operate in a contemporary setting. One can interrogate this event from the standpoint of the applicability of social contract theory and the racial contract theory. Questions can be asked about the shooting death of Martin as one evaluates which theoretical approaches provide the most meaningful and significant answer(s) to why and how Martin died. It is critical then to not let the debate about the social contract remain at an abstract level and assume that it is so firmly entrenched in every facet and aspect of our modern society that it is impossible to provide any meaningful or significant assessment of it. If one were to start the process of evaluating whether or not the social contract should be replaced, changed or left intact, then the ground-level perspective that the Martin shooting provides us is an invaluable resource for this type of analysis.

## Social Contract Versus the Racial Contract

In explaining his use of a racial contract as theoretical trope, Mills first delves into the history and origins of the social contract. Mills (ibid.: 3) offers the following introduction:

> We all understand the idea of a "contract," an agreement between two or more people to do something. The "social contract" just extends this idea. If we think of human beings as starting off in a "state of nature," it suggests that they then decide to establish civil society and a government. What we have, then, is a theory that founds government on the popular consent of individuals taken as equals.

This notion of a social contract is very familiar terrain for those properly seasoned in western philosophy and scholarship through the works of writers like Thomas Hobbes, John Locke, Jean-Jacques Rousseau and Immanuel Kant. It is standard practice to learn about the growth and development of western history from the standpoint of the role a conceptual framework for a social contract has played in this process. The history of the modern world only begins to make sense if we use the heuristic tool that the social contract provides. What made Europe *succeed* and the rest of the world *follow* this model of existence is retold through the story of how humans were led out of the state of nature by their ability to make a social contract with other humans. This established the framework for nation-states to establish various and democratic forms of governments. These governments would then establish and maintain order through the contractual agreement amongst equal men.

Mills (ibid.: 12) draws attention to the racial nature and implications of this dominant western narrative when he describes the role of the social contract in the formation of modern nation-states:

> *Politically, the contract to establish society and the government, thereby transforming abstract race-less "men" from denizens of the state of nature into social creatures who are politically obligated to a neutral state, becomes the founding of a racial polity, whether white settler states (where preexisting populations already are or can be made spare) or what are sometimes called "sojourner colonies," the establishment of a white presence and colonial rule over existing societies.*

What Mills correctly draws attention to is the fact that these race-less men become the foundation of this narrative. Whether it is Hobbes, Locke, Rousseau or Kant, scant attention is devoted to the racial implications of their work. It is typically assumed that the social contract narrative can not only explain European history, but that the history of the entire world can be accurately presented through a social contract lens. The social contract becomes the vehicle by which each state traveled to and entered the modern world. Everyone followed the European model in the exact manner as scholars such as Hobbes, Locke, Rousseau and Kant first presented and described the concept. With the sheer brutality and force embedded in the European colonial expansion project, it is not difficult to understand the appeal of social contract as a theory and as a human project that millions were subjected to both voluntarily and involuntarily.

It is from this vantage point that Mills (ibid.: 1–2) builds a case for the necessity and value of a racial contract. The starting point for the racial contract comes from what is left out of and not engaged in by western discourse:

> *... the fact that standard textbooks and courses have for the most part been written and designed by whites who take their racial privilege so much for granted that they do not even see it as political, as a form of domination. Ironically, the most important political system of recent global history—the system of domination by which white people have historically ruled over and, in certain important ways, continue to rule over nonwhite people—is not seen as a political system at all. It is just taken for granted; it is the background against which other systems, which we are to see as political, are highlighted.*

Mills adds another dimension to this dominant narrative with the case he builds for the necessity of a racial contract. The problem with the dominant narrative presented in western discourse is not just that it is inaccurate, but that it is infused with differential and detrimental power relations. The toxic mix of inaccurate and profound misunderstandings of historical and contemporary power relations scream out for an intervention. For those who do not live in the West and those that are not of non-western ancestry this narrative does not fit their conception of history nor does it help to explain their current conditions.

This intervention can be seen in the definition of a racial contract that Mills offers to challenge and supplant the dominant social contract. Put simply, Mills (ibid.: 10) asserts that:

> *... the Racial Contract—and the 'Racial Contract' as a theory, that is, the distanced, examination of the Racial Contract—follows the classical model in being both sociopolitical and moral. It explains how society was created or crucially transformed, how the individuals in that society were constituted, how the state was established,*

*and how a particular moral code and a certain moral psychology were brought into existence.*

This conveniently sets the table for an examination of what continues to be excluded from the dominant western social contract narrative. It also adds the element of the moral fabric for a particular re-reading of this social contract and what moral consequences are attached to this re-reading process. A simple correction or revisionist history then cannot be the goal of Mills's work because the actual lives of contemporary victims of this social contract are still being produced, contested and violently battled over. Mills highlights these points by suggesting that the goal of the racial contract must have a descriptive component, as well as a normative function (ibid.).

One way to understand Mills's project is by drawing attention to the fact that his works properly illuminate the significance of viewing western tradition from the vantage point of winners and losers. The narrative of a social contract stands firmly on the side of the victor. This understanding links directly to our historical and contemporary racial discourse. Mills (ibid.: 11) provides a way to understand how race and racism continue to operate in our society.

> ... but in any case the general purpose of the Contract is always the differential privileging of the whites as a group with respect to the nonwhites as a group, the exploitation of their bodies, land, and resources, and the denial of equal socioeconomic opportunities to them. All whites are beneficiaries of the Contract, though some whites are not signatories to it.

By inserting the concept of a racial contract as his key theoretical premise, Mills makes a compelling case for the explanatory power that race continues to hold for how our modern world operates. By analyzing Mills's work through western and non-western filters specific weaknesses in the traditional social contract can be highlighted, as well as the specific value the concept of a racial contract can have for understanding our historical development and our current state of affairs. It is also from this vantage point that current debates about reparations for African Americans can be initiated and debated.

## State of Nature Versus Better Natural State?

As previously discussed, the social contract never offered a fulfilling historical or philosophical narrative via the perspectives of the 'Fathers of Western discourse'—Hobbes, Locke, Rousseau or Kant—and it is important to adequately address the consequences of their critiques. The premise of this narrative has always been deeply flawed. There was never a simple dichotomy between those that lived in a state of nature and those that moved into a social contract. The reality is that the state of nature was the normal state of human affairs for at least 99 percent of the time that humans have been on earth. From an anthropological standpoint, this historical perspective of human life turns typical questions about "normal" and "natural" on their, respective, heads. This perspective immediately calls into question what is so appalling about 99 percent of our time on earth that a dramatic change in lifestyle was needed. The other key point is the notion that 99 percent of human history was based on a nomadic lifestyle and a social organization premised on family and extended family life units. This state of nature lifestyle was also dependent on a social contact, if for no other reason than mere survival. It was not possible to confront and successfully maneuver through the ecological and environmental conditions of that period without the implementation of tightly knit groups of humans working in concert. The daily challenges of finding food and maintaining shelter were embraced by these small clan units out of necessity for survival.

Mills's specific critique of the racial nature of this social contract explicitly acknowledges these anthropological insights about human history. In particular, Mills (ibid.: 13) claims:

> The role played by the "state of nature" then becomes radically different. In the white settler state, its role is not primarily to demarcate the (temporarily) prepolitical state "all" men (who are really white men), but rather the permanently prepolitical state or, perhaps better, nonpolitical state (insofar as 'pre' suggests eventual internal movement toward) of nonwhite men. The establishment of society thus implies denial that a society already existed; the creation of society requires the intervention of white men, who are thereby positioned as already sociopolitical beings. White men who are (definitionally) already part of society encounter nonwhite who are not, who are "savage" residents of a state of nature characterized in terms of wilderness, jungle wasteland.

What is significant for the social contract is not a generic transformation from state of nature to the social contract existence, but the specific story of European development. The nomadic and small family-unit existence that is paramount for human history still exists in parts of the western as well as the non-western worlds. These people are not, then, in a state of nature simply waiting to be delivered to a social contract existence. This is not "their" story, but is what their story would sound like from a European vantage point.

The salient point that Mills illustrates is that, to the extent that the existence of a social contract must rely on a movement from a state of nature to undergird its value and significance, this understanding of human history runs counter to the one based on anthropological knowledge of human history. Much of what the historical truisms that are claimed by the advancement a social contract narrative posits can easily be refuted from the standpoint of how groups of people, such as indigenous groups in North and South America, survived on a daily basis. In particular, Mills (1997:15) states:

> In part, then, the political contract simply codifies a morality that already exists, writing it down and filling in the details, so we don't have to rely on a divinely implanted moral sense, or conscience, whose perceptions may on occasion be distorted by self-interest. What is right and wrong, just an unjust, in society will largely be determined by what is right and wrong, just and unjust, in the state of nature.

Mills turns the question of morality on its head by claiming there would be no tangible differences in a state of nature or social contract society and this highlights the limited explanatory power of the western philosophical tradition. To buttress these observations Mills references multiple historical examples including genocide, slavery and de jure racism. This raises questions about how societies can produce a healthy moral structure and simultaneously develop just and moral traditions. The presentation of a traditional social contract-grounded perspective which suggests the only path towards social, moral, political and economic development is through a western-influenced perspective invariably leads to a Eurocentric bias through a very limited filter. This approach also misses the way in which morality and moral judgments are produced and navigated on a daily basis. To address this point, the next section considers a contemporary moral dilemma as seen through the filter of how race and racism operate today.

## Short Brutish Lives Déjà Vu?

The killing of Trayvon Martin provides a critical vantage point to evaluate Mills's assessment of the social contract, as well as his presentation of a racial contract. Martin's story is, on one level, all too common from the standpoint of the history of Africans in America—young, unarmed Black male shot to death while traveling near home and supposedly mistaken for the wrong "Nigger." Even with the added twist of the shooter, George Zimmerman, not being a police officer and being biracial (Latino and White), the death of Martin and the initial willingness of local authorities to allow Zimmerman to escape immediate arrest after the shooting has a very familiar ring to it. It is also a story that was very predictable and closely follows the lines of analysis that so many current and past Black scholars and activists have posited. Mills is no exception to this larger body of critical race work. There are areas of significance that his racial contract perspective highlights and his specific use of a racial contract lens provides important openings into the larger canon of western philosophy.

It is important to draw attention again to the fact that Mills wrote *The Racial Contract* 15 years before Martin was killed, but the circumstances that led to his death and the actual incident that transpired can clearly be seen in Mills's work. Specifically, Mills's section on space explains the conditions under which Martin could be *accidentally* shot by the *friendly neighborhood watchman*. In describing the way in which space is dominated by race, Mills (ibid.: 52) states:

> These traversals of space are imprinted with domination: prescribed posture of deference and submission for the black Other, the body language of no uppitiness (no "reckless eyeballing"); traffic-codes of priority ("my space can walk through yours and you must step aside"); unwritten rules for determining when to acknowledge the nonwhite presence and when not, dictating spaces of intimacy and distance, zones of comfort and discomfort ("thus far and no farther") ... lynching to proscribe and punish the ultimate violation, the penetration of black into white space.

Given the fact that Zimmerman admitted to killing Martin and that he believed Martin to be a potential criminal, he was closely following the racial codes for security and domination of space that Mills has described. Martin had entered a (White) gated space and it was Zimmerman's duty to protect this space from any suspicious-looking person(s)—particularly young, Black, hoody-wearing potential troublemakers—as he charged himself with the task of deciding exactly who was qualified to enter his (White) gated space. This was why Zimmerman could ignore unambiguous directions from the 911 operator to cease and desist his pursuit of Martin and why he was anxious for authorities to assume control over the crime scene immediately after the shooting. Zimmerman was certain with every fiber of his being that this suspicious young Black male (read: punk) was up to no good and that he not only had the right to intervene with a loaded gun, but that he was performing a civic/public duty. By the same racial token, if Martin had just not worn a menacing hoody and had he appeared less uppity, he could have safely traveled through that (White) gated space.

It is apparent that, at least initially, the Sanford Police Department tacitly supported Mills's White spatial domination thesis, since no charges were initially filed against Zimmerman; he was not administered a drug test nor were his hands examined for gunpowder residue. Conversely, Trayvon Martin's body was tested for drug use. Mills (ibid.: 53) would argue that this suggests:

> ... there is a sense in which the real polity is the virtual white polity, then, without pushing the metaphor too far, one could say that the nonwhite body is a moving bubble

*of wilderness in white political space, a node of discontinuity which is necessarily in permanent tension with it.*

It is significant to note that when these bodies come into tension, even lethal tension, there is a very predictable script of White domination and supremacy that is presented within a public setting. It is first assumed that the Black body is in the wrong space (e.g., the White gated community is Zimmerman's "home"); that the Black body is a threat (e.g., Zimmerman's comments about hoodies and those people); and that White intervention is needed, required and ultimately rewarded (e.g., Zimmerman is not arrested and received an outpouring of support on the web page set up for his legal defense). It could also be argued that with or without a "Stand Your Ground" law, the actual proof of innocence or guilt can always be determined by the White person's assessment of threat, danger and risk. The shooting deaths of young Black men in Florida, and all over the US, and the determination of the guilt or innocence of the accused have never been dependent on laws that are passed, observed and enforced. Mills (ibid.: 25) correctly draws upon American history and makes the argument for the existence of a slavery contract:

> *A classic statement of the slavery contract is the 1857 Dred Scott V. Sanford U.S. Supreme Court decision of Chief Justice Roger Taney, which stated that blacks had for more than a century before been regarded as beings of an inferior order, and altogether unfit to associate with the white race, either in social or political relations; and so far inferior, that they had no rights which the white man was bound to respect, and that the negro might justly and lawfully be reduced to slavery for his benefit.*

This allows one to connect the dots between not just how race functions on a personal level and in a public space, but how race operates in a historical frame and has been sanctioned and given legitimacy by the highest courts of the land. Martin represents another chapter that can be added to the book of truisms that Blacks have "no rights which the white man was bound to respect" and also the mythical "post-racial" period we have entered since the election of the nation's first African American president. The way in which this point is then reinforced on a daily basis adds credence to the existence of a racial contract. Literally, initially, no one was held responsible for Martin's death and nothing short of a social media-driven national social movement was needed to compel the state of Florida to charge Zimmerman with Martin's death several months later.

This racial script is unfortunately played out daily in the US and it results in the, at best, mistreatment or, at worst, death of young men of color on an all-too-frequent basis. Mills addresses the way in which this narrative is tied into the very fabric of our society. In particular, Mills (ibid.: 6) declares that:

> *Subpersons are humanoid entities who, because of racial phenotype/genealogy/culture, are not fully human and therefore have a different and inferior schedule of rights and liberties applying to them. In other words, it is possible to get away with doing things to subpersons that one could not do to persons, because they do not have the same rights as person. Insofar as racism is addressed at all within mainstream moral and political philosophy it is usually treated in a footnote as regrettable deviation from the ideal.*

This means the way that we learn about moral and political philosophy has a direct connection to the racial script we abide by. The tragic end that Martin confronted as a just-turned 17-year-old Black male in our society was not only predictable, it was preventable. The way in which

Mills presents the racial contract provides the analytical lens for understanding events such as Martin's death. It also advises on ways to intercede. The following questions, grounded in Mill's work, could be the starting point for the re-examination of the social contract and a pathway for exiting the racial contract. What would happen if the social contract was not taught in every high school and every college as the basis of western philosophy and history? What if the racial contract was used instead and everyone was required to learn about the racial space and identity he or she occupied historically, as well as in today's society? Could this radically transform our society and the world?

## Conclusion

Mills' presentation of a racial contract becomes salient for not just for an analysis of contemporary domestic issues, but his work also provides an invaluable tool to gain an understanding of how the production of race and racism continues as a foundational component within our society. To the extent that a racial contract has a life outside of academia, the spheres of power and influence can be uncovered and examined through the lens of Trayvon Martin's tragic death. Martin, traveling through the very well demarcated (White) gated space as understood by a gun-carrying George Zimmerman, was unaware of the racial contract and its connection with his life. When placed in the context of a social contract tradition that relies on an understanding of a linear development, some very noticeable limitations and weaknesses become apparent. For Martin, traveling to and from his father's girlfriend's home in Sanford, Florida was fraught with danger because he was not granted the social contract protection every American citizen is entitled because of a racial identity that stripped his social contract privilege of any meaning or significance. As Mills correctly identifies, the socially constructed meaning and significance of racial identity led to Martin's tragic death. It is through a racial contract lens that we can historically understand the way in which irrational and lethal fears of African American men have been sewn into the fabric of our society to such an extent that there are few safe spaces left for African American men.

Mills's racial contract can be shown to illuminate some new pathways, as well as placing a useful and critical lens on the applied and theoretical contributions a social contract can provide us with. How to develop these new and well-established openings is not as clear-cut and it also illustrates the way in which Mills encounters the same dilemmas that other anti-racist scholars and activists have experienced. As previously suggested, given the way these intellectual as well as physical, social, political, spiritual and economic battles have been disputed for centuries does not lend itself to quick-fix solutions or magical resolutions. Utilizing Mills's work as a weapon that is part of a larger arsenal does make a lot of sense from the vantage point of action occurring on a larger battlefield. Understanding the level in which Mill's meta-theoretical and historical work engages western discourse is a crucial point for assessing what tactics and strategies might be most successful and useful for anti-racist scholars and activists to adopt and develop. This brings us back to the previous points about how the social contract is raised by Mills and the master narrative that has been created in and around social contract theories and history. This material can be read as a European "victory story" and not as an actual history of humankind. This "story" continues to be a significant battlefield for not just for the development of a better or more accurate story, but also from the standpoint of real anti-racist work that needs to be done each every day. Whether or not this history is presented from the vantage point of a social or a racial contract, the reality has been and continues to be a distinctly western narrative; a narrative that is of very limited used to non-western populations both in the West and beyond. To the extent that Mills's explicit use of a racialized title draws attention to this accepted and traditional story and is able to re-focus a critical lens on it, the debate will not be resolved nor all of the outstanding issues answered. There are obviously powerful forces at play that allow for the continued reading of the social contract as disconnected, non-grounded universal narrative of progress and development to be consumed and utilized on a regular basis. The social contract will also still be used as a barometer to measure how much a particular individual or a society has moved out of the state of nature and into the proper modern state based on a social contract and an implied higher state of being. The fact that this basis of existence has been rooted in White bodies and in a certain level of material and resource-based wealth risks being hidden and marginalized, and suggests that anti-racist scholars and activists will have to carry the burden of finding effective methods for intervention. Attempts to highlight and draw attention to the exact racial hierarchy and power-relations that are drawn around this western dominance will be very much needed, and Mills's work fits in quite well within this tradition of resistance and speaking truth to power.

# References

Mills, Charles W. 1997. *The Racial Contract*. Ithaca, NY: Cornell University Press.

# Is it Easy Living in the Big Easy?: Examining the Lives of African American Emerging Adults in the Aftermath of Hurricane Katrina

### Farrah Gafford Cambrice

*I just wanted to go home. I did not care if there was mold. I did not care if it is ruined. I just wanted to be really close to my environment. It was not until I got to Georgia when I started to see how much the city was a part of me. Stuff that I did other people did not do. I was Catholic. People in Georgia would also ask me things like, "Why do you talk like that?" It would really frustrate me. I just felt so alienated. My grandmother was not in Georgia with us and my Auntie Nikki was gone. I think what I missed the most was the culture. It was the little things. They did not have crawfish. No snowballs, French bread, seasoning and red beans. But the little things do add up and when they are taken from you and it is like every which way you look everything is different. Eventually you are like, what do I have left?*
– (Briana Robinson, 21 years old, personal communication, May 29, 2013)[1]

Long before Hurricane Katrina, African American youth residing in New Orleans, Louisiana were an extremely vulnerable population. Of the families who lived in poverty, 91.2 percent were African American (Turner and Zedlewski 2006). In neighborhoods like the Lower Ninth Ward, the average household earned slightly more than $20,000 annually (Berube and Katz 2005). Additionally, many of the city's poorest families were living in some of the most segregated communities. The average African American family in New Orleans resided in neighborhoods in which nearly 82 percent of their neighbors were of the same race. Segregated neighborhoods in urban areas are typically associated with high crime and poverty rates, limited social networks and poor schools (ibid.).

The unprecedented damage of Hurricane Katrina created additional challenges for African American youth and their families. The initial images of residents stranded at the New Orleans Superdome and the Morial Convention Center were the first and most vivid indicators that African American families bore the brunt of Hurricane Katrina. Without credit cards, savings accounts or adequate transportation, the families who were forced to stay endured days of rising flood waters, heat and chaos before being evacuated from New Orleans. The destruction of New Orleans's physical structures and services left many families displaced for extended periods. As the opening description by Briana Robinson shows, some families relocated hundreds of miles away from New Orleans leaving youth to adjust to new schools, peers and life void of New Orleans' distinctive culture. While there has generally been a great amount of interest in how the storm affected African American

---

1    Pseudonyms are used to protect the anonymity of research participants in this study.

families in New Orleans, little research has focused on the experiences of African American adolescents who endured Katrina.

African American survivors of Hurricane Katrina, like Briana, are currently at critical junctures in their lives. They are no longer adolescents, but their transition into adulthood is not quite complete. Scholars refer to the stage between adolescence and adulthood as "emerging adulthood." Emerging adulthood occurs between age 18 and 25 and is a time for self-focus and the exploration of possibilities (Arnett 2000). The emerging adulthood concept also speaks to the extended or prolonged transition into full adulthood. Unlike fifty years ago, modern men and women are likely to delay more traditional markers of adulthood (i.e., marriage, children and leaving home) to pursue education and gain experiences that propel their careers (ibid.). Emerging adulthood, however, is not a uniform processes. Scholarship examining emerging adulthood suggests the importance of a "multiple institutional context" in adolescents' transition into adulthood (Settersten and Ray 2010: 175). The context can include, but is not limited to, higher education, labor markets, family and neighborhoods. While researchers do not agree on which aspects of the institutional context have the most or least influence on emerging adults, they typically agree that a person's institutional context can limit or foster any opportunities available during the stage (Furstenberg 2008; Hardaway and McLoyd 2008; Settersten and Ray 2010).

The goal of this chapter is to examine the lived experiences of some African American emerging adults in New Orleans post Hurricane Katrina. Based on the disproportionate impact of Hurricane Katrina on the lives of African Americans in New Orleans, it is likely the events surrounding the devastation and recovery continue to have a significant effect on the coming-of-age experiences of these emerging African American adults. Emerging adults are an important demographic group, as many are old enough to have experienced schools, neighborhoods and other aspects of life in New Orleans both pre and post Hurricane Katrina. Pre- and post-Hurricane Katrina schools and neighborhood experiences are part of the group members' institutional context that can either limit or foster opportunities as they transition into adulthood nearly a decade later. To understand the lived experiences of African American emerging adults in post-Katrina New Orleans, in-depth qualitative interviews were conducted with African American survivors of Hurricane Katrina who were between 18 and 25 years of age at the time of the interviews in 2013. The final sample consisted of 31 emerging adults (12 men and 19 women).

Life history interview data were collected from participants regarding school, family, neighborhood and general lived experiences before, during and after Hurricane Katrina. The interviews were loosely structured and prompts were used when needed to obtain more detailed information. Each participant was interviewed once and interviews lasted from 45 to 90 minutes. At the time of Hurricane Katrina, all of the participants were residing in the Greater New Orleans area. While participants had different evacuation experiences (i.e., where they settled after relocation, living arrangements during the evacuation and the duration of the evacuations), all eventually returned to live in New Orleans after the storm. The interviews were conducted either in the researcher's office or in local coffee shops or restaurants. The researcher offered each participant a $25 gift card as an incentive to participate in this inquiry. All participants consented to having their interview recorded and transcribed. To protect the confidentiality of participants, pseudonyms are used for each individual.

Examining the lives of African American emerging adults within a post-disaster context can benefit policy makers seeking to address the needs of youth who experience natural disasters. It has been nearly ten years since Hurricane Katrina. New Orleans officials and citizens have made important strides in the recovery and revitalization of the city. Once referred to as one of the worst in the nation, currently the New Orleans public school system receives recognition for improved graduation rates and test scores (Bassett

2010). Community activists and residents have also worked tirelessly to revitalize local neighborhoods, institutions and networks (Gotham et al. 2011). Yet, studies on post-Katrina New Orleans show variations in the timing and pace of the recovery and repopulation of the city. Notably, African American neighborhoods had some of the lowest citizen return rates, characterized by blocks of blight among restored homes and limited access to grocery stores and other amenities (Gafford 2010; Gotham et al. 2011). The uneven recovery rate of neighborhoods, the displacement of family members and friends and the disruption to the educational system are sure to have had a lasting impact on the lives of the city's African American youth. Emerging adults in the current study have had intimate insight into the city's devastation and recovery. Thus, it is likely that the narratives of these African American emerging adults will demonstrate whether the recovery of New Orleans has alleviated or created more challenges for minority youth as they transition into adulthood.

## Related Research on the Impact of Hurricane Katrina on African American Youth

Within weeks of the initial impact of Katrina many displaced families found refuge in shelters or new communities that were several hundred miles away from New Orleans. Nearly 125,000 young people from Louisiana were scattered across the United States—a disproportionate number were African Americans from New Orleans (Peek and Fothergill 2008). The embedded racism in the media's reporting of Hurricane Katrina did little to alleviate the negative attitudes and stereotypes that African Americans encountered during the evacuation period. In early 2006, a Houston area survey showed that nearly half of all Houstonians believed the decision to relocate residents from New Orleans to Houston had been a bad idea. One public official stated that families from New Orleans who caused problems in schools or committed crimes should be "shipped back" to New Orleans (Lavelle and Feagin 2006).

Not only was the racial hostility geared towards adults, children were also impacted by the negative attitudes. In participant observations of shelter operations in Lafayette, Louisiana, researchers observed how race affected interactions between white volunteers and African American evacuees (Fothergill and Peek 2006). Researchers provided examples of encounters where African American children were treated in rude or offensive manners by white volunteers (ibid.). African American participants in another study commented on how their children had been the victims of negative racial comments at their new schools (Hawkins and Maurer 2012:127).

Additionally, the displacement and relocation of residents resulted in the loss of an intricate web of social and familial networks. African American families are more likely to have extensive family (kin) networks rooted in New Orleans compared to white families (Litt 2008). Much of the communality and assistance among family and friends in New Orleans before Katrina centered on children. Members of the networks were responsible for raising money for other families, helping to transport children to and from school and providing temporary and/or long-term child care. Often these activities mitigate the stress and unexpected events that routinely occur in the lives of the working class and poor (Litt 2008). Researchers have examined how the loss of these networks effect youth. For example, Peek, Morrissey and Marlatt (2011) analyzed qualitative interviews with children and adults to assess the nature of post-disaster adjustments within households. Using a majority African American sample of residents who were displaced to Colorado after Katrina, researchers found 44 of the 55 children used words like "unhappy," "sad" or "depressed" to describe their feelings about living away from New Orleans (Peek et al. 2011). Peek and colleagues suggested that the discontent expressed by the youths was rooted, in part, in the disruption of crucial familial and friendship networks. Youth respondents missed their friends, family members and the familiarity of day-to-day routines (ibid.: 1387).

Research findings on the evacuation experiences of African American youth and their families are indeed important. However, these experiences provide only a partial understanding of how the city's African American youth were affected by the storm. Missing from the literature is an examination of the lived experiences of African American youth in the context of the city's lengthy recovery and revitalization period. African American youth who returned to New Orleans witnessed and experienced an overhaul to the city's public schools system. Before the storm, the city school system was in shambles. Out of 68 Louisiana parishes, Orleans Parish ranked 67 in academic achievement. Moreover, nearly 70 of the city's public schools had been rated academically unacceptable by the Louisiana Department of Education and several of the city's high schools had double-digit drop-out rates (Perry and Reneau 2012). Two months after Hurricane Katrina the Louisiana State Legislature voted to take into receivership 107 New Orleans Public Schools that performed at or below the state average in 2004–05. The schools were placed under the control of the Recovery School District (Cowen Institute 2010). In the revamped educational system, where charter schools outnumbered district operated schools, attendance zones were lifted and many of the city's new teachers were recruited from alternative certification programs like Teach for America (ibid.).

On the one hand, the new school system seems to be an improvement when compared to the troubled one that was in place before Katrina. According to a report issued by the Cowen Institute, public school performance in New Orleans, as measured by standardized test scores, has increased while the proportion of academically unacceptable schools in New Orleans has fallen (ibid.). On the other hand, there have been numerous problems associated with the new system. Tuzzolo and Hewitt (2006), for example, argue that the harsh and punitive discipline policies in the revamped school system continue to reinforce the "school-to-prison" pipeline for students. According to the authors, students attending public schools are subjected to metal detectors, the increased presence of security guards and police officers and suspensions for small infractions (ibid.: 66). McDonogh Senior High, a public school operated by the Recovery School District (RSD), had nearly 32 security guards for its student body that consisted of 775 students. In addition to the jail-like environment of some of the schools, Adamo (2007) points out that in 2006 and 2007, many of the RSD schools lacked books and food services, had overcrowded rooms and a large number of uncertified teachers, many of whom were not prepared for the challenges of the post-Katrina classroom. It is fair to say that the pre- and post-Katrina comparisons of the school system continue to be a source of ongoing academic and public debate. Perhaps one of the primary concerns should be how these changes have affected black students since they represented the majority of those attending public schools before and after Hurricane Katrina. Unfortunately, there has been very little scholarly attention devoted to the actual experiences of black students in post-Katrina New Orleans.

Neighborhood and housing recovery also presented challenges for blacks returning to post-Katrina New Orleans. Before Hurricane Katrina, many working-class black families lived in public housing. Nearly one year after Hurricane Katrina, 80 percent of public housing remained closed. By June 2006, federal housing officials announced the demolition of roughly 5,000 public housing units (Bullard and Wright 2009). After the storm, traditional public-housing units were replaced with mixed-income developments. Mixed-income communities were, however, met with a great deal of resistance by some of the city's black working-class residents who believed the closing of public housing was an attempt to rid the city of its black residents. Other concerns regarding mixed-income housing included the disruption of social ties created in previous communities. Only a small number of units in mixed-income developments would be reserved for public-housing tenants; thus, making it impossible for all the former residents who wished to return to do so (Inniss 2007; Bullard and Wright 2009).

Neighborhood recovery was not just difficult for public-housing residents, black middle-class families also experienced a slower rate of recovery than affluent and mostly white areas due to discriminatory practices of the Road Home Program. Heavily ravaged black middle-class neighborhoods in Gentilly and New Orleans East were some of the last neighborhoods to recover in the aftermath of the storm (Bullard and Wright 2009). Four years later, less than 50 percent of the residents in some black middle-class enclaves had returned (Gafford 2010). The loss of housing stock due to flooding also meant moving to a new neighborhood or living in partially repopulated neighborhoods. Several of these neighborhoods suffered from a "jack-o-lantern effect" or instances where there were blocks of darkness and blight among a handful of lighted and/or restored homes.

To date, much of the research on the impact of neighborhood revitalization and repopulation has centered on the experiences of homeowners and other stakeholders in community redevelopment. The importance of place in the lives of black adolescents and their coming-of-age experience, however, should not be underestimated. More than just places to stay, neighborhoods provide a space for interaction with peers and opportunities to develop mobility networks. New Orleans, in particular, includes neighborhoods that are known for being culturally rich and filled with family networks (Wright and Storr 2009; Gotham et al. 2011). In sum, various parts of the institutional context for black emerging adults in New Orleans are in a state of flux since Hurricane Katrina. If the multi-institutional context has a significant role in the lives of emerging adults, as scholars suggest, it is then necessary to examine the lives of African American youth who experienced post-Katrina New Orleans during their emerging adulthood years.

## Neighborhood Experiences of Emerging Adults

Flooding and/or wind damage from Hurricane Katrina affected nearly 80 percent of the New Orleans metropolitan area. The damage to neighborhoods was so extensive that many residents were displaced for months (Peek et al. 2011). Participants in this study spoke in-depth about how their neighborhoods and communities were affected by the storm:

> It looked like a bomb had gone off in the city, everything was dead, all the trees were dead, debris all over, Xs with these numbers and stuff on the houses. The smell was horrible. We had a sunken living room; it was full of water. My mom just broke down crying like everything she worked for was gone, you know. And it was just like we couldn't believe it. We couldn't believe it. (Darrell Smith, 22 years old, personal communication, June 12, 2013)

> Yeah we saw it the first time we came back over Thanksgiving break. It was crazy. Everything was still kind of dead. There were no businesses. And when we went to the house and my daddy opened the door. It was bad; we got 12 feet of water. And there was nothing left. We peeked in and tried to look but you couldn't save anything. I felt like I was very numb at that point. (Carla Thomas, 24 years old, personal communication, July 23, 2013)

Many of the participants interviewed lived in majority African American neighborhoods located in Eastern New Orleans and Gentilly. Before Hurricane Katrina these two areas housed identifiable African American middle-class enclaves. New Orleans East, which made up two-thirds of the corporate limits, was inhabited by many of the city's African American professionals, businesspeople and politicians; representing nearly 40 percent of the city's base (Pastor et al. 2006). The areas served as a refuge from many of the social problems associated with the inner city for middle-class African American families. However, they were located in some of the lowest-lying areas of the city. Race remains a determinant of class status and economic resources and minorities often have little choice but to settle in communities that are more prone to flooding or other forms of damage in the wake of disasters (Gladwin and Peacock 1997). Thus, neighborhoods, like Carla and Darrell's were more vulnerable during Hurricane Katrina.

Residents in majority black neighborhood are not only likely to be geographically vulnerable, but disasters can render residents socially vulnerable too. In the years following Hurricane Katrina participants explained how their neighborhoods felt less safe. For example, Alex Foster lived in Eastern New Orleans. During the interview, Alex shared his personal experience with crime in the context of his neighborhood:

> *Two days after my high school graduation my whole family went to Puerto Rico. That day before Puerto Rico, I went to the mall and my friend who lives two houses down, Crystal, she called and said, "did you leave the window open?" And I said, "no" and she said, "the window is open—somebody broke in your house." So I called my mom and she was panicking and everything and she called the police. [Mom] looked at the window and she broke down crying. Somebody broke in our house and we had security cameras all over. And we saw him come in the house go through my mom's window. What if I was home? I was only gone 15 minutes before he came there. Thank God, I wasn't home. What if he comes back again? It's just makes you uneasy—you never feel the same. (Alex Foster, 22 years old, personal communication, March 11, 2013)*

Tatiana Jackson had an encounter with crime in her post-Katrina neighborhood:

> *Before Katrina we stayed in Gentilly, close to Pontchartrain Park. It was nice and quiet. When we moved back, there was no peace. Last year, I went to the park and I heard gunshots. My mom called me trying to find me. I was sitting at the park. She was like they shot through the window. I tried to find somebody to walk me home. I saw police officers. My house was a crime scene. There was a bullet hole in the window. I slept by my friend's house that night. (Tatiana Jackson, 20 years old, personal communication, April 2, 2013)*

In addition to crime, participants in the study commented on how the neighborhood infrastructure (i.e., businesses, services and important amenities) drastically declined in the years following Hurricane Katrina. The decline seemed to adversely affect social activities for the emerging adults who grew up in heavily devastated spaces.

> *Interviewer: Before the storm, what did you and your friends do for fun?*
>
> *Julie Holmes: The mall, the movies and go by each other's house. We don't have a mall anymore. I know the Plaza (a shopping center that is no longer opened) wasn't much, but it was something. They had just built the movie theater. A lot of people use to go out and hang. We use to walk around the mall. We don't have anything now it seems*

*like. We had a Walmart and a Sam's Club. There are a lot of businesses that are not there. (Julie Holmes, 25 years old, personal communication, April 18, 2013)*

Nikki shared a similar response. She stated:

*Pre-Katrina New Orleans was the best. I just moved out the 8th ward to the East. At the time the East had businesses. It had the Grand (the movie theater). I was there the first night it opened. Now we have to drive across the city. We don't have any businesses. We have Family Dollars and Dollar Generals. I know on Reed or Bullard they have a Save-A-Lot [discount grocery]. They don't even give you grocery bags and there are no places that stay open 24 hours. (Nikki Jones, 21 years old, personal communication, April 24, 2013)*

Nikki and Julie's descriptions of the areas are accurate. The area's one shopping mall, Lake Forest Plaza, was demolished in 2007. Despite having nearly three-fourths of its pre-Katrina population, New Orleans East still lacks family entertainment (bowling, amusement parks or movie theaters), major shopping companies and other amenities that were present before Hurricane Katrina (Bullard and Wright 2009; Roberts 2010).

The decline in community infrastructure and the increase in the prevalence of crime have implications for African American emerging adults in a post-disaster context and for African American emerging adults, in general. Several sociologists have documented the deleterious effects on African American youth living in neighborhoods with high crime and poverty rates (see Pattillo 1999 and Jones 2010). Coming of age in a neighborhood with few businesses or places for leisure also results in youth missing out on constructive interactions with peers and neighbors. Emerging adults in this study claim to have lived in relatively stable neighborhoods before the storm. Many participants described their neighborhood as a place "where everyone knew everyone" and replete with neighbors who looked out for one another. One participant stated that her neighbors were like surrogate grandparents. Interview data show that the storm altered this social dynamic of many neighborhoods. Youth in devastated communities also miss out on possible employment opportunities as well as opportunities to cultivate networks that are important for future successes. In 2010, nearly 50 percent of Orleans Parish youth between the ages of 16 and 19 were unemployed (Cowen Institute 2010). This is not to say that respondents who grew up in heavily devastated spaces will not be successful; neighborhoods are only one part of the equation. These experiences simply demonstrate how the slow and uneven recovery associated with some neighborhoods in the aftermath of Hurricane Katrina could have further disadvantaged African American youth.

## Getting an Education in Post-Katrina New Orleans

Education is one of several factors that can facilitate one's smooth transition into adulthood. Yet, receiving a quality education appears to be one of the most challenging issues for the emerging adults in this study. Narratives from emerging adults highlight the complicated and often discouraging nature of education for African American youth living in New Orleans. Several participants currently attending public schools after Katrina spoke about uninterested teachers and counselors, disruptive students and an unchallenging curriculum:

> *Well many of the teachers at Carver High School were from Teach for America. They were young and most of them had just gotten out of college. I know for a fact that two or three were intimidated. You would hear it in their voices and they would do what the students told them to do. I didn't like it. I didn't like the fact that the students were the way they were. They were so disruptive. It was embarrassing. I don't know what they could've done. But you are supposed to make a stand on your first day. I guess what I know about the children I went to school with you supposed to prove yourself. They [the students] actually test you. If you don't do anything back they are going to keep doing it. (Tatiana Jackson, 20 years old, personal communication, April 2, 2013)*

> *I guess in public school sometimes when you are housed with individuals who don't take education seriously. You kind of get lost. It is okay that everybody else is mediocre. So it's like I was always like trying to go to the next lesson or I was always trying to get ahead but the teacher was just focused on the fact that everybody wasn't getting it. I had several situations where she would hand back the exams and you know a lot of the students would fail and I would be the one that passed. She never really acknowledged the fact that she could have in essence been wrong about me. I mean because she treated, a lot of teachers treated me really bad because my behavior and stuff like that. (Brent Taylor, 24 years old, personal communication, August 7, 2013)*

Despite public discourse promoting the notion that schools in New Orleans have improved drastically, data from this study suggest that problems still persist in the New Orleans Public School system. To be clear, the excerpts in this study are not representative of every student's experience with public school education in New Orleans, nor do the excerpts serve as a condemnation of all post-Katrina schools. The excerpts, however, do speak to various challenges that exist in schools in the aftermath of the disaster and lend support to previous research that questions whether or not the changes made to New Orleans's public schools benefit African American students. According to Buras (2011), the creation and destruction of schools in post-Katrina New Orleans has little to do with improving the academic performance of children of color. The reform, according to Buras, merely serves as a way for upper-class white entrepreneurs to obtain public and private funds to build new schools and manage charter schools around the city:

> *In New Orleans, white entrepreneurs have seized control of a key asset in the black communities—public schools—and through state assistance, charter school reform and plans for reconstruction, have built a profitable and exclusionary educational system that threatens to reinforce rather than challenge the political economy of New Orleans. (Ibid.: 304)*

It is also quite likely that, post Katrina, students are better able to develop comparative understandings of ideal-type school programs and curriculums after attending different schools during the evacuation period. In other words, the dispersal to non-New Orleans public schools in the initial aftermath of the storm might have shed light on their substandard education within the Orleans Parish school district. Several participants offered comparisons between the schools in New Orleans and the schools they attended while living in places like Atlanta, Charlotte and Dallas:

> *I took Spanish in Texas my 10th grade year. I had a real good teacher. I came back to New Orleans and the students were learning how to count in Spanish. I could have died. I wrote a children's book assignment in Texas and I come home and y'all still*

*doing colors and numbers. In Texas I knew the periodic table. When I got back to New Orleans, I was like y'all don't know the first five elements on the periodic table. The teacher wasn't teaching. (Tatiana Jackson, 20 years old, personal communication, April 2, 2013)*

*It was like they [the teachers] challenged you. If you didn't understand they would literally take the time out to help you … They prepare you for college. They give you everything that you need. My high school (in New Orleans) didn't do that. (Tina Brown, 19 years old, personal communication, March 20, 2013)*

*I had never been to a school that big and nice. It was a huge building like state of the art thing. Even though I went to the cream of the crop public schools [in New Orleans], I never been to a school that size. It had a big gym and an Olympic-size pool. The cafeteria had five lines and all these types of things. That really amazed me. Like wow what was this? (Regina Adams, 20 years old, personal communication, June 14, 2013)*

Public schools were not the only option for African American emerging adults in the post-disaster city. The troubled public school system in New Orleans is responsible for one of the city's most unique features: a robust network of private schools. Before Hurricane Katrina approximately 25,000 local students attended private schools; which was nearly one-third of the city's population of school-aged children (Newmark and De Rugy 2006). Despite the fact that most white families opted out of public schools and instead chose private and parochial schools at significantly higher rates than African American families, African American students still made up nearly 35 percent of the private school enrollment in New Orleans (Perry and Reneau 2012).

After Hurricane Katrina, private schools remained a viable option for African American working- and middle-class families. St. Mary's Academy, Xavier Preparatory High School and St. Augustine High School (known affectionately as "Prep" and "St. Aug," respectively) are historically Black institutions (HBIs) in New Orleans and serve as symbols of achievement and pride in the African American community. The schools have produced judges, local leaders and a long list of alumni who make valuable contributions to New Orleans (Vanacore 2013). Nine participants in the current study attended HBIs. Nearly all describe Black private Catholic schools as institutions that stress rules, discipline and structure. Natalie Green, a graduate of St. Mary's Academy, stated:

*We had nuns, so some were really nice but then they had some mean nuns as well. But they were supportive as well you know being a Catholic school and instilling those you know virtues … I'm older now so I can appreciate it, but at the time I didn't see why we had to have our skirts a certain length or why we had to wear a slip under our skirts. We had to wear certain shoes and not this shoe and all this other stuff but it was really discipline and shaping us into being, you know, women. You look at the young girls now and they don't have certain decorum about themselves, a sense of who they are. (Natalie Green, 24 years old, personal communication, July 26, 2013)*

Alison, a graduate of Xavier Prep, shared a similar sentiment about Xavier Prep:

*We couldn't wear nail polish or have hair color. Your color had to be subtle or you would get a demerit. You couldn't wear hoop earrings and only one per ear. We had a uniform. My sophomore year we couldn't wear pants anymore because the girls would sag [pull pants down low] their pants. We had to wear skirts. (Allison Lester, 21 years old, personal communication, June 6, 2013)*

Despite the strict nature of the Black Catholic schools discussed, former students hold a deep sense of admiration for their respective alma maters. Laura Jackson, a graduate of Xavier Prep, stated, "I grew to love Prep. I made friends. Real cool friends that I am still friends with today. I got involved in the marching unit, I was a flag twirler, and I was Ms. Sophomore. I loved it."

Darrin Collins, a graduate of St. Augustine, echoed similar sentiments: "I loved it because it was like, I really appreciated what they have. St. Aug is one of those schools it's just like tough love, you don't realize how mean or why somebody is being mean to you until you realize that they're doing it because they care."

For African American parents living in New Orleans, Catholic schools like Xavier Prep and St. Aug offer a better education than local public schools and they serve as a deterrent or antidote to the perils of "street life" by offering stern discipline (Dequine 2011). In their book, *Growing up African American in Catholic Schools*, Irvine and Foster (1996) state that Catholic school environments guide and empower African American students as they succeed in school and beyond. Specifically, Catholic schools acknowledge and support the community's efforts to nurture a strong Black identity and teachers' high expectation of the students (ibid.).

However, some former students interviewed for this project do not believe that HBIs prepared them for life beyond high school. Jerry, a graduate of St. Aug, stated:

*The classes [at St. Augustine] were basically the same as any regular public school and I know this because I've tutored people at public schools and it's basically the same material. There are no actual college preparatory classes at least when I was there. There was no dual enrollment [a program where you can take college courses while you are still a high school student]. The only thing they had was a class preparing you for the ACT and SAT and the college tours that was it ... it is a prestigious school compared to everything else [other schools in New Orleans].*

Laura, a premed major attending Xavier University of Louisiana, did not feel prepared when she started college:

*I don't think it prepared me for college. I just thought, by going to Xavier Prep; it was Xavier University preparatory school, I thought I was a shoo-in, but when I took classes [at the university] it was different. It is like y'all didn't prepare me for what was here in my face with college. I wish I would have the opportunity to learn more from my teachers. I wish they would've taught more.*

Nikki Gibson graduated from St. Mary's Academy and was somewhat ambivalent about whether or not she had been adequately prepared for college:

*Yes and no. I think St. Mary's challenged us but in a way I feel like we weren't really prepared because I had to take remedial math at Xavier so in that aspect I don't think it prepared us for it. I took Algebra I, Algebra II, Geometry, uh I believe I took Trigonometry as well. Yeah, but I still had [remedial courses] ... I don't know it may have just been for everybody just that transition from you know being a high school student to a college student.*

Although the Black private schools discussed here emphasize discipline and decorum, interview data leads one to question whether or not such institutions confer any significant advantage in the lives of African American youth in post-Katrina New Orleans vis-à-vis those attending public school. Both Laura and Nikki felt underprepared when they reached college while Jerry wanted more college preparatory classes. The narratives regarding educational experiences in post-Katrina New Orleans suggest a hierarchy in the education system. Whether or not they had attended public schools in the city, participants believed the public schools in New Orleans were at the bottom of the hierarchy. During their interviews participants described city schools with terms such as "not the best," "unchallenging" or "bad." On the other hand, private schools were believed to represent a better alternative to public schools or, as Briana Robinson put it, "In New Orleans if you were Black middle class you went to Catholic school if your parents could pay the tuition." Even though the value of a Catholic education has been identified among scholars, parents and former students, the reflections in the current study raise questions regarding the extent that African American emerging adults really benefited from attending majority Black private schools in post-Katrina New Orleans.

# Conclusion

What lies ahead for the emerging adults featured in this study? Having endured Hurricane Katrina and several years of the city's revitalization efforts (many of which are still underway), emerging African American adults are now making decisions regarding their future in New Orleans. When asked to discuss whether or not they saw New Orleans as a place where they could possibly build a future, the reactions of the respondents were mixed. Some participants were open to staying in New Orleans. Twenty-year-old Regina, for example, wants to return to New Orleans upon graduating from Spelman:

> *I do want to eventually settle here. I really like it and I want to come back home. Not just because of my family but I really just like the vibe. I like the people. I like the culture … A lot of people don't see the potential that is here. I see a lot of people my age who go to school and don't want to come back. They are like if I want to be successful I will just have to go somewhere else. I am happy that I see a lot of potential here. The city is already a great place but I think it could be so much better. I just wish other people could see that.*

Respondents like Natalie Tucker, however, questioned whether or not staying in New Orleans was a good move for her future:

> *It's funny to me because it's like a lot of people who I know who are from here it just seems like when they leave it's you know they have a better life, and I don't necessarily want to leave but I do want a better life … I don't know if it's the people or the city itself, the institution of the city or the government, I don't know. But it's just like … They're doing more in their life they're you know moving up and it just seems like there's a cap down here, you can only go so high you know. You know I could probably work my same job and be making two times the amount that I'm making here.*

On one hand, the desire of emerging adults to help New Orleans return to its better days seems more than appropriate. They are interested in challenging and ameliorating issues that adversely impact their transition into adulthood. The city's problem with crime, for instance, is intertwined with education and a lack of opportunity for youth. High suspension and expulsion rates in local schools have contributed to conditions which make it easier for black youth to engage in crime than to complete the requirements for high school (Tuzzolo and Hewitt 2006). In addition to helping to fix New Orleans, black emerging adults who desire to stay in the city might be the answer to another issue that has plagued the city for decades; the inability to keep and attract aspiring black professionals.

Recent data indicate that employment and upward mobility may indeed be a daunting task for African American emerging adults like the ones featured in this study. Despite the sense that New Orleans has benefited from an influx of skilled workers to the region in the aftermath of Hurricane Katrina, there are still disparities in employment rates and many fall along racial lines. There is almost a 20 percent gap between black and white male employment rates. Moreover, blacks in New Orleans still earn almost 50 percent less income than white households (Sellers et al. 2012).

The goal of this chapter was to examine whether post-Katrina New Orleans created or alleviated the challenges that existed for the city's black youth. The recovery of New Orleans is not just about the actual number of residents who return to neighborhoods or about how many new schools are built. In many ways, the strength of the city's recovery should be measured by how well some of its vulnerable populations are faring in the aftermath of the storm.

The data in this inquiry not only substantiate previous research findings on the uneven nature of the post-Katrina recovery, the findings also hint at persistent racial disparities in education, neighborhood quality and networks for African American emerging adults. Black emerging adults in this research live in spaces that are not only geographically vulnerable but socially vulnerable as well. In the post-Katrina context, emerging adult residents are personally affected by neighborhood crime and the city's inability—or unwillingness—to rebuild parts of the devastated infrastructure (i.e., businesses and public amenities). Participants in the study also articulate how the absence of grocery stores and shopping centers in their post-Katrina neighborhoods represent a drastic change in neighborhood quality. The findings from this research also raise questions regarding the state of education in post-Katrina New Orleans. Despite having received national recognition and praise, respondents still question the quality of education they receive in post-Katrina New Orleans. Several respondents express not feeling prepared for college even after attending some of the 'better' schools in New Orleans.

New Orleans is not the only context in which educational and neighborhood disparities exist for emerging African American emerging adults who have experienced a natural disaster. As such, future research projects should center on disasters such as tornadoes and earthquakes and the lived experiences of emerging adult in those areas. Ultimately, future studies on emerging African American adults, specifically, should examine whether or not racial disparities impacting African American emerging adults can be offset if provided adequate institutional resources.

# References

Adamo, Ralph. 2007. "Squeezing Public Education: History and Ideology Gang Up on New Orleans. *Dissent* 54(3): 44–51.

Arnett, Jeffrey. 2000. "Emerging Adulthood: A Theory of Development from Late Teens to Teens through the Twenties." *American Psychologist* 55(5): 469–80.

Bassett, Laura. 2010. "Post-Katrina, New Orleans Rescues a Drowning Public School System." *Huffington Post*, August 27. Retrieved October 17, 2013: http://www.huffingtonpost.com/2010/08/27/postkatrina-new-orleans-h_n_697374.html.

Berube, Alan and Bruce Katz. 2005. "Katrina's Window: Confronting Concentrated Poverty Across America." The Brookings Institution. Retrieved August 12, 2013: http://www.brookings.edu/research/reports/2005/10/poverty-berube.

Bullard, Robert and Beverly Wright. 2009. *Race, Place and Environmental Justice after Hurricane Katrina: Struggles to Reclaim, Rebuild, and Revitalize New Orleans and the Gulf Coast*. Boulder, CO: Westview Press.

Buras, Kristen. 2011. "Race, Charter Schools and Conscious Capitalism: On the Spatial Politics of Whiteness as Property and the Unconscionable Assault on Black New Orleans." *Harvard Educational Review* 81(2): 296–330.

Cowen Institute. 2010. "The State of Public Education in New Orleans: Five Years After Hurricane Katrina." Accessed November 12, 2013: http://www.coweninstitute.com/wp-content/uploads/2010/07/katrina-book.final_.CIpageSmaller.pdf.

Dequine, Kari. 2011. "St. Augustine High School Paddling Policy is 'Not Broken,' Marchers Say." *The Times-Picayune*, March 26. Retrieved November 1, 2011: http://www.nola.com/education/index.ssf/2011/03/st_augustine_high_school_paddl.html.

Fothergill, Alice and Lori Peek. 2006. "Surviving Catastrophe: A Study of Children in Hurricane Katrina." in *Learning from Catastrophe: Quick Response Research in the wake of Hurricane Katrina*, ed. Institute of Behavioral Science, University of Colorado at Boulder. Boulder, CO: Institute of Behavioral Science, University of Colorado, pp. 97–103.

Furstenberg, Frank. 2008. "The Intersections of Social Class and the Transition to Adulthood." New Directions for Child and Adolescent Development 119: 1–10.

Gafford, Farrah. 2010. "Rebuilding the Park: The Impact of Hurricane Katrina on a Black Middle-Class Neighborhood." *Journal of Black Studies* 41(2): 385–404.

Gladwin, Hugh and Walter G. Peacock. 1997. "Warning and Evacuation: A Night for Hard Houses." in *Hurricane Andrew: Ethnicity, Gender and the Sociology of Disaster*, eds. W.G. Peacock, B.H. Morrow, and H. Galdwin. New York, NY: Routledge, pp. 52–72.

Gotham, Kevin, Richard Campanella, Josh Lewis, Farrah Gafford, Earthea Nance and Mallikharjuna Avula. 2011. "Reconsidering the New Normal: Vulnerability and Resilience in Post-Katrina New Orleans." *Global Horizons: The Journal of Global Policy and Resilience* 4(2): 54–68.

Hardaway, Cecily and Vonnie McLoyd. 2008. "Escaping Poverty and Securing Middle Class Status: How Race and Socioeconomic Status Shape Mobility Prospects for African Americans during the Transition to Adulthood." *Journal of Youth Adolescence* 38(2): 242–56.

Hawkins, Robert and Katherine Maurer. 2012. "Waiting for the White Man to Fix Things: Rebuilding Black Poverty in New Orleans." *Journal of Sociology & Social Welfare* 39(1): 111–39.

Innis, Lolita. 2007. "A Domestic Right of Return?: Race, Rights and Residency in New Orleans in the Aftermath of Hurricane Katrina." *Third World Law Journal* 27(2): 325–73.

Irvine, Jacqueline and Michele Foster. 1996. *Growing up African American in Catholic Schools*. New York: Teachers College Press.

Jones, Nikki. 2010. *Between Good and Ghetto: African American Girls and Inner City Violence*. New Brunswick, NJ: Rutgers University Press.

Lavelle, Kristen and Joe Feagin. 2006. "Hurricane Katrina: The Race and Class Debate." *Monthly Review* 58(3): 52–66.

Litt, Jacquelyn. 2008. "Getting Out or Staying Put: An African American Women's Network in Evacuation from Katrina." *Feminist Formations*, 20(3): 32–46.

Newmark, Kathryn and Veronique De Rugy. 2006. "Hope After Katrina: Will New Orleans Become the New City of Choice?" *Education Next* 6(4): 13–21.

Pastor, Manuel, Robert Bullard, James K. Boyce, Alice Fothergill, Rachel Morello-Frosch and Beverly Wright. 2006. *In the Wake of the Storm: Environment, Disaster and Race After Katrina.* New York: Russell Sage Foundation. Retrieved April 22, 2015: http://www.dscej.org/images/pdfs/In%20The%20Wake%20of%20the%20Storm.pdf.

Pattillo, Mary. 1999. *Black Picket Fences: Privileges and Peril Among Black Middle Class.* Chicago, IL: University of Chicago Press.

Peek, Lori and Alice Fothergill. 2008. "Displacement, Gender, and the Challenges of Parenting after Hurricane Katrina." *NWSA Journal* 20(3): 69–106.

———, Bridget Morrissey and Holly Marlatt. 2011. "Disaster Hits Home: A Model of Displaced Family Adjustment After Hurricane Katrina." *Journal of Family Issues* 32(10): 1371–96.

Perry, Andre and Franz Reneau. 2012. "The Path of Education Reform toward Higher Education for African Americans in New Orleans." *Equilibrium: The State of Black New Orleans.* Houma, LA: Morgan Hill Publishing.

Roberts, Sally-Ann. 2010. "While Progress Made: N.O. East Still Lacking Many Vital Services." *WWLTV*, August 25. Retrieved November 1, 2013: http://www.wwltv.com/katrina-anniversary/New-Orleans-East-still-lacking-many-vital-services.html.

Sellers, Susan, Andre Perry, Petrice Sams-Abioudun, Alison Plyer and Elaine Ortiz. 2012. "Building an Inclusive, High Skilled Workforce for New Orleans' Next Economy." The Greater New Orleans Community Data Center. Retrieved January 3, 2013: (http://www.brookings.edu/~/media/Research/Files/Reports/2011/8/29%20new%20orleans%20index/08_neworleans_execsum.PDF).

Settersten, Richard and Barbara Ray. 2010. "What's Going on With Young People Today? The Long and Twisting Path to Adulthood." *The Future of the Children* 20(1): 19–41.

Smith, William, Walter Allen, and Lynette L. Danley. 2007. "Assume the Position … You Fit the Description: Psychosocial Experiences and Racial Battle Fatigue Among African American Male College Students." *American Behavioral Scientist* 51(4): 551–78: doi:10.1177/0002764207307742.

Turner, Margery and Sheila Zedlewski. 2006. "After Katrina: Rebuilding Opportunity and Equity into the *New* New Orleans." The Urban Institute. Retrieved October 10, 2012: http://www.urban.org/uploadedpdf/311406_after_katrina.pdf.

Tuzzolo, Ellen and Damon Hewitt. 2006. "Rebuilding Inequality: The Re-Emergence of the School to Prison Pipeline in New Orleans." *The High School Journal* 90 (2): 59–68.

US Department of Education. 2010. *Digest of Education Statistics.* Washington, DC: National Center for Educational Statistics.

Vanacore, Andrew. 2013. "Xavier Prep Community, in Shock, Fears Loss of a 'Sisterhood'." *The Times-Picayune*, February 21. Retrieved November 10, 2013: http://www.nola.com/education/index.ssf/2013/02/xavier_prep_community_in_shock.html.

Wright, Emily and Virgil Henry Storr. 2009. "There is No Place Like Home: Sense of Place and Community Recovery in the Ninth Ward After Katrina." *Journal of Urban Affairs* 31(5): 615–34.

# The Psychosocial Impact of Parental Incarceration on Children and their Caregivers

Sheridan Quarless Kingsberry, Sachin Karnik,
Natalie M. Fountain and Kelly Wetzel

Parental incarceration in the United States is an intensifying social problem with serious implications for both the individual and society (Elbogen and Johnson 2009; Huebner and Gustafson 2007; Murray and Farrington 2005). According to Western and Pettit (2010), 54 percent of prison inmates are the parents of children under the age of 17. This includes more than 120,000 mothers and 1.1 million fathers. Fully 2.7 million, or one in every 28, American children has a parent who is incarcerated (ibid.). Equally troubling are two particular trends that can have deleterious social consequences for our society in the future. First is the increasing rate of maternal incarceration and its impact on children. According to a 2010 revised U.S. Bureau of Justice Statistics (BJS) report by Glaze and Maruschak, between 1991 and 2007 the number of children with a father in prison increased by 77 percent while the number of children with a mother in prison doubled by 131 percent. Mothers have traditionally been, and continue to be, the key socializing and protective factor in the lives of children. Therefore, when mothers are incarcerated their children are often left behind with limited protective structures. These children must be socialized by "other mothers" and may be vulnerable to risk factors including abuse and neglect. The second troubling trend is the disproportionate number of Black children with incarcerated parents. In 2010, one in nine Black children (11.4 percent), one in 28 Hispanic children (3.5 percent) and one in 57 White children (1.8 percent) had an incarcerated parent or parents (Western and Pettit 2010). Black children with incarcerated parents tend to be poor and live in urban, violence-prone communities (Murray and Farrington 2005; Phillips et al. 2006; Woldoff and Washington 2008; Davies et al. 2008). Blacks comprised approximately 12.4 percent of the U.S. population in 2006, yet they represented about 35 percent of the country's state and federal prisoners (Darensbourg et al. 2010). When so many Black children are left without the protection, support and guidance of their parents—especially their mothers, who are responsible for providing their basic human needs (e.g., physiological, safety, belongingness and self-esteem)—they are less likely to achieve self-actualization and are more likely to grow into adults who make little or no positive contribution to their families, communities and the larger society (Maslow, as cited in Zastrow and Kirst-Ashman 2013).

Children with imprisoned parents experience lives that are disrupted, unstable and often result in their traumatization. Young children, given their vulnerable stages of development, are especially unable at times to articulate their distress. Instead, they may display their feelings and emotions in disruptive ways. At home, their caregivers are often overly stressed and are more likely to provide poor parenting responses to the children's negative behaviors (Dannerbeck 2005). Similarly, most schools are unprepared to handle disruptive students in the classroom. The general response of most educators is to: 1) send the student to time out or "redirect" rooms, 2) impose in-school suspension (ISS), or out-of-school suspension (OSS), or 3) expel the student. When these strategies are used to address the behaviors of children experiencing disruption and trauma the result is usually low academic performance and, ultimately, high rates of school dropout (Christle et al. 2005). These unintended consequences can lead to what researchers call the "school-to-prison pipeline" (ibid.).

More troubling is the increase in intergenerational incarceration. A growing number of studies show that children with incarcerated parents are more likely to engage in delinquency and become incarcerated like their parents (Phillips et al. 2006; Hairston 2007; Raimon et al. 2009; Wildeman 2009). A study by Davis and colleagues (2008) found that parental incarceration is associated with a variety of negative behaviors in children such as angry outbursts, emotional withdrawal, fighting and showing lack of respect for authority. These unconstructive behaviors can lead not only to negative school behavioral outcomes like poor grades and school dropout, but also to more serious social problems like substance abuse and juvenile delinquency. According to The National Fatherhood Initiative (2010), when compared to their counterparts who live with their married biological or adoptive parents, children who live apart from their biological fathers are about two to three times more likely to be poor, to use drugs, to experience educational, health, emotional and behavioral problems, to be the victims of child abuse and to engage in criminal behavior.

With an average prison sentence of seven years and an average time served of five years (Hairston 2009), increasing rates of parental incarceration will continue to have a profound and negative impact on Black children and their families for many years to come if sound interventions are not established immediately. These interventions require creative and long-term prevention strategies for children, their caregivers and their incarcerated parents. Additionally, the interventions require partnerships not only with children who have been impacted by incarceration, but also with their families, schools and their communities. The interventions also will require a multi-systems approach that addresses the bio-psycho-social impact of incarceration on children and their adult caregivers at the micro (individual and family), mezzo (organization) and macro (community) levels of practice.

## Literature Review

Parental incarceration has a profoundly negative impact on the family left behind. The spouses/partners, children and extended family members who assume the caretaking responsibilities of the children in the absence of their parents are usually overlooked and often forgotten as they go about their daily lives trying desperately to cope with the multiple economic, psychological and environmental risk factors that a parent's incarceration imposes upon them (Arditti et al. 2003; Kjellstrand and Eddy 2011). Although displaying commendable levels of strength and resilience, caregivers left behind, most with limited education, few financial resources and little social support, struggle financially, socially, emotionally and mentally (Dallaire and Wilson 2010). Thus, the adults left alone to carry the burden of caretaking and family maintenance, usually mothers, grandmothers or other female relatives, are often unable to adequately meet the needs of children with incarcerated parents.

Consequently, parental incarceration frequently results in maladjusted children whose social and emotional competence is often compromised (ibid.). Many children of incarcerated parents experience high rates of attachment insecurity (Poelhmann 2005) and high levels of anxiety and depression (Murray and Farrington 2008). These children also tend to suffer from increased stress, anxiety and trauma (Hairston 2007). Indeed, findings from a meta-analysis of small-scale studies reported by Puddefoot and Foster (2007) indicate that the effects of parental arrest and incarceration on a child's development are profound. The children may suffer from multiple psychological problems including trauma, anxiety, guilt, shame and fear. Negative behavioral manifestations can include sadness, aggression, emotional withdrawal, low self-esteem, a decline in school performance, truancy and the use of drugs and/or alcohol. Socially, they have poor peer relationships, difficulty with school and lack of respect for authority. Schools are not immune to the impact of parental incarceration. Given that schools are a major socializing agent, they are at the forefront of experiencing the problems children exhibit as a result of their parents' incarceration. Every day, students bring with them the social and emotional challenges they face at home. As a result, their adherence to rules may decline, leading schools to adopt disciplinary actions such as time out, re-directs, in-school suspensions (ISS), out-of-school suspensions (OSS) or expulsions.

A growing body of literature provides a clearer understanding of the devastating effect parental incarceration has on children and their families (Murray and Farrington 2008; Dallaire and Wilson 2010). Dallaire (2007) found that families affected by incarceration and criminal activity are exposed to proximal risk factors such as having *both* parents incarcerated, higher rates of familial incarceration, exposure to regular parental drug use and parental recidivism. The experience of contextual risk factors such as poverty, parental mental illness and substance abuse—when added to the stress of a parent's imprisonment—may help explain why children with incarcerated parents are at a heightened risk for negative outcomes (ibid.).

On average, children with an incarcerated parent can experience as many as three changes in caregivers (Hanlon et al. 2007). Children subjected to inconsistency in primary caregivers are likely to struggle with adjustment issues as they attempt to adapt to changes in social environments, parenting styles and school placements. This is especially pronounced when mothers are imprisoned, which is a growing phenomenon. In such cases, children typically receive care from a grandmother (Hairston 2007). Grandparent caregivers tend not to have completed high school, to be female, poor, unemployed and to struggle with financial and health issues (ibid.). The experience of these risk factors may further exacerbate an already fragile and stressed family (Dallaire 2007; Johnson 2012).

Another growing social problem is the troubling economic implications parental incarceration has for our society (Clear 2007; Sampson and Loeffler 2010). In 2007, $74 billion was spent on corrections, with the average cost per prisoner of $45,000 (Kyckelhahn 2013). Most convicted felons have difficulty finding employment after they are released from prison (Arditti and Few 2006). As a result, up to 60 percent are re-incarcerated within 36 months (Langan and Levin 2002). When formerly incarcerated parents are unable to find jobs that pay a living wage to support themselves and their families, not only are they unable to model our valued American work ethic for their children, they are also unable to pay taxes, buy homes or start businesses—all positive economic contributions to society. Instead, they remain a growing, and increasingly multigenerational, economic drain on society. The families of the incarcerated require financial support for housing through vouchers, food through food stamps and health and mental health services through Medicaid and Medicare, all of which are subsidized or paid for by other members of society.

Parental incarceration has numerous deleterious effects. It destroys family bonds and sentences children and the remaining parent(s)/parental figure(s) to a punishment they do not deserve. The establishment of programs and services to support a population that has too long been ignored is crucial to ending the cycle of delinquency and incarceration and in rebuilding vibrant and safe communities. Supporting these children will help them decrease problem behaviors in school and at home, improve their social and emotional competence, improve their academic outcomes and help to avoid the path to imprisonment taken by their parents; thus breaking the cycle of intergenerational incarceration (Wildeman 2009). When we strengthen and provide proven services to fragile families impacted by the incarceration of a parent, or parents, we can increase family stability which is a key element in reducing recidivism and rebuilding communities that have been damaged by crime and violence.

## Overview of the HOPE Project: A Community Partnership

In 2010, the Wilmington HOPE Commission, a non-profit organization in the city of Wilmington, Delaware, became concerned that children from two communities significantly impacted by crime and violence were facing a number of obstacles to their well-being. The city was ranked sixth in the nation for violent crime in 2011 (Blaine and Sauter 2013). The agency wanted to reduce the negative in-school behaviors of children with incarcerated parents since it believed those behaviors led to poor school behavioral outcomes and eventually juvenile delinquency and adult incarceration. The agency also wanted to provide support to caregivers by linking them to resources that would positively impact their children's well-being. Children attending three elementary schools that serve two of Wilmington's most economically, educationally and socially deprived communities were targeted for the project. The agency conceived the HOPE Project: A Community Partnership and partnered with the Delaware State University (DSU) Department of Social Work to implement and evaluate this pilot project.

The HOPE Project had two goals: (1) that 50 percent of the children in the program would show reduced negative in-school behavioral incidents each program year; and (2) that 50 percent of the parents/guardians would show increased engagement in school and/or community activities that may have direct impact on their children's in-school behavioral outcomes. The project used a variety of therapeutic strategies to engage the families. A combination of play, art, biblio and talk therapies was used with the children and case management. Also, parental and child assessments and a family improvement plan was used with the parents/guardians. The project also utilized an array of prevention, intervention and enrichment activities including, but not limited to, counseling, family networking sessions, a mother's support group and linkages to school and community activities and resources.

Throughout its duration the project engaged a variety of community partners to help deliver support services to the children and their families. Memoranda of agreements were established with the Center for Child Development and the Counseling Center to provide clinical services to the children and supervision of the Master's degree in Social Work students serving as case managers/graduate assistants on the project. Both agencies already had a presence in the three schools via licensed clinical social workers. Their staff also facilitated workshops for the families and children during the family networking sessions.

## Conceptual Model

When the effects of parental incarceration on the family left behind are examined, major difficulties such as lack of financial resources, deep emotional stress/worry, shame issues and the development and/or intensification of existing mental health/addiction issues are observed. All of these contribute to "familial disruption." The model depicted in Figure 5.1

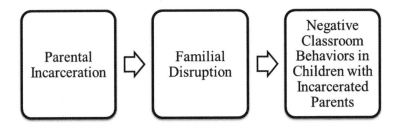

**Figure 5.1     Conceptual Model**

illustrates and hypothesizes a possible causal relationship between parental incarceration and negative classroom behavior where familial disruption is an intermediate variable.

There are many possible impacts of parental incarceration. Although only one, familial disruption, is depicted in the model it is important to be cognizant that others exist and can be part of the causal change of psychosocial processes that ultimately lead to a child's negative classroom behaviors. The fact that a parent is incarcerated has a significant cognitive and affective impact on a child. This impact is further reinforced by overall familial disruption. There exist parental difficulties such as a lack of employment skills and resources, mental health challenges and stigma. All of these affect families of the incarcerated such that there is a significant multidimensional and multi-systemic psychosocial impact. The families have significant stressors and issues of anxiety and abandonment that all intermix to create behavioral difficulties in the children of incarcerated parents.

To extend this model further in the context of the interventions performed in the HOPE Project, Figure 5.2 depicts the hypothesized impact of targeted interventions on familial disruptions and negative classroom behaviors. It further illustrates the overall research process where case management interventions are developed and implemented such that significant reduction of familial disruption is predicted and an overall increase in parenting effectiveness also is predicted.

In-school interventions are directly aimed at elementary school children in kindergarten through 5th grade who have experienced parental incarceration. These are psychotherapeutic interventions such as bibliotherapy, art therapy, play therapy and individual age-specific counseling aimed at reducing behavioral difficulties within the classroom.

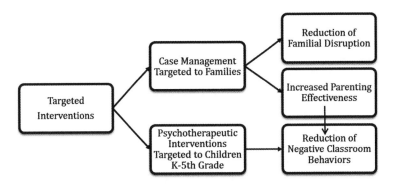

**Figure 5.2     Model of Targeted Interventions**

## Methodology

### Design

Institutional Review Board (IRB) permission was received prior to implementing the three-year pilot HOPE Project. The program evaluation was conducted during and at the end of the three-year project using a mixed method approach. Specifically, six data collection strategies, both formal and informal, were used although only five are reported in this chapter: 1) the project's data form collected demographic information on the children and families at the time of enrollment in the project; 2) a pre-test/post-test teacher assessment evaluated the children's in-class behavior at the time of enrollment and at the end of the school year in June; 3) a focus group was conducted at the end of year 3 of the project with a convenience sample of parents; 4) a teacher feedback meeting was held with a convenience sample of nine teachers from Bancroft Elementary School at the end of the project's third year; and 5) the project's monthly report generated bi-weekly feedback from (a) teachers on the children's in-class behavior (i.e., whether they were improving, remaining the same or regressing), (b) therapists (MSW students and the LCSW supervisors) on the children's therapeutic progress during counseling sessions and (c) parents during monthly meetings. The monthly report also served to ensure treatment fidelity; that is, that the project was being implemented as intended (Royse et al. 2010). This allowed problems to be identified and corrective measures to be implemented on an ongoing basis.

### Instrument

The teacher assessment was a pre-test/post-test 20-item scale developed by the project's staff and modeled on the Rutter behavior scales (Rutter et al. 1970). This instrument allowed teachers to measure children's behaviors in the classroom at the time of enrollment in the HOPE Project and at the end of the school year in June. An insufficient number of teacher assessments were completed in year 1, rendering data analysis impractical. Therefore, data are reported for year 2 and year 3 only. The 4-point rating scale assessed an array of in-class behaviors such as restlessness, fights, ability to focus, defiance and disobedience. Teachers used the 4-point rating scale (0 = never/almost never, 1 = 1–2 times a day, 2 = 3 or more times a day and 3 = 1–2 times a week) to assess the children's in-class behavior. Negative behaviors included the following: very restless, frequent fights, difficulty focusing, often defiant, threatens others, disobedient and bullies others. The lower the score a child received, the better their behavior. Ongoing monitoring was conducted and corrective measures were implemented throughout the year by the case managers/graduate assistants (GAs).

## Results

### Descriptive Data

Forty-seven (96 percent) of the 49 children who participated in the HOPE Project were Black, 30 (61 percent) were males and 38 (76 percent) were living with their mother. Fourteen of the children (29 percent) had a parent who was incarcerated at the time the child was enrolled in the project. An additional four children (8 percent) had parents who were incarcerated more than once during their enrollment in the project. Another 19 children (39 percent) had parents who had been incarcerated prior to their enrollment in the project. Only one child had both parents incarcerated while enrolled in the project. Additionally, 27 (55 percent) of the children had siblings enrolled in the project. Just over half (28, or 57 percent) of the children attended one school and most (32, or 65 percent) were enrolled in first through third grades. The 49 children represented 35 different families (see Table 5.1).

**Table 5.1    Demographics Characteristics of Project Participants by Program Year (Children N = 49: Families N = 35)**

|  | Year 1 | Year 2 | Year 3 | Total |
|---|---|---|---|---|
| **No. of Families** | 8 (23%) | 13 (37%) | 14 (40%) | 35 (100%) |
| **No. of Children** | 13 (27%) | 17 (35%) | 19 (39%) | 49 (101%)* |
| **Race/Ethnicity** | | | | |
| African American | 13 (28%) | 16 (34%) | 18 (38%) | 47 (100%) |
| Mixed Race | 0 (0%) | 1 (50%) | 1 (50%) | 2 (100%) |
| **Gender** | | | | |
| Female | 2 (11%) | 7 (37%) | 10 (53%) | 19 (101%)* |
| Male | 11 (37%) | 10 (33%) | 9 (30%) | 30 (100%) |
| **School** | | | | |
| Bancroft | 3 (11%) | 12 (43%) | 13 (46%) | 28 (100%) |
| Stubbs | 9 (60%) | 2 (13%) | 4 (27%) | 15 (100%) |
| Elbert Palmer | 1 (17%) | 3 (50%) | 2 (33%) | 6 (100%) |
| **Grade** | | | | |
| Kindergarten | 2 (29%) | 4 (57%) | 1 (14%) | 7 (100%) |
| First Grade | 2 (18%) | 2 (18%) | 7 (67%) | 11 (103%)* |
| Second Grade | 3 (30%) | 4 (40%) | 3 (30%) | 10 (100%) |
| Third Grade | 3 (27%) | 3 (27%) | 5 (45%) | 11 (99%)* |
| Fourth Grade | 2 (40%) | 1 (20%) | 2 (40%) | 5 (100%) |
| Fifth Grade | 1 (20%) | 3 (60%) | 1 (20%) | 5 (100%) |
| **Parental Incarceration** | | | | |
| Current (time of enrollment) | 0 (0%) | 6 (43%) | 8 (57%) | 14 (100%) |
| Past | 3 (16%) | 7 (37%) | 9 (47%) | 19 (100%) |
| Multiple | 2 (50%) | 2 (50%) | 0 (0%) | 4 (100%) |
| Unknown | 8 (67%) | 4 (33%) | 0 (0%) | 12 (100%) |
| **No. of Siblings Enrolled** | 10 (37%) | 8 (30%) | 9 (33%) | 27 (100%) |
| **Guardianship** | | | | |
| Mother Only | 10 (26%) | 12 (32%) | 16 (42%) | 38 (100%) |
| Father Only | 2 (67%) | 0 (0%) | 1 (33%) | 3 (100%) |
| Aunt and Father | 0 (0%) | 1 (100%) | 0 (100%) | 1 (100%) |
| Grandmother | 1 (20%) | 2 (40%) | 2 (40%) | 5 (100%) |
| Mother and Father | 0 (0%) | 2 (100%) | 0 (0%) | 2 (100%) |

*Note:* * Percentage totals are higher or lower than 100% due to rounding.

## Paired Sample t-Test Results

The *t*-test results shown in Table 5.2 indicate statistical significance in several categories, approaching significance in some categories and lack of statistical significance in one category. The significance level was set at p < .10 given the non-probability sampling used in the project. It should be noted that the psychometric instrument utilized for this study had four categories that were combined into two categories: Category 1) never/almost never and Category 2) one–three times a day because there was considerable overlap in the four categories as shown on the instrument. The four categories were: 1) never/almost never; 2) one to two times a day; 3) three or more times a day; and 4) one to two times a week. In an attempt to analyze the results with relative interpretative significance, categories 1 and 4 were combined and categories 2 and 3 were combined. Table 5.2 reflects this combination and paired sample *t*-tests were performed utilizing the combined paired pretest/posttest data.

**Table 5.2    Paired Sample *t*-Test From Year 2 and Year 3 of the HOPE Project**

| Negative Classroom Behavior | Pre-Test Mean | Post-Test Mean | Pre-Test SD | Post-Test SD | *t*-Test Results |
|---|---|---|---|---|---|
| 2nd Year Results (Never/Almost Never Category) (n = 12) | 6.7 | 8.3 | 3.3 | 3.8 | (p< .10) <br> * *t* = 0.05 (paired, one-tailed) <br> * *t* = 0.09 (paired, two-tailed) |
| 2nd Year Results (1–3 Time/ Day Category) (n = 12) | 6.9 | 5.4 | 2.8 | 3.9 | (p < .10) <br> * *t* = 0.08 (paired, one-tailed) <br> * *t* = 0.16 (paired, two-tailed) |
| 3rd Year Results (Never-Almost Never Category) (n=12) | 6.7 | 8.5 | 2.6 | 3.9 | (p < .10) <br> * *t* = 0.07 (paired, one-tailed) <br> * *t* = 0.14 (paired, two-tailed) |
| 3rd Year Results (1–3 Time/ Day Category) (n = 12) | 5.2 | 4.9 | 3.9 | 3.9 | (p < .10) <br> * *t* = 0.41 (paired, one-tailed) <br> * *t* = 0.81 (paired, two-tailed) |

Year 2 results from the combined category 'never/almost never' show the cohort of 12 children experienced a significant reduction ($t = 0.05$, one-tailed and $t = 0.09$, two-tailed) of negative classroom behaviors. These children, at pre-test, manifested higher levels of negative behaviors. The change in the mean score from 6.7 to 8.3 is indicative that students who were manifesting slight behavioral problems (i.e., never/almost never) showed an overall reduction of these behaviors since the post-test mean score is 8.3. It should be noted that a higher score in this category (i.e., never/almost never) indicates lower levels of negative behaviors, given the nature of the psychometric instrument utilized, judgments made by teachers, and the structure of 18 quantitative questions within the instrument. The standard deviation (SD) increased slightly from 3.3 to 3.8 indicating a small increase in the dispersion of raw scores. Since there is only a change of .5 between the two SD scores the cohort's overall dispersion around the mean is minimal. This could indicate greater consistency in the change of behavioral patterns within each child.

With regard to the combined category "one to three times a day," one-tailed paired *t*-test results also indicate a significant reduction of children's negative classroom behaviors in year 2. The one-tailed test provides more power to detect an effect in one direction by not testing the effect in the other direction. With regard to the current study, the reduction of negative behaviors was examined as "one-tail" and by setting the p value at .10 it can be stated that there is only an 8 percent probability that the difference between the pre- and post-test scores is due to chance factors. Hence, it can be said that the decrease in negative behaviors is statistically significant at the p level of .10 where case management and psychotherapeutic interventions were effective in decreasing negative classroom behavior.

Examination of year 3 results for the combined category "never/almost never" show there was a significant reduction of negative classroom behaviors among the cohort of 12 children as indicated by a one-tailed paired $t$-test result. The result of $t = 0.07$ is encouraging as it demonstrates there was a decrease of negative behaviors that were detected during pre-test. Results for the combined category "1 to 3 times a day" did not indicate a statistically significant reduction of negative classroom behaviors. The $t$-test results indicate there is 41 percent probability that the difference between the paired pre-test and post-test results was due to chance factors. Therefore, there is a 59 percent probability that the difference is due to case management and psychotherapeutic interventions. This is possibly indicative of other uncontrollable factors outside the purview of the interventions performed. With regard to the mean scores in the combined category "1 to 3 times a day," the post-test mean decreased slightly from 5.2 to 4.9 in year 3. The difference is negligible and gives further indication of other significant factors that may have been at work in the children's continued maintenance of their negative behaviors.

## Teacher Feedback Meeting

Most of the nine teachers from Bancroft Elementary School who participated in the teacher feedback meeting indicated that the HOPE Project was very helpful in re-directing the children's in-class behaviors and they wanted to see it continue. Several teachers gave specific examples of children who were better able to listen and follow directions and who were less confrontational with their peers and teachers. One teacher, describing a child that demonstrated significant improvement in her behavior, said, "I was so surprised by her behavior I wanted to know what was happening so it could keep happening." The teachers believed that many of the HOPE Project children seemed to display signs and symptoms of Attention Deficit Hyperactive Disorder (ADHD) and asked if the HOPE Project would provide training for them on the disorder and alert them of any students who had a positive diagnosis. They also identified four specific areas where the HOPE Project could be improved. One, they requested the staff introduce the project to all of the school's teachers early in the school year, preferably during their professional development training in August. The staff would make an oral presentation and provide teachers with program brochures and intake forms. Second, they requested the project staff have consistent office hours in the school so the project team would be more accessible to the teachers. Third, they asked that project staff meet monthly with teachers to discuss the students' in-class behavior. Last, they requested that graduate assistants spend time in the classroom observing the children. While teachers appreciated graduate assistants removing children from class for their therapy sessions, especially when they were being disruptive, they also believed the opportunity to observe the children's interactions with peers and their teacher would yield important information that could be useful during the therapeutic process.

### Focus Group Results

The focus group results are presented in two parts. The first shows how parents or caregivers perceived the program's effectiveness in reducing their children's negative school behavior. The second shows how parents or caregivers perceived the program's effectiveness in increasing their engagement in activities that had a direct impact on their children's behavior.

## Parents' Perception of the HOPE Project's Success in Reducing their Children's Negative In-School Behavioral Incidents (Project Goal #1)

Five (36 percent) of the 14 parents from year 3, all mothers, participated in the focus group. Together they parented seven (37 percent) of the children enrolled in year 3 of the project; four of the seven were enrolled in both year 2 and year 3. Of the seven children, six displayed negative behaviors on the teacher assessment pre-test. This was further confirmed during the initial parental assessment (with the parent/caregiver only) and child assessment (with the child only) conducted by the case managers/graduate assistants after enrollment in the project. Information from the assessments was used to develop the family improvement plan.

The overall theme gleaned from the parents was that the HOPE Project achieved Goal #1: it helped to reduce the children's negative behaviors both in school and at home. All four parents who initially reported behavioral issues said their children's behavior had improved. One parent said, "My son had behavior problems from last year up until now ... it has changed drastically. I used to get five, six phone calls a day [from the school] alone because of his behavior. Now I'm getting no phone calls at all. But if I do, it is something good that he's done. So it has, The HOPE Project has impacted his life." That particular child participated in The HOPE Project in year 2 and year 3 and earned the highest score in his school, for his grade level, on the state's standardized test in 2013. Another parent, whose child's behavior resulted in several suspensions during year 2 of the project, said that her daughter's behavior "improved a lot ... from last year to this year. She's changed a lot and I give it to the staff that she's worked with that come and get her from her class, and spend one-on-one time with her ... she really did a lot ... a whole turnaround from last year to this year." The focus group also indicated that the project helped to improve some children's academic achievement and self-confidence. The mother whose child did not demonstrate negative behavior during the parent and child assessments stated, "... from last year to this year she's [daughter] up on her reading level." This mother also indicated that her child gained confidence in her academic abilities, stating "It's the confidence that I [the child] know how to do this and I'm not acting up because I'm frustrated that I don't understand it."

## Parents' Perception of the HOPE Project's Success in Increasing their Engagement in School and Community Activities that had Direct Impact on their Children's Behavior (Project Goal #2)

The general theme that emerged regarding project Goal #2 was that parents appreciated being regularly informed about school and community activities by the case managers/

graduate assistants. One parent, referring to the graduate assistant who worked directly with her and her daughter said, "… she [the graduate assistant] always … you know … calls me and tells me different activities that's going on to be involved in and have my daughter come and be involved." Another parent stated, "… everyone in the whole project calls, lets me know about different programs, different things that are going on. Keeps me active and not at home, not doing anything. I can't do that. And the fact that she [the graduate assistant] even encourage me to be more involved, not only with my son's life, but with the school."

When asked to identify the barriers they encountered during their participation in the HOPE Project, three of five parents identified transportation as the biggest obstacle. One parent stated, "I would catch the bus … but sometimes I don't have the fare." Another parent said her health was the barrier that prevented her from attending some of the project's activities. Yet another parent said her job was the barrier because it conflicted with the time of day that many of the school and community activities were offered.

## Monthly Report Results

The monthly report collected data on a variety of project outputs and outcomes. However, only two, the children's psychosocial progress and the parents'/caregivers' engagement in school and community activities, are reported in this chapter.

### Children's Psychosocial Progress

In each monthly report the case managers/GAs provided a narrative update on the psychosocial progress of each child on his or her caseload. The average caseload was 10 children per academic year. The update identified whether the child's behavior improved, regressed or remained the same as the previous month. It also provided an assessment of which therapeutic strategies were working, or not, and which corrective measures had been or needed to be put in place to help improve the children's behaviors. Data were obtained from the children's teachers, parents/caregivers and from GAs' and therapists' via observations of the children during their bi-weekly therapy sessions. Overall, all of the children's behaviors improved as a result of the intervention over the three years of the project. Only one child, who was enrolled in the project all three years and who lived with his grandmother, demonstrated inconsistent behaviors which became more pronounced when the child's mother failed to show up to scheduled visits with the child. We learned that his mother became incarcerated and his father, who had been released from prison, was re-incarcerated.

### Parents'/Caregivers' Engagement in School and Community Activities

During the first two years of the project the case managers/GAs developed a resource book to inform parents about available and affordable school activities and community resources during the academic year and in the summer months. For year 1 and year 2 the GAs identified in the monthly report which activities they encouraged parents to attend. However, the precise number of parents attending the activities and the total number of activities was not collected until year 3. Between November 2012 and June 2013, eight (57 percent) of the 14 parents/caregivers attended a total of 86 workshops. Some parents attended one workshop but most attended four or five workshops per month. The types of workshops ranged from one centered on teaching parents how to identify signs and symptoms of ADD/ADHD in their children, to another emphasizing effective parenting skills, to a session on preparing for employment opportunities, to one that taught them how to educate their children about sexual molestation and sexual abuse.

It is important to note that both the number of parents attending the workshops and the number of workshops they attended increased between November 2012 and June 2013. For example, four parents attended a total of nine workshops in November and six parents attended 15 workshops in the months of May and June.

## Discussion

All five strategies used in the program evaluation indicate that the HOPE Project was successful in achieving its two goals of reducing children's negative in-school behaviors and increasing their parents'/caregivers' engagement in school and community activities. The data form captured relevant demographic information about the prospective families at intake. It did not, however, ask about parental incarceration status due to concerns about perceived stigma. This information was captured during the assessment process with parents/caregivers. Thus, during year 1 a few parents completed the intake form because they wanted assistance managing their children's negative in-school behavior, not because there was an incarcerated parent. Those families were allowed to remain in the project. This somewhat compromised the treatment fidelity (Royse et al. 2010), which was a limitation of the project. Future projects should request specific information about incarceration on the intake form that includes, but is not limited to: 1) the incarcerated parent's gender, 2) length of parent's incarceration, 3) state in which parent is incarcerated and 4) whether the parent has been previously incarcerated.

The pre-test/post-test teacher assessment captured different dimensions of each child's behavioral problems via the 18 quantitative questions. This was a strength of the instrument. It allowed teachers to identify the child's strengths using the two open-ended questions that provided a balanced perspective of the child's overall behavior. At the outset, the instrument was deemed to have both face and content validity. However, several limitations emerged during its implementation and data analysis. First, the instrument was not pilot tested with teachers prior to implementation. Second, teachers were not taught how to accurately utilize the assessment form by the project staff and some found it confusing to complete. Third, the four behavior categories identified in the *t*-test results were too similar and had to be combined during the data analysis. Fourth, due to teacher attrition some of the teachers who completed the pre-test were not the same ones who completed the post-test. All of these limitations compromised the validity and reliability of the instrument and thus the intervention. The project staff developed the teacher assessment because the literature did not suggest any valid and reliable instrument that captured the construct of behavioral problems among children with incarcerated parents. The teacher assessment should be revised and tested for increased validity and reliability before use in future programs.

Year 3 pretest/posttest teacher assessment results in the "one to three times a day" combined category indicated slight to no reduction of the children's negative classroom behaviors. There are two possible explanations for this outcome. First, the pre-test was administered at different times during the school year when the children enrolled in the program. Second, teachers experienced confusion when completing the instrument.

Additionally, given the small convenience sample used in the analysis for year 2 and year 3, which is another limitation, it is not possible to generalize these results to either the population of children with incarcerated parents in the three targeted schools or to the overall population of children with incarcerated parents. The project's results suggest the need for additional research with a much larger sample sizes, which may show similar or even improved results and where greater confidence in generalizability could be obtained.

Teacher feedback meetings confirmed that the project positively impacted the children's negative behaviors and yielded positive reports that are indicative of the teachers' perception of the children's overall improved behavior. The majority of teachers stated that the intervention was "working" because the children's behaviors had improved and they wanted to see the program continued. The meeting provided important feedback on how future projects can work more effectively with teachers to reduce the negative behavior of children who have incarcerated parents. Their suggestion that the project be introduced to all teachers early in the school year is an excellent one. The researchers recommend implementing the teachers' suggestion that project staff maintain office hours in the school to more easily engage and frequently meet with teachers. They also concur with teachers that graduate assistants spend time in the classroom observing the children, as this could result in the acquisition of invaluable information that can better inform the therapeutic process. These recommendations may help future programs better develop effective teacher partnerships and the delivery of services to the children. The meeting also uncovered teacher concerns about the number of children displaying signs and symptoms of ADHD. This observation was confirmed in the children's mental health assessments and addressed during their therapy sessions. While addressing ADHD was not a component of the HOPE Project, the researchers, nevertheless, agree that training teachers to better identify the signs and symptoms of ADHD will help them make timely referrals to social workers and other mental health specialists. Future projects should also consider educating parents about ADHD so that they can work with their children at home and become more effective partners with the school in managing their children's behaviors.

The focus group provided a qualitative first-hand account of the intervention performed from the parents'/caregivers' perspective (Dudley 2011). The evaluation gave parents an opportunity to provide feedback on the effectiveness of the project and share their barriers to full participation. The barrier cited by most of the parents was the lack of transportation to attend program activities. Future programs must include transportation in order to remove this barrier. A limitation of the evaluation process is that only one focus group was conducted at the end of year 3 of the project. The researchers recommend that future projects conduct focus groups at the end of each program year, so that the results would be more representative of all the parents participating in the project.

The strength of the project's monthly report is that it illustrated the children's psychosocial progress and the parents'/caregivers' engagement in school and community activities over the duration of the project. The report also documented the children's responses (behavioral improvement, non-improvement, or regression) to the various intervention strategies (art, play, biblio- and talk therapies) and the corrective measures that were developed when necessary. These reports captured the key outputs and outcomes of the project on a regular and consistent basis and were prepared monthly except for May and June when, due to limited school activities, they were combined.

Overall, the HOPE Project was shown to be a successful intervention strategy to help reduce the negative behaviors of children with incarcerated parents and increase the engagement of their parents/caregivers in school and community activities. Practitioners, including social workers (particularly those who work in schools), teachers, physicians and community nurses who work with these children and their families should be aware of the numerous emotional and psychological challenges and environmental risks these families face. They must also pay attention to protective factors such as stable and supportive caregivers and alternative caregivers, and promote secure attachment between the caregivers and children (Dallaire 2007) to improve the well-being of both. These protective factors have been shown to foster resiliency and positive growth and development in children whose parents are incarcerated (Denby 2012). There are no formal rituals and ceremonies when a child loses a parent or a parent loses a partner to incarceration (Dallaire and Wilson 2010). Unlike the array of resources and support available to families that are coping with death and divorce, few formal support systems are available in communities to help families cope with the loss of a parent due to incarceration (ibid.). More well-funded community-based programs that collaborate with schools, the criminal justice field and mental health practitioners, particularly those that are school-based, are needed if our country is truly serious about reducing the psychosocial impact of parental incarceration and interrupting the tragic cycle of intergenerational incarceration.

# References

Arditti, Joyce, and April Few. 2006. "Mothers' Reentry into Family Life Following Incarceration." *Criminal Justice Policy Review* 17(1): 103–23.
———, Jennifer Lambert-Shute and Karen Joest. 2003. "Saturday Morning at the Jail: Implications of Incarceration for Families and Children." *Family Relations* 52: 195–204.
Blaine, Charley, and Michael Sauter. 2013. "The Most Dangerous States in America." *Wall Street Journal*: http://247wallst.com/special-report/2013/10/04/the-most-dangerous-states-in-america/print/.
Christle, Christine, Kristine Jolivette and Charles Nelson. 2005. "Breaking the School to Prison Pipeline: Identifying School Risk and Protective Factors for Youth Delinquency, Exceptionality." *A Special Education Journal* 13(2): 69–88.
Clear, Todd. 2007. *Imprisoning Communities: How Mass Incarceration Makes Disadvantaged Neighborhoods Worse*. New York: Oxford University Press.
Dallaire, Danielle. 2007. "Incarcerated Mothers and Fathers: A Comparison of Risks for Children and Families." *Family Relations* 56: 440–53.
———, and Laura Wilson. 2010. "The Relation of Exposure to Parental Criminal Activity, Arrest, and Sentencing to Children's Maladjustment." *Journal of Child and Family Studies* 19: 404–18.
Dannerbeck, Anne. 2005. "Differences in Parenting Attributes, Experiences, and Behaviors of Delinquent Youth With and Without a Parental History of Incarceration." *Youth Violence and Juvenile Justice* 3: 199.
Darensbourg, Alica, Erica Perez and Jamilia Blake. 2010. "Overrepresentation of African American Males in Exclusionary Discipline: The Role of School-Based Mental Health Professionals in Dismantling the School to Prison Pipeline." *Journal of African American Males in Education* 1(3): 196–211.
Davies, Elizabeth, Diana Brazzell, N.G. La Vigne and Tracey Shollenberger. 2008. *Understanding the Experiences and Needs of Children of Incarcerated Parents: Views from Mentors*. Washington, DC: Urban Institute Justice Policy Center.
Denby, Ramona. 2012. "Parental Incarceration and Kinship Care: Caregiver Experiences, Child Well-being, and Permanency Intentions." *Social Work in Public Health* 27(1–2): 104–28.
Dudley, James. 2011. *Research Methods for Social Work: Being Producers and Consumers of Research*, 2nd edn. Boston, MA: Allyn & Bacon/Pearson.

Elbogen, Eric, and Sally Johnson. 2009. "The Intricate Link Between Violence and Mental Disorder: Results from the National Epidemiological Survey on Alcohol and Related Conditions." *The Archives of General Psychiatry* 66: 152–61.

Glaze, Lauren, and Laura Maruschak. Revised 2010. *Parents in Prison and their Minor Children.* Washington, DC: US Department of Justice, Bureau of Justice Statistics.

Hairston, Creasie. 2007. *Focus on Children with Incarcerated Parents: An Overview of the Research Literature.* Baltimore, MD: Annie E. Casey Foundation.

———. 2009. *Kinship Care When Parents are Incarcerated: What We Know, What We Can Do.* Baltimore, MD: Annie E. Casey Foundation.

Hanlon, Thomas, Steven Carswell and Marc Rose. 2007. "Research on the Caretaking of Children of Incarcerated Parents: Findings and their Service Delivery Implications." *Children and Youth Services Review* 29(3): 362–84.

Huebner, Beth, and Regan Gustafson. 2007. "The Effect of Maternal Incarceration on Adult Offspring Involvement in the Criminal Justice System." *Journal of Criminal Justice* 35(3): 283–96.

Johnson, Toni. 2012. Mapping the Critical Needs of Adolescent Children of Prisoners. *Social Work in Public Health* 27(1-2): 45–68.

Kjellstrand, Jean, and J. Mark Eddy. 2011. "Parental Incarceration During Childhood, Family Context, and Youth Problem Behavior Across Adolescence." *Journal of Offender Rehabilitation* 50(1): 18–36.

Kyckelhahn, Tracey. Revised 2013. *State Corrections Expenditures, FY 1982–2010.* Washington, DC: US Department of Justice, Bureau of Justice Statistics.

Langan, Patrick, and David Levin. 2002. *Recidivism of Prisoners Released in 1994* (NCJ 193427). Washington, DC: US Department of Justice, Bureau of Justice Statistics, Office of Justice Programs.

Murray, Joseph, and David Farrington. 2005. "Parental Imprisonment: Effects on Boys' Antisocial Behavior and Delinquency Through the Life-Course." *Journal of Child Psychology and Psychiatry* 46: 1269–78.

———. 2008. "Effects of Parental Imprisonment on Children." in *Crime and Justice: A Review of Research* (vol.37), ed. Michael Tonry. Chicago, IL: University of Chicago Press, pp. 133–206.

The National Fatherhood Initiative. 2010. "Facts on Father Absence": http://www.fatherhood. org/media/fatherhood-statistics.

Phillips, Susan, Alaattin Erkanli, Gordon Keeler, Jane Costello, Adrian Angold and Denise Johnston. 2006. "Disentangling the Risks: Parent Criminal Justice Involvement and Children's Exposure to Family Risks." *Criminology and Public Policy* 5: 677–702.

Poehlmann, Julie. 2005. "Representations of Attachment Relationships in Children of Incarcerated Mothers." *Child Development* 76: 679–96.

Puddefoot, Ginny, and Lisa Foster. 2007. *Keeping Children Safe When Their Parents are Arrested: Local Approaches That Work.* Sacramento, CA: California Research Bureau.

Raimon, Martha, Arlene Lee, and Philip Genty. 2009. *Sometimes Good Intentions Yield Bad Results: ASFA's Effect on Incarcerated Parents and Their Children. An Intentions and Results: A Look Back at the Adoption and Safe Families Act 121.* Urban Institute Center for the Study of Social Policy: http://ocfs.ny.gov/main/publications/PDF_StongerTogetherVol1.pdf.

Royse, David, Bruce Thyer and Deborah Padgett. 2010. *Program Evaluation: An Introduction,* 5th ed. Belmont, CA: Wadsworth, Cengage Learning.

Rutter, Michael, Jack Tizard and Kingsley Whitmore. 1970. *Education, Health and Behaviour.* London: Longman Group.

Sampson, Robert, and Charles Loeffler. 2010. "Punishment's Place: The Local Concentration of Mass Incarceration." *Daedalus* 139: 20–31.

Western, Bruce, and Becky Pettit. 2010. *Collateral Costs: Incarceration's Effect on Economic Mobility*. Washington, DC: The Pew Charitable Trusts.

Wildeman, Christopher. 2009. "Parental Imprisonment, the Prison Boom, and the Concentration of Childhood Disadvantage." *Demography* 46(2): 265–80.

Woldoff, Rachael, and Heather Washington. 2008. "Arrested Contact: The Criminal Justice System, Race, and Father Engagement." *Prison Journal* 88: 179–206.

Zastrow, Charles, and Karen Kirst-Ashman. 2013. *Understanding Human Behavior and the Social Environment*, 9th edn. Belmont, CA: Thompson-Brooks/Cole.

# "Sure there's Racism … But Homophobia—that's Different": Experiences of Black Lesbians Who are Parenting in North-Central Florida at the Intersection of Race and Sexuality

## Clare Walsh

This chapter explores the perspectives of black lesbians as they discuss their lives in a social world where they are challenged by racism because of their African American[1] racial identity and homophobia because of their lesbian sexual identity. There are almost 85,000 black lesbian and gay couples in the United States and they represent 14 percent of all same-sex couples living in the nation (Dang and Frazer 2004). This group is in a unique position given that their experiences are not the same as those of black heterosexual couples or those of couples composed of white lesbians or gay men. Little is known about this group since most sexuality research tends to focus on white lesbian and gay couples and most race-based research tends to focus on heterosexual couples.

Black same-sex couple's experiences highlight the unique circumstance found at the intersection of sexuality and race. For example, Dang and Frazer (ibid.) report that 53 percent of black lesbians and gay men interviewed in 2000 experienced racial discrimination and 42 percent experienced discrimination based on their sexual orientation. Furthermore, Biblarz and Savci (2010: 493), in their review of the scholarship on lesbian, gay, bisexual and transgender (LGBT) families, report that even though there has been significant progress in research on these families, "we know little about the unique family processes that may unfold when families are subjected to both the concomitants of racism and of homophobia." Black lesbians and gay men must negotiate the social world while being challenged by the interlocking oppressions of racism and heteronormativity/homophobia.

Racism and its impact on the lives of African Americans has been the focus of research for many scholars. Bonilla-Silva (2010: 8) argues that race is a socially constructed category since "notions of racial differences are human creations rather than eternal, essential categories." Nagel (2003: 6) explains that "current notions of *race* are centered exclusively on visible (usually skin color) distinctions among populations." Roberts (2011: x, original emphasis)

---

1   For this project, I use "black" and "African American" interchangeably since according to recent Gallup polls there is no strong consensus in the community for either term (Associated Press 2012) and since my participants also used these terms interchangeably and expressed no preference for either term.

further contends that "biologically, there is one human race. Race applied to human beings is a *political* division: it is a system of governing people that classifies them into a social hierarchy based on invented biological demarcations" (ibid.: 3, original emphasis) She further acknowledges that "race is the main characteristic most Americans use to classify each other" (ibid.). This classification system based on race has produced a social hierarchy, grounded in racism with oppression and mistreatment of black Americans by white Americans, ranging from the subtle and hard to observe (e.g., stereotyping by name to limit one's employment opportunities) to the blatant and easily noticed (e.g., lynching and murder) (Feagin 2000). The effects of racism are encountered in "everyday situations in workplaces, stores, schools, housing, and daily social interaction" and this racial segregation remains a fundamental feature of the U.S. social landscape (Collins 2000: 23), even influencing empirical research.

Several researchers have reported on the influence racism has had in the study of African American families (Chatters et al. 1994; Dilworth-Anderson et al. 1993; Staples 1971) and these findings inform the data analysis for this project. Much of the existing literature in family studies has been criticized for using the white, middle-class family as the standard for comparison to other groups. More often than not, the comparison of African American families with white families has shown the former to be *deviant* and as a result to become *pathologized*. Staples (1971:119) asserts:

> *Black family research has been characterized by the reiteration of unfounded myths and stereotypes which produce in the public mind the image of black families as a pathological social unit—a system incapable of rearing individuals who can adjust to the demands of a civilized society.*

He further notes that this deviant status has been used to formulate public policy that directly impacts the everyday lives of African American families. Ethnic minority families *are* different from white middle-class families, but that should not suggest that they be inherently relegated to a subordinate or deviant status.[2]

Many scholars have investigated attitudes of African Americans toward lesbians and gay men (Battle and Lemelle 2002; Ernst et al. 1991; Herek and Capitanio 1995; Jenkins et al. 2009; Lewis 2003; Schulte and Battle 2004). For example, Herek and Capitanio (1995) found that negative African American attitudes toward lesbians and gay men were widespread within the community, with African American men having a more negative attitude toward gay men than toward lesbians. The authors conclude that African American men had a greater tendency to see male homosexuality as unnatural vis-à-vis female homosexuality. Herek and Capitanio (1995) found the single most important predictor to more positive attitudes was whether or not a person believed homosexuality was beyond an individual's control. They also found more favorable attitudes toward lesbians and gay men were present if respondents had experienced personal contact with lesbians or gay men.

In another study, Lemelle and Battle (2004) explored the information gained from the National Black Politics Study. They pointed out that for African American women, age, income, education and urban residence were variables that were important to explain attitudes toward gay men. Specifically, they found older and more educated African American women who lived in big cities and had an increased level of income were more sympathetic to gay

---

2    This pathologizing of African American families is part of the cultural legacy of the 1965 Moynihan study of black families, *The Negro Family: The Case for National Action*. As Hill (2005: 13) reports, Moynihan implied that "the lack of socioeconomic progress by blacks was linked to weak dysfunctional female-headed families.". These black matriarchs were labeled as being unfit parents since they spent too much time working outside the home and not supervising their children; without supervision their children became social failures (Collins 2000).

men. For African American men, religious attendance was the only significant variable with more church attendance leading to less sympathetic attitudes toward gay men. Lemelle and Battle (2004:48) suggest "among the larger African American male population, more age, more money, more education or living in a big city does not impact attitudes toward gay males" as much as church teachings that enhance black masculinist homophobic attitudes. However, this body of research on African American attitudes on homosexuality misses an opportunity to investigate the complexity and diversity of both the LGBT community and the African American community since the research does not define sexuality in terms of race. For example, African American and white participants are asked to report on their attitude toward lesbians and gay men in general, not their attitude to African American lesbians or white gay men, specifically.

African American lesbians and gay men negotiate the social world as members of two minority groups. As African Americans, they negotiate the world through a racial lens and as a lesbian or gay man they negotiate the world as a sexual minority. Green describes this as being on the horns of a dilemma. He notes the men in his study are "alienated from Black community institutions because of their sexuality but less integrated into white, urban, gay community institutions because of their race" (Green 2007: 754). African Americans with a lesbian/gay identity *are* on the horns of a dilemma as they negotiate the social world as both a racial minority and as a sexual minority with varying levels of acceptability within each social group. Race is important to an individual's identity in the LGBT community and sexuality is important to their identity in the African American community.

This investigation provides a more focused discussion on the salience of participants' lesbian sexual identity as they negotiate their social world also as a racial minority. When participants articulate their lived experiences at the simultaneous and interlocking social oppressions of both racism and homophobia, they focus on a discussion of both/and (both racism and homophobia) as they stress that 'sexuality is bigger' and different.

## Data and Methods

Data for this analysis come from 10 interviews conducted with a non-random sample of 12 women who identify as African American/black and lesbian/gay and were living in Jacksonville, Florida between late 2012 and early 2013. Jacksonville, Florida was selected as it provided a unique opportunity to investigate the challenges faced by lesbians and gay men who were parenting in an area that is politically conservative and has historically been among the most segregated cities in the United States (Alderman et al. 2005; Taeuber and Taeuber [1965] 2009). This segregation and political conservatism create a social world where experiences with racism and homophobia might be more unique than those experiences in other less conservative and less segregated areas of the country. Jacksonville is also unique in that the 2010 U.S. Census highlighted the city as having the second largest population of LGBT parents in the United States. I recruited participants with the help of a gatekeeper[3] and while attending various Pride events in Jacksonville.

---

3    Pastor Val is quoted in *The New York Times* article discussing gay parenting in the South (Tavernise 2011) and has been a vocal supporter of the LGBT community in Jacksonville. She has been quoted in many newspaper articles and has been interviewed several times by local affiliates for nightly television news broadcasts. When asked if she would prefer I use a pseudonym for her in this project, Pastor Val noted she had no misgivings with the use of her given name.

Participants were between the ages of 25 and 45 and had been in their parenting relationship between two and 10 years. The number of children parented either solely or as a couple ranged from one to four and all the children were at least of elementary school age. Eight of the participants had children biologically in a previous heterosexual relationship. One participant bore the child she was raising with a partner through *in vitro* fertilization. And another participant was raising a child with her partner that she had adopted and they were fostering another child. Eight of those interviewed self-identified as having a middle-class socioeconomic status with three self-identified as working-class or blue-collar and one self-identified as being of low socioeconomic status since they were unemployed at the time of the interview. Nine of the participants lived in Jacksonville, Florida at the time of the interview and three individuals lived in other North Central Florida cities; cities with social, political and cultural views that mirror the conservatism of Jacksonville. All participants had 'come out,' or disclosed their sexual identity to their families, and were 'out' in varying degrees in other social situations like work or at their child(ren)'s school. Separate audiotaped semi-structured interviews were conducted with participants in public spaces like coffee shops and restaurants or in their home. The interviews ranged from 30 to 90 minutes in length and were transcribed for analysis. During analysis all participants' names and identifiable characteristics were changed to provide anonymity.

Rather than generating theory, I use a constructivist grounded theory approach (Charmaz 2006) to provide a conceptual frame that helps explain the ways black lesbians frame the challenges faced by their families today. A constructivist perspective of grounded theory is described by Charmaz in *Constructing Grounded Theory* (2006). She notes, "constructivist grounded theorists assume that both data and analyses are social constructions that reflect what their production entailed" (Charmaz 2006: 131). Analysis of the interviews leads to categorizing segments of data into codes which are refined and analyzed, creating an "analytic handle" to develop abstract ideas for interpreting each code (ibid.: 45). So, during the analysis of the data, the researcher is working in concert with the participants, through their narratives, to construct a view of their reality. Because I am paying attention to the reality of my participant's lives as it is constructed in interviews, I focused on explaining the *hows* and the *whats* (Charmaz 2006; Holstein and Gubrium 1995). I kept these questions in mind: *how* do participants frame their reality? And *what* do participants see as reality?

## Sure There's Racism ... But Homophobia—That's Different

Participants' overwhelmingly reported that race and racism were unremarkable for them on an everyday basis. While they valued the black community for support in a racist society, taught their children about racism and spoke of themselves as distinctly black in relation to their lesbianism, they also explicitly said that managing their racial identity and the associated racism were not part of their daily experience in the same way that sexuality and homophobia were. Moreover, they stressed how they frequently managed their sexual identity. In many of the interviews participants reflected on the ways they self-policed their lesbian identity in order to avoid conflict, to make others feel more comfortable or to make themselves feel more comfortable depending on the situation or the social spaces they found themselves. Many revealed that they regularly do not volunteer information about their sexual identity. They also noted, however, that their sexual identity was sometimes revealed by behaviors such as their gender presentation or that of their partner. All in all, participants told narratives revealing how they regulate their behavior in a social world that marginalizes their lesbian identity through homophobia. Before a discussion of how participants managed the visibility of their sexual identity, I provide an explanation for why they may be emphasizing their sexual identity as the more remarkable identity in their everyday lives.

## Everyday Homophobia as More Salient

The dearth of available research on black lesbians and gay men centers on how they often find themselves in a social world where they have been defined outside the realm of fully human because of their race and sexuality (Bennett and Battle 2001). With this in mind, I asked participants if they had experiences dealing with racism, homophobia or both. When asked explicitly if they had experienced racism all participants remarked that they had not dealt with specific instances in their everyday lives. Eva said, "I have never experienced any racism or anything toward being a lesbian." Sal indicated, "Let's see, not that I know of. I don't really even pay attention to [racism]." Nancy and Denelle also note that the most challenging issues for them center around sexuality. They said:

> Nancy: Yeah, [racism]'s not. It isn't as big an issue.
>
> Denelle: It's really not. I'd have to say more sexuality. I'm thinking.
>
> Nancy: Yeah, because we are faced with not being able to share.
>
> Denelle: Yeah, I think that sexuality is bigger. That's my answer because I don't think race so much.

As illustrated here, participants spoke of never having experienced racism and simply not paying attention to race. When asked, most acknowledged that dealing with issues of homophobia was more of a daily challenge than was dealing with issues of racism. When participants were asked about their experiences dealing with homophobia this is when, overwhelmingly, race *did* enter the discussion. The seeming erasure of race from their social identity does not mean race is not a consideration for them. As Greene (2002: 932–3) acknowledges, "we cannot make arbitrary assumptions about which of those identities is most salient to a given individual. Moreover, we cannot even assume that one identity is ever more important than the others." Participants' sentiments reflect the complexity of navigating the social world at the intersection of race and sexuality. Indeed, it is important to note again that when participants were asked about their experiences in dealing with homophobia, overwhelmingly race *did* enter the discussion.

Importantly, several participants compared their struggles with homophobia to the struggle for race rights during the Civil Rights Movement. Denelle pointed out that she sees overcoming homophobia as a continuation of this earlier civil rights work. She said:

> I think a lot of the issues that the gay community face are the same issues that blacks have faced as far as civil rights for years. And I think that the more people recognize that and come together that is the only way we are going to become the minority, I mean the majority, over being the minority, that we all are [stigmatized] for being the minority.

Here Denelle is articulating a parallel between the challenges of the gay and black communities suggesting that both are civil or human rights struggles. Denelle further asserted, "Once you have that behind your name, or you're labeled as GLBT, whether you're black, you're white, it doesn't matter, you are a minority now, point blank." For her, sexual identity is a marker of being a marginalized identity and one that she stresses as *mattering* beyond race and rendering race irrelevant. Denelle's way of speaking about her marginalized status, in terms of sexuality beyond race, makes sense in a social world that has interlocking racist and homophobic stereotypes of sexuality. These stereotypes make a claim to black lesbian sexuality quite complicated. As leading intersectional scholars argue, the combination of racism and homophobia have socially defined black sexuality in terms of heterosexuality; thus, rendering the idea of a black gay identity an impossibility (Collins 2005; Ferguson 2004).

Like Denelle, Taye and Fola indicate that their everyday experiences with homophobia are different and more remarkable than their experiences dealing with racism. They also compared the struggle for gay-related rights to the struggle for race-related rights. They suggest:

> Taye: *I think homophobia trumps racism on any day.*
>
> Fola: *It's the new racism.*
>
> Interviewer: *Oh yeah?*
>
> Taye: *Yeah, I believe that.*
>
> Fola: *At least that's what I think. It's the new racism [laughter].*
>
> Taye: *It trumps it, I think racism is something. I don't know it's kind of, I don't want to say it's archaic but, it's still very much real. But homophobia, that's something totally different, that's a different animal.*
>
> Fola: *This is just as bad, it's inhumane, to say that we can't have the same rights.*

Taye and Fola contend that a marginalized sexual identity is more salient for them than a marginalized racial identity. Importantly, they do not just say homophobia is more salient and leave it at that. They call it a *new racism*; thus, acknowledging the parallel between racism and homophobia. Taye does not negate racism as she later states that it is "still very much real. But homophobia, that's something totally different." Fola's comment about new racism and Taye's comment about homophobia being different from racism are not assertions that racism is no longer relevant. This point cannot be emphasized enough and their comments should not be read that way. Their comments do, however, underscore the idea of how homophobia currently impacts their everyday lives in different and significant ways than does race. This is a reminder of what Miller (2011: 561) argues. She suggests the challenge of "disentangling race from sexuality was often impossible." Participants' racial identity is so embedded in their sexual identity that in many social situations it is hard to tease them apart. As the participants emphasize the salience of homophobia, for example, they return again and again to reminders of how race is still relevant to their lived experiences.

For Eva, the salience of homophobia came after she began disclosing her sexual identity. Eva transitioned to a lesbian identity after a heterosexual marriage that lasted about 10 years. She notes that she has a different perspective now that she has a gay identity. She reveals: "Well when I was straight I was more committed to being an African American family. Now that I am gay, I am more committed, unfortunately I have to admit it, to being gay. My life and my fight is not for being African American, it is for being gay."

Salience of a marginalized sexual identity may, in fact, not develop because participants feel their racialized identity is unremarkable. Instead, acknowledgement actually highlights the fact they live in a social world at the intersection of race and sexuality. All participants, as black lesbians, experience an "everyday racism," a form of racism that is so recurrent and systemic that is taken for granted (Steinbugler 2012: 28). The everyday racism they experience is unremarkable because of the visibility of their racial identity. However, the invisibility of their lesbian identity gives their experiences with homophobia a more prominent status in their everyday lives. They regulate their behavior to maintain that invisibility. Just as Collins emphasizes, this increased salience of participants' marginalized sexual identity may be explained by the differences between racism and heterosexism. Collins (2005: 114) observes:

> *Blackness is clearly identifiable, and in keeping with assumptions of color blindness of the new racism, many Whites no longer express derogatory racial beliefs in public, especially while in the company of Blacks. In contrast U.S. society's assumption of heterosexuality along with its tolerance of homophobia imposes no such public censure on straight men and women to refrain from homophobic comments in public. As a result, closeted and openly LGBT people may be exposed to a much higher degree of interpersonal insensitivity and overt prejudice than the racial prejudice experienced by Blacks and other racial/ethnic groups.*

Participants are not *erasing* race, they are highlighting the visibility and distinct experiences they have of racism that operates differently than homophobia. This, then, makes it seem less remarkable in their daily lives. In fact, I argue that their statements need to be read as evidence that the institutional and social barriers of racism and homophobia have created a social hierarchy that oppresses them at the intersection of race *and* sexuality.

As explained in this section, it may seem that participants are claiming that the challenges they face dealing with a marginalized sexual identity are more remarkable in their daily lives when compared to the challenges they face when dealing with racism. However, on further examination they reveal that dealing with *both* homophobia *and* racism are important parts of their experience; it is a dynamic of the ways the different oppressions work in their daily lives that creates the difference in importance. Homophobia may be the *new racism*, but the old racism is still just as challenging as the participants in this project negotiate a racist and homophobic social landscape.

### Don't Want to Tense Nobody Up

Several participants note that managing a lesbian identity in the black community has been a particular challenge because sexuality is not a topic of conversation. Eva indicated: "I would say that the African American community outside of gay people are homophobic. It's taboo, we don't talk about it, we can sit down, we are not going to discuss it, it is very taboo."

Like Martinez and Sullivan (1998: 252) suggest, "homophobia in the African American community is a function of how 'out' the individual is; engaging in homosexual activity is not so much rejected as is talking about it." The silencing of any discussion relating to sexual identity in the black community is explored in this section.

As others have explained, because of homophobia in the black community, lesbian and gay sexuality is largely unspoken (Gomez and Smith 1990). Barbara Smith quotes a line from black lesbian writer Ann Allen Shockley (1987: 49), 'Play it, but don't say it,[4] noting "this is a

---

4    From: Shockley, Ann Allen. 1987. *The Black and the White of It*. Tallahassee, FL: Naiad Publishing.

line that capsulizes the general stance of the Black community on sexual identity and sexual orientation." Greene (2002: 938) further explains, "Quiet tolerance is usually contingent upon a lesbian's silence about her sexual orientation; open disclosure, discussion, or self-identification may give rise to serious conflicts." As detailed below, the participants in this study confirmed that the expectation of silence is true in their lives. They also stressed the way that homophobia for black women is different than for black men and they explain how they experience a racism-inflected homophobia.

One aspect of their everyday experiences of homophobia was the expectation that they *remain silent*. Shandee used the expression "don't ask don't tell" to described experiences she has had at church. She acknowledged:

> *Church is a, it's almost like "don't ask, don't tell", they haven't asked, I haven't told. I don't think they would have a problem with it. I mean, some people, you can tell. If you really are ordained by God, you'll be able to pick up on any type of signs of anything, but they're still loving. I'm the youth ministry coordinator over the kids, and I have a group of girls, and they do praise dances or whatever. So, I don't think if they ever to noticeably find out it would be an issue.*

Just as Moore (2011: 187) suggests, "this 'don't ask, don't tell' policy enabled the women to remain on good terms with family and old friends rather than cause a breach for a relationship their families did not want to fully acknowledge." Because Shandee is not openly discussing her sexuality, she is not sanctioned because of her lesbian identity.

Sal explains that she recognizes a potential source of conflict if she talks about her sexuality with her family or members of the black community. Because of this potential, she self-monitors her conversations to avoid talking about sexuality. She said:

> *So many people have their opinion within the black community to where it is like you know what, never mind. They're not that accepting. And when I say they, I mean my own family also. Yeah, you've got some people, well you've got a lot of people that always want to say how they feel and you don't want to really say something back because you know it's going to start a talk war, to a fight. And it's just, how can I describe it. Yeah, it's like a battle sometimes, where you are just like, you know what, and you just have to ignore 'em. And then when you do say something most likely it is not going to be nice at all. Like you can't just be like you know I can live my own life, do what I want to. They're like scht [whistles through teeth].*

She later reported that she has a strained relationship with her mother because of her lesbian status. Sal offers that she does not visit her mother because of the friction she feels when with her. She reveals:

> *My mom is from [the Caribbean]. A lot of people from down there say they have trouble. I guess being that it is so small and everybody's so narrow-minded to bigger things that they are just like, nah, that's it [throws hands up]. So it's hard for her. So I'm like if it's that hard, then I just won't come around. She'll say she's OK with it [sexuality] but not really.*

Sal's strategy is to not only keep silent about her sexuality, but to also avoid her family and her mother in particular. She is *covering*. As Moore (2010: 3) explains, "When in Black social spaces, many gay people do not express a public gay identity. Instead they seek to minimize what they believe is a stigmatized status by practicing 'covering.'" Covering was first described by Goffman (1963) in his discussion regarding stigma. He noted that covering and passing were similar management techniques for a social identity that may be sanctioned. Goffman (1963: 102) advised:

> The individual's object is to reduce tension, that is, to make it easier for himself and the others to withdraw covert attention from the stigma, and to sustain spontaneous involvement in the official content of the interaction. However, the means employed for this task are quite similar to those employed in passing—and in some cases identical, since what will conceal a stigma from unknowing persons may also ease matters for those in the know. This process will be referred to as covering (sic).

Examples of covering as a strategy for managing their sexual identity are described by other participants. Shandee's partner's family has several members who are not accepting of gay family members. She explained:

> [Partner's] family, her mother is one of those funny acting people, men are with women, women are with men she really doesn't say no, don't bring her around me. But, I don't go around, you know because of that. You know, she explained it to me. So if they have some type of family function I really just don't go. Don't care to go around, 'cuz I am who I am.

Here, Shandee describes how she and her partner practice covering by just not being around certain people. Ebony, who struggled to come out to her family, tells a similar story of how she would visit her relatives alone. She would not bring along her partner and the children when she visited her family. The children were from her partner's previous heterosexual relationships. She said:

> But I had never used to do that, 'cuz I knew how they felt. And I don't want to tense nobody up, so I didn't bring [the children, partner] around like that, you know. I didn't try to take them with me when I did go home and visit. I'd go by myself, you know what I'm sayin', and stuff, you know. I wanted to have a good visit. I didn't want nobody to be tensed up, and stuff, and that's how that part goes. And yeah, they've pretty much accept me as bein' gay right now.

Ebony is covering by not bringing her partner to family events and hoping this results in nobody being *tensed up*. She further discussed how she avoided interacting with her grandmother because of her grandmother's negative reaction to her sexual identity. Ebony noted:

> My grandmother, and she just recently stopped sayin' it, ah, a couple of years ago, well she always said God didn't make you like that, I don't like that and stuff. And me and my grandmamma was always real close, and um, I used to call her all the time. But then I stopped callin' her so much 'cuz every time I called her she'd be like, well you need to get your life together, God don't like that, and he didn't make you like that, this that and the other. And I'm like well how you gonna tell me Grandmamma, you know what I'm sayin'. He did make me. He did, what do you mean? He don't make no mistakes, right, yeah but He gave you choices, this that and the other, you know. And I used to get stressed out about it. And now, I'm just not gonna call her, you know what I'm sayin' or whatever, she don't tell me that anymore.

81

Here Ebony describes another strategy: avoidance. The strategies of avoidance that Sal, Shandee and Ebony describe may be part of what Moore has called a "narrative of respect." This narrative of respect is a type of covering strategy used by some black lesbians. Moore (2011: 196) reports her understanding of how black lesbians use a narrative of respect:

> While they act in a limited way around family, they frame this behavior using a narrative of respect rather than a feeling that they do not have the freedom to be gay, and in other ways reveal the importance of significant others in their lives. So while they may choose to downplay their gay identities during social interactions, they nonetheless remain clear in their refusal to give up or deny their gay sexuality. They may not kiss their partners during thanksgiving dinner, but they will have them sitting right with them at the family table.

Participants in this project also engage in a narrative of respect when they keep silent about their sexuality or "just don't go around" to family gatherings. This way of managing sexuality is distinctive for black lesbians.

Participants are also strategically managing the visibility of their lesbian sexual identity when they self-police or regulate their behavior to avoid unwelcome attention (Steinbugler 2005). Managing visibility includes practices where individuals interpret social cues from their social environments and modify their actions in public to avoid possible harassment or confrontation (Steinbugler 2012). Lasser and Tharinger (2003: 233) provide a more detailed definition. They suggest visibility management is the "dynamic and ongoing process of careful, planned decisions about whether they will disclose their sexual orientation, and, if they decide to disclose, to whom and how they disclose, and how they continue to monitor the presentation of their sexual orientation in different environments." As I have discussed in this section, the participants in this project spoke of how they often implement visibility management with their families.

Covering is significant in the lived experience of the participants in this project because it allows them to keep important family ties. For example, although Shandee does not speak of hiding her sexuality, she explains the way it works in a black family:

> They don't have a choice. Yeah, it was never secretive, I mean they are loving in their aspects, but I mean the only person that probably, she doesn't really shy away from it, if I was to say today I'm going to get married, she'd be like no I'm not coming, which is my aunt. But, everybody else would be there, I mean I've had a commitment ceremony and I didn't invite one of my aunts because she's in church, but of course, she showed up anyways, fussing. But, I mean, it is what it is, they don't care, they're pretty cool. They love me as who I am. If me and my partner came around, they wouldn't say oh, no, she couldn't come here. They'd be cool with it.

Shandee's family's reluctant acceptance of her sexuality has been described by other scholars investigating black families with lesbian or gay family members. Like Greene (2002: 938) reports, "because of the importance of family to African Americans, lesbians are not typically 'disowned,' or formally cut off from family members to the extent that their white counterparts may be."

## People Are Able to Pick Up on It

Lesbian identity management involves individual sexual identity self-disclosure (Miller 2011). For black lesbians, the tactics and strategies may be particularly important as they work to manage visibility and cover their sexual identity in order to maintain a connection to their families. Despite attempts to silence and manage their (in)visibility around members of the community concerning their sexual identity, there are sometimes breaches. Participants' narratives about these breaches and reluctant disclosures are revealing and bring attention to strategies undertaken when their sexual identity is made visible. A discussion of these narratives is provided here.

Despite self-policing and covering, some participants describe instances when their sexual identity is exposed. La'Rae describes a scene that took place in her workplace:

> *People assume, that I'm married to a man until they may see a picture. 'Cuz I would just say my kids this, my kids that. I never said my partner's kids or my partner and I kids, 'cuz I just don't talk like that. So I would just be like my kid's bad or my kids did this, my kid did that. Oh, I've got to go to the school to see about my kids. So people assumed, that I was married to a guy unless I showed them a family photo, and then they are like [pause, like thinking], but [laughter]. Then I'd have to explain that they're not really my kids. I didn't birth them. I don't have any, 'cuz I'll say my kids, my kids, my kids. And then, you may have worked with me for about two or three years and I say my kids, my kids, my kids. And then I'll say, and then somebody'll be pregnant, or somebody will say how contractions felt or something like that. And I'll be like sayin', ohh see that's why I could never be pregnant. And they be like, but wait a minute, but you've got three kids. Then I have to say well I didn't birth them. They're my partner's kids. Then I have to clarify what I mean by partner's kids, and then that's how people usually find out, that they are not my kids.*

At work, La'Rae did not voluntarily disclose her sexual identity because she did not want to make people or herself uncomfortable. Her management status in the workplace helped to deflect some harassment. La'Rae's example shows us how sexual identity can be revealed despite the self--policing work that black lesbians may do as they look to *not tense people up*.

Nancy and Denelle similarly tell a story of when covering is breached through their description of a situation that occurred at their child's school. They did not tell anyone at the school they were partners. However, one person did figure it out. They said:

> *Nancy: I mean one teacher knew. So for her it was OK. That teacher, she was fine with it, black lady, but the rest of them. I wouldn't feel comfortable. And we never told her, but she just knew.*

> *Denelle: She knew, the black teacher, yeah, and she was cool about it.*

> *Nancy: She mistakenly said it one day and then it was like, she was trying to blow it up like she never said anything [laughter].*

> *Denelle: Yeah she did, that's how we knew she knew [laughter].*

Nancy and Denelle highlight a scenario where they do not talk about their sexual identity, yet people "know." Even though a teacher figured it out, her sexual identity was still not talked about and the teacher even became an accomplice in the managing of their (in) visibility by keeping silent.

Zoey tells a different story of visibility management. She commented that her masculine gender expression marks her as gay. Furthermore, she recently married her (female) partner and does not want to draw attention to her sexuality by displaying her wedding ring. She explained:

> *I go to the gay events, and try to support the gay events, and stuff. And I feel as I get older I am trying to come out more. Like, I was really in the closet, but now I pretty much, people can look at me and say oh, she's gay. [chuckle] So, and you know I'm still uncomfortable wearing my band. I notice that I'll be like this [covers it up with other hand] or I'll keep my hand in my pocket, 'cuz I don't want people to be oh what's that, are you married, or something. So, I'm just getting used to it.*

When people notice she has a wedding ring and ask about her partner, Zoey is not comfortable revealing to others the fact that her partner is a woman. Zoey acknowledges that her masculine gender presentation makes her sexual identity visible to those around her. She works hard to cover the fact that she is married so that she does not further mark herself as lesbian by acknowledging that her partner is a woman.

Sal and Eva also talk about being more visible and marked with a lesbian sexual identity when the gender of a partner is revealed or is visible. Sal explained:

> *I think when I have a partner it makes it worse. Only as far as like getting to know the people, 'cause then they're sitting there looking at the both of us like what they be doing. Then they see the kids. What I can really go based on my last relationship, because she was the one with the most [five] kids. Everywhere we go we all had to go together and be together. So, when somebody introduce the kids they had to see both of us, teachers both of us. Um, the only thing I think, the only battle would be just somebody trying to understand like how does this family work. With myself and my [child] I don't think it's that hard for people. It's just like, well, that's her [child]. They don't really see, there is nobody else, to either compare or try to adjust, like well who's who and who does what. So I think it's real easy for people to accept me and my [child]. Well OK, that's OK.*

Eva has a feminine gender presentation (long hair, long fingernails and feminine style of clothing) and when she is with her more masculine-presenting partner, she is made visible as gay. She notes:

> *Well the women that I generally get with they look like studs, so there was no need to hide due to the fact that everybody would know, so if you just look at me and my son you would never suspect that I am gay. But if I had gotten with women who look more like me then I don't know if I would have been as open but when you get with someone that looks and dress and carries themselves more masculine than they do femme it just came out that it was just going to be open and I knew even before I decided what type of woman I was going to get with I knew from March 18, 2002, I was never going to be in the closet. That I was going to come out flaming [snaps fingers].*

Sal, Eva and Zoey highlight the importance of gender presentation in covering (or uncovering) their black lesbian identity.

The narratives presented in this section bring attention to how self-policing a lesbian identity is particularly important for black lesbians as they negotiate a social world where they are marginalized both as racial minorities and sexual minorities. Covering for black lesbians becomes not only important for avoiding exposure, it also becomes important in maintaining an invisible sexual identity after that marginalized sexual identity is exposed and breached. Participants explained that they work to cover their sexual identity in order to avoid conflict and discomfort from family members or others in the community (and for the most part they mean the black community). Yet, sometimes their sexual identity is revealed when they are seen with their partner or when the gender identity of their partner is revealed in conversation. Sometimes, despite the exposure of their sexual identity, other members of the community help maintain their invisibility in a silence of acceptance that is unique to the black community.

## Conclusion

Because black lesbians and gay men are members of both a racial minority group and a minority group based on their sexual identity, they face multiple oppressions. The lived experiences of black lesbians and their families provide scholars with an opportunity to explore the subtleties and nuances found at the intersection of sexuality and race. This chapter explores the ways participants explain the difference between homophobia and racism—a difference discussed as being separate from each other, but still intertwined. Participants talk of their marginalized sexual identity as being more salient than their racial identity when it is made visible, especially in the black community. Participants in this project explain that salience of their lesbian identity by talking about how racism is a *different animal*. This discussion of salience reveals that participants are reaffirming the simultaneity of oppressions in their lives but doing so with an assertion that the oppressions manifest differently in their lived experiences. Participants discuss how they managed the distinctive homophobia they find salient in their everyday lives by covering, not hiding, their gay identity. Covering is different from being invisible or closeted. I argue that it is a distinctively black lesbian way of resisting homophobia by negotiating doing so while they are simultaneously managing racism as they work to maintain ties with family. Finally, a discussion is provided where participants share many situations where people "knew" their identity because of a breach in their management of their behavior; specifically, their or their partner's gender presentation. These breaches remind us how gender expression is distinct in black lesbian communities and, as such, breaches that occur via gender presentation are important for understanding visibility management (its successes and its failures) since visibility management was important for helping participants avoid harassment and conflict with family members and other members of the black community.

This research is significant in providing examples of the ways participants explain the different forms of the oppression they experience. Race is not erased from their experiences, but it becomes less remarkable in certain circumstances, especially those in the African American community. "Sexuality was bigger," but race was still present. The interlocking oppressions of racism and homophobia create a system where the participants in this project are challenged as *both* black *and* lesbian. As the discussion in this chapter has suggested, it "really is not just gay, but African American gay" and sometimes "sexuality is bigger," even as racism is still present.

# References

Alderman, Jason, Gitanjali Gurudatt Borkar, Amanda Garrett, Lindsay Hogan, Janet Kim, Winston Le, Veronica Louie, Alissa Marque, Phil Reiff, Colin Christopher Richard, Peter Thai, Tania Wang and Craig Wickersham. 2005. "The Most Conservative and Liberal Cities in the United States." Berkeley, CA: The Bay Area Center for Voting Research.

Associated Press. 2012. "African American, Black American or Just American?" in *BlackNews.com*. Columbus, OH: Dante Lee International.

Battle, Juan and Anthony J. Lemelle Jr. 2002. "Gender Differences in African Attitudes Toward Gay Males." *The Western Journal of Black Studies* 26: 134–9.

Bennett, Michael and Juan Battle. 2001. "'We Can See Them: But We Can't Hear Them': LGBT Members of African American Families." in *Queer Families, Queer Politics: Challenging Culture and the State*, eds. M. Bernstein and R. Reimann. New York: Columbia University Press, pp. 53–67.

Biblarz, Timothy J. and Evren Savci. 2010. "Lesbian, Gay, Bisexual, and Transgender Families." *Journal of Marriage and Family* 72: 480–97.

Bonilla-Silva, Eduardo. 2010. *Racism Without Racists: Color-Blind Racism & Racial Inequality in Contemporary America*. Lanham, MD: Rowman & Littlefield.

Charmaz, Kathy. 2006. *Constructing Grounded Theory: A Practical Guide through Qualitative Analysis*. Thousand Oaks, CA: Sage Publications, Inc.

Chatters, Linda M., Robert Joseph Taylor and Rukmalie Jayakody. 1994. "Fictive Kinship Relations in Black Extended Families." *Journal of Comparative Family Studies* 25: 297–313.

Collins, Patricia Hill. 2000. *Black Feminist Thought: Knowledge, Consciousness, and the Politics of Empowerment*, 2nd edn. New York: Routledge.

———. 2005. *Black Sexual Politics: African Americans, Gender, and the New Racism*. New York: Routledge.

Dang, Alain and Somjen Frazer. 2004. "Black Same-Sex Households in the United States: A Report from the 2000 Census." New York: National Gay and Lesbian Task Force Policy Institute and National Black Justice Coalition.

Dilworth-Anderson, Peggye, Linda M. Burton and Leanor Boulin Johnson. 1993. "Reframing Theories for Understanding Race, Ethnicity, and Families." in *Sourcebook of Family Theories and Methods: A Contextual Approach*, eds. P.G. Boss, W.J. Doherty, R. LaRossa, W.R. Schumm, and S.K. Steinmetz. New York: Plenum Press, pp. 627–46.

Ernst, Frederick A., Rupert A. Francis, Harold Nevels and Carol A. Lemeh. 1991. "Condemnation of Homosexuality in the Black Community: A Gender-Specific Phenomenon?" *Archives of Sexual Behavior* 20: 579–85.

Feagin, J.R. 2000. *Racist America: Roots, Current Realities, and Future Reparations*. New York: Routledge.

Ferguson, Roderick A. 2004. *Aberrations in Black: Toward a Queer of Color Critique*. Minneapolis, MN: University of Minnesota Press.

Goffman, Erving. 1963. *Stigma: Notes on the Management of Spoiled Identity*. New York: Touchstone.

Gomez, Jewelle and Barbara Smith. 1990. "Talking about It: Homophobia in the Black Community." *Feminist Review* 34: 47–55.

Green, Adam I. 2007. "On the Horns of a Dilemma: Institutional Dimensions of the Sexual Career in a Sample of Middle-Class, Urban, Black, Gay Men." *Journal of Black Studies* 37: 753–74.

Greene, Beverly A. 2002. "Heterosexism and Internalized Racism among African Americans: The Connections and Considerations for African American Lesbians and Bisexual Women: a Clinical Psychological Perspective." *Rutgers Law Review* 54: 931–57.

Herek, Gregory M. and John P. Capitanio. 1995. "Black Heterosexuals' Attitudes Toward Lesbians and Gay Men in the United States." *The Journal of Sex Research* 32: 95–105.

Hill, Shirley A. 2005. *Black Intimacies: A Gender Perspective on Families and Relationships*, ed. J.A. Howard. Walnut Creek, CA: AltaMira Press.

Holstein, James A. and Jaber F. Gubrium. 1995. *The Active Interview, Qualitative Research Method Series 37*. Thousand Oaks, CA: Sage Publications.

Jenkins, Morris, Eric G. Lambert and David Baker. 2009. "The Attitudes of Black and White College Students Towards Gays and Lesbians." *Journal of Black Studies* 39: 589–613.

Lasser, Jon and Deborah Tharinger. 2003. "Visibility Management in School and Beyond: A Qualitative Study of Gay, Lesbian, and Bisexual Youth." *Journal of Adolescence* 26: 233–44.

Lemelle, Jr., Anthony J. and Juan Battle. 2004. "Black Masculinity Matters in Attitudes Toward Gay Males." *Journal of Homosexuality* 41: 47–51.

Lewis, Gregory B. 2003. "Black-White Differences in Attitudes toward Homosexuality and Gay Rights." *The Public Opinion Quarterly* 67: 59–78.

Martinez, Dorie Gilbert and Stonie C. Sullivan. 1998. "African American Gay Men and Lesbians: Examining the Complexity of Gay Identity Development." in *Human Behavior in the Social Environment from an African American Perspective*, ed. L.A. Lee. New York: The Haworth Press, pp. 243–64.

Miller, Shannon J. 2011. "African-American Lesbian Identity Management and Identity Development in the Context of Family and Community." *Journal of Homosexuality* 58: 547–63.

Moore, Mignon R. 2010. "Articulating a Politics of (Multiple) Identities: Sexuality and Inclusion in Black Community Life." *Du Bois Review: Social Science Research on Race* 7: 1–20.

———. 2011. *Invisible Families: Gay Identities, Relationships, and Motherhood Among Black Women*. Berkeley, CA: University of California Press.

Moynihan, Daniel Patrick. 1965. "The Negro Family: The Case for National Action." ed. US Department of Labor. Washington, DC: Office of Policy Planning and Research.

Nagel, Joane. 2003. *Race, Ethnicity, and Sexuality: Intimate Intersections, Forbidden Frontiers*. New York: Oxford University Press.

Roberts, Dorothy. 2011. *Fatal Invention: How Science, Politics, and Big Business Re-create Race in the Twenty-first Century*. New York: The New Press.

Schulte, Lisa J. and Juan Battle. 2004. "The Relative Importance of Ethnicity and Religion in Predicting Attitudes Towards Gays and Lesbians." *Journal of Homosexuality* 47: 127–42.

Staples, Robert. 1971. "Towards a Sociology of the Black Family: A Theoretical and Methodological Assessment." *Journal of Marriage and Family* 33: 119–38.

Steinbugler, Amy C. 2005. "Visibility as Privilege and Danger: Heterosexual and Same-Sex Interracial Intimacy in the 21st Century." *Sexualities* 8: 425–43.

———. 2012. *Beyond Loving: Intimate Racework in Lesbian, Gay, and Straight Interracial Relationships*. New York: Oxford University Press.

Taeuber, Karl E. and Alma F. Taeuber. [1965] 2009. *Residential Segregation and Neighborhood Change*. Piscataway, NJ: Transaction Publishers.

Tavernise, Sabrina. 2011. "Parenting by Gays More Common in the South, Census Shows," *New York Times*, January 18.

# PART III
# Education and the Economy

# Parental Expectations, Family Structure and the Black Gender Gap in Educational and Occupational Attainment: An Intersectional Approach to the Social Psychological Model of Status Attainment

Tomeka Davis and Taralyn Keese

For many years, White women trailed White men in educational attainment and college completion (DiPrete and Buchmann 2006; McDaniel et al. 2011). However, recent statistics indicate a reversal of this pattern as White men now trail White women in this regard (Buchmann and DiPrete 2006; McDaniel et al. 2011; U. S. Census Bureau 2012). While White women only began to reach parity with White men in the late 1980s, historically, Black women's educational attainment has always more closely matched that of Black men and Black women have surpassed Black men for longer in this regard (Brunn and Kao 2008; Buchmann and DiPrete 2006; DiPrete and Buchmann 2006; McDaniel et al,. 2011). More recently, structural economic change has made lower-skilled jobs scarce in the communities where Blacks reside (Wilson 1996) and, because Black men are less likely to complete college and therefore are less able to effectively compete in the new economy, many speculate that college-educated, early career women, regardless of race, will surpass young men on a number of labor market indicators (Autor and Wasserman 2013; Cauchon 2010; Luscombe 2010; Morello and Keating 2010; Hill et al. 2009). Yet there is little systematic empirical evidence to date supporting this claim (Autor and Wasserman 2013; Hill et al. 2009). Concern over this Black gender imbalance has led some to label the declining fortunes of Black men as a "crisis" (Boo 2003; Johnson et al. 1998; 2000; Kunjufu 2005; Legette 1999; Noguera 1997).

Despite the rhetoric surrounding this crisis, little empirical research addressing the Black gender gap in education has focused on potential explanations for the gap or how it affects the Black gender gap in early occupational outcomes (Buchmann and DiPrete 2006; DiPrete and Buchmann 2006). Since the late 1960s, status attainment researchers have shown that parental expectations matter for student's educational and occupational attainment (Bozick et al. 2010; Hossler and Stage 1992; Reynolds and Burge 2008; Sewell et al. 1969); yet little if any sociological research has examined the simultaneous influence of race and gender on parental expectations and the structural forces that moderate their influence. Two lines of research are relevant to understanding the importance of the simultaneous influence of race and gender on parental expectations. Existing scholarship highlights patterns of gender-specific childrearing within Black families, whereby girls and boys are socialized to meet divergent challenges shaped by the *intersecting* dynamics of race and gender oppression (Collins 2000; Lopez 2003). In particular, the high probability of entanglement in criminal activity and incarceration for Black male youth in urban communities is a critical concern (Alexander 2012; Ferguson 2002; Pettit and Western 2004; Smith and Fleming 2006). As a result of these gendered threats, the structural and cultural realities young Black men experience are often qualitatively different from those encountered by young Black women (Anderson 2000; Pattillo-McCoy 1999). These starkly different circumstances potentially influence the expectations Black parents have for their children, and to the extent that parental expectations impact children's life-course outcomes, ultimately shape adult gender differences in educational and occupational attainment. Fears of delinquency and hopes for education potentially wind up becoming *trade-offs* for the parents of boys. To better illustrate this scenario, consider the myriad of public figures who stepped forward after the Trayvon Martin/George Zimmerman verdict offering anecdotal evidence concerning the discussions they have with their sons about maintaining their safety in public spaces (Eligon 2013; Holder 2013). However, such public pronouncements about educational aspirations or expectations are not nearly as ubiquitous. Black parents may encourage their daughters, consciously or unconsciously, to do well in school and plan for college while they may be more concerned about behavioral outcomes for boys and consequently stress the importance of avoiding the dangers of the street and the criminal justice system (Anderson 2000; Smith and Fleming 2006).

In addition, one characteristic common among Black families that potentially moderates the effect of gender on parental expectations for Blacks is single-parent households. The prevalence of single-mother households among Blacks has commonly been used to explain poorer outcomes of African American men, especially compared to other groups (Moynihan 1965). These arguments assert that children living in single-mother households are exposed to poverty at a higher rate and experience negative outcomes as a result of economic hardship (Downey 1994; McLanahan 1985). These models also assert that mothers are not able to serve as suitable role models for sons (Autor and Wasserman 2013; Kunjufu 2007). Other scholars claim that the socioeconomic position of unmarried, low-income mothers compel them to view education as a means by which their daughters may escape a similar fate (Lopez 2003; Sharp and Ispa 2009), leading them to have higher educational expectations for daughters compared to sons. In the context of educational and occupational attainment, this would potentially propel Black women over their male counterparts.

The existing literature on how parental expectations influence the Black gender gap in educational outcomes is limited in quantity as well as in theoretical and methodological scope. Few studies directly examine the topic and only one uses a sociological frame (Lopez 2003); but it does not focus on African Americans. The list of shortcomings are more varied with regard to methodological scope: 1) only three studies have directly investigated the topic; two are qualitative and use extremely small samples sizes that focus disproportionately on single-mother families, thus, making it difficult to draw conclusions about the specific impact of family structure (Sharp and Ispa 2009; Smith and Fleming 2006); 2) none of the existing studies establish an empirical link between parental expectations and actual educational attainment and 3) none examine whether gendered parental expectations and the educational advantage they may confer Black women are converted into occupational advantage.

This chapter addresses the Black gender gap in educational and occupational attainment by assessing the impact of parental expectations on the schooling and labor-market outcomes of Black men and women from adolescence through early adulthood and the moderating influence of family structure on these outcomes. We use data from the 1997–2010 waves of the National Longitudinal Survey of Youth (NLSY) to address these questions. We test predictions regarding gendered expectations and family structure made by small-scale qualitative research using quantitative techniques and a nationally representative sample. Though we do not directly test the impact structural race and gender inequality have on parental expectations, we use these theories to frame our arguments and contextualize our findings.

## Race, Gender and Parental Expectations: Assessing Obstacles, Avoiding Fears

Since the late 1960s, status attainment researchers have shown that parental expectations matter for student's educational and occupational attainment (Bozick et al. 2010; Hossler and Stage 1992; Reynolds and Burge 2008; Sewell et al. 1969). Yet, despite the contributions of early status attainment research to the field of inequality, recent work highlights the shortcomings evident in earlier models (Bozick et al. 2010). At the time of its inception, status attainment research focused mainly on inequality among White men while the experiences of women and minorities were left unexamined. More recently, research investigating the experiences of minorities within the framework of the Wisconsin model supports the basic findings of the model among Blacks—the notion that parental expectations matter for future educational and occupational attainment (Cheng and Starks 2002; Hossler and Stage 1992; Kim et al. 2012; Portes and Wilson 1976)—but none of this work addresses how structural conditions specific to Blacks potentially moderate the impact of gender on attainment.

In addition, although there is a large body of literature on gender role socialization among Blacks (Blee and Tickmayer 1995; Burgess 1994; Hill 2001; Lewis 1975), the existing literature on gender differences in Black parental educational and occupational expectations is limited; both in terms of quantity and generalizabilty. The larger literature on gender role socialization among Black families argues that Blacks tend to reject traditional gender roles and favor more flexible gender role behavior. This tendency grew out of slavery and subsequent conditions that made adhering to rigid gender roles difficult for both Black women and men (Dill 1988; Hill 2001; Jones 1010). Yet, the neutral attitudes Black parents possess about gender roles do not extend to parental expectations regarding education as Black parents, Black mothers especially, tend to have higher educational expectations for daughters than sons (Jones and Shorter-Gooden 2003; Smith and Fleming 2006; Wood et al. 2007). This divergence may reflect the distinction between parental expectations and gender role socialization. Whereas gender role socialization is a 'gendering' process (i.e., a process whereby children are taught gender-specific behaviors which they are expected to enact as adults) (Messner 1990), the gender-specific expectations Black parents have for children are a product of the "race-gender experiences" (Lopez 2003) they anticipate their children will encounter and live through. Race-gender experiences refer to the specific kinds of inequality, discrimination, stereotypes or privilege individuals are confronted with based on their race and gender status. Within this framework the intent among Black parents is not to inculcate a set of gender-appropriate behaviors, but rather to ensure survival for their children by preparing them for specific challenges that confront Black female adults in society versus a divergent set of challenges that Black male adults face. For Black girls, these race-gender experiences reflect the necessity of economic independence for Black women that is produced by the poor economic position of Black men and the lower likelihood of marriage over the life course for Black women compared to White women (Barr and Simons 2012; Gibson-Davis et al. 2005; Hill 2006; Jones 2010; Wilson 1987). For Black boys, parental concerns for sons' well-being center on steering them clear of illegal activity, police, prison or worse: death as a result of community violence (Smith and Fleming 2006).

This idea that Black parenting is influenced by recognition of the dual impact that race *and* gender exert on well-being is rooted in intersectionality theory (Collins 2000; King 1988). First conceptualized by social theorists and activists in the Black womanist and feminist traditions (Beale 1979; Terrell 1904), intersectionality theory asserts that individuals may be subject to "several, simultaneous oppressions" and "to the multiplicative relationships among them" (King 1988: 47) which impact their material, psychological and physical circumstances. In other words, in understanding social outcomes, race and gender, as well as other dimensions of inequality including class, sexual orientation, etc., interact to produce unique consequences for individuals at any specific position within the "matrix" of inequality (Collins 2000).

The two existing studies which investigate the impact of race and gender of the child on the expectations of Black parents suggest that the higher educational expectations Black mothers potentially have for daughters are conditioned by these anticipated race-gender constraints (Sharp and Ispa 2009; Smith and Fleming 2006). Sharp and Ispa (2009) studied 15 low-income mothers and found they were more likely to talk about schooling as a way of protecting their daughters from following in their footsteps (i.e., being poor and having children at an early age). Mothers of daughters also expressed the expectation that daughters would be independent and self-reliant. Mothers of sons expressed more concern about protecting them from illegal activities and delinquent peer groups. Moreover, the mothers of sons expressed decidedly more fatalism with regard to the outcomes for their child, taking a "boys will be boys" attitude while the mothers of daughters were far more optimistic about their daughters' outcomes.

Smith and Fleming (2006) draw similar conclusions. They note that mothers' higher college aspirations for girls were driven by a fear that their daughters would be dependent (e.g., on men or public aid). For boys, parents were more concerned about the entanglements of criminal activity. The authors note, "In short, parents send their sons on trajectories that help them survive the streets and avoid confrontations with law enforcement and criminal elements" (ibid.: 85). Elsewhere they state:

> It seemed that they [parents] believed the best way to counter the temptation of inner-city criminal activity was to set up reasonable and flexible post-high school goals for their sons. These goals were ostensibly low-stress, low-pressure goals compared to the high-stress peer pressure to become involved in criminal activity. (Ibid.: 86).

Therefore, Smith and Fleming conclude that parents set lower educational expectations for boys as a way of countering and relieving some of the stress created by the higher expectations they established for avoiding delinquency.

## Family Structure as a Moderator of Parental Expectations

One characteristic common among African American families that potentially moderates the effect of gender on parental expectations for Blacks is single-parent households. In 1991, approximately 46.7 percent of Black children under the age of 18 lived in single-parent households compared to 16.4 percent of Whites (U.S. Census Bureau 2011). These estimates have remained relatively stable over time, rising to 50.4 percent and 18.5 percent respectively in 2009. In general, the sociological literature indicates that children raised in single-parent households, particularly single-mother households, have poorer outcomes on a number of social, educational and economic dimensions compared to children raised in two-parent families (Demuth and Brown 2004; McLanahan 1988; McLanahan and Booth 1989; McLanahan and Sandefur 1994; Thomson and McLanahan 2012). One reason for the increased risk of disadvantage among children raised by single mothers is the increased likelihood of poverty and economic hardship among female-headed households (McLanahan 1985; McLanahan and Percheski 2008; McLanahan and Sandefur 1994; Thomson and McLanahan 2012). Consequently, the prevalence of this family structure among Black households is often cited as a cause for the reproduction of poverty and economic disadvantage among African Americans across generations (McLanahan 2009; Moynihan 1965).

McLanahan and Booth (1989) note that parental expectations for children in single-mother households may differ from expectations for children in two-parent families in two contradictory ways. First, because of limited economic resources, greater time demands and more daily hassles and difficulties, single mothers may hold lower expectations for their children than two-parent families. However, while a lack of resources among single-parent households compared to two-parent families might explain the college completion gap between Blacks and Whites. This aspect of McLanahan and Booth's (1989) argument does not adequately explain the gender gap among Blacks.

A second way McLanahan and Booth contend expectations of children reared by single mothers differ from children in two-parent families is, as the authors note, "because of their own experience as breadwinners," single-mothers "may place a greater emphasis on children's attainment or a higher value on independence and nontraditional gender roles" (ibid.: 562). The latter explanation falls in line with Sharp and Ispa's (2009) and Smith and Fleming's (2006) findings, for daughters at least. Yet, would these experiences influence boys raised in single-mother households similarly? There is little rigorous scholarly research on the matter (Bush 2004), though many have been critical of the efforts of single Black mothers and contend they are unable to impart boys with (stereotypical) masculine attitudes and behaviors deemed necessary for success (Kunjufu 2005, 2007; Moynihan 1965). However, scholarly literature which examines parents raising children of the opposite sex finds little evidence to support the notion that these children are less successful than children raised by same-sex parents (Biblarz and Stacey 2010; Downey et al. 1998; Downey and Powell 1993; Powell and Downey 1997), though none of this research has focused on Blacks specifically.

Recent quantitative research is mixed with regard to how the educational attainment of young Black males is affected by family structure. Autor and Wasserman (2013: 27) argue that growing up in a single-parent household hampers the educational attainment of men compared to women and ultimately lowers their labor-market prospects, in part because boys growing up in economically poor and female-headed households do not have "positive or stable same sex role-models present." Hill and colleagues (2009) find that Black males raised in single-mother homes fare worse on a host of social outcomes (employment, educational attainment, incarceration and out-of-marriage parenthood) than Black females raised in mother-only homes. Buchmann and DiPrete (2006) found that growing up in father-absent homes had the strongest negative effect on the college completion of Black men compared to any other race-gender group, though they contend that this finding does not support the same-sex hypothesis; presumably because the finding did not apply to girls or to both Whites and Blacks. Powell and Parcel (1997) found the opposite effect: that women's educational attainment suffered as a result of growing up in a non–two–parent family, but not men's. Other research indicates that the educational expectations of Black fathers has less influence on the educational aspirations of their children than the expectations of Black mothers, presumably (the authors claim) because Black students are less likely to reside with their fathers (Cheng and Starks 2002). On the other hand, using 1992 data from the National

Educational Longitudinal Study (NELS), Reynolds and Burge (2008) found that Black girls reported getting significantly more educational encouragement from mothers *and* fathers compared to Black boys. Biblarz and Raftery (1999) find no evidence of significant gender differences regarding the effects of alternative family forms (including single-mother, single-father and step-parent households) on educational and occupational attainment—alternative families had the same effect on men and women. Similarly, Amato and Keith (1991) also fail to find evidence for the idea that family disruption affects the educational attainment of minority men. Thus, it is unclear whether the effects of family structure on parental expectations or adult educational and economic outcomes are gendered.

## Occupational Attainment and the Black Gender Gap

One interesting irony regarding the Black gender gap is that despite the long-term educational attainment advantage Black women have had over Black men, to date, most research indicates Black men retain a wage advantage over Black women (Browne 2000; Browne and Misra 2003; Conrad 2001, 2008; Danzinger and Ratner 2010; Padavic and Reskin 2002). However, some emerging research indicates that many labor-market outcomes are trending toward gender convergence and that Black women are beginning to surpass Black men on some labor-market outcomes like employment rates (Danzinger and Ratner 2010). Others forecast the educational advantage women are gaining over men will lead women of all races to surpass men on wages, especially men from lower SES backgrounds (Autor and Wasserman 2013; Hill et al. 2009). Among Blacks, this emerging trend makes sense in light of the decline of the American manufacturing sector where relatively unskilled and less-educated Black men were able to find work for many years (Wilson 1987, 1996). Others contend a primary reason for the decline in employment outcomes among Black men are attributable to increasingly high rates of incarceration (Holzer 2009; Western et al. 2001; Western and Wildeman 2009). Yet, to date, little if any existing research has examined whether Black women convert the educational advantage they maintain over Black men into any occupational advantage.

Intersectionality theory is also useful in helping derive predictions regarding the various ways labor-market outcomes differ for Black men and women (see Browne and Misra 2003 for a more detailed review). Intersectionality might predict that there is a hierarchical gender gap between Black men and women such that Black women face a disadvantage compared to Black men of the same educational and class background (i.e., for Black women, race and class represent a "double jeopardy") (Beale 1979; King 1988). Other intersectionality theorists posit that Black men and women's experiences are qualitatively different due to the combination of race and gender, rather than additive or hierarchically stratified (Collins 2000). A third group sees race and gender intersecting to create a hierarchical stratification among Blacks that is the opposite of patterns among Whites: Black women are advantaged, or have access to more resources, in comparison to Black men because they are perceived as less visible (Purdie-Vaughns and Eibach 2008) or less threatening to White men (Sidanius and Pratto 2001). The gender differences in educational attainment among Blacks potentially support this third position, but in this case because Black women possess higher levels of human capital in the form of education. Given the existing lack of attention devoted to this issue in the literature, we address the differences between Black men and women in this regard.

# Hypotheses

Based on the literature we have outlined, we generate the following hypotheses:

- *Hypothesis 1—Gender Influences*: Black parents are more likely to have greater concerns regarding delinquency for males and these heightened concerns for delinquency will lead to lower high school achievement and lower educational attainment compared to females. This lower educational attainment will result in lower occupational status for males.
- *Hypothesis 2—Mother-only Households as a Moderator of Gender Influences*: Black parents are likely to have higher educational expectations for females than males and this effect is potentially moderated by family structure. Single mothers may have heightened educational expectations for daughters and these higher expectations will result in higher achievement and higher educational attainment. This higher educational attainment will result in higher occupational status for female respondents compared to male respondents.

# Data and Measures

We use data from the National Longitudinal Survey of Youth 1997 (NLSY) and its successive waves to examine the impact of gender and family structure on the expectations Black parents have for their children. The NLSY is a nationally representative, longitudinal study conducted by the U.S. Department of Labor (through the Bureau of Labor Statistics) that follows approximately 8,984 respondents who were age 12 to 16 at the start of the survey (in 1997) through adulthood. The NLSY contains information gained from thousands of respondent and parental queries covering the years between 1997 and 2010. Our primary samples consist of the full subsample of Blacks in the NLSY (N=2,335) and limited subset of Black male and female respondents (N=527). Table 7.1 below displays the means and descriptions of variables in our analysis for the limited subsample.

Parents of youth over the age of 15 (born in 1980 or 1981) were asked to rate the percent chance their child would: 1) have a high school diploma by age 20; 2) serve time in jail or prison by age 20; 3) be a parent by age 20; 4) have a four--year college degree by age 30 and 5) work more than 20 hours per week by age 30. We use two of these measures, "expect child to be in jail by age 20" and "expect child to have a college degree by age 30," since they reflect the core concepts of our research question. We acknowledge that our parental expectation measures do not directly test parental perceptions of children's future race-gender experiences, yet, to the extent that we find any evidence of racial and gender differences in parental expectations and particularly parental expectations for incarceration for young Black males, our approach embodies a new and important contribution to prior research and invites future research to address the issue as previous research (Sharp and Ipsa 2009; Smith and Fleming 2006) encouraged our query.

Our family structure indicator is a dichotomous measure distinguishing biological mother-only households from all other family forms assessed in the first wave of data collection (1997).[1] We use transcript-reported grade-point average (GPA) in Wave 3 of the

---

1    Biblarz and Raftery (1999) note the inclusion of specific controls matter because some controls, like family SES, reduce the impact of family structure, largely because SES mediates the impact of family structure on adult outcomes. However, in our case, excluding it leads to considerably

**Table 7.1 Descriptive Statistics for Limited Black Subsample (Unweighted)**

| Variable | Variable Coding and Description | Mean (SD) | NLSY Wave/Year | N (% missing) |
|---|---|---|---|---|
| Gender | Female = 1 | .537 (.499) | Wave 1/1997 | 527 (0%) |
| Family Structure | Biological mother only family = 1 | .505 (.500) | Wave 1/1997 | 527 (0%) |
| Parental Expectations for Jail by Age 20 | Parents of youth over the age of 15 were asked to rate the percent chance their child would be in jail by age 20. | 3.996 (12.566) | Wave 1/1997 | 526 (.190%) |
| Parental Expectations for College Degree by Age 30 | Parents of youth over the age of 15 were asked to rate the percent chance their child would have a college degree by age 30 | 71.695 (31.487) | Wave 1/1997 | 527 (0%) |
| Adolescent Academic Outcomes | Transcript-reported high school grade point average | 267.826 (56.107) | Wave 3/1999 | 386 (26.755%) |
| Educational Attainment | Highest year of schooling completed by respondent | 13.242 (2.556) | Wave 14/2010 | 521 (1.139%) |
| Occupational Status | Hauser and Warren Total SEI scores based using updated coding scheme developed by Frederick (2010). NLSY respondents list occupation and industry worked in; answers coded according to 2002 Census 4-digit codes | 33.381 (12.977) | Wave 14/2010 | 527 (0%) |
| Mother's Education | Highest year of schooling completed by mother | 12.431 (2.121) | Wave 1/1997 | 492 (6.641%) |
| Negative Peer Influence Index | Composite of percentage of peers who: 1) smoke regularly, 2) get drunk more than once a month, 3) belong to a gang, 4) use illegal drugs, 5) cut class or school, 6) have had sex | .236 (.691) | Wave 1/1997 | 527 (0%) |

NLSY97 to measure adolescent academic outcomes. In the NLSY this variable is measured on a scale ranging from 0–500 where 100 is equivalent to a GPA of 1.00, 200 is equivalent to a GPA of 2.00, and so forth. For example, a GPA of 296 on the 0–500 scale is equivalent to 2.96 on a 5-point scale.[2] We use the highest year of schooling completed to measure adult educational attainment. This variable is measured at each round of data collection and we use the indicator collected in the most recent round (2010). The variable ranges from having completed 1st grade to having completed 8 years of post-secondary schooling (phrased in the data set as "8th year of college").[3]

We measure early occupational status with socioeconomic index (SEI) scores for occupation detailing the NLSY respondent's occupation and industry of employment. Of the many available SEI scores, we use the Hauser and Warren 1997 Total SEI, which is based on a formula that builds on critiques of and updates earlier occupational status scales (Duncan 1961; Nakao and Treas 1994). Hauser and Warren use prestige scores (the general level of social standing enjoyed by the incumbents of an occupation) as part of the criterion for the SEI score (based on ratings of occupations by respondents in the General Social Survey), but also base it on characteristics of the work force from the 1990 Census; including the percentage of people in an occupation who had completed one or more years of college and the percentage of workers in an occupation who earned more than $14.30 per hour. We use Hauser and Warren SEI scores that have been updated by Frederick (2010) using 2002 Census codes. The existing research on male-female labor-market outcomes tends to emphasize earnings differentials and focuses less on other indicators of position in the labor-market hierarchy, like occupational status (see Browne and Misra 2003 for a review). For our purposes, occupational status may be a more suitable measure of occupational stratification since, as some argue, some of its components, like occupational prestige, may be less

---

poorer model fit. The inclusion of mother's education did not appear to reduce the impact of family structure, at least in terms of significance. In fact, family structure is a significant predictor of all of our endogenous variables except parental expectations. We might find more cause for concern if the inclusion of mother's education led to fewer significant relationships.

2   We do not control for prior academic achievement which might presumably have some effect on parental expectations, especially for college, because we lack an indicator of prior academic achievement that occurs before our parental expectations measure, which is measured at Wave 1.

3   One problem that arose in preparing the data for analysis were missing values resulting from item non-response—legitimate skips or eligibility requirements for particular questions in the survey. Although the Black subsample in NLSY was composed of 2,335 respondents, only 800 Black respondents were 15 years old at the first wave of data collection and thereby eligible for the parental expectations questions. In addition, of these remaining Blacks, there were 264 who were valid skips (i.e., persons who were not employed) and non-interviews on questions relating to current occupation in 2010. The first concern that arises with missing data is the nature of the missingness—whether the data is missing at random or completely at random (MAR or MCAR), or is dependent on some specific factor (non-ignorable missing or missing not at random, MNAR). Many researchers contend that it is valid to treat item non-response cases as MCAR and therefore suitable to use statistical methods like multiple imputation or full information maximum likelihood to account for missing values because missingness is not a function of the dependent variable (Allison 2001; Schafer and Graham 2002). On the other hand, these researchers also note that listwise deletion produces unbiased regression estimates when data is MCAR.

We experimented with a number of different methods to account for missingness, including listwise deletion with the exclusion of item nonresponse cases and maximum likelihood estimation with the full Black subsample. Our multivariate results, in terms of the size and significance of our coefficients, were largely similar across these different methods (with the exception of the gender coefficient for expectations for jail by 20). However, model-fit indices were superior for the full Black subsample, so we present them here. We used the software program MPlus (version 5.1) to generate our path coefficients; the default estimator in the program is maximum likelihood, which managed the remaining missing values. We also refrain from using the sampling weights, since it led to the loss of an additional 165 cases.

influenced by gender discrimination or some of the other forces that impact the gender gap in wage differentials alone (e.g., sex segregation, part-time work, etc.) (England 1979; Fox and Suschnigg 1989; Magnusson 2009).[4] SEI scores are scaled from 0 to 100 so that higher scores indicate an occupation has higher prestige, income and educational requirements than occupations with lower scores.

We include two controls at various points in the model to capture theoretically relevant characteristics that potentially affect parental expectations and schooling outcomes. An abundance of research indicates that higher SES parents have higher expectations for children and that children from higher SES homes have higher grades and educational attainment (Jencks 1972; Sewell et al. 1969). We use mother's years of completed education as a proxy for parental SES.[5] In addition, peer groups also impact adolescent academic outcomes and the existing literature on peer influence suggests that peers play a role in shaping student academic outcomes (Bowen and Bowen 1999; Greenman 2013). We create an index for negative peer influences using six items from NLSY that measure negative peer behavior. These items include: percent of peers who smoke regularly, percent of peers who get drunk more than once a month, percent of peers who belong to a gang, percent of peers who use illegal drugs, percent of peers who cut class or school and percent of peers who have had sex. The Cronbach's alpha for the scale is .84.[6]

## Analytic Strategy

Figure 7.1 displays our final model specification which we derived after analyzing all possible theoretically relevant paths, including covariances between observed variables as well as covariances between error terms. We trimmed these models iteratively; the final model we specify proved to be the best-fitting one. We control for mother's education and negative peer influence at various points along the gender-attainment path. We include the interaction between family structure and respondent gender in the analysis of expectations only since it had little impact and added no benefit to model fit at later points in the path

---

4    Others, including Hauser and Warren (1997), argue that occupational status for women is affected by the same structural forces that reduce wages for women. To account for this, they calculate separate occupational status scores for male workers and female workers, as well as a combined score for all workers (the total SEI score). We use the total SEI score as our measure of occupational status in order to compare men and women on a similar scale, as recommended by Hauser and Warren (1997). Though some argue that the total SEI scale disadvantages women (Boyd 1986), Hauser and Warren contend that one way to account for some of the structural forces that disadvantage women in the labor market in the SEI scale, like the overwhelming supply of part-time work for women, is to include all workers in the scale but to adjust the earnings portion of the scale for part-time/full-time status and weeks worked, which they did in the creation of the total SEI scale. Despite this concern, women in our sample still manage to surpass men in occupational standing. For this reason, our estimate of the impact of education on the Black gender gap in occupational status may be a conservative indicator of the extent to which Black women outpace Black men.
5    Biblarz and Raftery (1999) note the inclusion of specific controls matter because some controls, like family SES, reduce the impact of family structure, largely because SES mediates the impact of family structure on adult outcomes. However, in our case, excluding it leads to considerably poorer model fit. The inclusion of mother's education did not appear to reduce the impact of family structure, at least in terms of significance. In fact, family structure is a significant predictor of all of our endogenous variables except parental expectations. We might find more cause for concern if the inclusion of mother's education led to fewer significant relationships.
6    We do not control for prior academic achievement which might presumably have some effect on parental expectations, especially for college, because we lack an indicator of prior academic achievement that occurs before our parental expectations measure, which is measured at Wave 1.

between gender and educational/occupational attainment in supplemental analyses. We use a limited subsample of Black respondents in our descriptive results, but, given the utilities of SEM programs, we use the full subsample of Blacks in our final regression models.

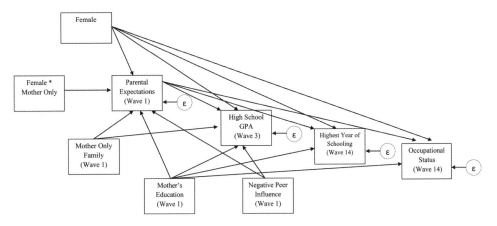

**Figure 7.1    Final Model Specification**

# Results

## Descriptive Results

Tables 7.1 and 7.2 display the unweighted means and standard deviations for the variables in our analysis. Table 7.1 shows that the sample is evenly split between males and females and that about half of the sample lived in a single-mother household at Wave 1. This figure is consistent with national statistics regarding the percentage of Black children living in single-mother households (US Census Bureau 2011). On average, parents estimated that their children had a 4 percent chance of going to jail by age 20 and a 72 percent change of getting a four-year college degree by 30, but these figures differed by gender. Table 7.2 shows that Black parents estimated sons had a 5 percent chance of going to jail by age 20, while this figure was only 2 percent for daughters. Similarly, parental expectations for college for daughters were significantly higher than parental college expectations for college for sons (75.5 percent versus 67 percent respectively). Female respondents also had significantly higher high school GPA, significantly more years of schooling and significantly higher occupational status scores than males. Differences between respondents from mother-only families compared to other family types, as well as between males and females from mother-only families largely reflect these same patterns. Table 7.3 shows the pairwise correlations between the variables in the analyses. Consistent with qualitative research (Smith and Fleming 2006), parental expectations for jail are inversely related to parental expectations for college (r = -.30). As parental expectations for jail increase, expectations for education decrease. From this, we would expect that the higher expectations Black parents have for incarceration for sons will have a detrimental impact on their educational and subsequent occupational outcomes compared to daughters.

**Table 7.2    Descriptive Statistics by Gender and Family Type for Limited Black Subsample (Unweighted)**

| Variable | Males | Females | Mother Only | Other Family | Males—Mother Only | Females—Mother Only |
|---|---|---|---|---|---|---|
| Parental Expectations for Jail by Age 20 | 5.354* (14.213) | 2.830 (10.848) | 5.596** (15.436) | 2.372 (8.465) | 7.565* (17.235) | 3.865 (13.488) |
| Parental Expectations for College Degree by Age 30 | 67.172 (33.059) | 75.594** (29.573) | 67.711 (32.403) | 75.755** (30.047) | 63.872 (34.187) | 71.113+ (30.454) |
| High School Grade Point Average | 257.077 (52.202) | 276.198*** (57.712) | 257.134 (57.842) | 277.874*** (52.619) | 249.000 (49.174) | 263.486+ (63.305) |
| Highest Year of Schooling | 12.717 (2.487) | 13.690*** (2.533) | 12.660 (2.417) | 13.830*** (2.563) | 12.398 (2.455) | 12.892+ (2.367) |
| Occupational Status | 31.173 (12.419) | 35.285*** (13.168) | 31.364 (11.877) | 35.437*** (13.732) | 29.709 (11.864) | 32.832* (11.735) |
| N | 244 | 283 | 266 | 261 | 124 | 141 |

*Note:* Mean difference significant at + p < .10, * p < .05, ** p < .01, *** p < .001 (two-tailed tests); higher mean in bold. Standard deviations in parentheses.

**Table 7.3    Pairwise Correlations**

| | Parental Expectations for Jail by 20 | Parental Expectations for College by 30 | High School GPA | Highest Year of Schooling | Occupational Status | Mother's Education | Negative Peer Index |
|---|---|---|---|---|---|---|---|
| Parental Expectations for Jail by 20 | | | | | | | |
| Parental Expectations for College by 30 | -.302*** | | | | | | |
| High School GPA | -.130*** | .307*** | | | | | |
| Highest Year of Schooling | -.249*** | .485*** | .525*** | | | | |
| Occupational Status | -.147*** | .366*** | .332*** | .572*** | | | |
| Mother's Education | -.112** | .300*** | .192*** | .411*** | .339*** | | |
| Negative Peer Index | .150*** | -.161*** | -.185*** | -.130** | -.132** | -.054 | |

*Note:* + p < .10; * p < .05; ** p < .01; *** p < .001 (two-tailed tests).

## Multivariate Results

Table 7.4 displays the results of the structural equation models for parental expectations for incarceration and education respectively. We use separate models for each set of parental expectations to simplify interpretation. As with our descriptive results, gender has a significant direct effect on highest year of schooling completed and occupational status in Tables 7.4 and 7.5 though the effect of gender on status is only marginally higher (primarily because education is also included in the model, which has a much stronger effect). Across all of our models, the maximum likelihood estimates indicate that, after controlling for other relevant influences, Black female respondents complete about one-tenth of a standard deviation more schooling than Black male respondents. Meanwhile, even after controlling for education, the occupational status for Black women is about 4 percent of a standard deviation greater than Black men. Moreover, for every additional one standard deviation increase in completed schooling, occupational status increases by one-half standard deviation.

Table 7.4 shows that Black parents estimate sons have a significantly higher chance of going to jail by the time they are 20 years of age compared to daughters. However, this effect does not vary depending on family structure since the interaction between gender and mother-only families is not significant. In other words, parents of children in other family structures, including married parents, have the same expectations for sons' delinquency as single mothers. These expectations for incarceration carry over to educational attainment. When parents have higher expectations for incarceration respondents have significantly lower educational attainment ($\beta$ = .187). On the other hand, higher parental expectations for delinquency do not directly impact occupational status.

Table 7.4 also shows significant gender differences in parental expectations for a college degree in both Black subsamples. Black parents expect daughters to have a significantly higher chance than sons of getting a college degree by the age of 30 ($\beta$ =.164). As was the case with expectations for jail, this effect is also not moderated by family structure. Married parents as well as single mothers have higher educational expectations for Black daughters compared to Black sons. Moreover, parental expectations for a college degree impact all later educational and occupational outcomes. Parental expectations for college have a significant positive impact on high school GPA, highest year of schooling and occupational status. For example, a one standard deviation increase in parental expectations for college leads to a one-third standard deviation increase in grade point average and completed schooling. In turn, a one standard deviation increase in completed schooling leads to a one-half standard deviation increase in occupational status.

Model fit is considerably better for the parental expectations for college measure in Table 7.4. Though $\chi^2$ statistics are significant in both the model for expectations for jail as well as expectations for college, other model fit indicators, including the RMSEA (which reflects the difference between the population covariance matrix and the model-implied covariance matrix estimated with the sample data (Kline 2005) and CFI (which compares the specified model to a worst-case model where all of the variables are unrelated) indicate reasonably good model fit for parental expectations for college model (Hooper et al. 2008). The general rule for CFI is that values greater than .90 indicate good fit. A RMSEA below .05 indicates close approximate fit while values between .05 and .08 suggest reasonable fit (Kline 2005). Values of .10 or below for the SRMR (which reflects overall differences between observed and predicted correlations) are considered favorable (ibid.).

**Table 7.4** Standardized Maximum Likelihood Estimates for Impact of Gender and Family Structure on Parental Expectations and Educational and Occupational Attainment among Blacks (Full Black Subsample)

| | Jail by 20 | | | | College Degree by 30 | | | |
|---|---|---|---|---|---|---|---|---|
| | Parental Expectations for Jail by Age 20 | High School Grade Point Average | Highest Year of Schooling | Occupational Status | Parental Expectations for College Degree by 30 | High School Grade Point Average | Highest Year of Schooling | Occupational Status |
| Parental Expectations | | -.010 (.060) | -.187*** (.033) | .032 (.042) | | .189*** (.043) | .297*** (.029) | .104* (.043) |
| High School Grade Point Average | | | .359*** (.024) | | | | .307*** (.025) | |
| Highest Year of Schooling | | | | .519*** (.023) | | | | .469*** (.028) |
| Female | -.116* (.047) | .228*** (.025) | .119*** (.020) | .042* (.022) | .164*** (.043) | .206*** (.024) | .118*** (.019) | .036+ (.022) |
| Mother Only | .028 (.047) | -.061** (.024) | -.046** (.019) | | -.075+ (.044) | -.055* (.024) | -.048** (.019) | |
| Gender* Mother Only | .057 (.056) | | | | .055 (.051) | | | |
| Mother's Education | -.101** (.036) | .197*** (.025) | .274 (.020) | .095*** (.023) | .271*** (.032) | .147*** (.028) | .222*** (.021) | .082*** (.024) |
| Negative Peer Index | .157*** (.034) | -.103*** (.025) | | | -.111*** (.032) | -.087*** (.025) | | |
| R2 | .062 | .109 | .352 | .318 | .111 | .142 | .396 | .326 |
| χ2(df) | 1845.543 (26) | | | | | 192.753(26) | | |
| CFI / TLI | .832 / .709 | | | | .907 / .840 | | | |
| RMSEA | .071 | | | | .052 | | | |
| SRMR | .093 | | | | .065 | | | |
| N | 2,335 | | | | 2,335 | | | |

*Note*: Standard errors in parentheses. + p < .10; * p < .05; ** p < .01; *** p < .001 (two-tailed tests).

Table 7.5 shows the decomposition of these effects. The direct effect of gender on highest year of completed schooling and occupational status is significant, as Tables 7.4 and 7.5 show. However, we also expect that gender exerts indirect effects on educational and occupational attainment through parental expectations for incarceration and educational attainment. Hypotheses 1 predicts that parents are likely to have concerns about delinquency for male children and this should result in lower educational and subsequent occupational outcomes. Both aspects of this hypothesis are supported. Gender has a significant indirect effect on completed schooling via expectations for jail (p = .022) and on occupational status through the gender → expectations for jail → highest year of schooling path (p = .011). Similarly,

**Table 7.5    Decomposition of Gender Effect on Educational and Occupational Attainment among Blacks (Full Black Subsample)**

| Panel A: Decomposition of Female Through Jail by 20 | Highest Year of Schooling Completed | Occupational Status |
|---|---|---|
| Direct Effects: Female | -.187*** | .032 |
| | (.033) | (.042) |
| Sum of Indirect Effect: Female | .022* | .008 |
| | (.010) | (.006) |
| Specific Indirect Effects | | |
| Female → Parental Expectations for Jail by 20 | .022* | .004 |
| | (.010) | (.005) |
| Female → Parental Expectations for Jail by 20 → Grade Point Average | .000 (.002) | |
| Female → Parental Expectations for Jail by 20 → Highest Year of Schooling | | .011* (.005) |
| Female → Parental Expectations for Jail by 20 → Grade Point Average → Highest Year of Schooling | | .000 (.001) |
| N | 2,335 | |

| Panel B: Decomposition of Female Through College by 30 | Highest Year of Schooling Completed | Occupational Status |
|---|---|---|
| Direct Effect: Female | .118*** | .036+ |
| | (.019) | (.022) |
| Sum of Indirect Effect College by 30: Female | .058*** | .044*** |
| | (.016) | (.013) |
| Specific Indirect Effects | | |
| Female à Parental Expectations for College Degree by 30 | .049* | .017* |
| | (.014) | (.009) |
| Female à Parental Expectations for College Degree by 30 à Grade Point Average | .009* (.003) | |
| Female à Parental Expectations for College Degree by 30 à Highest Year of Schooling | | .023*** (.007) |
| Female à Parental Expectations for College Degree by 30 à Grade Point Average à Highest Year of Schooling | | .005** (.002) |

*Note:* + p < .10; * p < .05; ** p < .01; *** p < .001 (two-tailed tests).

the indirect effect of gender on highest year of schooling is significant through parental expectations for college (p = .049) and the parental expectations for college → GPA path (p = .017). Thus, Black female respondents in the NLSY have more education because their parents have higher educational expectations, which lead to higher academic achievement in high school. The indirect effect of gender on occupational status through the same paths (gender → expectations for college degree by 30 → highest year of schooling) equals .023 and .005 (gender → expectations for college degree by 30 → GPA → highest year of schooling) and is statistically significant. This means that Black females have higher occupational status as a result of parental expectations for college and the effects expectations have on high school academic achievement and completed education.

## Making a Case for Racialized Expectations

One question that potentially arises here is whether gendered expectations are specific to Blacks or if the same pattern exists among Whites. This seems crucial to making the case that parental expectations, and ultimately outcomes shaped by those expectations, are rooted in the race-gender experiences Black parents anticipate for their children. We compared the means on the parental expectations items for our limited subsample of Blacks and a similar limited subsample of Whites in the NLSY (again those respondents who were eligible for the parent expectation questions and who had complete data on the employment question in Wave 14) and on the larger sample of *all* Blacks and Whites who responded to the parental expectations question.[7]

These results are shown in Table 7.6. The results reveal significant variation by race and gender. Consistent with our hypothesis, the parents of Black males are more likely than the parents of White males to have higher expectations that their sons will be incarcerated by the age of 20. On the other hand, parental expectations for college do not differ by race within gender group. Parental expectations for college are lower for males than females regardless of race—parents have higher college expectations for White girls than White boys and for Black girls than Black boys. Thus, parents expect that girls will go farther in school than boys, regardless of race, while they expect Black males have a higher probability of incarceration. The lack of racial differences between Blacks and Whites on parental expectations for college do not challenge our hypotheses regarding the dual nature of race and gender constraints. Rather, our findings underscore the main tenets of intersectionality theory by highlighting the complexities that arise in its study. As McCall (2005) notes, different contexts reveal different configurations of inequality. In this context, inequality in parental expectations are configured differently depending on the type of expectation—some expectations are both raced and gendered (incarceration), while others are only gendered (college).

---

7    Using different samples for the mean comparison tests could be avoided with multiple imputation, but few if any SEM programs are compatible with multiply imputed data, so we are unable to use it to replace missing values. Consequently, we attempt to demonstrate the strength of the differences between race/gender groups using all of the data available in NLSY, though we show these results for our limited subsample to maintain consistency with other portions of the paper.

**Table 7.6    Mean Comparisons of Parental Expectations by Race for Subsample of Blacks and Whites (Unweighted)**

| | Limited Subsample (Listwise Deletion) | | All Nonmissing Respondents (Pairwise Deletion) | |
|---|---|---|---|---|
| **Panel A: Means** | **Parental Expectations for Jail by Age 20** | **Parental Expectations for College Degree by Age 30** | **Parental Expectations for Jail by Age 20** | **Parental Expectations for College Degree by Age 30** |
| Black Males | 5.354 (14.213) N = 44 | 67.172 (33.059) N = 244 | 6.862 (17.251) N = 390 | 64.016 (34.429) N = 387 |
| White Males | 3.890 (11.705) N = 810 | 68.044 (32.687) N = 810 | 3.481 (10.913) N = 813 | 66.697 (33.753) N = 811 |
| Black Females | 2.830 (10.848) N = 283 | 75.594 (29.573) N = 283 | 2.773 (10.539) N = 410 | 72.379 (31.974) N = 404 |
| White Females | 1.687 (7.705) N = 748 | 74.047 (29.528) N = 748 | 1.672 (7.175) N = 809 | 74.226 (29.945) N = 806 |

*Note:* Standard deviations in parentheses.

| | Limited Subsample (Listwise Deletion) | | All Nonmissing Respondents (Pairwise Deletion) | |
|---|---|---|---|---|
| **Panel B: Mean Comparisons** | **Different from White Males? (Significance Level)** | **Different from White Females? (Significance Level)** | **Different from White Males? (Significance Level)** | **Different from White Females? (Significance Level)** |
| **Parental Expectations for Jail by 20** | | | | |
| Black Males | Yes (.10) | | Yes (.001) | |
| White Females | Yes (.001) | | Yes (.001) | |
| Black Females | | Yes (.10) | | Yes (.05) |
| **Parental Expectations for College by 30** | | | | |
| Black Males | No | | No | |
| White Females | Yes (.001) | | Yes (.001) | |
| Black Females | | No | | No |

*Note:* Mean difference significance calculated using t-tests (two-tailed).

# Discussion

This chapter offers an examination of the relationship between parental expectations and the Black gender gap in educational and occupational attainment. Previous research suggests that the intersecting dynamics of race and gender oppression and the divergent life experiences parents anticipate boys and girls will encounter based on these oppressions lead parents to emphasize and reward different types of behavior among boys and girls (Lopez 2003; Sharp and Ipsa 2009; Smith and Fleming 2006). Our results largely support this literature. Parents had significantly higher expectations for incarceration for male respondents than female respondents and these expectations for incarceration were inversely related to expectations for college. Conversely, parents had significantly higher expectations that daughters would obtain a four-year college degree by age 30 than would sons. These gender differences in parental expectations mediated significant gender differences in high school grades and in the end, educational attainment and occupational status.

On the other hand, we also hypothesized that gender differences in parental expectations would be even larger among single-mother families; however, this hypothesis was not supported in our multivariate analyses. In fact, the latter revealed that the gendered pattern of expectations occur among all family types and are not limited to single-mother households. With regard to the "crisis" among Black men, this suggests that the macro-structural dynamics (i.e., intersecting dynamics of race and gender oppression in American society) dictating gendered concerns and expectations for children among Black parents may overshadow meso-level family characteristics that have often been cited as risk factors for poor adult outcomes among Black men especially (Autor and Wasserman 2013; Moynihan 1965; Sampson 1987). Thus, regardless of family type, structural and environmental factors that shape serious threats in the lives of young Black men and women may be at the forefront of parental agendas. The ubiquity of these expectations across family type signals the persistent influence of structural race and gender inequality in the lives of Black youth and Black families.

Our findings should not be interpreted as an indictment of poor parenting among Black parents. The common adage that Black mothers "raise their daughters and love their sons" (Hill 2002; Kunjufu 2007) is a quintessential example of how deficit models are often used to explain racial inequality by attributing the unfortunate circumstances of, in this case, Black men, to the shortcomings of Black culture. On the contrary, we argue that parents identify the principal threat endangering their children and govern them accordingly. Since parents perceive that those threats vary by gender, parental fears and the expectations that accompany them dictate different strategies to address these divergent concerns, as previous research contends (Smith and Fleming 2006).

In terms of methodological limitations, we surmise the expectation for jail measure is limited in that it asks parents to rate the probability of their child being incarcerated before age 20. This is certainly a young age and we would expect that parental expectations for the probability of incarceration might be higher if the age ceiling were increased to 30 or if the question asked about the probability of incarceration over the life course. Moreover, few parents may want to face the possibility of such a negative turn of events for their children. We believe the limitations of this measure yield smaller racial differences in parental expectations for incarceration than would be seen if the question were broader.

With regard to our statistical models, the models we present here are simple yet robust. Our model-fit indices suggest that our models fit the data reasonably well, though there is room for improvement. Of course, sample size drives power and our results, in terms of statistical significance, are even more favorable when we are able to use all available data instead of having to limit our sample based on missingness. Nevertheless, given the paucity of research in the area, our work can be viewed as an exploratory analysis for future researchers to build on. Methodologically, this might include variations in model specifications, but also adding more theoretically relevant factors that make our account even more complex. For example, future research should consider addressing how specific neighborhood influences impact parental expectations. Urban sociologists studying the impact of neighborhood conditions on parenting strategies have long noted the difficulties of raising children in high-poverty, high-crime neighborhoods (Anderson 2000; Furstenberg et al. 1999; Jarrett 1997). Negative neighborhood conditions might exacerbate gendered expectations among parents, especially given the concerns these neighborhoods raise for delinquency among male youth. In addition, scholars argue that young men and women of color have specific race-gender experiences in school (Ferguson 2002; Lopez 2003) and in the labor market (Browne and Kennelly 1999; Kennelly 1999; Lopez 2003; Pager 2003). Consequently, future research might consider how these distinctive early experiences also contribute to the occupational gap between Black men and women.

While we find significant gender differences in high school academic achievement, educational attainment and occupational status, critics might concede that the magnitude of these differences, despite their statistical significance, is substantively small, leaving Black female youth/adults, arguably, in no better position than Black male youth/ adults. In other words, Black men *and* Black women are still relatively low in the educational and occupational hierarchy. For example, before controlling for other factors, the average high school GPA for males is 2.6, while the average GPA for females is 2.8. Similarly, the difference between men and women in educational attainment is around 1 year, while the difference in occupational status is about 4 points. For some, these findings potentially provoke a broader question: if both Black men and Black women are doing poorly, to whom should policymakers direct their attention and resources? Given our results, and the rhetoric surrounding the "crisis" among Black men, can or should policymakers comfortably say that one group should be prioritized over the other? This is a difficult question, yet our results point to one potential policy solution that would shrink the differences between them: eliminating the structural circumstances that lead to shamelessly high incarceration rates among Black men that contribute to reduced parental expectations. For example, if policymakers reshape the structures that create the 3–4 point difference in parental expectations for jail between male and female respondents, it is likely that the differences in educational expectations would be reduced in a corresponding manner. However, it would not completely close the parental expectations gap between males and females. Thus, while our results have specific implications for the Black gender gap, we urge policymakers to remain vigilant about reducing Black-White inequality that reduce opportunities for Blacks regardless of gender.

# References

Alexander, Michelle. 2012. *The New Jim Crow: Mass Incarceration in the Age of Colorblindness.* New York: New Press.

Allison, Paul. 2001. *Missing Data.* Thousand Oaks, CA: Sage.

Amato, Paul and Bruce Keith. 1991. "Separation from a Parent during Childhood and Adult Socioeconomic Attainment." *Social Forces* 70(1): 187–206.

Anderson, Elijah. 2000. *Code of the Street: Decency, Violence, and the Moral Life of the Inner City.* New York: W.W. Norton.

Autor, David and Melanie Wasserman. 2013. "Wayward Sons: The Emerging Gender Gap in Labor Markets and Education." Retrieved on March 20, 2013: http://content.thirdway.

org/publications/662/Third_Way_Report_NEXT_Wayward_Sons-The_Emerging_Gender_Gap_in_Labor_Markets_and_Education.pdf.

Barr, Ashley and Ronald Simons. 2012. "Marriage Expectations among African American Couples in Early Adulthood: A Dyadic Analysis." *Journal of Marriage and Family* 74(4): 726–42.

Beale, Francis. 1979. "Double Jeopardy: To be Black and Female." in *The Black Woman: An Anthology*, ed. T. Cade. New American Library: New York, pp. 90–100.

Biblarz, Timothy and Adrian Raftery. 1999. "Family Structure, Educational Attainment, and Socioeconomic Success: Rethinking the 'Pathology of Matriarchy.'" *American Journal of Sociology* 105(2): 321–65.

——— and Judith Stacey. 2010. "How Does the Gender of Parents Matter?" *Journal of Marriage and Family* 72(1): 3–22.

Blee, Kathleen and Ann Tickamyer. 1995. "Racial Differences in Men's Attitudes about Women's Gender Roles." *Journal of Marriage and Family* 57(1): 21–30.

Boo, Katherine. 2003. "The Black Gender Gap." *Atlantic Monthly* 291(1): 107–9.

Bowen, Natasha and Gary Bowen. 1999. "Effects of Crime and Violence in Neighborhoods and Schools on the School Behavior and Performance of Adolescents." *Journal of Adolescent Research* 14(3): 319–42.

Boyd, Monica. 1986. "Socioeconomic Indices and Sexual Inequality: A Tale of Scales." *Canadian Review of Sociology and Anthropology* 23: 457–80.

Bozick, Robert, Karl Alexander, Doris Entwisle, Susan Dauber and Kerri Kerr. 2010. "Framing the Future: Revisiting the Place of Educational Expectations in Status Attainment." *Social Forces* 88(5): 2027–52.

Browne, Irene. 2000. "Opportunities Lost? Race, Industrial Restructuring, and Employment among Young Women Heading Households." *Social Forces* 78(3): 907–29.

——— and Ivy Kennelly. 1999. "Stereotypes and Realities: Images of African American Women in the Labor Market." in *Latinas and African American Women at Work*, ed. I. Browne. New York: Russell Sage Foundation, pp. 302–26.

——— and Joya Misra. 2003. "The Intersection of Gender and Race and the Labor Market." *Annual Review of Sociology* 29: 487–513.

Brunn, Rachel and Grace Kao. 2008. "Where Are All The Boys? Examining the Black Gender Gap in Post-Secondary Attainment." *Du Bois Review* 5(1): 137–60.

Buchmann, Claudia and Thomas DiPrete. 2006. "The Growing Female Advantage in College Completion: The Role of Family Background and Academic Achievement." *American Sociological Review* 71(4): 515–41.

Burgess, Norma. 1994. "Gender Roles Revisited: The Development of the 'Woman's Place' Among African American Women in the United States." *Journal of Black Studies* 24(4): 319–401.

Bush, Lawson. 2004. "How Black Mothers Participate in the Development of Manhood and Masculinity: What Do We Know About Black Mothers and Their Sons?" *The Journal of Negro Education* 73(4): 381–91.

Cauchon, Dennis. 2010. "Gender Pay Gap Is Smallest On Record." *USA Today*, September 14.

Cheng, Simon and Brian Starks. 2002. "Racial Differences in the Effects of Significant Others On Students' Educational Expectations." *Sociology of Education* 75(4): 306–27.

Collins, Patricia Hill. 2000. *Black Feminist Thought: Knowledge, Consciousness, and the Politics of Empowerment*. New York: Routledge.

Conrad, Cecilia. 2001. "Racial Trends in Labor Market Access and Wages: Women." in *America Becoming: Racial Trends and their Consequences*, eds. N. Smelser, W.J. Wilson and F. Mitchell. Washington, DC: National Academy Press, pp. 124–50.

———. 2008. "Black Women: The Unfinished Agenda." *The American Prospect* 19(10): A12–A15.

Danzinger, Sheldon and David Ratner. 2010. "Labor Market Outcomes and the Transition to Adulthood." *The Future of Children* 20(1): 133–58.

Demuth, Stephen and Susan Brown. 2004. "Family Structure, Family Processes, and Adolescent Delinquency: The Significance of Parental Absence versus Parental Gender." *Journal of Research in Crime and Delinquency* 41(1): 58–81.

Dill, Bonnie Thorton. 1988. "Our Mother's Grief: Racial and Ethnic Women and the Maintenance of Families." *Journal of Family History* 13(1): 415–31.

DiPrete, Thomas and Claudia Buchman. 2006. "Gender-Specific Trends in the Value of Education and the Emerging Gender Gap in College Completion." *Demography* 43(1): 1–24.

Downey, Douglas. 1994. "The School Performance of Children from Single-Mother and Single-Father Families: Economic or Interpersonal Deprivation?" *Journal of Family Issues* 15 (1): 129–47.

————— and Brian Powell. 1993. "Do Children in Single-Parent Households Fare Better Living with Same-Sex Parents?" *Journal of Marriage and Family* 55(1): 55–71.

—————, James Ainsworth-Darnell and Mikaela Dufur. 1998. "Sex of Parent and Children's Well-Being in Single-Parent Households." *Journal of Marriage and Family* 60(4): 878–93.

Duncan, Otis. 1961. "A Socioeconomic Index for All Occupations." in *Occupations and Social Status*, ed. A. Reiss. New York: Free Press, pp. 109–38.

Eligon, John. 2013. "Florida Case Spurs Painful Talks Between Black Parents and Their Children." *New York Times*. July 18, 2013, Page A11.

England, Paula. 1979. "Women and Occupational Prestige: A Case of Vacuous Sex Equality." *Signs* 5(2): 252–65.

Ferguson, Ann Arnett. 2002. *Bad Boys: Public Schools in the Making of Black Masculinity*. Ann Arbor: University of Michigan Press.

Frederick, Carl. 2010. "A Crosswalk for Using Pre-2000 Occupational Status and Status Codes with Post-2000 Occupation Codes." Retrieved on January 8 2013: http://www.ssc.wisc.edu/cde/ cdewp/2010-03.pdf.

Fox, John and Carole Suschnigg. 1989. "A Note on Gender and the Status of Occupations." *The Canadian Journal of Sociology* 14: 353–60.

Furstenberg, Frank, Thomas Cook, Jacquelynne Eccles, Glen Elder and Arnold Sameroff. 1999. *Managing to Make It: Urban Families and Adolescent Success*. Chicago, IL: University of Chicago Press.

Greenman, Emily. 2013. "Educational Attitudes, School Peer Context, and the 'Immigrant Paradox' in Education." *Social Science Research* 42(3): 698–714.

Gibson-Davis, Christina, Kathryn Edin and Sara McLanahan. 2005. "High Hopes but Even Higher Expectations: The Retreat from Marriage among Low-Income Couples." *Journal of Marriage and Family* 67(5): 1301–12.

Hauser, Robert and John Robert Warren. 1997. "Socioeconomic Index of Occupational Status: A Review, Update, and Critique." in *Sociological Methodology* (volume 27), ed. A. Raftery. Cambridge: Blackwell, pp. 177–298.

Hill, Carolyn, Harry Holzer and Henry Chen. 2009. *Against the Tide: Household Structure, Opportunities, and Outcomes among White and Minority Youth*. Kalamazoo, MI: W.E. Upjohn Institute for Employment Research.

Hill, Shirley. 2001. "Class, Race, and Gender Dimensions of Child Rearing in African American Families." *Journal of Black Studies* 31(4): 494–508.

—————. 2002. "Teaching and Doing Gender in African American Families." *Sex Roles* 47(11/12): 493–506.

—————. 2006. "Marriage among African American Women: A Gender Perspective." *Journal of Comparative Family Studies* 37(3): 421–40.

Holder, Eric. 2013. Attorney General Eric Holder Addresses the NAACP Annual Convention. July 16, 2013. Retrieved September 6, 2013: http://www.justice.gov/iso/opa/ag/speeches/2013/ag-speech-130716.html.

Holzer, Harry. 2009. "The Labor Market and Young Black Men: Updating Moynihan's Perspective." *The Annals of the American Academy of Political and Social Science* 621(1): 47–69.

Hooper, Daire, Joseph Coughlan and Michael Mullen. 2008. "Structural Equation Modeling: Guidelines for Determining Model Fit." *Electronic Journal of Business Research Methods* 6: 53–60.

Hossler, Don and Frances Stage. 1992. "Family and High School Experience Influences on the Postsecondary Educational Plans of Ninth-Grade Students." *American Educational Research Journal* 29(2): 425–51.

Jarrett, Robin. 1997. "African American Family and Parenting Strategies in Impoverished Neighborhoods." *Qualitative Sociology* 20(2): 275–88.

Jencks, Christopher. 1972. *Who Gets Ahead? The Determinants of Economic Success in America.* New York: Basic Books.

Johnson, James, Walter Farrell and Jennifer Stoloff. 1998. "The Declining Social and Economic Fortunes of African American Males: A Critical Assessment of Four Perspectives." *The Review of Black Political Economy* 25(4): 17–40.

———, Walter Farrell, and Jennifer Stoloff. 2000. "An Empirical Assessment of Four Perspectives on the Declining Fortunes of the African-American Male." *Urban Affairs Review* 35(5): 695–716.

Jones, Charisse and Kumea Shorter-Goodwin. 2003. *Shifting: The Double Lives of Black Women in America.* New York: Harper Collins.

Jones, Jacqueline. 2010. *Labor of Love, Labor of Sorrow: Black Women, Work, and the Family from Slavery to the Present.* New York: Basic Books.

Legette, William. 1999. "The Crisis of the Black Male: A New Ideology on Black Politics." in *Without Justice for All: The New Liberalism and Our Retreat from Racial Equality,* ed. A. Reed. Boulder, CO: Westview Press, pp. 291–326.

Kennelly, Ivy. 1999. "'That Single-Mother Element': How White Employers Typify Black Women." *Gender and Society* 13(2): 168–92.

Kim, Youngmi, Michael Sherraden and Margaret Clancy. 2012. "Do Mothers' Educational Expectations Differ by Race, Ethnicity, or Socioeconomic Status?" *Economics of Education Review* 33: 82–94.

King, Deborah. 1988. "Multiple Jeopardy, Multiple Consciousness: The Context of a Black Feminist Ideology." *Signs* 14(1): 42–72.

Kline, Rex. 2005. *Principles and Practice of Structural Equation Modeling.* New York: Guilford Press.

Kunjufu, Jawanza. 2005. *Countering the Conspiracy to Destroy Black Boys.* Chicago, IL: African American Images.

———. 2007. *Raising Black Boys.* Chicago, IL: African American Images.

Lewis, Diane. 1975. "The Black Family: Socialization and Sex Roles." *Phylon* 36(3): 221–37.

Lopez, Nancy. 2003. *Hopeful Girls, Troubled Boys: Race and Gender Disparity in Urban Education.* New York: Routledge.

Luscombe, Belinda. 2010. "Workplace Salaries: At Last, Women on Top." *Time,* September 1.

Magnusson, Charlotta. 2009. "Gender, Occupational Status, and Wages: A Test of Devaluation Theory." *European Sociological Review* 25(1): 87–101.

McCall, Leslie. 2005. "The Complexity of Intersectionality." *Signs* 30(3): 1771–800.

McDaniel, Anne, Thomas DiPrete, Claudia Buchmann and Uri Shwed. 2011. "The Black Gender Gap In Educational Attainment: Historical Trends and Racial Comparisons." *Demography* 48(3): 889–914.

McLanahan, Sara. 1985. "Family Structure and the Reproduction of Poverty." *American Journal of Sociology* 90(4): 873–901.

———. 1988. "Family Structure and Dependency: Early Transitions to Female Household Headship." *Demography* 25(1): 1–16.

———. 2009. "Fragile Families and the Reproduction of Poverty." *The Annals of the American Academy of Political and Social Science* 621(1): 111–31.

——— and Karen Booth. 1989. "Mother-Only Families: Problems, Prospects, and Politics." *Journal of Marriage and Family* 51(3): 557–80.

——— and Christine Percheski. 2008. "Family Structure and the Reproduction of Inequalities." Annual *Review of Sociology* 34: 257–76.

——— and Gary Sandefur. 1994. *Growing Up With a Single Parent: What Helps, What Hurts.* Cambridge, MA: Harvard University Press.

Messner, Michael. 1990. "Boyhood, Organized Sports, and the Construction of Masculinities." *Journal of Contemporary Ethnography* 18(4): 416–44.

Morello, Carol and Dan Keating. 2010. "More U.S. Women Pull Down Big Bucks." *Washington Post*, October 7.

Moynihan, Daniel. 1965. *The Negro Family: The Case for National Action.* Washington, DC: US Department of Labor.

Nakao, Keiko, and Judith Treas. 1994. "Updating Occupational Prestige and Socioeconomic Scores: How the New Measures Measure Up." in *Sociological Methodology* (volume 24), ed. P. Marsden. Cambridge: Blackwell, pp. 1–72.

Noguera, Pedro. 1997. "Reconsidering the 'Crisis' of the Black Male in America false." *Social Justice* 24(2): 147–64.

Padavic, Irene and Barbara Reskin. 2002. *Women and Men at Work.* Thousand Oaks, CA: Sage.

Pager, Devah. 2003. "The Mark of a Criminal Record." *American Journal of Sociology* 108(5): 937–75.

Pattillo-McCoy, Mary. 1999. *Black Picket Fences: Privilege And Peril Among The Black Middle Class.* Chicago, IL: University of Chicago Press.

Pettit, Becky and Bruce Western. 2004. "Mass Imprisonment and the Life Course: Race and Class Inequality in U.S. Incarceration." *American Sociological Review* 69(2): 151–69.

Portes, Alejandro and Kenneth Wilson. 1976. "Black-White Differences in Educational Attainment." *American Sociological Review* 41(3): 414–31.

Powell, Brian and Douglas Downey. 1997. "Living In Single-Parent Households: An Investigation of the Same-Sex Hypothesis." *American Sociological Review* 62(4): 521–39.

Powell, Mary Ann and Toby Parcel. 1997. "Effects of Family Structure on the Earnings Attainment Process: Differences by Gender." *Journal of Marriage and Family* 59(2): 419–33.

Purdie-Vaughns, Valerie and Richard Eibach. 2008. "Intersectional Invisibility: The Distinctive Advantages and Disadvantages of Multiple Subordinate-Group Identities." *Sex Roles* 59(5/6): 377–91.

Reynolds, John and Stephanie Burge. 2008. "Educational Expectations and the Rise in Women's Post-Secondary Attainments." *Social Science Research* 37(2): 485–99.

Sampson, Robert. 1987. "Urban Black Violence: The Effect of Male Joblessness and Family Disruption." *American Journal of Sociology* 93(2): 348–82.

Schafer, Joseph and John Graham. 2002. "Missing Data: Our View of the State of the Art." *Psychological Methods* 7(2): 147–77.

Sewell, William, Archibald Haller and Alejandro Portes. 1969. "The Educational and Early Occupational Attainment Process." *American Sociological Review* 34(1): 82–92.

Sharp, Elizabeth and Jean Ispa. 2009. "Inner-City Single Black Mothers' Gender-Related Childrearing Expectations and Goals." *Sex Roles* 60(9/10): 656–68.

Sidanius, Jim and Felicia Pratto. 2001. *Social Dominance: An Intergroup Theory of Social Hierarchy And Oppression*. Cambridge: Cambridge University Press.

Smith, Michael and Michael Fleming. 2006. "African American Parents in the Search Stage of College Choice: Unintentional Contributions to the Female to Male College Enrollment Gap." *Urban Education* 41(1): 71–100.

Terrell, Mary Church. 1904. "The Progress of Colored Women." *Voice of the Negro* 1: 292.

Thomson, Elizabeth and Sara McLanahan. 2012. "Reflections on Family Structure and Child Well-Being: Economic Resources Vs. Parental Socialization." *Social Forces* 91(1): 45–53.

US Census Bureau. 2011. "Living Arrangements of Children 2009." Washington, DC: US Census Bureau. Retrieved March 11, 2013: http://www.census.gov/prod/2011pubs/p70-126.pdf.

———. 2012. "Educational Attainment in the United States: 2009." Washington, DC: US Census Bureau. Retrieved on October 9, 2012: www.census.gov/prod/2012pubs/p20-566.pdf.

Western, Bruce and Christopher Wildeman. 2009. "The Black Family and Mass Incarceration." *The Annals of the American Academy of Political and Social Science* 621(1): 221–42.

———, Jeffrey Kling and David Weiman. 2001. "The Labor Market Consequences of Incarceration." *Crime and Delinquency* 47(3): 410–27.

Wilson, William Julius. 1987. *The Truly Disadvantaged: The Inner City, the Underclass, and Public Policy*. Chicago, IL: University of Chicago Press.

———. 1996. *When Work Disappears: The World of the New Urban Poor*. New York: Vintage.

Wood, Dana, Rachel Kaplan and Vonnie McLoyd. 2007. "Gender Differences in the Educational Expectations of Urban, Low-Income African American Youth: The Role of Parents and the School." *Journal of Youth and Adolescence* 36(4): 417–27.

# Real Effects of Attitudes about the Value of Education and Social Structure on the Black/White Academic Achievement Gap

Ervin (Maliq) Matthew and Littisha Bates

## Introduction

Contemporary education research accepts as a given there is a direct and measurable effect of students' attitudes on academic performance. For this reason, attitudinal factors are cited as a partial explanation for known racial and social class gaps (Pino and Smith 2004). Particularly, the effects of student attitudes on white-black disparities in grades and test scores has been discussed for several decades (including Ogbu 1978; Fordham and Ogbu 1986; Mickelson 1990; Ainsworth-Darnell and Downey 1998; Tyson et al. 2005; Harris and Robinson 2007; Harris 2011).

Some scholars argue that the influence of attitudes on academic achievement pales in comparison to structural factors that debilitate the academic achievements of black students, such as family background, socioeconomic status and family size (Ainsworth-Darnell and Downey 1998, Tyson 2002). Questions abound about whether students consciously consider the pay-offs of academic performance during the majority of their school years (Tyson 2002). Nevertheless, it is generally assumed there is some relationship, conscious or otherwise, between attitudes toward school and students' perceptions of prospects for future success in the adult world (Mickelson 1990).

In this chapter, we establish that both attitudes about education and those about effects of social structure have meaningful impacts on academic achievement. We demonstrate that positive attitudes about education help decrease the performance gap between black and white students, whereas these effects are countered by disparities in attitudes about social structure since blacks perceive more structural barriers to success than do whites. Our overall models show that the black/white academic performance gap exists clear of known control variables and that only the positive attitudes that black and white students share about school prevent the gap from being overwhelmingly wider.

## Attitudes about Education and Social Structure

Individual perception of the correlation between academic effort and life outcomes is known as "effort optimism" (Ogbu 1983). As the basis for their assertion that black students underperform relative to whites in school partly because they exert less effort in the classroom, Fordham and Ogbu (1986) posit that black and white students differ in optimism about the relationship of academic success to future life opportunities. The authors claim that blacks hold pessimistic views on the value of schooling while whites do not. However, counter to Fordham and Ogbu's claim, several researchers (Coleman et al. 1966; Ainsworth-Darnell and Downey 1998; Akom 2003; Tyson et al. 2005; Harris 2008) empirically demonstrate that black students actually have positive attitudes about education. Matthew (2011) reconciles these two positions by arguing that positive attitudes about education—which he finds are shared by both black and white students—do not preclude racial disparities in pessimism about the effects of social structure, but rather work as an offsetting force to diminish its effects. Resultantly, black students simultaneously accept individual agency through education as a route to future prosperity while acknowledging social structure as an impediment to commensurate rewards for their efforts. This latter finding supports a hypothesis by Mickelson (1990) that students hold multidimensional and complex views about the importance of education to their futures. However, the two papers differ in their findings about the influences of these beliefs on relevant outcomes. This discrepancy invites investigation into whether these divergent attitudes are useful for explaining a portion of the black/white academic achievement gap and whether the same interplay that informs optimism about future life opportunities also significantly affects school performance.

Although consensus has, ostensibly, been reached on the matter of whether blacks report similar attitudes toward school as those of white students, the question of how to reconcile these attitudes with the enduring black/white academic achievement gap remains unresolved. One of the most influential explanations for this presumed attitude-achievement paradox is forwarded by Mickelson (1990). She claims that expressed positive attitudes about education are the result of the adoption of a societal meritocratic ideology of upward mobility and that both black and white students are quick to espouse the tenets of this ideology without regard to the likelihood that they will benefit from their efforts. Simultaneously, knowledge of the ways in which education pays off, or fails to do so, for members of different groups in society leads students to form more rational predictions about how their education will translate into life opportunities for them. At its heart this perspective posits that belief in individual agency fails to impact student performance. Conversely, contemplation of likely payoffs to effort produce concrete beliefs which manifest themselves in ways that are measurable by student performance. The author finds support for her hypothesis that concrete social structural considerations (but not abstract, meritocratic ones) vary by race and concludes that her primary premise is sound.

Recent research justifies skepticism of Mickelson's conclusion. In their review of this debate, Downey, Ainsworth and Qian (2009) report mixed results from researchers who aim to determine whether the positive attitudes of black students about education impact their classroom performance and whether results for blacks are comparable to those of students from other racial groups. The authors conclude that black students likely experience a greater challenge in translating their attitudes into academic outcomes than do whites, but that their optimism is genuine and rational or, at the very least, no less rational and sincere than that of other racial groups. Harris and Robinson (2007) provide evidence that black students manifest their enthusiasm for school through pro-school behaviors and that deficiencies in prior skills, rather than lack of effort, mute their ability to translate this affinity into performance at levels paralleling whites. Akom (2003) and Perry (2005) even highlight a positive black achievement ideology as conscious resistance to the societal assertion of black intellectual inferiority relative to whites. This body of research acknowledges a belief in academic success as integral to—rather than counter to—racial authenticity among blacks. Finally, Sum and colleagues (2007) highlight a significant financial payoff for academic attainment among black males. This finding provides support for beliefs among blacks that education is the key to a more desirable future, even if the payoffs are not commensurate with those enjoyed by whites. In light of these claims, there is little reason that beliefs about payoffs to education should be considered rational only if blacks assume that they are being undersold, rather than that they benefit from academic achievement. This is particularly true once we allow that blacks, like many other groups, are more likely to make within-group comparisons than between-group assessments.

Our research suggests a reconsideration of Mickelson's (1990) model as we are skeptical of the theory that beliefs about social structure render irrelevant—rather than merely offset—the effects of a general belief in mobility through education. Contrary to this contention, we posit that ideological beliefs about the importance of education for both black and white students are grounded in rational recognition of the role that achievement plays in future prosperity and do have a measurable effect on academic performance. Research on the effects of these very attitudes on optimism about the future reveal that positive attitudes about school do contribute significantly to more favorable optimism about the future. Black students, unlike whites, merely temper their expectations for success in light of perceived structural barriers, but they do not dismiss such expectations entirely (Matthew 2011). A similar finding with regard to academic performance would indicate that positive attitudes about school do have a positive effect, but that this positive effect is countered by the influence of concerns about negative impacts of social structure. This neutralization of influence between the opposing sets of attitudes might result in an observed black/white gap that is similar to the size of said gap in models that do not account for these social psychological factors.

If Mickelson's argument is that black students consider social mobility through education to be unrealistic, then this fails to be borne out in findings which suggest that blacks are overwhelmingly *more* optimistic about the probability of being able to improve their standings relative to previous generations than are whites (Matthew 2011). Given the net of perceptions of both individualistic and structural influences on future life opportunities, black students still express optimism that they will arrive at satisfactory outcomes (albeit to a lesser degree than whites). It is not feasible to expect that a disparity in academic performance need be informed only by negative perceptions of social structure. More likely is the consideration that both positive attitudes about education and negative attitudes about structural barriers influence academic performance, but that the effects of these attitudes are not sufficient for explaining the achievement gap between black and white students. It is this claim that we aim to support through the results of our analysis.

# Data and Methods

## Data

This chapter utilizes data from the National Educational Longitudinal Study of 1988 (NELS:88). Data collection for NELS:88–2000 began during the 1987–88 school year and gathered a nationally represented longitudinal sample of 8th-graders in the United States.

Data were collected in five waves (1987–88, 1990, 1992, 1994 and 2000) and information was gathered from students, parents, teachers, school administrators and student transcripts.

This study uses data from both the second (1992) follow-up and restricted high school transcripts (1992). We choose the second follow-up for three reasons. First, students are in 12th grade at the time of data collection. This is meaningful because the relationship between academic achievement and future opportunities is most salient to school-age students as they look toward high school graduation and subsequent college enrollment or entry into the labor force. Second, the differentiation between attitudes about school and social structure is made by Matthew (2011) using these data, making a test of the concepts captured by these variables fairly straightforward. Finally, the availability of students' high school achievement records via restricted data makes this an ideal dataset for examining the effects of these attitudes on achievement.

The original sample consists of 12,144 students. For our analysis, we have limited the sample based on two criteria: valid data on the dependent variables and racial designation. To be included in the analysis, students must have valid grade-point average (GPA) and SAT data. In order to examine Mickelson's (1990) claims the sample has also been limited to black and white students, leaving a final sample of 6,300[1] students for the GPA analysis and 4,900 students for the analysis of SAT scores. The generalizability of these data is an improvement over Mickelson's study which uses a regionally limited purposive sample consisting of students from eight high schools in Los Angeles, California. We are examining the nature of a national academic achievement gap, therefore using national data is inherently more reliable.

**Table 8.1    Summary Statistics, NELS 88:92**

|  | Entire Sample | Non-Hispanic White | Non-Hispanic Black |
|---|---|---|---|
| High School GPA | 2.70 | 2.77 | 2.31 |
| SAT Score | 914.25 | 934.72 | 773.33 |
| Socioeconomic Status | -0.06 | 0.02 | -0.38 |
| **Student's Gender (vs. Males)** | | | |
| Female | 52.0% | 51.4% | 54.8% |
| **Attitudes About Academic Achievement (agree = 1)** | | | |
| "Education is important for getting a good job later on" | 97.1% | 96.9% | 97.1% |
| "It is important to get a good education" | 85.1% | 82.8% | 93.7% |
| **Attitudes about structural influence on life opportunities (agree = 1)** | | | |
| "In my life luck is more important the hard work for success" | 10.0% | 9.2% | 15.3% |
| "Every time I try to get ahead, someone or something stops me" | 22.7% | 21.4% | 32.6% |

---

1    Due to restricted data regulations sample sizes are rounded.

In an effort to more robustly measure the impact of students' own attitudes on the black/white gap in academic achievement we use two measures of achievement as our dependent variables. The first measure is student's GPA, which is a continuous index of self-reported grades in math, English, social studies and science. This variable ranges from 0.50 (most grades below D on four major subjects) and 4.00 (all grades are A for four major subjects). Our second dependent variable is standardized exam performance, referred to as SATREV in the dataset, and is a composite variable that comes from the restricted transcript data. This variable consolidates test scores on the SAT, ACT and PSAT on a single band-scale (Curtin et al. 2002). The methodology as well as SAS code for the variable creation can be found in the restricted data documentation. ACT scores were converted to the SAT scale in order to enable comparisons between students regardless of the college entrance exam taken. In an effort to measure the standardized exam performance of students who had neither SAT nor ACT scores, PSAT results were rescaled to approximate SAT scores.

Both race and student attitudes are focal independent variables for our analysis. Student's race comes from the composite race variable in the data and is measured as a simple dummy variable with non-Hispanic white as the reference group. Student attitudes are measured using student responses on a number of questions concerning education and structure. Since this chapter centers on the question of whether attitudes about school and social structure affect the academic performance gap between blacks and whites, we use students' response to the following question: "How strongly do you agree or disagree that education is important for getting a good job?" We also include students' response to "How important is it to get a good education?" as a proxy for views about education. This variable captures general attitudes about education rather than its value as a vehicle for future occupational attainment. Prior research has noted the consistency with which black students claim to have favorable attitudes toward school (Mickelson 1990; Ainsworth-Darnell and Downey 1998; Tyson et al. 2005; Harris 2011), a finding mirrored in Matthew's (2011) analysis that makes use of these same variables.

Mickelson (1990) finds that disproportionately negative perceptions of social structure cause injury to blacks' academic performance relative to whites. Consequently, we account for such perceptions in our analyses. While NELS does not offer ideal variables that measure perceptions of societal opportunity structure directly, available measures allow us to assess student perceptions of how external factors impact their ability to convert effort into favorable outcomes. Attitudes about factors that are beyond the control of the individual are captured in student responses to the following questions: "How strongly do you agree or disagree that when trying to get ahead, someone/something is always stopping you?" and "How strongly do you agree or disagree that good luck is more important than hard work?" Each of the attitudinal questions is measured on an ordinal scale with the options for three of the four being "strongly agree," "agree," "disagree" and "strongly disagree." The one exception is the question that measures the general importance of receiving a good education, for which response options are "very important," "somewhat important" and "not important." In an effort to more accurately measure general student attitudes we collapse the responses for each question into two categories. For the three questions ranging from "strongly agree" to "strongly disagree," we collapse "strongly agree" and "agree" into "agree" and "disagree" and "strongly disagree" into "disagree." While we acknowledge that collapsing categories may result in suppressing some variance between categories (e.g., the difference between "disagrees" and "strongly disagrees"), we argue that the substantive meaning of disagreeing, for example, is the same no matter the strength (i.e., strongly) of the disagreement (Matthew 2011). The new categories, "agree" and "disagree,'" are coded so that "agree" = 1 and the findings represent support for each attitudinal statement. Using the same logic, the final question has also been collapsed and recoded so the "very important" = 1 and "somewhat or not important" = 0.

We also control for student's sex and socioeconomic status (SES) (Heyneman 2005). Sex is a simple dichotomy with female as the reference group. Student's SES is measured using a composite variable from the dataset. This measure accounts for parental education, occupation and income. The SES measure is continuous and ranges from -2.8 to 2.8 with higher numbers representing a higher/better SES standing.

We use ordinary least square regression to examine the effects of attitudes about social structure and school on black/white disparities in academic performance. Missing data are dealt with using multiple imputation as outlined by Allison (2002). The imputations were carried out using the PROC MI procedure in SAS 9.3. The OLS regression was carried out using the PROC REG procedure in conjunction with the MIANALYZE command in SAS 9.3. We do not impute on the dependent variables and all models account for the appropriate sample weights.

## Results

Table 8.1 provides an overview of the sample characteristics as well as the difference between black and white students on all variables used in the analysis. For both measures of achievement, black students score significantly lower than their non-Hispanic white counterparts. Black students also come from homes that score lower on the SES index compared to their non-Hispanic white counterparts.

Although there is no difference in the proportion of black students who agree with the statement "education is important for getting a good job" compared to whites, a significantly higher proportion of black students report that getting a good education is very important relative to whites. A significantly lower proportion of whites students compared to blacks agree "that good luck is more important than hard work" and "that when trying to get ahead, someone/something is always stopping you." These finding suggests that there is variation in both achievement and attitudes between white and black students.

Tables 8.2 and 8.3 present the regression results for GPA and SAT scores, respectively. Model 1 in both tables examines the bivariate relationship between race and achievement. Model 2 in Tables 8.2 and 8.3 add in the measure for student's sex and SES background. This model serves as our baseline when assessing the independent impact of the four attitudinal measures. In Models 3–6, we individually examine the impact of each of the four attitudinal measures on the achievement gap between white and black students. Model 7 is our full model. In Model 1 of Table 8.2 we find that non-Hispanic white students report having higher GPAs than their non-Hispanic black counterparts by .44 points. Model 2 adds student's sex and SES. Consistent with prior literature, female students report higher GPAs than their male counterparts and students who are higher on the SES index report higher GPAs compared to those who are lower on the index. Once both student's sex and SES are accounted for, we see a decrease in the black/white GPA gap.

In Model 3, agreement with the statement "education is important for getting a good job" results in reports of higher GPAs, as evidenced by the significant and positive coefficient. As expected, based on the lack of variation between whites and blacks on this attitudinal measure, the inclusion of this measure does very little to change the GPA gap between black and white students. However, inclusion of the measure "How important is it to get a good education" in Model 4 widens the GPA gap. This finding supports Ainsworth-Darnell and Downey's (1998) suggestion that the gap might be larger if not for the more positive attitudes about education expressed by blacks (93.7 percent of blacks report getting a good

**Table 8.2    High School GPA OLS Results**

| | Model 1 | | Model 2 | | Model 3 | | Model 4 | | Model 5 | | Model 6 | | Model 7 | |
|---|---|---|---|---|---|---|---|---|---|---|---|---|---|---|
| **Student's Race (vs. Non-Hispanic White)** | | | | | | | | | | | | | | |
| Black | -0.44 | *** | -0.33 | *** | -0.33 | *** | -0.36 | *** | -0.32 | *** | -0.31 | *** | -0.34 | *** |
| Socioeconomic Status | | | 0.28 | *** | 0.28 | *** | 0.27 | *** | 0.28 | *** | 0.27 | *** | 0.25 | *** |
| **Student's Gender (vs. Male)** | | | | | | | | | | | | | | |
| Female | | | 0.20 | *** | 0.19 | *** | 0.18 | *** | 0.19 | *** | 0.19 | *** | 0.16 | *** |
| **Attitudes About Academic Achievement** | | | | | | | | | | | | | | |
| "Education is important for getting a good job later on" | | | | | 0.40 | *** | | | | | | | 0.32 | *** |
| "It is important to get a good education" | | | | | | | 0.27 | *** | | | | | 0.22 | *** |
| **Attitudes about structural influence on life opportunities** | | | | | | | | | | | | | | |
| "In my life luck is more important the hard work for success" | | | | | | | | | -0.27 | *** | | | -0.18 | *** |
| "Every time I try to get ahead, someone or something stops me" | | | | | | | | | | | -0.24 | *** | -0.19 | *** |
| Intercept | 2.75 | *** | 2.66 | *** | 2.26 | *** | 2.43 | *** | 2.67 | *** | 2.70 | *** | 2.23 | *** |
| R2 | 0.031 | | 0.129 | | 0.137 | | 0.146 | | 0.140 | | 0.147 | | 0.171 | |

*Source*: National Educational Longitudinal Study of 1988: 92.
*Note*: Due to restricted data regulations all sample sizes have been rounded: N = 6,300; * p <. 05; ** p < .01; *** p < .001.

**Table 8.3    SAT Scores OLS Results**

| | Model 1 | Model 2 | Model 3 | Model 4 | Model 5 | Model 6 | Model 7 |
|---|---|---|---|---|---|---|---|
| **Student's Race (vs. Non-Hispanic White)** | | | | | | | |
| Black | -157.46 *** | -116.30 *** | -116.10 *** | -120.01 *** | -116.08 *** | -109.28 *** | -112.23 *** |
| Socioeconomic Status | | 106.38 *** | 106.18 *** | 105.35 *** | 105.48 *** | 101.36 *** | 100.44 *** |
| **Student's Gender (vs. Male)** | | | | | | | |
| Female | | -22.34 . | -23.06 ** | -25.52 * | -25.58 * | -25.52 * | -29.95 *** |
| **Attitudes About Academic Achievement** | | | | | | | |
| "Education is important for getting a good job later on" | | | 55.28 *** | | | | 36.86 *** |
| "It is important to get a good education" | | | | 44.54 *** | | | 30.62 *** |
| **Attitudes about structural influence on life opportunities** | | | | | | | |
| "In my life luck is more important the hard work for success" | | | | | -66.87 *** | | -42.65 *** |
| "Every time I try to get ahead, someone or something stops me" | | | | | | -81.57 *** | -73.76 *** |
| Intercept | 931.31 *** | 917.07 *** | 863.18 *** | 879.80 *** | 923.76 *** | 932.67 *** | 873.91 *** |
| R2 | 0.045 | 0.193 | 0.194 | 0.198 | 0.200 | 0.214 | 0.220 |

*Source:* National Educational Longitudinal Study of 1988:92.

*Note:* Due to restricted data regulations all sample sizes have been rounded. N = 4,900; * p <. 05; ** p < .01; *** p < .001.

education to be very important compared to 82.8 percent of whites). Model 4 also suggests that agreement with the concept that it is very important to get a good education has a positive impact on GPA.

Models 5 and 6 include measures that tap students' attitudes about structural influences on life opportunities. Agreement with the statements "In my life luck is more important than hard work for success" and "Every time I try to get ahead, someone or something stops me" result in reports of lower GPAs. However once controlling for these attitudes, we see a decrease in the GPA gap between white and black students. In the full model, Model 7, both the direction and significance of the covariates remain as they were in the previous models. Although the GPA gap is reduced across the models, a gap still exits net of both control variables and the four attitudinal measures. These covariates explain 17 percent of the variation in students' GPAs.

The results of the OLS for SAT scores are almost identical to the findings for GPA. This suggests that the findings are fairly robust. This set of covariates explains more variation in SAT scores than it did in regard to GPA (22 percent vs. 17 percent). Consistent with prior research and our descriptive statistics, non-Hispanic white students outscore their non-Hispanic black counterparts on the SAT. Model 2 in Table 8.3 shows that some of the gap in achievement is explained by sex and SES. However, net of these factors, white students continue to outperform their black counterparts.

Agreement with the statement "Education is important for getting a good job" results in higher achievement test scores as evidenced by significant and positive coefficient in Model 3 in Table 8.3. As expected, based on the lack of variation between whites and blacks, the inclusion of this measure does very little to influence the gap for SAT scores. However the inclusion of the measure "How important is it to get a good education" in Model 4 widens the gap in SAT scores. Just as with GPA, we find that negative attitudes about structure result in lower SAT scores while, simultaneously, closing the black/white gap in SAT scores (see Models 5 and 6). Finally, accounting for all four of the attitudinal measures when predicting SAT scores narrows the black/white achievement test score gap.

# Discussion

In this chapter, we examined the impact of student attitudes about school and structural barriers on the achievement gap. Contrary to the argument of Mickelson (1990), our findings suggest that both positive attitudes toward the potential rewards of educational achievement as well as negative attitudes toward structural barriers impact student achievement. Specifically, we find that those attitudes, referred to as "abstract" by Mickelson (1990), have very real effects on the academic achievement gap between blacks and white students. When we account for these attitudes we see a narrowing of the black/white gap in both GPA and SAT scores.

Although positive attitudes about education are expressed by both black and white students, academic success appears to carry a stronger intrinsic value among blacks than among whites as evidenced by the significantly higher percentage of blacks who agree that getting a good education in general is very important. We know from prior research that black students have long reported a strong affinity toward school (Coleman et al. 1966; Ainsworth-Darnell and Downey 1998; Tyson et al. 2005; Harris 2006) and our research provides evidence that there is, indeed, a tangible payoff to this. Our findings that these "abstract" attitudes narrow the achievement gap, evidenced here using two distinct measures of achievement, should signal to scholars the importance of regarding attitudes about education as one of the few factors that actually contracts the black/white achievement gap. This is in direct opposition to the popular argument that they are accountable for expanding it.

In contrast to positive beliefs of academic agency, black students internalize skepticism about the impediments of structural barriers to their potential outcomes as a result of educational success. These negative attitudes lower both GPA and SAT scores. However, when these perceptions of structural barriers are controlled for, we see a slight narrowing of the gap. Although students' positive attitudes about the possible rewards of educational success and their negative attitudes about structural barriers facilitate a narrowing of the gap, we still see racial disparities in both GPA and SAT scores. This indicates that attitudes about education should be regarded—as suggested by Ainsworth-Darnell and Downey (1998)—as a strong moderator that blunts the full impact of the structural disadvantages that face many black students.

Our findings indicate a significant influence of attitudes about school on the black/white academic achievement gap. We do, however, stop short of claiming that all that is needed to eliminate this disparity is an attitude adjustment on the part of blacks. On the contrary, we assert that the attitudes expressed by these students reflect a rational assessment of the impacts of the competing forces of agency and structure on their life opportunities. While Mickelson claims there is no rational reason for black students to believe in the payoffs of schooling, Sum and colleagues (2007) show the marked financial benefit of academic attainment among black males, which supports our position that educational attainment serves as a tangible and perceivable vehicle toward desirable future outcomes for black students as well as for their white counterparts. Likewise, negative perceptions that blacks have of social structure are a legitimate response to a system in which the assertion of black identity in school or in overall society is still sometimes perceived as "oppositional" behavior (Lundy 2003).

# Conclusion

This chapter offers several critical revelations with regard to the impact of attitudes on the black/white achievement gap. First, we demonstrate an impact of both positive attitudes about individual agency and negative perceptions of social structure on academic achievement. Relatedly, we show that, rather than having no impact on the black/white achievement gap, attitudes about agency actually serve as a significant counterforce to those on the effect of social structure on future outcomes.

The conclusions drawn from our research offer insight that calls for greater acknowledgment of the complexity of student attitudes about the payoffs of academic success. In one way, these findings lend support to Mickelson's claim that black students' relative distrust of the meritocratic promise of education contributes to the size of the black/white achievement gap. On the other hand, we find no reason to assume that this skepticism precludes positive effects of the favorable views about education that researchers have found among black students.

Despite the significance of the findings in this chapter, there are some limitations. First, our measures of attitudes about structural barriers do not specifically ask respondents to consider the role of race in determining whether hard work and motivation will pay off for them. Additionally, given Tyson's (2002) contention that prior academic achievement predicts present attitude about investing in education, the direction of causality between attitudes and achievement yet remains to be resolved. One might also consider the changing importance of these attitudes and the development of these attitudes across the academic career. Furthermore, with the changing landscape of the student population in the US, future studies must include a range of racial/ethnic groups as well as foreign-born students in order to truly understand the relationship between attitudes and achievement. Finally, we caution that our findings, though significant, fall short of explaining the entire black/white gap in achievement as our overall models account for 17 percent of the gap in GPA and approximately 22 percent of the disparity in standardized exam scores, respectively. Despite these limitations, this chapter makes a contribution to the existing literature by empirically demonstrating the relevance of both stated attitudes about education and attitudes about social structure. Paying due respect to the effects of *both* sets of attitudes is mandatory if we are to fully comprehend the resiliency of the black/white academic achievement gap in the United States.

# References

Ainsworth-Darnell, James and Douglas B. Downey. 1998. "Assessing the Oppositional Culture Explanation for Racial/Ethnic Differences in School Performance." *American Sociological Review* 63: 536–53.

Akom, A.A. 2003. "Reexamining Resistance as Oppositional Behavior: The Nation of Islam and the Creation of a Black Achievement Ideology." *Sociology of Education* 76: 305–25.

Allison, Paul. 2002. "Missing Data: Quantitative Applications in the Social Sciences." *British Journal of Mathematical and Statistical Psychology* 55: 193–6.

Coleman, James C., Ernest Q. Campbell, Carol J. Hobson, James McParland, Alexander M. Mood, Frederic D. Weinfeld and Robert L. York. 1966. *Equality of Educational Opportunity*. Washington, DC: US Government Printing Office.

Curtin, Thomas R., Steven J. Ingels, Shiying Wu and Ruth Heuer. 2002. *National Education Longitudinal Study of 1988: Base-Year to Fourth Follow-up Data File User's Manual (NCES 2002-323)*. Washington, DC: US Department of Education, National Center for Education Statistics.

Downey, Douglas B., James W. Ainsworth and Zhenchao Qian. 2009. "Rethinking the Attitude-Achievement Paradox Among Blacks." *Sociology of Education* 82: 1–19.

Fordham, Signithia and John U. Ogbu. 1986. "Black Students' School Success: Coping with the 'Burden of Acting White.'" *The Urban Review* 18: 176–206.

Harris, Angel L. 2006. "I (Don't) Hate School: Revisiting 'Oppositional Culture' Theory of Blacks' Resistance to Schooling." *Social Forces* 85: 797–834.

———. 2008. "Optimism in the Face of Despair: Black-White Differences in Beliefs About School as a Means for Upward Social Mobility." *Social Science Quarterly* 89: 608–20.

———. 2011. *Kids Don't Want to Fail: Oppositional Culture and the Black-White Achievement Gap*. Cambridge, MA: Harvard University Press.

——— and Keith Robinson. 2007. "Schooling Behaviors or Prior Skills? A Cautionary Tale of Omitted Variable Bias within Oppositional Culture Theory." *Sociology of Education* 80: 139–57.

Heyneman, Stephen P. 2005. "Student Background and Student Achievement: What is the Right Question?" *American Journal of Education* 112: 1–9.

Lundy, Garvey F. 2003. "The Myths of Oppositional Culture". *Journal of Black Studies* 33: 450–67.

Matthew, Ervin (Maliq). 2011. "Effort Optimism in the Classroom: Assessing Black and White Student Attitudes on the Role of Academic Achievement in Gaining Life Opportunities." *Sociology of Education* 84: 225–45.

Mickelson, Roslyn Arlin. 1990. "The Attitude-Achievement Paradox among Black Students." *Sociology of Education* 63: 44–61.

Ogbu, John. 1978. *Minority Education and Caste*. New York: Academic Press

———. 1983. "Minority Status and Schooling in Plural Societies. *Comparative Education Review* 27: 168–90.

Perry, Theresa. 2005. "Up from Parched Earth." in *Young, Gifted, and Black: Promoting High Achievement Among African-American Students*, eds. T. Perry, C. Steele and A. Hilliard III. New York: Beacon Press, pp. 1–87.

Pino, Nathan W. and William L. Smith. 2004. "African American Students, the Academic Ethic, and GPA." *Journal of Black Studies* 35: 113–31.

Sum, Andrew, Ishwar Khatiwada, Joseph McLaughlin and Paulo Tobar. 2007. "The Educational Attainment of the Nation's Young Black Men and Their Recent Labor Market Experiences: What Can Be Done to Improve Their Future Labor Market and Educational Prospects?" Boston, MA: Center for Labor Market Studies, Northeastern University.

Tyson, Karolyn. 2002. "Weighing In: Elementary-Age Students and the Debate on Attitudes toward School among Black Students." *Social Forces* 80: 1157–89.

———, William Darity, Jr. and Domini R. Castellino. 2005. "It's Not a 'Black Thing': Understanding the Burden of Acting White and Other Dilemmas of High Achievement." *American Sociological Review* 70: 582–605.

# African American Women Workers in the Postindustrial Period: The Role of Education in Evaluating Racial Wage Parity among Women

Katrinell M. Davis

## Introduction

Over the past fifty years substantial changes in the demographic characteristics of women in the workforce have had a significant impact on their relative earnings. Black women's earnings first began to increase, relative to similarly situated White women, in the 1950s (King 1993; Sokoloff 1992; Blau and Beller 1992). One of the factors that contributed to this improvement is the steady increases in Black women workers' average level of education attainment between 1940 and 1980 (Sokoloff 1992; Blau and Beller 1992). While White women's educational attainment improved from 8.8 years to 12.5 years between 1940 and 1980, Black women's average educational attainment doubled from 6.2 years to 12 years during this time (King 1993: 1109). These trends, in addition to other factors including declining fertility rates (Bianchi 1995), led to shifts in wage convergence among white and Black women workers by the mid- to late 1970s (King 1995; Sokoloff 1992). Relative income gains among White and Black women have also been attributed to Black women's occupational upgrades (Blau and Beller 1992; Goldin 1990) and anti-discrimination laws that helped them gain access to public sector and professional jobs (Grodsky and Pager 2001; Darity and Mason 1998; Blau and Beller 1994).

Despite these influences, wage disparities among White and Black women have increased substantially since the 1980s. In fact, between 1979 and 2005, the racial wage gap between young White and Black women nearly tripled (Pettit and Ewert 2009: 469). Given the shifts in wage disparities between women workers, research has emerged to examine declines in wage parity primarily between Black and White women. Some researchers analyzing persistent wage gaps between women interpret racial variations in wages to demographic and attitudinal attributes (Smith 2005; Neal 2004; Moss and Tilly 2001). Meanwhile, other scholars argue that wage gaps among women are related to racial differences in the structure of opportunity available to women workers (Branch 2011; Pettit and Ewert 2009) in addition to declining labor conditions (Kalleberg et al. 2000; Tilly 1996), a waning public sector premium (Newsome and Dodoo 2002) and the increasing wage inequality in the postindustrial labor market (Bernhardt et al. 2001, 1995).

In light of evidence indicating conflicting conclusions regarding the effect of human capital investments on wage gaps among women workers, this study is designed to re-examine the relationship between educational attainment and wage parity among White, Black and Latin American women workers. While educational investments are key in gaining entry into occupations, previous research indicates that human capital investments do not solely determine who competes for and succeeds in acquiring power, prestige and status within the workplace (Glenn 2002; Hum 2000; Collins 1990). Therefore, I join other researchers in assuming that education matters (Wilkie 1985). However, the extent to which educational attainment is related to relative wage trends among women is addressed in this analysis for the purposes of clarity and discussion.

## Literature Review

### The Effect of Human Capital on Wages

Research within the social demographic tradition draws heavily on human capital theory. Proponents of human capital theory claim that earnings are largely based on individual investments in schooling and work experience. According to human capital theorists, labor is paid according to the worker's productivity and the importance of their skill to the labor market (Reid 2002; Danziger and Gottschalk 1995).

Social demographic scholars attribute persistent racial gaps in wages to compositional changes in the labor force (Neal 2004). According to Neal, between the 1980s and the 1990s the composition of the labor market changed with the influx of well–educated White women and low skilled Black women. Neal contends that wage gaps between White and Black women widened because low-skilled Black women were not well-positioned to compete with highly educated White women in the labor market. Meanwhile, the income gaps between White women and Latin American women have been attributed to Latin American women's immigrant status, low levels of education and minimal experience in the US labor market (Melendez 1993; Ortiz 1995). Latinas also have a high likelihood of holding low-income jobs in the lower-level service sector (Tienda and Guhleman 1985).

Accordingly, studies in this tradition attribute earnings inequality to the perceived intentions and attitudes that workers bring to the labor market (Hall and Farkas 2011; Moss and Tilly 2001). Hall and Farkas' (2011) study examined how racial/ethnic variations in wages were related to cognitive skills and attitudinal traits as measured by scores that identified educational expectations and inspirations, self-esteem and level of assertiveness. Hall and Farkas reported that women of color who appear to be assertive and confident are not viewed favorably by employers. This is particularly true for young African American women who Hall and Farkas (ibid.) claimed have been portrayed as "untrustworthy and unreliable" "welfare queens" (Gilens 1996) or as abrasive "loudies" who lack self–control" (Hall and Farkas 2011: 1281). According to Hall and Farkas, Black women earn less than White women, especially at the beginning of their employment careers, due to their cognitive skill deficits and their perceived attitudinal/behavior traits. For Latina women, cognitive skills did not significantly influence initial wages. However, their attitudinal traits played a role in shaping their wage growth throughout their careers.

## Variations in Job Opportunity

Researchers also contend that racial wage gaps among women are related to Black women's disproportionate concentration in low-paying jobs (Pettit and Ewert 2009; Malveaux 1986; Jones 1985). Like African American men, African American women have a long history of being segregated into the lowest-paid jobs where they work; even in jobs wherein workers share the same level of educational training (Jones 1985). For instance, African American women working for tobacco factories in Virginia were concentrated in jobs as re-handlers who sorted, stripped and hung tobacco leaves as part of the re-drying process (ibid.: 137). As tobacco manufacturing firms began to grow with the increasing popularity of cigarettes and the mechanization of the industry, these firms started hiring White women in large numbers as skilled operatives while African Americans continued to perform the manual labor.

King (1993) suggests that the occupational movement of Black women into administrative work had more to do with hiring preferences among employers than the workers' skills and educational credentials. King's analysis of Black women's journey into clerical work illustrates how their increasing similarity to White women in terms of education did not impact their transition from domestic work to clerical work or substantially improve their economic well-being. King (ibid.) notes in this study that African American women appear to have acquired the necessary educational qualifications for clerical work well before they were hired in large numbers. King (ibid.) presents data illustrating that for decades employers typically overlooked Black female laborers, even when they had the necessary level of education. For instance, in 1940 clerical and sales work employed almost 60 percent of White women with high school degrees while only 7 percent of African American women employed in clerical positions possessed a high school diploma. Nearly 70 percent of high school-educated African American women workers at this time held low-level service jobs. According to King, service jobs remained the occupational niche for high school-educated Black women until 1980 despite their steady improvements in educational attainment (ibid.: 1101).

# Data and Methods

## Study Rationale and Method

While social demographic and labor opportunity arguments are useful explanations of racial wage disparities among women, researchers have paid less attention to the wage inequality that exists among similarly situated workers. Neal (2004) assumes that wage inequality among women can be explained by racial differences in educational attainment. Structural researchers focus more on the nature of African American women's opportunity structure, including Browne (2000) and Branch (2011), and attribute wage differences to occupational segregation by race. However, few researchers have specified how wage inequality varies among workers with similar levels of education (King 1993; Malveaux 1986).

This research helps fill this empirical gap by documenting the relationship between educational attainment and wage differences among White, Black and Latin American women. Although some of the general patterns presented here, including the deteriorating relative economic status of less educated women, are known (Browne 2000; King 1993), this analysis offers a disaggregated look at wage inequality in order to establish important distinctions among women workers representing different race/ethnicity and class locations in the postindustrial era. Two questions guide this investigation. First, to what degree is wage parity among White, Black and Latin American women workers mediated by educational attainment? Second, how does the relationship between educational attainment and wages differ for low- and high-wage earners?

## Data

The findings in this chapter derive from a large and nationally representative sample of Census data drawn from the Integrated Public Use Microdata Series (IPUMS). For the purposes of this analysis, I randomly selected a 1 percent sample from the IPUMS database for years 1960 through 2000. With these data I examine wage gaps among women workers at different levels of the earnings distribution through an analysis of earnings ratios by education group.

## Method

In this analysis I explore inter- and intra-group differences in wage variations. Median estimates are used to compute the inter-group earnings ratios among women workers, which illustrate shifts in wage inequality among women by education over a forty-year period. In order to assess the extent to which wage inequality is related to race, education and wage group, intra-group comparisons capture wage inequality by level of education at different levels of the earnings distribution. I explore earnings ratios by education and percentile across race and year. I also explore within wage group inequality by estimating the ratio of 90th-percentile median earnings to 10th-percentile median earnings.

## Dependent and Independent Variables

Gross and net effects of education on logged earnings are estimated by utilizing the Ordinary Least Squares (OLS) regression method. The natural logarithm of earnings served as the dependent variable in order to capture the proportional changes in earnings. The covariates in this analysis include a range of variables that are instrumental in shaping wage inequality among women including occupation, sector of employment, region of residence, metropolitan status, age, age squared, marital status, number of children, usual hours workers, weeks employed last year and dummy variables representing different levels of educational attainment.

Unless otherwise indicated, the sample in this analysis consists of individuals aged 25 to 64 who are in the labor market. I exclude workers under age 25 who may still be developing their skill set, in addition to individuals who did not report wages and their employment status to the Census from this analysis. Lastly, I do not include more race and ethnic groups other than Black, White and Latin Americans in this analysis. This remains a significant area for future research.

This analysis illustrates the race- and class-specific implications of shifts in the relationship between educational attainment and wage inequality among women. Tables 9.1 and 9.2 demonstrate the nature of wage inequality among women workers by illustrating postindustrial-era shifts in the percentage of employed women workers by level of education, mean earnings by level of education, race/ethnicity, and year, in addition to earnings ratios between workers with advanced education and those with only a high school education.

Table 9.3 further demonstrates the class- and race-specific trajectories of earnings ratios by percentile and level of education. In order to measure the impact of education on wages for women workers, evidence in Tables 9.4 through 9.6 capture racially distinctive shifts in the impact of different levels of education by year and race. Following the presentation of this evidence, I discuss the implications of these findings.

# Results

**Table 9.1    Percentage of Employed Female Workers by Level of Education, Year and Race/Ethnicity**

|  | All | Black | White | Latin |
|---|---|---|---|---|
| **1960** | | | | |
| High School Education | 34% | 18% | 36% | 34% |
| Associate Level of Education | 12 | 6 | 13 | 12 |
| Bachelor's Level of Education | 8 | 5 | 9 | 8 |
| **1970** | | | | |
| High School Education | 40 | 32 | 42 | 41 |
| Associate Level of Education | 13 | 10 | 14 | 13 |
| Bachelor's Level of Education | 11 | 6 | 11 | 11 |
| **1980** | | | | |
| High School Education | 43 | 38 | 44 | 43 |
| Associate Level of Education | 20 | 19 | 21 | 20 |
| Bachelor's Level of Education | 15 | 11 | 16 | 15 |
| **1990** | | | | |
| High School Education | 35 | 36 | 35 | 35 |
| Associate Level of Education | 32 | 31 | 32 | 32 |
| Bachelor's Level of Education | 21 | 17 | 22 | 21 |
| **2000** | | | | |
| High School Education | 29 | 34 | 29 | 29 |
| Associate Level of Education | 34 | 35 | 35 | 34 |
| Bachelor's Level of Education | 27 | 18 | 29 | 27 |

Throughout the period of study the results presented in Table 9.1 support the well-established finding that the female workforce continues to improve its level educational attainment throughout the postindustrial era (Corcoran 1999). This illustrates the extent to which the educational distribution of women workers varies across racial groups over time. According to the estimates in Table 9.1, women workers of all race groups experienced large gains in their educational attainment between 1960 and 2000. Prior to 1980, most of these women workers operated in the labor market with only a high school education. After 1980 more women workers became college educated. Between 1980 and 2000 the percentage of White and Latin American women nearly doubled from 16 to 29 percent and 15 to 27 percent, respectively.

The educational upgrade that White and Latin American women workers experienced between 1980 and 2000 was not as substantial among African American women workers. Similar to other women in the workplace, the percentage of Black women with advanced college experience increased by at least threefold. However, unlike White and Latin American women, the increase in the percentage of Black women obtaining a high school education as well as some college experience outpaced the percentage of Black women with an advanced level of college education.

**Table 9.2    Median Earnings by Race/Ethnicity, Education and Year, 1960–2000 (in 2013 dollars)**

| | 1960 | 1970 | 1980 | 1990 | 2000 |
|---|---|---|---|---|---|
| **Black** | | | | | |
| High School | $9,039 | $18,300 | $19,754 | $24,920 | $27,000 |
| Some College | $15,720 | $17,100 | $11,421 | $13,929 | $21,195 |
| Bachelor's Degree | $25,545 | $37,500 | $33,621 | $44,500 | $47,250 |
| **White** | | | | | |
| High School | $20,695 | $23,635 | $21,530 | $24,167 | $22,950 |
| Some College | $23,973 | $23,700 | $23,166 | $29,583 | $32,509 |
| Bachelor's Degree | $31,047 | $39,300 | $32,397 | $45,247 | $51,873 |
| **Latin** | | | | | |
| High School | $20,043 | $23,100 | $19,754 | $21,360 | $22,275 |
| Some College | $23,001 | $23,100 | $21,390 | $26,700 | $28,350 |
| Bachelor's Degree | $30,261 | $38,100 | $31,316 | $42,720 | $44,550 |
| **Earnings Ratios between Workers with Bachelor's Degree and High School Education** | | | | | |
| Black | 2.8 | 2.0 | 1.7 | 1.8 | 1.8 |
| White | 1.5 | 1.7 | 1.5 | 1.9 | 2.3 |
| Latin | 1.5 | 1.6 | 1.6 | 2.0 | 2.0 |

*Note:* All wages calculated with the Consumer Price Index Multipliers for 2010 dollars.

Table 9.2 displays the median earning among women workers by level of education, race/ethnicity and year. This table illustrates two important findings regarding earning trends among similarly situated women workers between 1960 and 2000. First, even when educational differences are eliminated there is a great deal of wage inequality among women; especially by race and level of education. With the exception of high school-educated Black women after 1980, who earned more than their White and Latin American women counterparts, Black women between 1960 and 2000 typically earned less than White and Latin American women workers.

Second, earnings ratios between workers with a high school education and a bachelor's degree also demonstrates contrasting trends in earning differences throughout the period of study. Among Black women, earnings ratios between high and low educated workers declined from 2.83 in 1960 to 1.75 in 2000. At the same time, earnings ratios among low and high educated White and Latin American women workers increased during this time. Among White women, their earnings ratios increased from 1.50 in 1960 to 1.87 in 2000. Meanwhile, Latin American women workers saw their earnings ratios between low and highly educated workers increase from 1.51 in 1960 to 2.0 in 2000.

**Table 9.3**     **Earnings Ratios by Level of Education, Earnings Percentile, Year and Race, 1960–2000**

|  | 1960 | 1970 | 1980 | 1990 | 2000 |
|---|---|---|---|---|---|
| **ALL** | | | | | |
| **Earnings Ratio by Percentile (Among High/Low Education Category)** | | | | | |
| 10th | 2.04 | 0.67 | 1.52 | 1.43 | 1.01 |
| 90th | 1.38 | 1.68 | 0.90 | 1.45 | 1.84 |
| **Earnings Ratio 90/10 Percentile** | | | | | |
| High School | 10.3 | 8.8 | 8.7 | 8.2 | 8.2 |
| Associate Level of Education. | 9.0 | 12.0 | 10.1 | 10.3 | 8.7 |
| Bachelor's Level of Education | 6.9 | 7.9 | 8.9 | 7.7 | 7.3 |
| **WHITE WOMEN** | | | | | |
| **Earnings Ratio by Percentile (Among High/Low Education Category)** | | | | | |
| 10th | 1.92 | 0.72 | 1.51 | 1.38 | 1.05 |
| 90th | 1.38 | 1.58 | 0.95 | 1.45 | 1.68 |
| **Earnings Ratio 90/10 Percentile** | | | | | |
| High School | 10.0 | 8.5 | 8.7 | 8.2 | 7.3 |
| Associate Level of Education | 9.1 | 12.1 | 9.7 | 10.3 | 8.8 |
| Bachelor's Level of Education | 7.2 | 8.2 | 9.1 | 8.4 | 7.8 |
| **BLACK WOMEN** | | | | | |
| **Earnings Ratio by Percentile (Among High/Low Education Category)** | | | | | |
| 10th | 3.80 | 0.44 | 1.59 | 1.28 | 1.16 |
| 90th | 1.68 | 4.21 | 0.38 | 1.49 | 4.03 |
| **Earnings Ratio 90/10 Percentile** | | | | | |
| High School | 9.2 | 10.6 | 7.8 | 12.9 | 10.9 |
| Associate Level of Education | 10.5 | 10.4 | 16.8 | 10.0 | 7.8 |
| Bachelor's Level of Education | 4.1 | 4.0 | 9.1 | 5.1 | 5.3 |
| **LATINAS** | | | | | |
| **Earnings Ratio by Percentile (Among High/Low Education Category)** | | | | | |
| 10th | 2.04 | 0.67 | 1.52 | 1.43 | 1.01 |
| 90th | 1.38 | 1.70 | 0.89 | 1.45 | 1.84 |
| **Earnings Ratio 90/10 Percentile** | | | | | |
| High School | 10.3 | 8.7 | 8.7 | 8.2 | 8.2 |
| Associate Level of Education | 9.0 | 11.7 | 10.1 | 10.3 | 8.7 |
| Bachelor's Level of Education | 6.9 | 7.7 | 8.9 | 7.7 | 7.3 |

Findings in Table 9.3 demonstrate the nature of earnings inequality among workers by percentile between 1960 and 2000. Table 9.3 displays earnings ratios between those that fall within the 90th and 10th percentile by level of education. On the whole, earnings inequality among women workers with an advanced college education increased between 1960 and

2000. At the same time, while high school-educated White and Latin American women workers saw declines in their earnings ratios throughout the period of study, high school-educated Black women experienced a net increase in the earnings differences between 90th- and 10th-percentile earners.

**Table 9.4    Effects of Education on Logged Wages of High School-Educated Women Workers by Race and Year**

| Race/Model | 1960 | 1970 |
|---|---|---|
| **White Women** | | |
| Model 1: Gross Effect | 0.303** (0.005) | 0.335** (0.003) |
| Model 2: Net Effect | 0.200** (0.003) | 0.188** (0.002) |
| **Black Women** | | |
| Model 1: Gross Effect | 0.494** (0.014) | 0.479** (0.007) |
| Model 2: Net Effect | 0.273** (0.011) | 0.243** (0.006) |
| **Latinas** | | |
| Model 1: Gross Effect | 0.408** (0.004) | 0.364** (0.002) |
| Model 2: Net Effect | 0.244** (0.003) | 0.214** (0.002) |

*Note:* *=p < .05; **p < .005; standard errors are in parentheses.

Previous tables illustrate that women workers have benefited from acquiring more education. At the same time, there is evidence that there may be other factors shaping the economic well-being and wage inequality that can diminish the impact of education. In order to observe how the impact of education is shaped by other mediating factors including age, marital status, region of residence, number of children and occupational status, Tables 9.4 through to 9.6 compare the net and gross effects of having a certain level of education on logged wages between 1960 and 2000.

Table 9.4, which illustrates the effects of having a high school education on logged wages, shows that all women saw increases in the gross effect of having a high school diploma between 1960 and 2000. For instance, similar to trends among Black and Latin American women, White women saw the gross effect of having a high school diploma increase from .303 in 1960 to .907 in 2000. Regardless of their racial/ethnic differences, women workers also saw the net effect of having a high school diploma decline throughout the period of study. While the decline in the net effect of having a high school diploma declined more drastically among Black women, White women workers received the least benefit from this level of education throughout the period of study.

**Table 9.5    Effects of Education on Logged Wages of Women with an Associate's Level of Education by Race and Year**

| Race/Model | 1960 | 1970 | 1980 | 1990 | 2000 |
|---|---|---|---|---|---|
| **White Women** | | | | | |
| Model 1: Gross Effect | 0.412** | 0.282** | 0.531** | 0.857** | 1.052** |
| | (0.007) | (0.004) | (0.004) | (0.005) | (0.010) |
| Model 2: Net Effect | 0.249** | 0.243** | 0.243** | 0.302** | 0.202** |
| | (0.005) | (0.003) | (0.003) | (0.003) | (0.006) |
| **Black Women** | | | | | |
| Model 1: Gross Effect | 0.944** | 0.490** | 0.324** | 0.995** | 1.020** |
| | (0.026) | (0.0010) | (0.011) | (0.012) | (0.015 |
| Model 2: Net Effect | 0.200** | 0.324** | 0.154** | 0.437** | 0.516** |
| | (0.019) | (0.009) | (0.009) | (0.008) | (0.012) |
| **Latinas** | | | | | |
| Model 1: Gross Effect | 0.539** | 0.317** | 0.487** | 0.803** | 0.877** |
| | (0.007) | (0.003) | (0.004) | (0.004) | (0.006) |
| Model 2: Net Effect | 0.279** | 0.268** | 0.254** | 0.336** | 0.397** |
| | (0.005) | (0.003) | (0.003) | (0.003) | (0.004) |

*Note:* $* = p < .05$; $** p < .005$.

Table 9.5 illustrates the net and gross effects of having an associate's level of education by race/ethnicity and year. Similar to gross effect trends among high school-educated women workers, those with an associate level of education saw the gross effect of having this level of education increase throughout the period of study. At the same time evidence in Table 9.5 illustrates that the net effect of having this level of education benefits some women more than others. For instance, both Black and Latin American women experienced increases in the net effect of having an associate's level of education, especially after 1980. Meanwhile, White women saw the net effect of having an associate's level of education on logged wages decline from .249 in 1960 to .202 in 2000.

Table 9.6, which presents the gross effects of having a bachelor's level of education by race/ethnicity and year, illustrates that this level of education has played an increasingly significant role in shaping women's earnings throughout the period of study. For instance, the gross effect of having a bachelor's level of education for White women increased from .320 in 1960 to 1.568 in 2000. At the same time, when we consider net effect trends among women workers we see that the impact of possessing this level of education varied by race. Data in this table illustrates that Black women benefit most from having a bachelor's degree than their White and Latina counterparts throughout the period of study. At the same time Table 9.6 illustrates that the net effect of having a bachelor's level of education increased among White and Latin American women. However, the net effect of having a bachelor's level of education declined among Black women from 1.066 in 1960 to .881 in 2000.

Table 9.6    Effects of Education on Logged Wages of Women with a Bachelor's Level of Education by Race and Year

| Race/Model | 1960 | 1970 | 1980 | 1990 | 2000 |
|---|---|---|---|---|---|
| **White Women** | | | | | |
| Model 1: Gross Effect | 0.320** | 0.778** | 0.875** | 1.357** | 1.568** |
| | (0.011) | (0.004) | (0.004) | (0.005) | (0.009) |
| Model 2: Net Effect | 0.092** | 0.479** | 0.378** | 0.574** | 0.489** |
| | (0.008) | (0.003) | (0.003) | (0.004) | (0.007) |
| **Black Women** | | | | | |
| Model 1: Gross Effect | 1.378** | 1.254** | 0.833** | 1.407** | 1.673** |
| | (0.098) | (0.013) | (0.012) | (0.013) | (0.016) |
| Model 2: Net Effect | 1.066** | 0.685** | 0.422** | 0.658** | 0.881** |
| | (0.07) | (0.012) | (0.010) | (0.009) | (0.013) |
| **Latinas** | | | | | |
| Model 1: Gross Effect | 0.457** | 0.843** | 0.866** | 1.293** | 1.418** |
| | (0.011) | (0.004) | (0.004) | (0.005) | (0.006) |
| Model 2: Net Effect | 0.160** | 0.491** | 0.413** | 0.594** | 0.700** |
| | (0.008) | (0.003) | (0.003) | (0.003) | (0.005) |

*Note:* *=$p < .05$; **$p < .005$.

## Summary and Conclusion

This analysis examined the relationship between education, race and ethnicity, wages and time by focusing on workers who are between ages 25–64 and paying close attention to how human capital traits relate to wage disparities among these full-time, work-reliant women. Findings from this study illustrate that cognitive skills do improve wage growth and disparities. However, we also see that these findings have race- and class-specific trajectories. Evidence presented in this chapter that reflects a decreasing significance of postsecondary education among African American women indicate that there is also a need to explore the extent to which the jobs that Black women work have become devalued in recent years.

There is also a need to complement these empirical findings with grounded explanations of how institutional and normative factors have shaped the structure of opportunities available to women workers. Descriptive statistics and multilevel models can identify important factors affecting wage parity; but outcomes such as career mobility are also influenced by state action (Howard 1997) as well as business actions (Appelbaum et al. 2003; Fligstein 2001) that are difficult to measure with survey data. For instance, based on Hall and Farkas's (2011) findings about how employers perceive African American women's assertiveness and confidence, there is a need to gather more empirical evidence that illustrate how cognitive biases about African American women impacts their employment outcomes over time. If the perceived or actual behavioral traits that African American women with advanced education present to employers negatively affects their returns within the workplace it is likely that we could learn a great deal from exploring the motivations and the consequences of work rules as well as the placement and promotion strategies employed by firms that employ them in large numbers. By examining shifts in workplace culture and economic returns in the jobs African American women predominately work we gain an opportunity to learn more about the mechanisms that help create class- and race-specific variations in economic returns to educational investments in the postindustrial era.

# Bibliography

Appelbaum, Eileen, Annette Bernhardt and Richard J. Murnane, editors. 2003. *Low Wage America: How Employers are Reshaping Opportunity in the Workplace.* New York: Russell Sage.

Bernhardt, A., M. Morris, M. Handcock and M. Scott. 2001. *Divergent Paths: Economic Mobility in the New American Labor Market.* New York: Russell Sage Foundation.

———, Martina Morris and Mark S. Handcock. 1995. "Women's Gains or Men's Losses? A Closer Look at the Shrinking Gender Gap in Earnings." *The American Journal of Sociology* 101(2): 302–28.

Bianchi, Suzanne. 1995 "Changing Economic Roles of Women and Men." in *The State of the Union,* ed. Reynolds Farley. New York: Russell Sage Foundation, pp. 202–25.

Blau, Francine D. and Andrea H. Beller. 1992. "Black-White Earnings Over the 1970s and 1980s: Gender Differences in Trends." *The Review of Economics and Statistics* 74(2): 276–86.

Branch, Enobong Hannah. 2011. *Opportunity Denied: Limiting Black Women to Devalued Work.* New Brunswick, NJ : Rutgers University Press.

Browne, Irene. 2000. "Opportunities Lost? Race, Industrial Restructuring, and Employment among Young Women Heading Households." *Social Forces* 78(3): 907–29.

Budig, Michelle J. and England, Paula. 2001 "The Wage Penalty for Motherhood." *American Sociological Review* 66(2): 204–25.

Collins, Patricia Hill. 1990. *Black Feminist Thought: Knowledge, Consciousness, and the Politics of Empowerment.* Boston, MA: Unwin Hyman.

Corcoran, Mary. 1999. "The Economic Progress of African American Women." in *Latinas and African American Women at Work,* ed. I. Browne. New York: Russell Sage Foundation, pp. 35–60.

Danziger, Sheldon and Peter Gottschalk. 1995. *America Unequal.* Cambridge, MA: Harvard University Press.

Darity, William and P. Mason. 1998. "Evidence on Discrimination in Employment: Codes of Color, Codes of Gender." *Journal of Economic Perspectives* 12: 63–90.

——— and S. Myers. 1998. *Persistent Disparity: Race and Economic Inequality in the United States Since 1945.* New York: Edward Elgar Publishing.

Farkas, George, Paula England, Keven Vicknair and Barbara Kilbourne. 1997. "Cognitive Skill, Skill Demands of Jobs, and Earnings among Young European-American, African-American, and Mexican-American Workers." *Social Forces* 75(3): 913–40.

Fligstein, Neil. 2001. *The Architecture of Markets: An Economic Sociology of Twenty-First Century Capitalist Societies.* Princeton, NJ: Princeton University Press.

Fosu, Augustin Kwasi. 1997. "Occupational Gains of Black Women Since the 1964 the Civil Rights Act: Long-Term or Episodic?" *The American Economic Review* 87(2): 311–14.

Gilens, Martin. 1996. "'Race Coding' and White Opposition to Welfare." *American Political Science Review* 90(3): 593–604.

Glass, Jennifer, Marta Tienda and Shelley A. Smith. 1988. "The Impact of Changing Employment Opportunities on Gender and Ethnic Earnings Inequality." *Social Science Research* 17(4): 242–76.

Glenn, Evelyn Nakano. 2002. *Unequal Freedom: How Race and Gender Shaped American Citizenship and Labor.* Cambridge, MA: Harvard University Press.

Goldin, Claudia. 1990. *Understanding the Gender Gap: An Economic History of American Women.* New York: Oxford University Press.

Gordon, Linda. 1994. *Pitied But Not Entitled: Single Mothers and the History of Welfare.* New York: Free Press.

Grodsky, E. and D. Pager. 2001. "The Structure of Disadvantage: Individual and Occupational Determinants of the Black-White Wage Gap." *American Sociological Review* 66: 542–67.

Hall, Matthew and George Farkas. 2011. "Adolescent Cognitive Skills, Attitudinal/Behavioral Traits and Career Wages." *Social Forces* 89(4): 1261–85.

Higginbotham, Elizabeth. 1994. "Black Professional Women: Job Ceilings and Employment Sectors." Pp. 113-131 in *Women of Color in U.S. Society*, eds. Maxine Baca Zinn and Bonnie Thornton Dill. Philadelphia, PA: Temple University Press.

Holzer, H. and M. Stoll. 2002. "Employer Demand for Welfare Recipients by Race." Assessing the New Federalism. Discussion Paper No. 01-07. Washington, DC: Urban Institute.

Howard, Christopher. 1997. *The Hidden Welfare State: Tax Expenditures and Social Policy in the United States.* Princeton, NJ: Princeton University Press.

Hum, Tarry. 2000. "A Protective Niche? Immigrant Ethnic Economies and Labor Market Segmentation." in *Prismatic Metropolis: Inequality in Los Angeles*, eds. Lawrence D. Bobo, Melvin L. Oliver, James H. Johnson Jr. and Abel Valenzuela Jr. New York: Russell Sage Foundation, pp. 279–314.

Hunter, Tera W. 1997. *To 'Joy My Freedom: Southern Black Women's Lives and Labors After the Civil War.* Cambridge, MA: Harvard University Press.

Johnson, Michael R, and Ralph R. Sell. 1976. "The Cost of Being Black: A 1970 Update." *American Journal of Sociology* 82: 183–9.

Jones, Jacqueline. 1985. *Labor of Love, Labor of Sorrow: Black Women, Work, and the Family from Slavery to the Present.* New York: Vintage Books.

***Juhn, C. and K. Murphy. 1997. "Wage Inequality and Family Labor Supply." *Journal of Labor Economics* 15: 72–97.

Kalleberg, A., B. Reskin, and K. Hudson. 2000. "Bad Jobs in America: Standard and Non-Standard Employment Relations and Job Quality in the United States." *American Sociological Review.* 65:256–278.

Kennelly, Ivy. 1999. "'That Single-Mother Element': How White Employers Typify Black Women." *Gender and Society* 13: 168–92.

King, Mary C. 1995. "Human Capital and Black Women's Occupational Mobility." *Industrial Relations* 34(2): 282–98.

———. 1993. "Black Women's Breakthrough into Clerical Work: An Occupational Tipping Model." *Journal of Economic Issues* 27(4): 1097–125.

Malveaux, Julianne. 1986. "Comparable worth and its impact on Black women." in *Slipping Through the Cracks: The Status of Black Women*, eds. Margaret C. Simms and Julianne Malveaux. New Brunswick, NJ: Transaction Books, pp. 40–69.

McCall, Leslie. 2001. "Sources of Racial Wage Inequality in Metropolitan Labor Markets: Racial, Ethnic, and Gender Differences." *American Sociological Review* 66(4): 520–41.

McLafferty, Sara and Valerie Preston. 1992. "Spatial Mismatch and Labor Market Segmentation for African-American and Latina Women." *Economic Geography* 68(4): 406–31.

Melendez, Edwin. 1993. "Latino Race Relations Understanding Poverty." *Sage Abstracts* 3:42.

Mincer, Jacob and Solomon Polachek. 1974. "Family Investments in Human Capital: Earnings of Women." in *Marriage, Family, Human Capital, and Fertility*, ed. Theodore W. Schultz. Cambridge, MA: NBER Books, National Bureau of Economic Research, Inc., pp. 76–111.

Morris, Edward W. 2007. "'Ladies' or 'Loudies'?: Perceptions and Experiences of Black Girls in Classrooms." *Youth & Society* 38(4): 490–515.

Moss, Philip I. 1988. "Employment Gains by Minorities, Women in Large City Government, 1976–83." *Monthly Labor Review* 111: 11.

———, and Chris Tilly. 2001. *Stories Employers Tell: Race, Skill, and Hiring in America.* New York: Russell Sage.

Neal, D. 2004. "The Measured Black-White Gap Among Women Is Too Small." *Journal of Political Economy.* 112: 1–28.

Newsome, Yvonne, and F. Nii-Amoo Dodoo. 2002. "Reversal of Fortune: Explaining the Decline in Black Women's Earnings." *Gender and Society* 16(4): 442–64.

Ortiz, Vilma. 1995. "A Profile of the Demographic and Socio-Economic Characteristics of Latino Families." in *Latino Families: Developing a Paradigm for Research, Practice and Policy*, eds. Ruth Zambrana and Maxine Baca Zinn. Newbury, CA: Sage Publications, pp. 25–50.

Pettit, Becky and Stephanie Ewert. 2009. "Employment Gains and Wage Declines: The Erosion of Black Women's Relative Wages Since 1980." Demography 46(3):469–492.

Reid, L. 2002. "Occupational Segregation, Human Capital, and Motherhood: Black Women's Higher Exit Rates From Full-Time Employment." *Gender and Society* 16: 728–47.

Reskin, Barbara F., and Patricia A. Roos. 1990. *Job Queues, Gender Queues: Explaining Women's Inroads into Male Occupations*. Philadelphia, PA: Temple University Press.

Royster, Deirdre A. 2003. *Race And The Invisible Hand: How White Networks Exclude Black Men From Blue-Collar Jobs*. Berkeley: University of California Press.

Segura, Denise. 1992. "Walking on Eggshells: Chicanas in the Labor Force." in *Hispanic in the Workplace*, eds. Stephen Knouse, Paul Rosenfeld and Amy Culbertson. Newbury, CA: Sage Publications, pp. 173–93.

Smith, Sandra. 2005. "Don't Put My Name on It": Social Capital Activation and Job–Finding Assistance among the Black Urban Poor." *The American Journal of Sociology* 111(1):1–57.

Smith, Vicki. 1998. "The Fractured World of the Temporary Worker: Power, Participation, and Fragmentation in the Contemporary Workplace." *Social Problems* 45(4): 411–30.

Sokoloff, Natalie J. 1992. *Black Women and White Women in the Professions: Occupational Segregation by Race and Gender, 1960–1980*. New York: Routledge.

Spalter-Roth, Roberta, and Cynthia Deitch. 1999. "I Don't Feel Right Sized: I Feel Out Sized: Gender, Race, Ethnicity, and the Unequal Costs of Displacement." *Work and Occupations* 26: 446–82.

Tienda, Marta and Patricia Guhleman. 1985. "The Occupational Position of Employed Hispanic Women." in *Hispanics in the U.S.*, eds. George Borjas and Marta Tienda. New York: Academic Press, pp. 243–74.

———, Shelley A. Smith, and Vilma Ortiz. 1987. "Industrial Restructuring, Gender Segregation and Sex Differences in Earnings." *American Sociological Review* 52: 195–210.

Tilly, Chris. 1996. *Half a Job: Bad and Good Part-Time Jobs in a Changing Labor Market*. Philadelphia, PA: Temple University Press.

Wilkie, Jane Riblett. 1985. "The Decline of Occupational Segregation between Black and White Women." *Race and Ethnic Relations* 4: 67–89.

Wilson, George. 2009. "Downward Mobility of Women from White-Collar Employment: Determinants and Timing by Race." *Sociological Forum* 24(2): 382–401.

Woody, Bette. 1989. *Black Women in the New Services Economy: Help or Hindrance in Economic Self-Sufficiency?* Wellesley, MA: Wellesley College, Center for Research on Women.

# Race, Class and Nativity: A Multilevel Analysis of the Forgotten Working Class, 1980–2009

Lori Latrice Martin, Hayward
Derrick Horton and Teresa A. Booker

Despite some claims that the US has entered a post-racial era there is mounting evidence that the economic divide between blacks and whites is as great today, if not greater, than decades ago (Dawson and Bobo 2009; Gines 2010). Racial disparities in the types and levels of assets owned provide some of the most clear and convincing evidence of the enduring racial divide that has characterized the nation for centuries (Martin 2013; Ozawa and Huan-yui 2000; Todd and Savitskey 2005). The impact of the Great Recession on racial and ethnic minority groups, relative to whites, is one recent example of the continuing significance of race (Allegretto and Pitts 2010; Davis et al. 2012; Katkov 2011). Studies have shown that the overall net worth for Asians, blacks and Hispanics fell more sharply than the overall net worth for whites (Kochhar et al. 2011). While we are only beginning to understand the effects of the Great Recession on the American economy, our understanding of the role that race may or may not have played may be impacted by the limited scope of existing research. For one, research about the impact of the Great Recession on blacks tends to ignore the economic and ethnic diversity that has always characterized the black population (Martin 2013). Also, current studies tend to focus almost exclusively on either overall net worth or home ownership, thus ignoring other key components of the average American's portfolio like savings, stock ownership and real estate beyond the primary residence (Estrada 2006; Freeman 2003; Feeman 2005; Martin 2010; Oliver and Shapiro 2006; Ozawa and Huan-yui 2000). Existing studies also tend to be descriptive in nature (Kochhar et al. 2011). In this chapter, we conduct a multilevel analysis of housing values and interest, dividends and rental income to gain a better understanding of the impact of the Great Recession on blacks, particularly those with membership in the forgotten working-class. The following research questions are examined: 1) Were race and class significant determinants of home ownership, housing values and interest, dividends and rental income before and after the Great Recession? 2) Did other factors, including nativity, explain some of the variations in home ownership, housing values and interest, dividends and rental income, particularly for blacks with membership in the forgotten working–class? 3) Were the predictors of the outcomes under study significantly different for native and foreign-born blacks, and if so, in what ways? 4) What are the theoretical and methodological implications of the study findings?

## The Great Recession

Recessions are, in many ways, a normal part of any business cycle. Recessions describe a period whereby there is a substantial decline in economic activity. The decline is observable not in one particular industry but across the economy. The decline, to qualify as a recession, must last a few months and may be visible in real Gross Domestic Product (GDP). Recessions tend to occur after a period when an economy has enjoyed a relatively high level of activity and then decreases to a relatively low level of activity. However, the Great Recession experienced by millions of Americans was, by all accounts, very different. There were fears that without government intervention the US economy would spiral into the abyss of another Great Depression (Martin 2013).

A number of factors helped bring about the Great Recession which began circa 2007 and ended in 2009. The rise and fall of housing prices was one cause. The sale of financial instruments on Wall Street, which were discovered to be of relatively little value, was another cause. Katkov (2011) cites several other key factors including employment rates and the US as a global economic partner. According to Katkov, employment rates fell in manufacturing and other sectors in the decades leading up to the Great Recession which placed the economy in a very vulnerable position. Millions of manufacturing jobs were lost between 1979 and 2007. At the same time millions of jobs were added in the service and finance industries. Katkov contends there is little need for many jobs in sales when so little is being produced. Such an imbalance places Americans and the health of the economy at risk. Additionally, the role of the US in the global market led to a loss of revenue from imports, the disappearance of manufacturing jobs and a decline in investments at home due to increased investments abroad.

The impact of the Great Recession could have been worse for the nation were it not for affirmative action on the part of the administration of President Barack Obama. Whether the choices made were prudent will be debated for decades to come. There is little debate, however, about whether or not certain groups were disproportionately affected by the recession than others. Whether race or class mattered more, particularly for blacks, is part of a larger ongoing debate in sociology which has filled the pages of hundreds of academic journal articles for decades.

## Race versus Class and the Great Recession

A recent study by the Pew Research Center found that blacks were among the groups hardest hit by the recent economic crisis where overall net worth was concerned (Kochhar et al. 2011). Blacks were also impacted in other key ways. Racial differences in unemployment rates (Allegretto and Pitts 2010) and housing foreclosures (Rugh and Massey 2010) are two areas that have garnered a lot of attention.

Unemployment rates for blacks were higher than for whites well before the Great Recession. In the 1970s unemployment rates for blacks were almost twice as high as the unemployment rates for whites. At its highest point the unemployment rate for blacks in the 1970s was 14.8 percent. The highest point for whites during the same time period was 8.5 percent. A decade later, according to the Bureau of Labor Statistics, black unemployment was about 20 percent. For whites, unemployment rates never exceeded 10 percent during the 1980s. Black unemployment was 14.2 at its highest point in the 1990s, compared to 7.5 for whites. In the years leading up to the Great Recession blacks continued to be unemployed at substantially higher levels than their white counterparts. Such was also the case following the recession. While the unemployment rate for the country peaked near 10 percent in 2009, black unemployment was well over 16 percent. In the case of black youth unemployment, nearly half were unemployed in 2010. Black male unemployment during this same year was 19 percent and black female employment was 13. Data from the bureau also showed that unemployment rates were even higher for college-educated blacks than for college-educated whites following the Great Recession. Blacks with some college education were unemployed at a rate of 12.4 compared to 7.6 for whites. The unemployment rate for blacks with at least a four-year degree was 7.9 compared to 4.3 for whites.

The overrepresentation of blacks in certain industries may help explain why blacks were especially impacted by the recession. About 64 percent of black male workers and almost 76 percent of black women were employed in one of the following sectors leading up to the Great Recession: public administration, education and health services, wholesale and retail trade, manufacturing and professional and business services (Allegretto and Pitts 2010). Blacks are unemployed at higher rates than whites and are over-represented in certain sectors due to a number of factors, including racial discrimination and prejudice (Prager et al. 2009).

Not only did the labor-force participation of blacks place the group at risk in the years leading up to the Great Recession, the fact that some blacks were targeted by financial lending institutions was another contributing factor. The National Association of the Advance of Colored People (NAACP) found that blacks were 30 percent more likely to receive high-interest rate loans than whites. This was the case for black and white borrowers with identical qualifications. The findings were consistent across the income spectrum. The US Department of Housing and Urban Development (HUD) also found that blacks were over-represented in the receiving of subprime loans. The overrepresentation of blacks receiving subprime loans could be described as an epidemic since blacks across the country were impacted. In the case of New York City, subprime financing accounted for a quarter of all loans in more than 50 percent of census tracts. Moreover, black neighborhoods were home to nearly half of all the subprime lending in the entire city (Martin 2013).

Despite these findings, some have theorized that race has declined in significance while others contend that the old racism that dominated American society has simply been replaced by the new racism; also known as "colorblind racism" (Bonilla-Silva 2014). If race has declined in significance it should no longer be a factor in determining variations in the levels and types of assets owned. The present study tests these frameworks by examining whether or not race alone accounts for the observed variations or whether other social and demographic variables account for the differences in the levels of interest, dividends, rental income and housing values, as well as or in addition to the likelihood of owning a home, a savings account, stocks or rental property beyond the primary residence. Social class position and nativity are among the factors that have not been adequately studied. These variables are particularly important in understanding racial social stratification.

## Economic and Ethnic Diversity within the Black Population

The black population has always been ethnically and economically diverse; however, sociologists have often ignored this fact (Dodoo 1997; Fu 2007; Martin 2010, 2013; Robinson, 2010). The black middle class and the underclass receive a lion's share of attention in the literature despite the finding that blacks, historically, are more likely to be working class and despite the fact that middle-class blacks are less secure of maintaining their middle-class status than most other racial groups in America (Horton et al. 2000). Although some scholars have devoted attention to the black working class (Arena, 2005, 2011) far more research is needed.

That Blacks hail from virtually every corner of the globe is also often overlooked. Most sociologists have all but abandoned examinations of the experiences of black immigrants in America (Alba 1995; Dodoo 1997). An exception may be found in a recent article by Fu (2007) which explores intermarriage and pan-ethnicity in the US. Some in the popular press have focused on ethnic diversity within the black population and some have even hailed black immigrants as a modern-day model minority (Robinson 2010). The failure to empirically consider the economic and ethnic diversity that characterizes and shapes the black experience in America has limited our understanding as it relates to economic inequality in contemporary America. This point is especially important as we continue to explore risk factors surrounding the Great Recession and as we seek to predict ways of limiting the effects of subsequent economic downturns on vulnerable populations in the decades that follow.

## Data and Methods

Understanding the determinants of home ownership and housing values, interest, dividends and rental income for individuals with membership in the working class is key, especially for the black working class. To that end, we analyzed Public Use Microdata for 1980, 1990, 2000 and 2009 which allows us to explore a host of economic and social variables as they relate to the dependent variables selected. Specifically, we were able to determine the race, gender, age, educational attainment, marital status, social class position, number of children, region and nativity of respondents leading up to the Great Recession and for the time period associated with the recession's end. All respondents were at least 25 years of age and identified as the head of household.

We compared non-Hispanic black and white respondents. We created a series of dummy variables for gender, marital status, region, nativity and social class position. These variables have consistently been shown to explain variations in the overall economic well-being of racial groups in America. We compared males and females, and married with non-married. In our analysis we also compared respondents living in the Northeast, Midwest and West with respondents in the South. Following the methodological approach used by Horton et al. (2000), we also created dummy variables to measure social class position: middle class, working class and bottom class.

We analyzed the data using logistic regression analysis and hierarchical linear modeling. Additionally, we used logistic regression analysis as it is an appropriate methodological approach for analyses where the dependent variable is dichotomous. Since our objectives include explaining variations in the likelihood of homeownership and the likelihood of having interest, dividends and rental income, logistic regression analysis is appropriate. The first set of models examined the variations in home ownership for blacks and whites with membership in the working class. A separate model was estimated for each of the years under consideration. The next set of models also focused on homeownership, but was restricted to native-born blacks. Again, separate models were estimated for 1980, 1990, 2000 and 2009. We then fit models for foreign-born blacks in the working class for the same time periods. We employed the same strategy for understanding variations in the likelihood of having interest, dividends and rental income for the working class by race and then by nativity.

To assess variations in housing values and interest, dividends and rental income we used hierarchical linear modeling. Specifically, we estimate a series of random intercept models. We expected that variations in housing values and interest, dividends and rental income may exist not only at the household level, but at the metropolitan level, given the role of the housing market, for example, in precipitating the Great Recession. We estimated models for blacks and whites in the working class and then we estimated models for blacks in the working class by nativity. Separate models were estimated for 1980, 1990, 2000 and 2009.

The values for housing and interest, dividends and income were adjusted for inflation to allow for comparability over time.[1] We included the use of log transformations for the dependent variables housing values and interest, dividends and rental income for better model fits.

# Findings

We found similarities and differences between blacks and whites by social class. For example, we found that between 1980 and 2009 whites in the working class had the highest number of children of all social groups. For blacks, respondents with membership in the middle class had the highest number of children (See Tables 10.1a and 10.1b). For blacks and whites, respondents with membership in the bottom class were older than respondents in either the middle or working classes. Whites, regardless of class, were older than their black counterparts. Whites also reported higher levels of education than blacks in each of the years considered and for each of the socioeconomic groups explored. Blacks and whites in the middle class had higher levels of education than their counterparts in either the working or bottom classes.

Housing values and interest, dividends and rental income were greater for whites than for blacks, regardless of social class position both before and after the Great Recession. On average, middle-class whites had homes valued around $176,000 in 1980, compared to middle-class blacks with housing values of about $119,000. In the years before the Great Recession housing values for middle-class whites exceeded $205,000 compared to only $135,000 for comparable blacks. As the recession came to a close, in 2009, housing values for whites in the middle class was almost $273,000 compared to just under $193,000 for blacks.

Disparities were also evident for those with membership in the working class. Working-class whites had homes valued about $121,000 in 1980, $123,000 in 1990, nearly $130,000 in 2000 and over $170,000 in 2009. For working-class blacks, housing values were, on average, less than $81,000 in 1980, about $88,000 in 1990, $94,000 in 2000 and about $135,000 in 2009.

We took a closer look at social class position for blacks by nativity. We found that foreign-born blacks had higher levels of membership in the middle class than native-born blacks in 1980, 1990, 2000 and 2009. More foreign-born respondents reported that they were working class than native-born blacks between 1980 and 2000. More native-born respondents reported being members of the bottom class than foreign-born respondents in each year. As expected, blacks (regardless of nativity) were overwhelmingly represented among the working class than either the bottom or middle class. In the decade before the Great Recession 55.56 percent of native-born black respondents were working class, compared to 62.12 percent of foreign-born respondents. By 2009 52.76 percent of native-born blacks were working class and 62.20 percent of foreign-born blacks were working class. See Table 10.2 below.

---

1    1999 constant dollars.

145

**Table 10.1a  Means and Standard Deviations for Blacks by Social Class, 1980–2009**

| | 1980 | | | 1990 | | | 2000 | | | 2009 | | |
|---|---|---|---|---|---|---|---|---|---|---|---|---|
| | Middle Class | Working Class | Bottom Class | Middle Class | Working Class | Bottom Class | Middle Class | Working Class | Bottom Class | Middle Class | Working Class | Bottom Class |
| No. of Children | 1.28 (1.41) | 1.45 (1.58) | 1.06 (1.60) | 1.11 (1.20) | 1.26 (1.32) | 0.89 (1.32) | 1.02 (1.17) | 1.12 (1.25) | 0.74 (1.11) | 0.87 (1.12) | 0.93 (1.18) | 0.54 (0.99) |
| Age | 41.38 (11.98) | 42.87 (13.05) | 57.28 (17.11) | 42.58 (11.62) | 43.80 (12.80) | 59.27 (17.78) | 43.26 (11.28) | 44.14 (12.22) | 60.43 (16.89) | 46.30 (11.85) | 47.33 (12.57) | 62.92 (15.82) |
| Education | 7.25 (1.82) | 6.03 (2.08) | 4.21 (2.14) | 7.82 (1.36) | 6.80 (1.77) | 5.10 (2.24) | 7.98 (1.10) | 7.24 (1.43) | 5.83 (2.14) | 8.36 (2.10) | 7.05 (2.06) | 5.62 (2.37) |
| Occupational Score | 39.77 (6.60) | 23.34 (4.02) | 2.85 (4.82) | 39.98 (6.61) | 23.27 (4.27) | 2.51 (4.70) | 41.43 (6.40) | 23.55 (4.73) | 2.38 (4.89) | 41.65 (6.44) | 23.43 (4.85) | 2.09 (4.63) |
| Income | $39,510.66 ($26,306.35) | $25,888.34 ($18,361.08) | $9,943.95 ($4,335.63) | $42,493.54 ($33,899.57) | $25,123.87 ($19,852.85) | $9,898.67 ($10,530.37) | $44,791.44 ($43,441.13) | $28,191.97 ($28,645.58) | $12,879.60 ($19,566.16) | $45,537.13 ($43,697.91) | $26,611.80 ($23,589.12) | $13,122.38 ($14,720.97) |
| Housing Value | $119,093.50 ($79,927.91) | $80,959.45 ($23,974.93) | $57,523.89 ($10,032.64) | $138,479.15 ($110,261.67) | $88,288.66 ($77,808.60) | $66,302.28 ($67,996.43) | $135,424.62 ($115,361.75) | $94,018.04 ($82,882.27) | $78,903.84 ($86,196.16) | $192,720.11 ($208,633.75) | $134,503.25 ($159,237.14) | $118,242.44 ($175,697.83) |
| Interest, Dividends and Rental Income | $674.60 ($4,844.78) | $264.47 ($2,510.93) | $218.89 ($2,145.61) | $787.18 ($4,441.66) | $276.86 ($2,207.57) | $276.76 ($2,223.31) | $946.35 ($7,903.85) | $415.10 ($4,897.74) | $586.62 ($6,410.21) | $785.47 ($7,117.71) | $263.61 ($3,907.12) | $408.45 ($5,124.03) |
| Business Income | $2,612.45 $(14,057.82) | $562.99 ($5,100.28) | $76.30 ($1,895.84) | $2,301.06 $(13,765.61) | $612.87 ($5,285.84) | $98.07 ($1,775.36) | $2,025.33 ($15,445.08) | $805.60 ($7,910.02) | $248.32 ($3,733.30) | $1,576.60 ($12,839.61) | $667.81 ($6,216.62) | $241.30 ($3,262.47) |

*Source:* Public Use Microdata Samples (PUMS) of the US Census for years 1990, 2000 and 2009.

**Table 10.1b  Means and Standard Deviations for Whites by Social Class, 1980–2009**

| | 1980 | | | 1990 | | | 2000 | | | 2009 | | |
|---|---|---|---|---|---|---|---|---|---|---|---|---|
| | Middle Class | Working Class | Bottom Class | Middle Class | Working Class | Bottom Class | Middle Class | Working Class | Bottom Class | Middle Class | Working Class | Bottom Class |
| No. of Children | 1.099 (1.25) | 1.05 (1.25) | 0.41 (0.92) | 0.94 (1.12) | 0.93 (1.12) | 0.35 (0.81) | 0.88 (1.12) | 0.84 (1.10) | 0.29 (0.72) | 0.78 (1.08) | 0.74 (1.05) | 0.29 (0.75) |
| Age | 44.96 (13.06) | 45.19 (14.10) | 65.94 (15.46) | 45.43 (12.91) | 45.57 (13.89) | 67.48 (15.46) | 46.43 (12.29) | 46.60 (13.13) | 68.90 (15.00) | 49.19 (12.64) | 49.52 (13.19) | 69.29 (14.95) |
| Education | 7.69 (1.51) | 6.01 (1.92) | 5.28 (2.27) | 8.05 (1.20) | 7.19 (1.58) | 5.99 (2.15) | 8.16 (1.03) | 7.51 (1.34) | 6.60 (1.94) | 8.66 (2.08) | 7.53 (2.11) | 6.55 (2.36) |
| Occupational Score | 41.07 (7.52) | 24.93 (4.01) | 2.45 (4.92) | 41.30 (7.61) | 24.87 (4.16) | 2.08 (4.59) | 42.37 (7.39) | 24.96 (4.67) | 1.67 (4.22) | 42.47 (7.33) | 24.63 (4.54) | 1.40 (3.87) |
| Income | $57,620.50 ($37,632.97) | $35,764.32 ($22,897.82) | $18,461.12 ($20,001.19) | $63,384.47 ($54,972.67) | $35,187.55 ($27,247.06) | $19,617.38 ($19,495.04) | $69,462.05 ($73,246.40) | $37,567.60 ($34,859.45) | $24,588.11 ($31,434.25) | $66,408.23 ($69,941.13) | $34,784.13 ($32,316.29) | $22,055.14 ($27,436.26) |
| Housing Value | $175,861.50 ($100,294.41) | $121,247.40 ($72,918.85) | $101,726.97 ($76,431.39) | $192,368 ($140,278.91) | $123,064.70 ($104,794.23) | $108,127.68 ($104,363.56) | $205,257.85 ($180,137.05) | $129,800.79 (161,180.24) | $126,824.44 ($134,403.11) | $272,605.73 ($335,679.14) | $172,285.77 ($198,886.89) | $180,176.65 ($275,476.29) |
| Interests, Dividends and Rental Income | $3,684.22 ($12,884.23) | $1,566.43 ($6,378.65) | $4,303.24 ($12,611.84) | $4,137.06 ($12,093.87) | $1,762.89 ($6,759.75) | $5,119.83 ($12,410.07) | $4,722.00 ($19,208.04) | $1,830.77 ($10,708.00) | $6,308.53 ($20,850.95) | $37,803.06 ($18,574.26) | $1,369.14 ($9,962.63) | $5,073.36 ($20,376.06) |
| Business Income | $6442.05 ($23,768.58) | $2,049.68 ($10,718.95) | $265.35 ($3,969.69) | $6,068.81 ($24,021.39) | $2,208.35 ($11,239.70) | $204.07 ($3,334.63) | $6,140.71 ($29,733.82) | $2,401 ($14,050.62) | $1,050.73 ($9,364.88) | $4,994.03 ($25,463.93) | $1,814.33 ($11,445.21) | $811.15 ($8,302.05) |

*Source:* Public Use Microdata Samples (PUMS) of the US Census for years 1990, 2000, and 2009.

**Table 10.2     Blacks and Social Class Position by Nativity, 1980–2009**

|  | 1980 | | 1990 | | 2000 | | 2009 | |
|---|---|---|---|---|---|---|---|---|
|  | Native | Foreign | Native | Foreign | Native | Foreign | Native | Foreign |
| Middle Class | 8.93 | 12.93 | 10.28 | 17.72 | 13.77 | 20.26 | 14.51 | 19.55 |
| Working Class | 57.78 | 63.66 | 56.86 | 65.25 | 55.56 | 62.12 | 52.76 | 62.20 |
| Bottom Class | 33.28 | 23.40 | 32.86 | 17.03 | 30.67 | 17.63 | 32.73 | 18.25 |

*Source:* Public Use Microdata Samples (PUMS) of the US Census for years 1990, 2000 and 2009.

Table 10.3 includes the results of the descriptive analysis we restricted to blacks in the working class by nativity. In each year, with the exception of 1980, foreign-born blacks in the working class reported having more children than native-born blacks. We also found that, on average, native-born blacks were relatively older than foreign-born blacks in 1980, 1990, 2000 and 2009. At the same time, the results show that foreign-born blacks had higher levels of education than native-born blacks, both prior to and following the Great Recession.

Our findings also indicate that housing values were higher for foreign-born blacks in the working class over the past few decades than for native-born blacks in the working class. Housing values for foreign-born blacks in the working class were $105,402.20 in 1980 while the housing values for similar native-born blacks were $80,443.21 during the same year. By 2000 housing values were, on average, nearly $150,000 for foreign-born blacks in the working class and only about $90,000 for native-born blacks in the same social class. Nine years later housing values for foreign-born blacks in the working class exceeded $200,000 and housing values for native-born blacks in the working class was only $125,515.

Differences on interest, dividends and rental income between native- and foreign-born blacks in the working class were observed between 1980 and 2009. Again, foreign-born blacks fared better although the gap between the two groups was not as great. For example, foreign-born blacks in the working class had interest, dividends and rental income of about $354 in 1980, $445.91 in 1990, $649.42 in 2000 and $394.30 in 2009. Native-born blacks in the working class reported interest, dividends and rental income in 1980 of about $261. By 1990, this group reported interest, dividends and rental income that was, on average, $267.02. Prior to the Great Recession native-born blacks in the working class had interest, dividends and rental income in the amount of $395. The average income, dividends and rental income for native-born blacks in the working class was only $246.78 in 2009. On average, neither foreign-born nor native-born blacks in the working class saw declines in the value of their homes at the end of the recession. However, they did experience declines in their levels of interest, dividends and rental income. Our results also showed that, while the percentage of native-born black homeowners in the working class stay about the same between 1980 and 2009, the percentages of foreign-born blacks in the working class steadily grew (see Table 10.4).

Tables 10.5–10.9 include results of the logistic regression analyses. Table 10.5 shows that, even after controlling for nativity, age, gender, region, education, marital status and number of children, blacks in the working class were less likely to own homes when compared with similar whites between 1980 and 2009. Table 10.6 displays the determinants of home ownership for native-born blacks in the working class. The next table, Table 10.7, shows similar results for foreign-born blacks in the working class on homeowners.

**Table 10.3    Means and Standard Deviations for Blacks in the Working Class by Nativity, 1980–2009**

| | 1980 | | 1990 | | 2000 | | 2009 | |
|---|---|---|---|---|---|---|---|---|
| | Foreign | Native | Foreign | Native | Foreign | Native | Foreign | Native |
| No. of Children | 1.33 (1.50) | 1.45 (1.58) | 1.31 (1.37) | 1.26 (1.32) | 1.27 (1.33) | 1.11 (1.25) | 1.18 (1.31) | 0.90 (1.16) |
| Age | 41.67 (12.21) | 42.92 (13.08) | 42.07 (11.95) | 43.90 (12.84) | 43.64 (11.19) | 44.19 (12.03) | 46.41 (11.79) | 47.54 (12.66) |
| Education | 6.43 (2.06) | 6.01 (2.08) | 7.00 (1.93) | 6.79 (1.75) | 7.31 (1.69) | 7.24 (1.04) | 7.30 (2.40) | 7.02 (2.01) |
| Occupational Score | 23.01 (4.28) | 23.35 (4.07) | 22.93 (4.54) | 23.29 (4.25) | 22.97 (5.00) | 23.60 (4.70) | 22.71 (5.04) | 23.52 (20.40) |
| Income | $25,074.61 ($17,690.81) | $25,923.06 ($18,388.38) | $27,400.96 ($19,997.62) | $24,991.33 ($19,836.39) | $30,176.35 ($29,001.15) | $28,021.73 ($28,608.52) | $28,722.32 ($23,345.40) | $26,339.91 ($23,606.84) |
| Housing Value | $105,402.20 ($59,416.33) | $80,443.21 ($55,275.73) | $170,965.80 ($101,780.74) | $84,724.30 ($74,584.81) | $148,952.32 ($94,989.12) | $89,993.91 ($80,464.46) | $206,852.57 ($194,743.37) | $125,515.43 ($151,872.89) |
| Interest, Dividends and Rental Income | $354.44 ($2,165.82) | $260.63 ($2,524.54) | $445.91 ($2,282.98) | $267.02 ($2,161.37) | $649.42 ($6,052.87) | $395.00 ($4,785.15) | $394.30 ($4,830.63) | $246.78 ($3,771.47) |

*Source:* Public Use Microdata Samples (PUMS) of the US Census for years 1990, 2000 and 2009.

**Table 10.4    Blacks and Home Ownership in the Working Class by Nativity, 1980–2009**

| | 1980 | | 1990 | | 2000 | | 2009 | |
|---|---|---|---|---|---|---|---|---|
| | Native | Foreign | Native | Foreign | Native | Foreign | Native | Foreign |
| Owner | 51.33 | 35.19 | 51.20 | 37.92 | 51.10 | 43.63 | 51.98 | 50.13 |
| Renter | 48.67 | 64.81 | 48.80 | 62.08 | 48.90 | 56.37 | 48.02 | 49.87 |

*Source:* Public Use Microdata Samples (PUMS) of the US Census for years 1990, 2000 and 2009.

**Table 10.5** **Logistic Regression Analysis for Blacks and Whites in the Working-Class for Homeownership, 1980-2009**

|  | 1980 | 1990 | 2000 | 2009 |
|---|---|---|---|---|
| Intercept | -5.3241*** | -5.4616*** | -5.1805*** | -5.0723*** |
| Black | -0.7851*** | -0.7967*** | -0.8528*** | -0.9501*** |
| Foreign | -0.4740*** | -0.4257*** | -0.5701*** | -0.4267*** |
| Age | 0.1726*** | 0.1770*** | 0.1593*** | 0.1515*** |
| Age$^2$ | -0.00134*** | -0.00128*** | -0.00112*** | -0.00102*** |
| Female | -0.0371*** | -0.1387*** | -0.1140*** | -0.0661*** |
| Northeast | -0.4235*** | -0.1875*** | -0.2605*** | -0.1893*** |
| Midwest | 0.0743*** | 0.0774*** | 0.0308*** | 0.0768*** |
| West | -0.3156*** | -0.4498*** | -0.5399*** | -0.5302*** |
| Education | 0.0930*** | 0.0970*** | 0.1328*** | 0.1372*** |
| Married | 1.4283*** | 1.2584*** | 1.2838*** | 1.3920*** |
| No. of Children | 0.1789*** | 0.0931*** | 0.0967*** | 0.0803*** |
| Likelihood Ratio | 367,037.551*** | 402,446.178*** | 406,970.626*** | 91,266.1782*** |
| N | 1,763,687 | 2,010,652 | 2,077,147 | 446,898 |

*Note:* * p < 0.05; ** p < 0.01; *** p < 0.001; **** p < 0.0001.
*Source:* Public Use Microdata Samples (PUMS) of the US Census for years 1990, 2000 and 2009.

**Table 10.6** **Logistic Regression Analysis for Native-Born Blacks in the Working-Class for Homeownership, 1980–2009**

|  | 1980 | 1990 | 2000 | 2009 |
|---|---|---|---|---|
| Intercept | -6.5262*** | -6.9074*** | -5.9377*** | -6.1182*** |
| Age | 0.1799*** | 0.1917*** | 0.1414*** | 0.1313*** |
| Age$^2$ | -0.00130*** | -0.00130*** | -0.00086*** | -0.00074*** |
| Female | -0.0788*** | -0.2668*** | -0.1792*** | -0.1133*** |
| Northeast | -0.8452*** | -0.8626*** | -0.8000*** | -0.7159*** |
| Midwest | -0.1481*** | -0.2770*** | -0.3436*** | -0.3955*** |
| West | -0.3928*** | -0.7322*** | -0.8129*** | -0.8751*** |
| Education | 0.1482*** | 0.1551*** | 0.1941*** | 0.2280*** |
| Married | 1.3214*** | 1.1623*** | 1.1247*** | 1.3062*** |
| No. of Children | 0.1078*** | 0.0519*** | 0.0463*** | 0.0277** |
| Likelihood Ratio | 48,112.7258*** | 51,975.1370*** | 53,163.1661*** | 12,649.9863*** |
| N | 210,552 | 104,586 | 261,957 | 52,032 |

*Note:* * p < 0.05; ** p < 0.01; *** p < 0.001; **** p < 0.0001.
*Source:* Public Use Microdata Samples (PUMS) of the US Census for years 1990, 2000 and 2009

Notable differences were observed where gender was concerned. For the most part, the effects of age, region, education, marital status and number of children were directionally similar between 1980 and 2009. Gender was a significant predictor of homeownership for native-born blacks in the working class in each of the decades, but it was not a significant predictor of homeownership for foreign-born blacks in the working class in 1980 or in 1990. By 2000, in the decade leading up to the recession, foreign-born black women in the working class were more likely to own homes than their similar male counterparts, net of the effect of social and demographic variables included in the model. Native-born black women in the working class were less likely to own homes than their male counterparts in 1980, 1990, 2000 and 2009. The findings point to potential differences in the experiences of native- and foreign-born female heads of household with membership in the working class. Foreign-born females may have access to assets that are not as accessible to native-born females, which explains at least part of the observed differences.

**Table 10.7    Logistic Regression Analysis for Foreign-Born Blacks in the Working Class for Homeownership, 1980–2009**

|  | 1980 | 1990 | 2000 | 2009 |
|---|---|---|---|---|
| Intercept | -6.5275*** | -8.3030*** | -5.8001*** | -5.6565*** |
| Age | 0.1846*** | 0.2309*** | 0.1290*** | 0.1270*** |
| Age² | -0.00139*** | -0.00175*** | -0.00077*** | -0.00073*** |
| Female | -0.0604 | 0.0439 | 0.0714* | 0.2353*** |
| Northeast | -0.6099*** | -0.5599*** | -0.4604*** | -0.6748*** |
| Midwest | -0.02089* | -0.2578*** | -0.5256*** | -0.7006*** |
| West | -0.3683** | -0.6111*** | -0.6881*** | -0.7959*** |
| Education | 0.0538*** | 0.1425*** | 0.1473*** | 0.1532*** |
| Married | 0.9289*** | 0.8968*** | 0.7282*** | 0.7172*** |
| No. of Children | 0.2258*** | 0.1372*** | 0.2077*** | 0.1854*** |
| Likelihood Ratio | 1,593.9097*** | 2,312.4241 | 3,286.8964*** | 115.1484*** |
| N | 8,985 | 12,475 | 22,474 | 6,703 |

*Note:* * p < 0.05; ** p < 0.01; *** p < 0.001; **** p < 0.0001.
*Source:* Public Use Microdata Samples (PUMS) of the US Census for years 1990, 2000 and 2009.

Tables 10.8–10.10 contain the results of the logistic regression analyses on the dependent variable interest, dividends and rental income. The results, as shown in Table 10.8, show that between 1980 and 2009, blacks in the working class were less likely to have interest, dividends and rental income when compared with similar whites. Racial disparities in the likelihood of having interest, dividends and rental income were found in 1980, 1990, 2000 and 2009.

**Table 10.8    Logistic Regression Analysis for Blacks and Whites in the Working Class for Interests, Dividends and Rental Income, 1980–2009**

|  | 1980 | 1990 | 2000 | 2009 |
|---|---|---|---|---|
| Intercept | -4.4922*** | -4.9000*** | -6.7026*** | -5.7863*** |
| Black | -1.5327*** | -1.4292*** | -1.2612*** | -1.2489*** |
| Foreign | 0.0776*** | 0.0182* | -0.0347*** | -0.1403*** |
| Age | 0.0423*** | 0.0309*** | 0.0505*** | 0.0523*** |
| Age2 | -0.00003*** | 0.000074 | -0.00005*** | -0.00007*** |
| Female | 0.0698*** | -0.0402*** | -0.0989*** | -0.2834*** |
| Northeast | 0.3918*** | 0.3680*** | 0.3463*** | 0.2351*** |
| Midwest | 0.4085*** | 0.3127*** | 0.3057*** | 0.1519*** |
| West | 0.0986*** | 0.1104*** | 0.1444*** | 0.1347*** |
| Education | 0.2764*** | 0.3450*** | 0.4391*** | 0.2554*** |
| Married | 0.3906*** | 0.2868*** | 0.2806*** | 0.1127*** |
| No. of Children | -0.1598*** | -0.1492*** | -0.1173*** | -0.1047*** |
| Likelihood Ratio | 262,476.459*** | 271,697.326*** | 290,902.164*** | 49,531.4560*** |
| N | 1,763,687 | 2,010,652 | 2,077,147 | 446,898 |

*Note:* * $p < 0.05$; ** $p < 0.01$; *** $p < 0.001$; **** $p < 0.0001$.
*Source:* Public Use Microdata Samples (PUMS) of the US Census for years 1990, 2000 and 2009

**Table 10.9    Logistic Regression Analysis for Native-Born Blacks in the Working Class for Interests, Dividends and Rental Income, 1980–2009**

|  | 1980 | 1990 | 2000 | 2009 |
|---|---|---|---|---|
| Intercept | -6.4292*** | -7.1507*** | -7.9862*** | -7.6147*** |
| Age | 0.0619*** | 0.0525*** | 0.0555*** | 0.0623*** |
| Age2 | -0.00026*** | -0.00016*** | -0.00014*** | -0.00019 |
| Female | -0.00705 | -0.1959*** | -0.1809*** | -0.3207*** |
| Northeast | 0.3108*** | 0.4775*** | 0.2479*** | 0.2927*** |
| Midwest | 0.3519*** | 0.3003*** | 0.1697*** | 0.0921 |
| West | 0.2059*** | 0.3129*** | 0.1829*** | 0.2202*** |
| Education | 0.2810*** | 0.3924*** | 0.4478*** | 0.3008*** |
| Married | 0.4758*** | 0.3919*** | 0.3315*** | 0.2486*** |
| No. of Children | -0.1549*** | -0.1876*** | -0.1574*** | -0.1418*** |
| Likelihood Ratio | 9,004.6233*** | 11,286.0790*** | 11,912.0810*** | 2,072.4339*** |
| N | 210,552 | 214,324 | 261,957 | 52,032 |

*Note:* * $p < 0.05$; ** $p < 0.01$; *** $p < 0.001$; **** $p < 0.0001$.
*Source:* Public Use Microdata Samples (PUMS) of the US Census for years 1990, 2000 and 2009.

**Table 10.10    Logistic Regression Analysis for Foreign-Born Blacks in the Working Class for Interests, Dividends and Rental Income, 1980–2009**

|  | 1980 | 1990 | 2000 | 2009 |
|---|---|---|---|---|
| Intercept | -6.3990*** | -6.3915*** | -5.7476*** | -6.4204*** |
| Age | 0.1103*** | 0.0746*** | 0.0508*** | 0.0598* |
| Age$^2$ | -0.00077*** | -0.00043** | -0.00016 | -0.00022 |
| Female | -0.2389** | -0.0994 | -0.2105*** | -0.3484** |
| Northeast | 0.4295*** | 0.2749*** | 0.1901*** | 0.3146** |
| Midwest | 0.3426* | 0.1362 | 0.0518 | -0.3873 |
| West | 0.1594 | 0.0117 | 0.1556 | -0.1116* |
| Education | 0.1492*** | 0.2746*** | 0.2288*** | 0.2034*** |
| Married | 0.1621 | 0.2335*** | 0.1130* | 0.1368 |
| No. of Children | -0.0810*** | -0.0766*** | -0.0403* | -0.1133* |
| Likelihood Ratio | 300.6313*** | 476.3064*** | 584.3291*** | 196.2001*** |
| N | 8,985 | 12,475 | 22,474 | 6,703 |

*Note:* * $p < 0.05$; ** $p < 0.01$; *** $p < 0.001$; **** $p < 0.0001$.
*Source:* Public Use Microdata Samples (PUMS) of the U.S. Census for years 1990, 2000 and 2009.

Age and education had positive effects on the likelihood of both native- and foreign-born blacks in the working class possessing interest, dividends and rental income between 1980 and 2009. Married respondents, regardless of nativity, had greater odds of having the dependent variable than non-married respondents over time. As the number of children increased, the likelihood of having interest, dividends and rental income decreased for native- and foreign-born blacks in the working class between 1980 and 2009.

Gender was not a significant determinant of interest, dividends and rental income for native-born blacks in the working class in 1980. However, between 1990 and 2009 native-born black women in the working class were significantly less likely to possess interest, dividends and rental income than their male counterparts. For foreign-born black women in this social class there was no statistically significant difference between them and their male counterparts. However, in the decades leading up to the Great Recession foreign-born black women were less likely to own interest, dividends and rental income than similar males.

Native-born black respondents in the working class in the South were less likely to have interest, dividends and rental income than similar blacks in other regions. For foreign-born blacks in the working class this was the case for those living in the Northeast. For the most part, region was not a statistically significant predictor of interest, dividends and rental income for foreign-born blacks in the working class.

The results of the multivariate analyses are presented in Tables 10.11–10.15. The results show that, for the analyses conducted on housing values and on the levels of interest, dividends and rental income, hierarchical linear modeling is appropriate because variations exist at the metropolitan statistical area level.

Table 10.11 Multivariate Analysis of (log) Housing Values for Black and Whites in the Working Class, 1980–2009

| | 1980 | 1990 | 2000 | 2009 |
|---|---|---|---|---|
| Intercept | 10.2000*** | 9.5751*** | 9.2925*** | 16.5754*** |
| Black | -0.3792** | -0.2832*** | -0.2696*** | 0.6067*** |
| Foreign | 0.1242*** | 0.1947*** | 0.1380*** | 0.2296*** |
| Age | 0.01828*** | 0.03771*** | 0.02468*** | -0.1123*** |
| Age$^2$ | -0.00019*** | -0.00029*** | -0.00018*** | 0.000785*** |
| Female | 0.02287*** | 0.02588*** | -0.01246*** | -0.00239 |
| Northeast | 0.1929*** | 0.5695*** | 0.2926*** | 0.2505*** |
| Midwest | 0.0387*** | -0.09343*** | 0.09042*** | -0.08719*** |
| West | 0.3689*** | 0.2121*** | 0.4176*** | 0.6747*** |
| Education | 0.09519*** | 0.1264*** | 0.1402*** | -0.01755*** |
| Married | 0.2053*** | 0.2965*** | 0.30301*** | -0.7419*** |
| No. of Children | 0.002785*** | 0.01791*** | 0.02687*** | -0.02524*** |
| Between MSA Variance | 0.04438*** | 0.1224*** | 0.07480*** | 0.09633*** |
| Within MSA Variance | 0.2758*** | 0.4728*** | 0.4855*** | 33.3291*** |
| -2 Log Likelihood | 1,464,699 | 2,933,317 | 3,346,875 | 1,806,175 |
| MSAs | 256 | 250 | 284 | 285 |
| N | 944,208 | 1,403,606 | 14,739,920 | 446,898 |

*Source:* Public Use Microdata Samples (PUMS) of the US Census for years 1990, 2000 and 2009.

Table 10.12 Multivariate Analysis of (log) Interest, Dividend and Rental Income for Black and Whites in the Working Class, 1980–2009

| | 1980 | 1990 | 2000 | 2009 |
|---|---|---|---|---|
| Intercept | 2.2853*** | 2.9801*** | 3.1305*** | 3.2946*** |
| Black | -0.3196*** | -0.5335*** | -0.2569*** | -0.3323*** |
| Foreign | 0.2663*** | 0.2739*** | 0.2315*** | 0.3258*** |
| Age | 0.1133*** | 0.09034*** | 0.04896*** | 0.04250*** |
| Age$^2$ | -0.00056*** | -0.00031*** | -00000368 | 0.000045 |
| Female | -0.03414*** | -0.1103*** | -0.1545*** | -0.1121*** |
| Northeast | 0.07771*** | 0.03800*** | -0.09373*** | -0.08050* |
| Midwest | -0.05070*** | -0.1045*** | -0.1286*** | -0.1694*** |
| West | 0.1680*** | 0.07298*** | 0.1452*** | 0.2227*** |
| Education | 0.08203*** | 0.1202*** | 0.1424*** | 0.09140*** |
| Married | -0.00060 | 0.07638*** | 0.01965** | 0.07241*** |
| No. of Children | -0.09160*** | -0.1095*** | -0.03979*** | -0.01730 |
| Between MSA Variance | 0.02191*** | 0.03339*** | 0.04343*** | 0.06255*** |
| Within MSA Variance | 2.5348*** | 3.0969*** | 4.1332 | 5.1719*** |
| -2 Log Likelihood | 2,381,339 | 2,669,826 | 2,412,606 | 384,077.2 |
| MSAs | 256 | 250 | 284 | 285 |
| N | 631,841 | 672,642 | 566,601 | 85,648 |

*Source:* Public Use Microdata Samples (PUMS) of the US Census for years 1990, 2000 and 2009.

**Table 10.13    Multivariate Analysis of (log) Housing Values for Native-Born Blacks in the Working Class, 1980–2009**

|  | 1980 | 1990 | 2000 | 2009 |
|---|---|---|---|---|
| Intercept | 10.2839*** | 9.7342*** | 9.7802*** | 18.6774*** |
| Age | 0.008477*** | 0.03284*** | 0.01107*** | -0.1168*** |
| Age$^2$ | -0.00012*** | -0.00027*** | -0.00007**** | 0.000650*** |
| Female | -0.04607*** | -0.03627*** | -0.07847*** | 0.04659* |
| Northeast | 0.4052*** | 0.9644*** | 0.6533*** | 0.7479*** |
| Midwest | 0.06246*** | 0.03049 | 0.1636*** | 0.4185*** |
| West | 0.5810*** | 0.5912*** | 0.6749*** | 1.0536*** |
| Education | 0.07463*** | 0.08861*** | 0.09617*** | -0.1536*** |
| Married | 0.2011*** | 0.2395*** | 0.2145*** | -1.0404*** |
| No. of Children | -0.01198*** | -0.00478** | -0.00038 | -0.00075 |
| Between MSA Variance | 0.06529*** | 0.1440*** | 0.08707*** | 0.09063*** |
| Within MSA Variance | 0.3503*** | 0.4252*** | 0.4352*** | 4.3610*** |
| -2 Log Likelihood | 152,217.9 | 218,398.2 | 269,337.9 | 224,483.7 |
| MSAs | 251 | 250 | 284 | 273 |
| N | 84,705 | 109,738 | 133,850 | 52,019 |

*Source:* Public Use Microdata Samples (PUMS) of the US Census for years 1990, 2000 and 2009.

**Table 10.14    Multivariate Analysis of (log) Interest, Dividend and Rental Income for Native-Born Blacks in the Working Class, 1980–2009**

|  | 1980 | 1990 | 2000 | 2009 |
|---|---|---|---|---|
| Intercept | 3.0191*** | 2.5021*** | 5.4697*** | 4.7446*** |
| Age | 0.1052*** | 0.1181*** | 0.01232 | 0.02009 |
| Age$^2$ | -0.00064*** | -0.0068*** | 0.000145 | 0.000041 |
| Female | -0.2257 | 0.2995*** | -0.2571*** | -0.5759*** |
| Northeast | 0.1242* | 0.2312*** | 0.1543*** | 0.4204** |
| Midwest | 0.04723 | 0.01974 | 0.001598 | 0.2111 |
| West | 0.2125** | 0.2290*** | 0.2542** | 0.4518** |
| Education | 0.008774 | 0.06567*** | -0.01203 | 0.04079 |
| Married | -0.03997 | 0.05835 | 0.03256 | 0.07584 |
| No. of Children | -0.00354 | -0.04864*** | 0.01464 | 0.04378 |
| Between MSA Variance | 0.03076*** | 0.03048*** | 0.05247*** | 0.02202 |
| Within MSA Variance | 2.9109*** | 3.5231*** | 4.7482*** | 5.7792*** |
| -2 Log Likelihood | 79,465.0 | 83,607.4 | 96,359.1 | 13,189.0 |
| MSAs | 251 | 250 | 284 | 273 |
| N | 20,320 | 20,387 | 21,898 | 2,870 |

*Source:* Public Use Microdata Samples (PUMS) of the US Census for years 1990, 2000 and 2009.

Table 10.15    Multivariate Analysis of (log) Housing Values for Foreign-Born Blacks in the Working Class, 1980–2009

|  | 1980 | 1990 | 2000 | 2009 |
|---|---|---|---|---|
| Intercept | 10.2620*** | 11.1479*** | 10.7228*** | 18.2869*** |
| Age | 0.02184*** | 0.007686 | 0.003580 | -0.1052*** |
| Age$^2$ | -0.00026*** | -0.00006 | -0.00002 | 0.000622*** |
| Female | -0.00986 | -0.00331 | -0.01039 | -0.1821*** |
| Northeast | 0.3675*** | 0.7543*** | 0.3682*** | 0.2733* |
| Midwest | -0.03643 | -0.2640** | 0.1612** | 0.5102*** |
| West | 0.6567** | 0.6594*** | 0.6514*** | 0.7341*** |
| Education | 0.05399*** | 0.04032*** | 0.04043*** | -0.116*** |
| Married | 0.1946*** | 0.1420*** | 0.1319*** | -0.5423*** |
| No. of Children | -0.00424 | 0.007831 | 0.01958**** | -0.1314*** |
| Between MSA Variance | 0.08357*** | 0.1341*** | 0.07251*** | 0.1575*** |
| Within MSA Variance | 0.2769*** | 0.2446*** | 0.2698*** | 3.2725*** |
| -2 Log Likelihood | 2,894.4 | 6,979.2 | 15,229.7 | 27,068.3 |
| MSAs | 251 | 250 | 284 | 273 |
| N | 8,985 | 4,731 | 22,474 | 6,703 |

*Source:* Public Use Microdata Samples (PUMS) of the US Census for years 1990, 2000 and 2009.

We found in each year that blacks in the working class had lower levels of interest, dividends and rental income and housing values than their white counterparts between 1980 and 2009. We found interesting similarities and differences between native- and foreign-born blacks in the working class on housing values and interest, dividends and rental income—especially between the decade leading up to the Great Recession and the period when it ended. For native- and foreign-born blacks in the working class, interest, dividends and rental income increased, as education increased in 1980, 1990 and 2000. By 2009, after the Great Recession, the directional effect was the opposite. As education decreased the levels of interest, dividends and rental income increased. More educated blacks, regardless of nativity, may have had to tap into their savings, stocks and ownership of real estate beyond their primary residences to pay debts, sustain themselves through a period of unemployment or to invest in creating a business—all of which are not directly measured here.

Being married had a positive effect on the levels of interest, dividends and rental income owned by blacks in the working class, regardless of nativity. However, this was the case in the decades leading up to the Great Recession. By the end of the Great Recession married blacks in the working class did not do as well as non-married blacks. Given that black men and black women are relatively disadvantaged when compared with other racial and ethnic groups, they may not benefit economically as much from marriage as other groups. Consequently, withstanding an economic downturn like the Great Recession may have an even greater impact on married blacks in the working class than non-married blacks where interest, dividends and rental income are concerned. If one spouse were to lose their job the couple may have to tap into interest, dividends and rental income to make ends meet only to have the other spouse go through a similar experience. A non-married individual may not have to tap into these assets to the extent that a married couple might.

# Discussion

The Great Recession was felt by virtually every American. Many Americans even took to the streets to protest the economic inequality that existed in the nation. Chants of "We are the 99 percent!" could be heard across the nation. While few escaped the claws of the Great Recession, some groups were hit harder than others, partly because of this nation's history of institutional inequality. Racism, racial discrimination and prejudice have placed blacks at an institutional disadvantage. Consequently, it is not an anomaly that blacks would be disproportionately impacted by an economic downturn like the Great Recession. However, two salient questions are: to what extent were some within the black population hit harder than others and why has this area been under-examined. More attention must be devoted to the ethnic and economic diversity that exists within the black population. Although blacks continue to have the shared experience of being a racial minority in America, and while racism still exists, there are factors which place some at great risk than others.

The present study fills a gap in the literature on racial inequality by going into greater depth about the likelihood of homeownership and interest, dividends and rental income for members of the forgotten working class, especially for native-born blacks in the working class. Our findings showed that race and class were significant determinants of homeownership, housing values and interest, dividends and rental income. The findings support race-based theories. However, our findings also showed that other factors, including nativity, explain some of the variations in homeownership, housing values and interest, dividends and rental income, particularly for blacks with membership in the forgotten working class. The results further revealed similarities and differences in the determinants of the outcomes under study for native- and foreign-born blacks, including where gender, education and marital status are concerned. Our results provide support for the continuing significance of the race thesis, as blacks in the working class lagged behind similarly situated whites in each year considered. Our results are also a call for scholars to revisit assimilation theories and their relevance for the black population. Our results further show the need for more research on the role of gender in light of the Great Recession.

Future research should also take into account the types of resources available to native- and foreign-born females. Additionally, future research should also explore differences within the foreign-born population by ancestry. Clearly, asset poverty is a serious issue facing the black population and understanding what places blacks at risk of becoming asset poor is critical to addressing this pressing social problem.

# References

Alba, Richard. 1995. "Assimilation's Quiet Tide." *Public Interest* 119: 3–19.

Allegretto, Sylvia and Steven Pitts. 2010. "The State of Black Workers before the Great Recession," Research Brief. University of California Berkeley Labor Center.

Arena, John. 2005. "Bringing Back in the Black Working Class: A Critique of the "Underclass" and Urban Politics Literature." Conference Papers, American Sociological Association, pp. 1–24.

———. 2011. "Bringing In the Black Working Class: The Black Urban Regime Strategy." *Science & Society* 75(2): 153–79.

Bonilla-Silva, Eduardo. 2014. *Racism without Racists*. Lanham, MD: Rowman and Littlefield Publishers.

Davis, Shannon N., Shannon K. Jacobsen and Julia Anderson. 2012. "From the Great Recession to Greater Gender Equality? Family Mobility and the Intersection of Race, Class, and Gender." *Marriage & Family Review* 48(7): 601–20.

Dawson, Michael C., and Lawrence D. Bobo. 2009. "One Year Later and the Myth of a Post-Racial Society." *Du Bois Review: Social Science Research On Race* 6(2): 247–9.

Dodoo, F. Nii-Amoo. 1997. "Assimilation Differences among Africans in America," *Social Forces* 76(2): 527–46.

Estrada, Vanesa. 2006. "Getting and Keeping a Home: Black/White Homeownership Transitions in the US, 1969–2003." Conference Papers, American Sociological Association.

Freeman, Lance. 2003. "Making Progress?: Black Homeownership at the End of the 20th Century." Conference Papers, American Sociological Association.

———. 2005. "Black Homeownership: The Role of Temporal Changes and Residential Segregation at the End of the 20th Century." *Social Science Quarterly* 86(2): 403–26.

Fu, Vincent Kang. 2007. "How Many Melting Pots? Intermarriage, Pan Ethnicity, and the Black/Non-Black Divide In the United States." *Journal Of Comparative Family Studies* 38(2): 215–37.

Gines, Kathryn T. 2010. "From Color-Blind to Post-Racial: Blacks and Social Justice in the Twenty-First Century." *Journal of Social Philosophy* 41(3): 370–84.

Horton, Hayward Derrick, Beverlyn Lundy Allen, Cedric Herring and Melvin E. Thomas. 2000. "Lost in the Storm: The Sociology of the Black Working-Class, 1850 to 1990." *American Sociological Review* 65(1): 128–37.

Katkov, Alexander. 2011. "The Great Recession of 2008–2009 and Government's Role." ASBBS Annual Conference, Las Vegas. 18(1): 898–906.

Kochhar, Rakesh, Richard Fry and Paul Taylor. 2011. "Wealth Gap Rise to Record Highs Between Whites, Blacks, Hispanics Twenty-to-One." *Pew Research Social and Demographic Trends*. Washington, DC.

Martin, Lori Latrice. 2010. "Non-Married Women and Black Ethnicity: An Analysis of the Likelihood of Homeownership." *Western Journal of Black Studies* 34(3): 325–36.

———. 2013. *Black Asset Poverty and the Enduring Racial Divide.* Boulder, CO: First Forum Press.

Oliver, Melvin and Thomas Shairpo. 2006. *Black Wealth/White Wealth.* New York: Routledge.

Ozawa, Martha N., and Tseng Huan-yui. 2000. "Differences in Net Worth Between Elderly Black People and Elderly White People." *Social Work Research* 24(2): 96.

Prager, Devah, Bruce Western and Bart Bonikowski. 2009. "Discrimination in a Low Wage Labor Market: A Field Experiment." *American Sociological Review* 74: 777–99.

Robinson, Eugene. 2010. *Disintegration: The Splintering of Black America.* New York: Doubleday.

Rugh, Jacob S. and Douglas S. Massey. 2010. "Racial Segregation and the American Foreclosure Crisis." *American Sociological Review* 75(5): 629–51.

Todd, Jennifer, and Douglas Savitskey. 2005. "A Model of Race Discrimination Based Upon Wealth Inequality: A Rational Choice Agent-Based Approach." Conference Papers, American Sociological Association.

# PART IV
# Health Wellness

# What Do We Really Know: Revisiting the Stress-Health Relationship for Black Females Across the Lifespan

Claire M. Norris, Krista D. Mincey, Brian Turner
and Makeda Roberts

Black females have often been viewed as a monolithic demographic with minimal to non-existent variance in lived experience. As a result of years of marginalization, it is without wonder that the current mental health literature continuously fails to dissect the vast deviations that actually exist among black females. Mullings's work encourages researchers to incorporate an intersectional focus which highlights how race and gender are, in some sense, "not additive but rather interlocking, interactive, and relational categories, 'multiplicative' … 'simultaneous' … 'mutually constituted' … and characterized by 'the articulation of multiple oppressions'" (Mullings 2005: 80). Moreover, the life course perspective calls researchers to consider how age embodies a system of stratification that differentially exposes groups to certain types and amounts of stressors, shapes their coping strategies and, in turn, creates variations in psychological distress. To understand mental health variations among black women across age, this research operates within a stress-health framework which maintains that researchers must understand how the unequal distributions of stress exposure (i.e., type and source of stress) and the coping strategies that groups draw on differentially affect mental health outcomes across social groups (Pearlin 1989; Thoits 2010).

Despite sociological efforts that seek to understand how variations in age create and maintain social disparities in mental health outcomes (Adkins et. al., 2009; Hamilton-Mason et al., 2009; Mirowsky and Ross, 1992; Norris and Miller, 2014), few researchers have attempted to understand how the stress-health process occurs over time among black females. Therefore, this study seeks to understand the effects of age on the stress-health relationship for black women. Specifically, we examine differences in how stress exposure and access to coping strategies affect psychological distress for black adolescent girls, emerging adults and young adults. Consequently, this work widens our intersectional focus on mental health disparities in three distinct ways.

First, although community studies conducted in the 1950s and 1960s drew attention to how social groups' structural position affected their exposure to stressors, variations to coping strategies and, in turn, their emotional health (Hollingshead and Redlich 1958; Srole et al. 1960), empirical research on black female health experiences are scant. Furthermore, black females are viewed outside the norm because black females' experiences have not been calculated as a valid entity in the greater American female narrative. Our work allows for an expansion of that narrative by understanding how stress and coping strategies impact psychological distress for black females at three critical stages: adolescence, emerging adulthood and young adulthood.

Second, the process of understanding the interaction of race- and health-related outcomes is a function of the close examination of the role that stress and coping play in the everyday lived experience of black females (Pieterse et al. 2013). Thus, this research utilizes panel data to empirically track the stress-health process for black females across age. By employing panel data our study allows for the measurement of variation in how black females' experiences with stress and coping strategies impact their levels of psychological distress over time. More importantly, our work contributes to scholarly discourse on black women's health throughout womanhood.

Finally, our findings move beyond pure sociological research and into applied sociological research where we provide recommendations on ways to help black females cope with stress. By offering concrete recommendations our work provides practitioners a platform to develop successful interventions geared toward helping black females deal with stress based on their age and the type of stress they experience. It is believed that tailoring interventions with the elements of age and stress in mind will increase the success of interventions by providing black females with practical ways to deal with stress that consider their life phase and the type of stress they encounter.

The following sections build on conceptual frameworks that address the stress-health relationship among black females. A description of the methods, the sample from which our results are generated and the variables we analyze will also follow. We conclude with a discussion of the implications of our research for future studies.

## Adapting a Model for Black Females

Lazarus and Folkman's (1984) classic transactional model of coping highlights how variables influence stress and coping strategies and, consequently, mental health outcomes. Several researchers point out that for blacks and other ethnic groups in America, the actual experience of stress and the coping styles employed are indigenous to the experiences, history, resources and success of the group (Akbar 1991; Anderson 1991; Miranda and Matheny, 2000). The theory of acculturative stress is unique due to its inclusion of the effects of such variables on the mental health of blacks. The multiple interactions of the theory of acculturative stress make it an appropriate model for the study of stress in black women across the lifespan.

The transactional model of coping originally proposed by Lazarus and Folkman (1984) and modified by Anderson (1991) starts from the premise that stress is a causal factor in creating deleterious mental health outcomes for individuals. The transactional model identifies three levels of stressors that can impact a person's level of functioning. Level I stressors include chronic and environmental stressors such as poverty and whether or not one lives in a safe environment). Level II stressors are more central and include death, major life events, illnesses, job loss and divorce. These stressors may be considered reasonable in their possibility of occurring, but they are not considered to be chronic. They are more fluid events that can occur and create marked stress reactions. However, they generally do not require a long-term commitment of resources. Finally, Level III stressors are described as events that are disruptive to one's daily functioning, such as stress related to social roles, social interactions, etc. Because negative stress responses are found in individuals with limited resources as they seek to address consistent stressful events that deplete resources necessary for healthy responding, Level III stressors are the cornerstone in the assessment of the stress-health relationship (Bandura 1997; Neal-Barnett 2003; Neal-Barnett and Crowther 2000). Moreover, it is postulated that the persistence of Level III stressors operate as the greatest predictor of negative health outcomes in blacks (Anderson 1991).

## Coping Strategies and Mental Health for Black Females

The transactional model of coping also addresses coping strategies, both ineffective and effective, that impact mental health outcomes. Groups that have inadequate or ineffective coping strategies are more vulnerable to the deleterious effects of life's stressors (Bovier et al. 2004; Mabry and Kiecolt 2005). Faulty coping styles, or ineffective coping, tend to have negative impacts on individuals' mental health outcomes. Faulty coping refers to the employing of irrational thinking or behaviors to cope with stressful situations such as drug use, drinking and violence (Anderson 1991). We argue that, although faulty coping tends to have pernicious effects on one's psychological health, the effects can vary over the life course. Because faulty coping carries social and economic consequences that may be difficult to manage, as individuals become older, we argue, faulty coping will have a greater effect on individuals' psychological health over time.

Conversely, effective coping styles such as appraisals and internal coping (i.e., self-esteem, self-efficacy, prayer, exercise and problem solving) strongly correlate with positive mental health outcomes (Bovier et al. 2004; Mabry and Kiecolt 2005). That is, groups that have higher levels of positive appraisals of situations tend to report better mental health outcomes. Increased levels of self-esteem, self-efficacy, prayer and exercise have been shown to have positive effects on an individual's mental health (Anderson 1991; Bovier et al. 2004). To understand these affects across age for black women, we argue that these skills may become more developed and, therefore, more meaningful over time. Thus, we expect that internal coping strategies such as prayer, self-efficacy and self-esteem will more likely have an impact on young adults as compared to adolescents or emerging adults.

Additionally, social support theorists emphasize the "social" dimension of support as a critical link in understanding the mediating effects of social support on mental health. Social support is defined as "a social network's provision of psychological and material resources intended to benefit an individual's ability to cope with stress" (Cohen 2004: 676). Thus, groups with inadequate social support systems are likely to report higher levels of psychological distress (Thoits 2010). Although research reveals how social support systems are vital in mediating the harmful effects of life's stressors on mental health (Cohen 2004; Thoits 2010), this may not apply to young black women. Black women are usually embedded in strong, homogeneous networks that cannot offset the psychological consequences of stress (Mullings 2005). Stack (1974) maintains that while social networks often assist in black women's daily needs, they draw from a resource-poor network that has high demands of reciprocity. Hence, we argue that black women may perceive inadequate levels of social support as they age and over time that social support may have less of a positive influence on black women's mental health.

Despite health researchers' efforts to understand the relationship between age and psychological distress for women, the age patterns of black females' mental health processes across their life trajectory remain relatively unclear in the mental health literature (Adkins et al. 2009; Akbar 2003; Jones et al. 2007; Neal-Barnett 2003; Neal-Barnett and Crowther 2000; Norris and Miller 2014). Therefore, the purpose of this study is to understand the effects of age on the stress-health model for black women. Specifically, this study seeks to answer the question, "how do stress exposure and coping strategies affect Black females over time using panel data?"

# Methods

## Data

Data for this project came from the National Longitudinal Study of Adolescent Health and include a representative sample of adolescents living in the United States who were in grades 7–12 in 1994 and 1995 (Harris et al. 2009). This research enlists the use of Add Health Public Use Data. Wave 1 Public Use Data consist of a combination of In-Home, In-School, Parent and Add Health Vocabulary Picture Data (when available). The primary sampling technique used for the Add Health study was a clustered school-based design in which students were selected for inclusion from a sample of 80 high schools that had an 11th grade and at least 30 students. These high schools helped to identify a total of 52 feeder schools—schools that included a 7th grade and matriculated at least five students to the high school—resulting in a core sample of 132 schools.

Four waves of data were gathered, beginning in 1994 and ending in 2008. Our analysis is based on the first (1994–95), third (2001–02) and fourth (2008–09) waves. Wave 2 was excluded due to the close interval between it and Wave 1. Over 90,000 students completed an in-school interview in Wave 1 (ibid.). From each school a random sample of approximately two hundred students was selected for an in-home interview, for a total of 12,105 completed in-home interviews. In Waves 3 and 4, 15,170 and 15,701, respectively, original Wave 1 respondents were re-interviewed. There are 6,504 respondents in the Wave 1 public use dataset, with 4,882 and 5,114 of these respondents found in the public use data of Waves 3 and 4 public use data respectively. For the purposes of this paper, we employ a smaller subset of the total sample representing panel members interviewed in Waves 1, 3 and 4 (approximately 4,118 respondents). Of these, our analysis is based on the 566 black girls and women who were interviewed in all three waves.

Our primary interest in this study is to examine the effects of stress exposure and coping strategies on psychological distress as young black girls age into womanhood. As such, we control for race and gender. In the first wave of the study, respondents' average age was 16, by the third wave they were, on average, 22 years old, and by the fourth and final wave of the study, they had aged into young adulthood reporting a mean age of 29 years. In addition to changes taking place over time, we are also seeking to isolate the impact of being black and female on a person's experience with depressive symptoms. Gender is a 0, 1 variable where 0 equals female and 1 male. The intention of this chapter is *not* to examine gender or race differences, but to focus on transitions black female women as a group experience. As such, we selected only blacks and females for analysis. Race is assessed in much the same way as a dummy variable where 0 equals respondents of all other races and 1 equals black respondents.[1]

---

[1]  It is important to note that because some questions were inappropriate at certain age periods, some measures were not used across all waves. For example, a question concerning performance in school was not asked to young adults. Therefore, we use ([1]) to indicate that a measure was only used in Wave 1, ([3]) for Wave 3, and ([4]) for Wave 4. Additionally, there were some variations in the way the questions were asked over time. We indicated those changes with superscripts. For example, the depression scale was slightly modified in Wave 3. However, if a measure was consistently used in all waves, no symbol was used.

## Measures (Dependent variable)

*Psychological distress*

Distress was measured using a modified 10-item Center for Epidemiological Studies Depression (CES-D) Scale. Respondents were asked to think about the past seven days and report how frequently—ranging from rarely (0) to most of the time (3)—they experienced a variety of symptoms. Specifically, respondents were asked how frequently they felt: (1) bothered by things that usually did not bother them, (2) that they could not shake the blues, (3) that they were just as good as other people (reverse coded), (4) they had trouble keeping their mind on what they were doing, (5) depressed, (6) too tired to do things, (7) happy (reverse coded) ([1,4]), (8) that you enjoyed life (reverse coded), (9) sad, and (10) that people disliked them. Items were summed and responses ranged from 0 to 30 ([1,4]) and 0 to 27 ([3]). Our modified psychological distress scale was internally consistent for Wave 1 (Cronbach's alpha of 0.80), Wave 3 (Cronbach's alpha 0.82) and Wave 4 (Cronbach's alpha of 0.85).

## Independent variables

*Stress*

As previously mentioned, this study draws on the transactional coping framework (Anderson 1991) to operationalize stressors for black females. Anderson calls for researchers to understand stressful experiences at three levels: Level I (i.e., environment and poverty stressors), Level II (i.e., major life events) and Level III (i.e., hassles and social role strains).

*Level I stress.* Several measures were used to assess environmental strain. Interviewers ([3,4]) were asked whether (1) or not (0) they felt safe in their or the respondent's neighborhood. We also assessed the interviewer's perception of whether the home where the respondent lived was well kept ([1,4]). Responses ranged from "home needs no repairs" (1) to "home needs major repairs" (4). Interviewers were also asked whether or not there were signs of alcohol and smoking in the home ([1]). Responses were coded "yes" (1) and (0) "no." To assess overcrowding respondents were asked the number of people that lived in their household ([3,4]).

To conceive a poverty measure respondents were asked whether they ([3,4]) or their parents or guardian ([1]) received welfare assistance. Responses were coded "yes" (1) and (0) "no."

*Level II stress.* To tap major life events, respondents were asked whether or not (1) they had ever been expelled from school ([1]), (2) had a mother or father die and (3) whether a family member or friend attempted suicide within the last 12 months. Respondents were also asked whether they were sexually abused by a parent/caregiver ([3,4]) and/or by someone other than a parent ([4]). Responses were coded "yes" (1) and (0) "no."

*Level III stress.* Level III stressors varied across each wave. In Wave 1 respondents were asked (1) whether they had trouble paying attention in school and (2) whether they had trouble with homework ([1]). Responses ranged from "never" (1) to "almost everyday" (3). To operationalize respondents' exposure to social role stressors, respondents were asked whether they had trouble getting along with other students ([1]). Responses ranged from "never" (1) to "almost everyday" (3). Additionally, respondents were asked whether they had a serious argument with a parent about their behavior in the last 12 months ([1]). Respondents that indicated they had an argument with a parent or guardian were coded as (1) and those who indicated they did not have a serious argument with their parent or guardian were coded as (0). In Wave III respondents were also asked whether they felt they had limited access to a (1) car or (2) computer ([2]). Responses were coded "yes" (1) and "no" (0).

165

In Wave IV respondents were asked if they had one or more of the following chronic conditions ([4]): cancer, high cholesterol, high blood pressure, diabetes, heart disease, migraines, asthma, chronic bronchitis and emphysema. Respondents were also asked to report whether or not they provided financial support to a parent in the last year ([4]). Finally, respondents were asked whether (1) or not (0) they felt they had been mistreated because of their race, age, sex and/or religion ([4]).

## Coping strategies

*Faulty coping.* To measure faulty coping respondents were asked whether in the last 12 months they used drugs (i.e., marijuana), got into a fight ([1,3]) or drank excessively. Responses were coded (1) "yes" and (0) "no."

## Effective coping strategies.

*Appraisal.* To measure respondents' perception of appraisals or perceived susceptibility they were asked whether they expected to be killed by age 21 ([1]), live to age 35 ([3]) and whether they expected to get HIV ([3])/AIDS ([1,3]).

*Self-esteem.* A series of 4 items were used to create a self-esteem scale ([1,3]). Respondents were asked whether they (1) have a lot of good qualities, (2) have a lot to be proud of, (3) like themselves just the way they are and (4) feel like they are doing everything just about right. Items were summed and ranged from (4) low self-esteem to (20) high self-esteem.

*Self-efficacy ([4]).* Respondents were asked the following questions to assess their levels of self-efficacy. Within the last 30 days have they "felt unable to control important things," "felt that difficulties were piling up so high that they could not overcome them," "felt confident in their ability to handle personal problems" (reverse coded) and "felt things were going their way" (reverse coded). Responses were coded "never" (0) to "very often" (4). Responses were summed ranging from 0 (low levels of self-efficacy) to 16 (high levels of self-efficacy).

*Cognitive problem solving.* To assess Wave I respondents' cognitive problem-solving styles a 4-item scale was constructed. Respondents were asked (1) when you have a problem one of the first things you do is get as many facts about the problem as possible; (2) when you are attempting to find a solution to a problem you usually try to think of as many different ways to approach the problem as possible; (3) when making decisions you generally use a systematic method for judging and comparing alternatives and (4) after carrying out a solution to a problem you usually try to analyze what went right and what went wrong. Items were summed and range from 0 (negative problem solving) to 20 (positive problem solving).

Wave III respondents were asked (1) whether you go out of your way to avoid having to deal with problems in your life and (2) do you go with your "gut feeling" and don't think much about the consequence of each alternative. Responses were coded from "strongly agree" (5) to "strongly disagree" (1). Items were summed. Higher values indicate lower levels of cognitive problem solving.

*Prayer and exercise.* Two measures were also used to assess respondents' effective coping: prayer and exercise. In Waves 1, 3 and 4 respondents were asked how often they pray.

Responses were coded (4) "at least once a day," (3) "at least once a week," (2) "at least once a month," (1) "less than once a month" and (0) "never." In Waves 1 and 3 respondents were also asked how many times during the past week did they exercise (i.e., jogging, walking, karate, jumping rope, gymnastics or dancing) ([1,3]). Responses were coded as (0) "not at all," (1) "one or two times," (2) "three or four times" or (3) "five or more times." Respondents were asked how many times during the week did they walk for exercise ([4]).

*Perceived social support.* Measures for perceived social support adequacy varied by each wave. In Wave 1 ([1]) respondents were asked how much do they feel (1) adults care about them, (2) teachers care about them, (3) parents care about them and (4) friends care about them. Responses were coded as (1) "not at all," (2) "very little," (3) "somewhat," (4) "quite a bit" and (5) "very much." Wave 3 asked respondents ([3]) in the past seven days how many times did you just "hang out" with friends or talk on the telephone for more than five minutes. Wave 4 asked young respondents the number of close friends they had ([4]), including people with whom they felt at ease with to talk to about private matters that they can call on for help. Responses were coded as (1) "having no close friends," (2) "one to two friends," (3) "three to five friends," (4) "six to nine friends" and (5) "ten or more friends." Higher values index greater perceived perceptions of support.

# Analyses

To understand how the stress process operates for black females across age we employed a series of ordinary least squares [OLS] regression tests across Waves 1, 3 and 4. Finally, to ensure that none of the independent variables were sufficiently correlated to cause problems in the estimation of regression coefficients, we performed multicollinearity tests with tolerance diagnostics. All computed values were above 0.4. These values are sufficient to exclude multicollinearity (O'Brien 2007).

# Results

## Black Adolescent Girls

Table 11.1 shows OLS regression estimates of stress exposure and coping strategies on psychological distress for adolescent black girls. Starting with stress exposure, we found that the type of stress exposure that negatively impacts adolescent girls' psychological distress tends to be associated with elements in the context of family and friends. We found that the only Level I stressor that had an impact on black adolescent girls' mental health was evidence of smoking in the home. Evidence of smoking in the home had a positive, direct effect on psychological distress. Our findings also show a significant relationship between Level II stressors and psychological distress. Black adolescent girls that were exposed to Level II stressors (i.e., expulsion from school, parent death and/or family/friend suicide attempt) reported higher levels of stress than those not exposed to Level II stressors. Finally, for Level III stressors we found *only* problems with peers to have a negative impact on black adolescents' psychological health. That is, black adolescent girls who reported having problems with peers reported higher levels of psychological distress than those who did not report problems with peers.

**Table 11.1**   **Unstandardized Ordinary Least Squares (OLS) Regression of Stress Exposure and Coping Strategies on Psychological Distress, for Adolescent Black Girls**

| Variables | Model A Black Adolescent Girls (Ages 12–20) | |
| --- | --- | --- |
| | B[1] | Std. Error |
| Constant | 7.321** | 2.139 |
| **Level I Stress** | | |
| *Environmental* | | |
| Safe Environment | 0.395 | 0.608 |
| Well-Kept | 0.250 | 0.221 |
| Smoking in Home (Yes) | -0.866* | 0.451 |
| Drinking in Home (Yes) | 0.798 | 0.915 |
| *Poverty* | | |
| Parent Receives Welfare Assistance (Yes) | 0.883 | 0.518 |
| **Level II Stress** | | |
| *Major Life Events* | | |
| Expelled from school | 0.707 | 0.396 |
| Biological Parent Die | 1.929** | 0.663 |
| Family Attempt Suicide (Yes) | 2.403** | 0.751 |
| **Level III Stress** | | |
| *Hassles* | | |
| Problems Paying Attention in School | -0.42 | 0.202 |
| Problems with Homework | 0.318 | 0.186 |
| *Social Roles* | | |
| Getting Along with Peers | 0.747*** | 0.168 |
| Argued with Parents | 0.131 | 0.389 |
| **Faulty Coping Strategies** | | |
| Drug Usage (Yes) | 0.808 | 0.511 |
| Fighting | 0.747* | 0.389 |
| Binge Drinking | 0.376 | 0.367 |
| **Effective Coping Strategies** | | |
| *Appraisal* | | |
| Expected to be Killed by 21 | 0.696** | 0.236 |
| Expected to Get AIDS | -0.283 | 0.297 |
| Self-Esteem | 0.473*** | 0.048 |
| *Internal Coping* | | |
| Prayer | -0.135 | 0.136 |
| Exercise | -0.160 | 0.172 |
| Cognitive Problem Solving | -0.219** | 0.074 |
| *Social Interaction* | | |
| Perceived Social Support (Adult) | -0.866*** | 0.247 |
| Perceived Social Support (Teacher) | -0.227 | 0.174 |
| Perceived Social Support (Parent) | 0.182 | 0.333 |
| Perceived Social Support (Friends) | -0.746*** | 0.204 |

*Note:* 1 $p \leq .05$, **$p \leq .01$, ***$p \leq .001$ (on a two-tailed test); N= 600; R2 = 0.414.

Moving to coping strategies (i.e., faulty coping and effective coping), we found that *only* fighting had a significant effect on psychological distress for black adolescent girls. Drug abuse and binge drinking had no significant effect on psychological distress for black adolescent girls.

Turning to effective coping strategies, we found that black adolescent girls who reported negative appraisals (i.e., believed that they would be killed by age 21) reported greater psychological distress symptoms than those who had positive appraisals (i.e., believed they would live past age 21). Additionally, black adolescent girls who had higher levels of self-esteem also reported lower levels of psychological distress.

Finally, for perceived social support we found that only perceived social support from an adult or friend mattered. That is, adolescents who reported perceived social support adequacy (from an adult or friend) had lower levels of psychological distress. Perceived support from a teacher or parent had no significant effect on psychological distress for adolescent girls.

## Black Emerging Adult Women

Table 11.2 presents OLS regression estimates of stress exposure and coping strategies (i.e., faulty and effective strategies) on psychological distress. We found no significant relationship between Level I stressors (i.e., safe environment, overcrowding and poverty) and psychological distress. We did, however, find a significant relationship between Level II stress (i.e., major life events) and psychological distress. Black emerging adult women who reported that they had been sexually abused by their parent had higher levels of psychological distress than those who did not report sexual abuse by a parent. Finally, we found no significant relationship between Level III (i.e., daily hassles) stressors and psychological distress.

Moving to coping strategies, we found that only one faulty coping strategy (i.e., fighting) had a significant effect on psychological distress. Black emerging adult women who reported fighting had significantly higher levels of psychological distress than their counterparts who did not report fighting. However, we found that appraisals significantly affected black emerging women's psychological health. Individuals who reported they expected to be killed by 35, or that they would contract HIV/AIDS, also reported higher levels of psychological distress. Additionally, black emerging adult women with higher levels of self-esteem also had lower levels of psychological distress. Black emerging adult women who reported poorer problem-solving strategies also reported higher levels of psychological distress. Finally, black emerging adult women who reported spending less time with their friends also reported higher levels of psychological distress.

## Young Black Women

Table 11.3 presents OLS regression estimates of stress exposure and coping strategies (i.e., faulty and effective coping strategies) on psychological distress for young black women. We start with the relationship between stress exposure and psychological distress. For young black women we found that Level I environmental stressors (i.e., safe environment, well-kept building and number of people in home) had no significant effect on young black women's psychological health.

However, unlike adolescents and emerging adults, young black women who received welfare assistance reported greater levels of psychological distress symptoms than their

**Table 11.2    Unstandardized Ordinary Least Squares (OLS) Regression of Stress Exposure and Coping Strategies on Psychological Distress, for Emerging Adult Black Women**

| Variables | Model A Emerging Adult Black Women (Ages 18–27) | |
| --- | --- | --- |
| | **B[1]** | **Std. Error** |
| Constant | 18.012 | 1.802 |
| **Level I Stress** | | |
| *Environmental* | | |
| Safe Environment | -0.083 | 0.654 |
| No. of People in Home | 0.074 | 0.113 |
| *Poverty* | | |
| Receives Welfare Assistance (Yes) | 0.648 | 0.558 |
| **Level II Stress** | | |
| *Major Life Events* | | |
| Sexual Abuse by Parent | 2.143* | 0.899 |
| Biological Parent Die | 0.611 | 0.611 |
| Family Attempt Suicide (Yes) | 0.271 | 0.747 |
| **Level III Stress** | | |
| *Hassles* | | |
| Access to Car (No) | 0.160 | 0.375 |
| Access to Computer (No) | 0.499 | 0.376 |
| **Faulty Coping Strategies** | | |
| Drug Usage (Yes) | 0.978 | 0.519 |
| Fighting | 1.948* | 0.886 |
| Binge Drinking | 0.061 | 0.232 |
| **Effective Coping Strategies** | | |
| Expected to be Killed by 35 | 1.105*** | 0.277 |
| Expected to Get HIV | 0.846* | 0.425 |
| Self-Esteem | -0.620*** | 0.084 |
| Prayer | -0.173 | 0.174 |
| Exercise | -0.016 | 0.076 |
| Cognitive Problem Solving | -0.405*** | 0.094 |
| Perceived Social Support (Friends) | -0.235** | 0.078 |

*Note:* 1 p ≤ .05; ** p ≤ .01; *** p ≤ .001 (on a two-tailed test); N = 497; R2 = 0.278.

counterparts who did not receive welfare assistance. We also found a significant relationship between Level II stressors (i.e., major life events) and psychological distress. That is, young black women who reported that their biological mother and/or father died had greater levels of psychological distress. Finally, for Level III stressors, young black women who reported that they had a chronic illness (such as cancer, high cholesterol, high blood pressure, diabetes, heart disease, migraines, asthma, chronic bronchitis and/or emphysema) also reported greater levels of psychological distress than those who did not report a chronic illness.

**Table 11.3    Unstandardized Ordinary Least Squares (OLS) Regression of Stress Exposure and Coping Strategies on Psychological Distress, for Young Black Women**

| Variables | Model A Young Black Women (Ages 26–34) | |
|---|---|---|
| | B[1] | Std. Error |
| Constant | 19.783*** | 1.277 |
| **Level I Stress** | | |
| *Environmental* | | |
| Safe Environment | -0.389 | 0.273 |
| Well-Kept | 0.413 | 0.641 |
| No. of People in Home | 0.066 | 0.104 |
| *Poverty* | | |
| Receives Welfare Assistance (Yes) | 0.746* | 0.374 |
| **Level II Stress** | | |
| *Major Life Events* | | |
| Sexual Abuse | 0.809 | 0.465 |
| Biological Parent Die | 1.169** | 0.441 |
| Family Attempt Suicide (Yes) | -0.617 | 0.690 |
| **Level III Stress** | | |
| *Hassles* | | |
| Chronic Illness | 0.421* | 0.201 |
| Provide Financial Support to Parent | 0.011 | 0.389 |
| *Social Roles* | | |
| Perceived Discrimination | 0.532 | 0.416 |
| **Faulty Ineffective Coping** | | |
| Drug Usage (Yes) | 0.046 | 0.529 |
| Binge Drinking | -0.002 | 0.417 |
| **Effective Coping Strategies** | | |
| Self-Efficacy | -1.019*** | 0.062 |
| Prayer | -0.290* | 0.144 |
| Exercise | 0.075 | 0.159 |
| Perceived Social Support (Friends) | -0.362 | 0.203 |

*Note:* 1 $p \le .05$; ** $p \le .01$; *** $p \le .001$ (on a two two-tailed test); N = 491; R2 = 0.482.

Moving to coping strategies for young black women, we found that faulty coping had no significant effect on young black women's psychological distress. However, for effective coping, we found that self-efficacy and praying had significant effects on black women's psychological health. That is, black women who reported higher levels of self-efficacy also reported lower levels of psychological distress symptoms. Additionally, black women who reported increased amounts of prayer had lower levels of psychological distress.

## Discussion/Implications

Health researchers acknowledge that there are social group disparities in the type and amount of stress exposure and the coping strategies that social groups draw on to mitigate the harmful psychological effects of stress (Pearlin 1989; Thoits 2010). This study sought to understand how differences in stress exposure and coping strategies impacted black females across age. As findings from this study show, black females are a heterogeneous group whose varied experiences over time, from adolescence to young adulthood, impact their health outcomes in different ways based on the level of stress they encounter and the resources available to them to deal with the stress in their life.

Similar to findings by Sanchez, Lambert and Ialongo (2012), our findings demonstrate that peer life events (e.g., life events happening to their peers) have a negative impact on depressive symptoms for black males and females in middle school. This study reported that girls' psychological distress is associated with stressful elements within the context of family and friends. Our findings, which show that perceived social support from an adult or friend positively affected black females' psychological distress levels, is similar to research by Mariano and colleagues (2011) who convincingly argued that strong relationships with parents, friends and teachers are the most meaningful support sources for youth.

As mentioned by Sanchez and colleagues (2012), interventions could focus on helping adolescents develop a support system with their peers and adults (other than their parents) as a means to deal with the stressors they face. Additionally, interventions could focus on helping adolescents develop a group of specific coping techniques they can use to deal with the stress they face. By teaching adolescents specific ways they can cope with stress they have tools at their disposal to help them deal with stress even if they have a lack of external resources. Programs could also focus on opportunities that increase positive self-image in this group as it relates to community, gender, race/ethnicity and supportive networks and modes of positive behaviors.

For emerging adults, findings reported black females with higher self-esteem had lower psychological distress. This could be a function of a decrease in access to external resources which cause black females to look within to deal with the stress. Due to the transitional stage for emerging adults, interventions could focus on assisting them through this intermediate period and the stress that could arise from transitions (Hood et al. 2013). Additionally, these interventions could also involve family members of these emerging adults so that family members are better prepared to provide support through this transitional phase (ibid.). Interventions could also focus on promoting greater engagement in pro-social behaviors (e.g., helping others, personal investment in the community and values development), occupational support and trainings, continued supportive networks and connections to positive peers among emerging adults as a means to deal with stress.

For young adult black females, findings reported that those with higher levels of self-efficacy and engagement in prayer had lower psychological distress, similar to work by Kohn-Wood and colleagues (2012) who reported that religious coping independent of church attendance and clergy support was related to fewer psychological distress symptoms in blacks. To assist young adults in dealing with stress, interventions could focus on developing strategies and skills around prayer not related to religious affiliation but focused on connectedness to self and reflection of one's environment (i.e., meditation). Interventions could also focus on increasing self-efficacy within this group through skill development and other practices that increase self-esteem.

Future research could enhance the predictive nature of the relationship between stress and health outcomes for women across the life cycle by employing the following measures. First, drawing on qualitative approaches will provide a more comprehensive understanding of stress exposure and the coping strategies that effect health outcomes. This rich information will help create stronger quantitative stress and health measures and, in turn, help develop more meaningful models that adequately address health and health disparities. Second, we believe that understanding the effects of stress on health from a biosocial approach provides a more holistic perspective on the stress-health relationship. Thus far, the stress-health research presents segregated biological and sociological models. A nexus between the two disciplines would strengthen the stress-health model and, consequently, better inform policy makers on how to address health and health disparities.

# Bibliography

Adkins, Daniel E., Victor Wang, Matthew E. Dupre, J.C.G. Edwin and Glen H. Elder. 2009. "Structure and Stress: Trajectories of Depressive Symptoms Across Adolescence and Young Adulthood." *Social Forces* 88(1): 31–60.

Akbar, Naim. 1991. "The Evolution of Human Psychology for African Americans." *in Black Psychology*, edited by R.L. Jones. Hampton, VA: Cobb & Henry Publishers, pp. 99–123.

———. 2003. *Akbar Papers in African Psychology*. Tallahassee, FL: Mind Productions and Associates.

Amodeo, Maryann, Margaret L. Griffin, Irene Fassler, Cassandra Clay and Michael A. Ellis. 2007. "Coping with Stressful Events: Influence of Parental Alcoholism and Race in a Community Sample of Women." *Health and Social Work* 32(4): 247–57.

Anderson, Louis P. 1991. "Acculturative Stress: A Theory of Relevance to Black Americans." *Clinical Psychology Review* 11: 685–702.

Anshel, Mark. 1996. "Coping Styles among Adolescent Competitive Athletes." *The Journal of Social Psychology* 136: 311–23.

Bandura, Albert. 1997. *Self-efficacy: The Exercise of Control*. New York: W.H. Freeman and Company.

Beutler, Larry E., Rudolf H. Moos and Geoffrey Lane. 2003. "Coping, Treatment Planning and Treatment Outcome: Discussion" *Journal of Clinical Psychology* 59 (10): 1151–67.

Bovier, Patrick A., Eric Chamot and Thomas V. Perneger. 2004. "Perceived Stress, Internal Resources, and Social Support as Determinants of Mental Health among Young Adults." *Quality of Life Research* 13(1): 161–70.

Cohen, Sheldon. 2004. "Social Relationship and Health." *The American Psychologist* 59(8): 676–84.

Hamilton-Mason, Johnnie, J. Camille Hall and Joyce E. Everett. 2009. "And Some of Us are Braver: Stress and Coping among African American Women." *Journal of Human Behavior in the Social Environment* 19: 463–82.

Harris, Kathleen M., Carolyn Halpern, Eric Whitsel, Jon Hussey, Joyce Tabor, Pamela P. Entzel and J. Richard Udry. 2009. *The National Longitudinal Study of Adolescent Health: Research Design*: http://www.cpc.unc.edu/projects/addhealth/design.

Hollingshead, August B. and Frederick C. Redlich. 1958. *Social Class and Mental Illness: A Community Study*. New York: Wiley.

Hood, Kristina, Joshua Brevard, Anh Bao Nguyen and Faye Belgrave. 2013. "Stress Among African American Emerging Adults: The Role of Family and Cultural Factors." *Journal of Child & Family Studies* 22(1): 76–84.

Jones, Hollie L., William E. Cross and Darlene C. DeFour. 2007. "Race-related Stress, Racial Identity Attitudes, and Mental Health among Black Women." *Journal of Black Psychology* 33(2): 208–31.

Jung, John and Hari Khalsa. 1989. "The Relationship of Daily Hassles, Social Support, and Coping to Depression in Black and White Students." *Journal of General Psychology* 116(4): 407–17.

Kohn-Wood, Laura. P., Wizdom P. Hammond, Tiffany F. Haynes, Kelly K. Ferguson and Brittany A. Jackson. 2012. "Coping Styles, Depressive Symptoms and Race During the Transition to Adulthood." *Mental Health, Religion, & Culture* 15(4): 363–72.

Lazarus, Richard S. 1966. *Psychological Stress and the Coping Process*. New York: McGraw Hill.

——— and Susan Folkman. 1984. *Stress, Appraisal and Coping*. New York: Springer Publishing Company.

Lincoln, Karen D., Linda M. Chatters and Robert J. Taylor. 2005. "Social Support, Traumatic Events, and Depressive Symptoms among African Americans." *Journal of Marriage and Family* 67: 754–66.

Lu, Luo. 1991. "Daily Hassles and Mental Health: A Longitudinal Study." *British Journal of Psychology* 82: 441–47.

Mabry, Beth and Jill Kiecolt. 2005. "Anger in Black and White: Race, Alienation, and Anger." *Journal of Health and Social Behavior* 46(1): 85–101.

Marcus-Newhall, Amy and Timothy R. Heindle. 1998. "Coping with Interracial Stress in Ethnically Diverse Classroom: How Important are Allport's Contact Conditions?" *Journal of Social Issues* 54(4): 813–30.

Mariano, Jenni M., Julie Going, Kayla Schrock and Kelli Sweeting. 2011. "Youth Purpose and the Perception of Social Supports among African American Girls." *Journal of Youth Studies* 14(8): 921–37.

Miranda, Alexis O. and Kenneth B. Matheny. 2000. "Socio-Psychological Predictors of Acculturative Stress among Latino Adults." *The Journal of Mental Health Counseling* 22(4): 306–17.

Mirowsky, John, and Catherine Ross. 1992. "Age and Depression." *Journal of Health and Social Behavior* 33(3): 187–205.

Mullings, Leith. 2005. "Resistance and Resilience: The Sojourner Syndrome and the Social Context of Reproduction in Central Harlem." *Transforming Anthropology* 13(2): 79–91.

Neal-Barnett, Angela M. 2003. *Soothe Your Nerves: The Black Woman's Guide to Understanding and Overcoming Anxiety, Panic, and Fear*. New York: Simon & Schuster.

——— and Janis H. Crowther. 2000. "To Be Female, Anxious, Middle-Class, and Black." *Psychology of Women Quarterly* 24(2): 132–40.

Norris, Claire and Paige Miller. 2014. "Growing up Black and Female: Life Course Transitions and Depressive Symptoms." in *What the Village Gave Me: Conceptualizations of Womanhood*, eds. D. Davis-Maye, A.D. Yarber, and T.E. Perry. Lanham, MD: University Press of American, Inc., pp. 107–21.

O'Brien, Robert, M. 2007. "A Caution Regarding Rules of Thumb for Variance Inflation Factors." *Quality and Quantity* 41(5): 673–90.

Pearlin, Leonard. I. 1989. "The Sociological Study of Stress." *Journal of Health and Social Behavior* 30: 241–56.

Pieterse, Alex L., Robert T. Carter and Kilynda V. Ray. 2013. "Racism-Related Stress, General Life Stress, and Psychological Functioning among Black American Women." *Journal of Multicultural Counseling and Development* 41: 36–46.

Rutherford, Alexandra and Norman S. Endler. 1999. "Predicting Approach-Avoidance: The Role of Coping Styles, State Anxiety, and Situational Appraisal." *Anxiety, Stress, and Coping* 12: 63–84.

Sanchez, Yadira M., Sharon F. Lambert and Nicholas S. Ialongo. 2012. "Life Events and Depressive Symptoms in African American Adolescents: Do Ecological Domains and Timing of Life Events Matter?" *Journal of Youth & Adolescence* 41(4): 438–48.

Shorter-Gooden, Kumea. 2004. "Multiple Resistance Strategies: How African American Women Cope with Racism and Sexism." *The Journal of Black Psychology* 30(3): 406–25.

Srole, Leo, Thomas S. Langner, Morris K. Opler and T.A.C Rennie. 1960. *Mental Health in the Metropolis: The Midtown Study.* New York: McGraw-Hill.

Stack, Carol B. 1974. *All Our Kin: Strategies for Survival in a Black Community.* New York: Harper and Row.

Staples, Robert and Leanor B. Johnson. 1993. *Black Families at the Crossroads: Challenges and Prospects.* San Francisco, CA: Jossey-Bass Inc.

Steward, Robbie J., Ik J. Han, Darrick Murray, William Fitzgerald, Douglas Neil, Frank Fear and Martin Hill. 1998. "Psychological Adjustment and Coping Styles of Urban African American High-school Students." *Journal of Multicultural Counseling & Development* 26: 70–83.

Thoits, Peggy A. 2010. "Stress and Health: Major Findings and Policy Implications." *Journal of Health and Social Behavior* 51(S): S41–S53.

Utsey, Shawn O., Joseph G. Ponterotto, Amy L. Reynolds and Anthony A. Cancelli. 2000. "Racial Discrimination, Coping, Life Satisfaction, and Self-esteem among African Americans." *Journal of Counseling and Development* 78: 72–80.

West, Lindsey M., Roxanne A. Donovan and Lizabeth Roemer. 2009. "Coping with Racism: What Works and Doesn't Work for Black Women." *Journal of Black Psychology* 36(3): 331–49.

Zaff, Jonathan F., Ronald L. Blount, Layli Phillips and Lindsey Cohen. 2002. "The Role of Ethnic Identity and Self-Construal in Coping among African Americans and Caucasian American Seventh Graders: An Exploratory Analysis of Within-group Variance." *Adolescence* 37(148): 751–73.

# "We Need a New Normal": Sociocultural Constructions of Obesity and Overweight among African American Women

Angelique Harris, David Nelson, Kimberly
Salas Harris, Barbara A. Horner-Ibler and Edith Burns

## Introduction

Obesity/overweight has disproportionately impacted African American communities. Specifically, it has had a particularly negative impact on African American women who have the highest rates of obesity and overweight across all gender and racial/ethnic demographics (Ogden et al. 2013). Most clinical research examining obesity emphasizes comorbidities associated with excessive weight gain including hypertension, heart disease and diabetes (Kopelman 2007). However, previous intervention research examining these comorbidities among African Americans women has failed to consider sociocultural factors and barriers associated with obesity and overweight. Using data from six focus groups and Black feminist theory as the theoretical framework, this chapter examines the perceptions of, and experiences with, obesity and overweight among a sample of African American women in Milwaukee, Wisconsin. The findings suggest that sociocultural factors influencing obesity and overweight include poverty, a lack of access to resources, perceptions of overweight as "normal" and the association of 'skinny" with negative connotations. Focus group participants also highlight the importance of community assets and resources (e.g., religion, spirituality and the importance of "word of mouth" in passing along health information) as ways to address obesity and overweight within their community. These findings are discussed along with the implications they have for community health researchers in addressing this health issue among African American women.

## Background

While responding to the increasing rates of obesity and overweight among African American women, in 2011 United States Surgeon General Dr. Regina M. Benjamin was quoted in the *New York Times* as saying, "Oftentimes you get women saying, 'I can't exercise today because I don't want to sweat my hair back or get my hair wet … When you're starting to exercise, you look for reasons not to, and sometimes the hair is one of those reasons"

(O'Connor 2011). This controversial statement received a great deal of criticism. However, it also initiated discussions within the African American community about the importance of hair and body image and its influence on exercise and obesity/overweight among African American women. As an African American women herself, Benjamin's quote speaks to the various sociocultural barriers that influence perceptions of beauty, body image and health among African American women. Hair can be one of the factors that inadvertently helps to fuel excessive weight gain caused by decreased physical activity and low levels of exercise among African American women since some African American women are hesitant to engage in physical activity at the expense of "messing up" a hair style that may be costly and/or time consuming to reproduce after exercise (Pulvers et al. 2004; Cachelin et al. 2002; Stevens et al. 1994). In essence, Benjamin is speaking to the sociocultural construct of beauty and its impact on health among African American women. This sociocultural construction of beauty and health has implications for researchers addressing the problem of obesity and overweight among African American women.

The sociological perspective of health care differs from that in the medical field, in large part due to the emphasis placed on the sociocultural constructs of health and illness. Social constructionism is a theoretical framework central to medical sociology that examines how social forces such as poverty and perceptions of body image affect health, illness and disease (Conrad and Barker 2010). Importantly, social constructionism argues that illness is experienced and understood differently by varying social and cultural groups and that individual, social, cultural, economic and environmental factors influence perceptions of illness and health care (Lupton 2000; Freund and McGuire 1999). As such, perceptions of health and the body vary among individuals and social and cultural groups.

## Obesity and Overweight:

Obesity is defined as excessive body fat or having a body mass index (BMI) greater than 30 $kg/m^2$ (Centers for Disease Control 2012a). Overweight is defined as weighing more than what is considered normal for one's height—having a BMI between 25 and 30 $kg/m^2$ (ibid.). Obesity- and overweight-related conditions include hypertension, type 2 diabetes, stroke, heart disease, increased risk for cancers and respiratory problems (Kopelman 2007).

According to the World Health Organization (2013), obesity and overweight is a worldwide epidemic. Currently, there are over 1 billion overweight and 500 million clinically obese adults worldwide, with 115 million obese people living in developing nations. Particularly troubling is the high rate of excessive weight gain among youth as over 40 million children under the age of five are considered obese (ibid.). Additionally, over one-third of the US population is obese and rates of obesity and overweight vary by race, gender, class and economic status (Centers for Disease Control 2013).

African Americans have the highest rates of obesity and overweight compared to all other racial/ethnic groups and among women in this nation (49.5 percent) (Office of Minority Health 2013). Approximately 80 percent of African American women are overweight or obese. Additionally, they are 80 percent more likely to be obese than White women (ibid.). African American women have demonstrated the largest increase in obesity from early childhood to young adulthood. In 2011, for example, African American high school girls were more likely to be obese (18.6 percent) than White girls (7.7 percent). Also, in 2009–10 25.7 percent of African American children were obese compared to 14.6 percent of White children (ibid.).

The greatest geographical concentrations of overweight and obese Americans are in the Southern and Midwestern regions of the United States, respectively (Centers for Disease Control 2013). In the state of Wisconsin 29.7 percent of the population is obese (ibid.) and

62.8 percent are overweight (Centers for Disease Control 2012b). In the city of Milwaukee 31 percent are obese and 37 percent are overweight (Chen et al. 2011). Also, low-income African Americans in Milwaukee have higher rates of obesity relative to the rates of Whites (Wisconsin Department of Health Services 2008).

Much of the excessive weight gain for African American females is due to the lack of physical activity and high levels of sedentary behavior—defined as less than 20 minutes of continuous physical activity weekly (Martin et al. 2004). For example, in their study of sedentary behavior among Americans Barnes and Schoenborn (2003) found that 72 percent of women and 64 percent of men were inactive. African American women have the lowest rate of physical activity or are more sedentary than women of other races (Martin et al. 2004; Adams-Campbell et al. 2000). According to the Office of Minority Health (2013), in 2011 55.5 percent of African American adults were physically inactive compared to 44.1 percent for Whites. Specifically, 68 percent of African American women reported less than 20 minutes of leisure-time physical activity per week (Cowie et al. 1993) and 40–82 percent of African American women are inactive or have very low activity levels (Macera et al. 2003; Crespo et al. 1996; Kushner et al. 1995; Washburn et al. 1992).

Many intervention strategies have been implemented to decrease obesity and overweight through a focus on reducing the behaviors associated with these conditions, such as one's poor nutritional intake and physical inactivity. Poor nutritional intake behaviors associated with weight gain include inadequate intake of fruit, vegetables and fiber and the excessive intake of calories, refined sugar and sodium. Intervention strategies to reduce these behaviors include dietary education and prescription medicines to increased physical activity (Di Noia et al. 2013; Parrill and Kennedy 2011; Elliot Brown et al. 1998). Physical inactivity includes low levels of all types of actions and, in particular, vigorous physical activities which contribute to one's fitness. These interventions have had a limited impact on changing the behaviors associated with obesity and overweight and have not consistently resulted in sustained weight loss and maintenance among study participants, regardless of race. A possible explanation for the lack of effect of these prescriptive or educational interventions is that they do not consider theoretically important cognitive and behavioral prerequisites to health behavior, nor do they consider sociocultural factors such as poverty and perceptions of body image and beauty on obesity and overweight within different populations.

## Poverty

According to the Centers for Disease Control (CDC) (2013), obesity and overweight are correlated with income and class as lower-income women are more likely to be obese than higher-income women. Even though African Americans only comprise 12.8 percent of the US population in 2011, they totaled 23.6 percent of the population below the poverty level. According to researchers, poverty is one of the primary barriers to positive health and it is associated with a number of obesity and overweight risk factors; particularly, limited access to healthy food (Drewnowski and Specter 2004; Drewnowski 2003) and increased sedentary behaviors (Dutton et al. 2004b; Martin et al. 2004).

Healthy and more nutritiously rich foods cost significantly more money and take more time to prepare than processed foods which tend to be high in fat and calories (Drewnowski and Specter 2004; Drewnowski 2003). As these healthier foods are often more expensive to purchase, they are not also not readily available to poor people living in urban African American neighborhoods and communities (Andreyeva et al. 2008). These communities often face a shortage of healthy foods and are known in the health literature as "food deserts" (Walker et al. 2010). Relatedly, communities with an overabundance of fast food restaurants and small corner stores that sell high-fat and calorie-processed foods are known as "food swamps" (Fielding and Simon 2011; Rose et al. 2009). Compared to Whites, African Americans are much more likely to live in communities characterized as food deserts and food swamps (Karpyn and Treuhaft 2009). Consequently, access to healthy food is largely compromised and one's consumption of high-calorie foods increases the rates of obesity and overweight within this community.

Poverty not only influences diet, it is also strongly associated with sedentary behavior (Levine 2011). African American women have the highest rates of sedentary behavior compared to their White female counterparts and African American men (Dutton et al. 2004a; Martin et al. 2004). This behavior is associated not only with the desire to not "sweat out" their hair as Benjamin (O'Connor 2011) notes, but with a compromised ability to afford the financial costs of participating in regular physical activity. These costs include gym memberships, work-out equipment, childcare and the (in)ability of many women to exercise in a safe and aesthetically pleasing environment (Nies et al. 1999; Wilbur et al. 2002). Low-income and minority communities have fewer recreational facilities and exercise spaces than wealthier and predominately White neighborhoods (Moore et al. 2008; Powell et al. 2006). These costs are temporal in addition to monetary. Since the majority of African American households are female headed, many women have neither the time, money nor energy to exercise (Nies et al. 1999; Burke et al. 1996; Kahn, Williamson and Stevens 1991).

## Sociocultural Constructs of the Body

In addition to poverty and a lack of resources, the existing literature suggests that perceptions of body image and beauty (e.g., culture) play a major role in obesity and overweight among African American women (Cachelin et al. 2002; Gore 1999; Allen et al. 1993; Kumanyika et al. 1993). Culture is the inherited lens through which the individual perceives and understands the world that she or he inhabits and is socialized to live within (Swartz 1997; Blumberg 1987). Language, tradition, knowledge and even perceptions of reality are culturally constructed. In particular, perceptions of the body are not only socially constructed; they are socioculturally constructed in that different social and cultural groups have unique understandings and perceptions of body image. According to Bakhshi (2001: 374), "Body image can be described as a combination of a person's perceptions, feelings and thoughts about his/her body and their general physical appearance." Certain groups, such as African Americans and Latinos, for example, endorse a large body size, particularly among women, as attractive or ideal (Cheney 2010; Cachelin et al. 2006, 2002; Demarest and Allen 2000; Fitzgibbon et al. 2000). Within these cultures, larger body sizes for women are often socially constructed to symbolize health, beauty, sexual attractiveness, wealth and being a good mother/wife (Pompper and Koenig 2004; Bush et al. 2001; Nasser 1988). As such, in a society that includes multiple racial/ethnic and cultural groups, it is to be expected that there will be multiple understandings of, and definitions for, obesity and overweight (Cachelin et al. 2002; Bush et al. 2001; Demarest and Allen 2000).

African American women typically have a broad definition of, and acceptance for, different body sizes. Accordingly, they judge higher body weight and greater weight gain as normal (DeBate et al. 2001; Allen et al. 1993). Evidence for this notion is gleaned from studies indicating that African American women, compared to comparable Whites and women of other racial/ethnic groups, have heavier body ideals (Botta 1999, 2000, 2003; Burke et al. 1996). Additional studies have concluded that, regardless of size, African American women report less dissatisfaction with their bodies than White women (DeBate et al. 2001; Altabe 1998). Likewise, African American girls report less body image dissatisfaction than White girls

(Sherwood et al. 2003; Flynn and Fitzgibbon 1996; Parnell et al. 1996). Research findings suggest that the oppression and segregation that African American women have historically endured has helped them construct positive cultural standards of body image and beauty (Banks 2000; Byrd and Tharps 2001). This enables them to reframe the standards of beauty and body acceptance among African American women and within larger African American cultures.

Body image issues and subsequent constructions of beauty that many African American women experience are more likely to be influenced by skin complexion (Hunter 2005; Russell Wilson and Hall, 1992), hair length and, as described above, hair texture (Spellers 2002; Byrd and Tharps 2001; Rooks 2001; Banks 2000). Historically, African American women with lighter skin and longer, straighter hair have more access to resources and are treated more favorably than their darker-skinned counterparts with shorter, curly hair (Byrd and Tharps 2001). Therefore, among African Americans, skin and hair issues may be of greater concern than body size (Hunter 2005; Byrd and Tharps 2001; Banks 2000; Russell et al. 1992). This highlights the different sociocultural constructions of body image.

Sociocultural frameworks of the body are often based on varied definitions of healthy body sizes. African American women challenge the traditional BMI measures and have much more liberal definitions of healthy body sizes that often include being, technically, obese and overweight (Gore 1999; Kumanyika et al. 1993). BMI has been used since the 1940s to measure and define normal or desired body weight and size. It is calculated by dividing the weight of the person by the square of their height (Kuczmarski and Flegal 2000). However, women, women of color specifically, have consistently resisted accepting this scientific definition of obesity and overweight. BMI has often been criticized as being an inaccurate measure because, in part, it imposes a "White Body Norm" ideal onto other racial/ethnic groups to whom the measure may not adequately apply (Wagner and Heyward 2000). These "normal" body types and definitions, along with standard definitions of beauty, do not fit the cultural norm. The social and cultural issues facing people and their communities impact not only their ability and desire to reduce body weight, but, as shown above, also the perception of what is considered overweight and obese (Fitzgibbon et al. 2000; Gore 1999; Kumanyika et al. 1993). In summary, most of the existing literature has observed that poverty and cultural constructions of the body are among the most important factors influencing obesity and overweight among African American women.

## Theoretical Framework

As described above, sociocultural factors have significant influence on perceptions of body weight and the ability and desire to reduce body weight. These constructs of body image, combined with poverty, are among the most influential factors impacting obesity and overweight among African American women. Black feminist thought is used as the theoretical framework to analyze how sociocultural forces shape the consciousness of African American women as it provides a uniquely shaped world-view based on their experiences and perceptions (Collins 2000). Black feminist thought is linked to traditional Western African customs and is rooted in the history and experiences of African American women in the US (Collins 2000). In explaining African American women's standpoint, Black feminist theorist and author, Patricia Hill Collins (1995: 339) writes:

> *Black women's political and economic status provides them with a distinctive set of experiences that offers a different view of material reality than that available to other groups. The unpaid and paid work that Black women perform, the types of communities in which they live, and the kinds of relationships they have with others*

*suggest that African American women, as a group, experience a different world than those who are not Black and female ... these experiences stimulate a distinctive Black feminist consciousness concerning that material reality.*

In order to examine the issues pertaining to obesity and overweight among African American women, six focus groups were conducted with African American women from a Milwaukee neighborhood that has high rates of obesity, overweight and poverty. Understanding the sociocultural factors influencing rates of obesity and overweight among African American women is vital in reducing rates of health inequalities within this population. It is also important to help shift and expand understandings of the body and health and how they are perceived across sociocultural groups.

## Methods

This study is part of a larger health intervention program targeting African American women in Milwaukee. The project team consists of researchers from two major academic institutions and a community health clinic. The team has formed a partnership with representative women from the local community who are participating on a project advisory board that is helping to direct the work on this study. The overall purpose is to test a health intervention that incorporates motivational interviewing counseling (a technique using motivation to elicit behavioral change) (Rollnick and Miller 1995), conducted with the aid of community health workers from the local neighborhood (Brownstein et al. 2011; World Health Organization 2007). Primary outcome measures are health-related behaviors (i.e., change in exercise and nutritional intake patterns). A series of focus groups were used to conduct a needs assessment to guide the design of the motivational interviewing counseling sessions.

### Recruitment

In an effort to obtain a broad sample of African American women, flyers describing the project were distributed throughout the target neighborhood (e.g., coffee shops, churches and beauty salons). Staff at the community-based health clinic also approached potential participants. Twenty-two women responded and were arbitrarily divided into two groups to optimize participant input. The groups met twice a month to discuss various personal and community issues that influence health and rates of obesity and overweight in this community. Each focus group centered loosely on a particular topic: 1) defining health issues within the community, 2) body image among African American women in the community, 3) religion/spirituality, 4) upbringing/family, 5) community assets that promote health and 6) next steps that should be taken to address health and excessive weight gain among women in the community.

### Sample

All of the women were drawn from the same working-class neighborhood that is approximately one square mile and located in central Milwaukee. The area is as well-known for its high rates of civic and community engagement as it is for poverty and crime. This community is primarily comprised of female-headed African American households with an average yearly income of $22,466 (Weber and Frazer 2012). This community was selected for this inquiry because of its high rates of obesity and poverty, as well as its predominantly African American population.

The first "wave" of responders recruited additional participants. The women were asked to attend as many sessions as possible, with each meeting drawing 12–15 participants. All 22 women completed a demographic and health survey before joining their first group session.

## Data Analysis

Results from the demographic and health surveys were entered into SPSS for descriptive analysis. All focus group discussions were recorded with a digital voice recorder and transcribed. All transcriptions received a line-by-line analysis and were coded for key themes and concepts. The average focus group lasted approximately 63 minutes, with a range from 57 minutes to 72 minutes.

# Results

## Participants

All of the 22 women who completed the survey and participated in the focus groups identify as African American and their average age is 54. Two of the participants are legally married; although neither was living with their spouse at the time of this investigation. A vast majority of the participants earned below $8,500 per year. All but one of the focus group participants are obese or overweight and the average weight for the group is 180 pounds. Most have their high school diploma or GED and all identified as being religious or spiritual.

## Focus Groups

Similar themes recurred throughout all of the six topic sessions and they highlight the importance that sociocultural factors have on obesity and overweight in this community. The themes were: 1) social barriers (e.g., lack of money, resources and reliable health care that women have), 2) general disagreement over the medical definition of normal body size and the continued use of the BMI to calculate body size and 3) the inclusion of religion and spirituality as community assets and how these may be used to help promote health.

## Social Barriers

Focus group participants noted that the women in their community had, overall, poor health. For example, one participant stated, "The health here is actually poor. African-American women health is poor." Focus group participants listed a number of barriers they felt directly influence obesity and overweight and the overall health of African American women in their community. These barriers included poverty and the lack of adequate health care services. Commenting specifically on the lack of job opportunities in their community, one focus group participant noted, "It's hard to find a job ... A lot of us don't have no jobs."

Another said, "We don't have enough money for one. I'm just going to put that out there." In addition to lack of jobs, many felt it was simply difficult to find (healthy) food, particularly at the end of the month: "And at the end of the month them [food] stamps don't stretch. And at the end of the month you scratching out of your cabinets to make a meal so you take whatever is left to make a meal."

All focus group participants discussed how difficult it was to find reliable health care. One participant explained, "My thing is finding a good reliable physician because I'm a person that if you goin' take care of me, I want that person that's good to keep taking care of me. But once you get them and you get comfortable with them. They leave and I don't like that."

## The "Normal" Body

When asked about the overall health concerns facing women within their community, none of the women in the focus groups mentioned obesity or being overweight. Health concerns discussed included heart disease, high blood pressure and diabetes. Although these health issues are all related to obesity and overweight the women did not explicitly discuss it. When asked about obesity and overweight the respondents discussed their disagreement with the use of scientific measurements to determine what a normal body weight is and that they had different conceptualizations of thin than what would have been found within other communities.

Focus group participants were extremely critical of the continued use of the BMI to measure and define obesity and overweight. One participant noted, "We need a new normal." When asked to elaborate she stated, "Maybe I'm thinking wrong but the chart that they have up is going by 5'8" and I should be 140. Maybe they should allow me to be 150 or something. I don't know. See the normal might be wrong. But then also what is healthy? Just because you're big doesn't mean you have a disease." Another respondent agreed saying:

> They say I'm obese. I'm heavy; I've never been real, real thin. You know obesity is anything over whatever the normal is. It's not necessarily being fat but it's like I'm not 140. Then I'm obese. I'm not 110 then I'm obese. That's why I said obesity is anything that over the normal on the chart. You just not fitting into that normal thing you know, for your height and your weight.

When asked how obesity and body size should be measured they stated it should be based on how the client feels. One person said:

> I think you should measure it according to how you feel because BMI, everybody knows that doesn't work. Height and weight and all that we know that doesn't work for certain cultures. I think that we should measure it on how you feel. You know when certain things aren't suppose to be there. You know that's not healthy. But you have to get rid of that and the hips. You have to get rid of that also. But if you know that you are eating right and you can walk up a flight of stairs without breathing hard, or you can do normal things without being out of breath, I would measure that I'm healthy. I walk up 100 flight of stairs, well I will say 25 flights of stairs, and I wasn't out of breath.

When asked to discuss how thin is perceived, focus group participants did not highlight anything positive about being thin or about weight loss. Participants were asked what a "thin woman looks like to them" and all but one participant responded negatively. They stated that thin women look "anorexic," "skinny," "they need to gain weight ... I need to go feed her." In general, they were critical as to whether or not such women were actually healthy.

## Religion and Spirituality as Community Assets

Although focus group participants described the many challenges that they and other women in the community experience, they also discussed the many assets found within this community and how they can be used to help promote healthier lifestyles. Assets centered on the importance of religion and spirituality. Specifically, respondents noted how religion and spirituality provide not only mental health support, but also a sense of fulfillment to go along with a place that can promote health and social justice. Focus group participants also noted the importance of "word of mouth" transmissions to address community health concerns as well as the importance of other African American women in the community who provide information about community health concerns.

All focus group participants identified themselves as religious or spiritual. Moreover, they made a distinction between the two. One participant explained:

> To me, a religion is a name of a church or domination that you go to ... like Church of God in Christ, or Baptist. But a spiritual person to me is someone who I think puts Jesus Christ first in their life. Someone who, you know, goes to church and practices what they hear on Sundays and Wednesdays or however often that they go. So that's the difference.

Additionally, participants agreed that they feel their religion or spiritual belief promotes health. For example, one participant stated, "God promises us divine health in His Word. But in order to walk in the divine health that He promises us you know there are some conditions to that. We have to exercise. We have to eat right. We have to, you know, take care of ourselves mentally, physically and spiritually." Participants argued that most churches in the community do little to promote healthy eating and living. However, there is space for that type of education within their churches. It is especially important, they noted, if the pastor is on board and works to promote healthy living among congregants. A participant stated:

> Because the pastor is doing it [congregants] want to do it. Most of the time people want to do what their pastor is doing. They want to just let him know that they support him as he loses weight. So it makes a big difference if the pastor is practicing what he is preaching. Especially if you can see a difference in him.

## Community Self-Care

According to focus group participants, using word of mouth is the most effective way of reaching the African American women in their community to inform them on health and weight loss issues. For example, one participant explained, "Word of mouth is going into the corner store and you see a flyer in there and you just so happen go to pick it up and then you read it." Another, "Then you pass the word along. That's how I found out about this [focus group]." A key community asset, one that is responsible for the "word of mouth" and overall care that has proven to be an invaluable resource for these participants and the women in their community, comes from African American women in the community. Focus group participants argued that many women in their community had what is known as "a motherly instinct, that there's trouble, the mother is right there to help you out. The momma always has your back, health problems, they gonna get you to a doctor."

## Discussion

Black feminist theory is used to analyze data from focus groups made up of African American women from a community in Milwaukee. Findings indicate that the anticipated sociocultural barriers such as poverty and limited access to health care are important, but these may be offset to some degree by the identification of community assets such as high levels of spirituality and shared religious resources. The perceptions of body image described by the groups highlight a disconnection with the commonly accepted medical definitions of obesity and overweight. This may explain the limited success of prior obesity interventions. Understanding the sociocultural perceptions of obesity and overweight among African American women is vital if these rates, as well as the comorbidities within this population, are to be reduced. Moreover, they will have important implications for health promotion programs targeting these women. These data also help to expand understandings of sociocultural constructions of health issues and the body.

A consistent theme found within all of the focus groups was the alternative understandings of health. Although the respondents discussed the comorbidities associated with obesity and overweight, such as high blood pressure and diabetes, they do not see excessive weight gain as a health issue with their community. This could be from a lack of knowledge concerning how obesity leads to negative health conditions and their experiences that non-overweight individuals may also suffer from these conditions as well.

Although prior research highlights the importance of different perceptions of body image and obesity (Gore 1999; Kumanyika et al. 1993) and the relationship between poverty and health, most has excluded discussions on the importance of religion and spirituality in the lives of women and how it influences perceptions of obesity and body image. First, the religious beliefs of these women allow for both tolerance of obesity and overweight. As one respondent notes, her religion requires that she "accept everyone." This is the case regardless of body size and health status. Additionally, the religious institutions in which these women participate often provide food for congregants. More often than not these meals are not healthy and are high in fat and calories.

Focus group participants also highlight the importance of relying on community members for health-related information. The passing of information via word of mouth is a very important strategy for obtaining community information and services. They also believe that relying primarily on word of mouth, as well as obtaining help from other community members and leaders, is vital in promoting health within their community. Increasingly, health promoters and researchers are emphasizing the importance of community health workers (CHWs), trusted people from the local community who will serve as conduits between members of the community and health care providers and services (Brownstein et al. 2011; World Health Organization 2007), as they are vital in the development of any community -focused health care promotion program. CHWs provide a number of resources for community members, health care researchers and practitioners, as they can help researchers understand community issues and help community members understand community health issues and inequalities. These focus group findings suggest that using CHWs is a successful strategy for implementing behavior change. Women in the focus group specifically emphasize their belief that health promoters often overlook them. As one participant explained, "I think there are specific things that African Americans are at risk for, and they should target us. We are at risk for it, and a White person is not at risk, so we should be targeted." Furthermore, all of the women are concerned about their health: "We are stereotyped. Black people don't go to the doctor, but that's not true. We're women first and were happy that we are in studies, but we basically are women, of different colors." These comments speak to the lack of health care resources in some urban minority communities. Despite this deficiency, these women acknowledge the importance of self-motivation for behavior change and convey an intuitive grasp of "patient activation," or the understanding and skill to address one's health care needs (Greene and Hibbard 2012).

## Conclusion

Black feminist theory argues that the life experiences of African American women greatly influence sociocultural perceptions of reality (Collins 2000), which includes health. Analysis of the data within this frame allows for a better understanding of the sociocultural issues associated with obesity and overweight among the African American women. Importantly, the women here believe that poverty and perceptions of body image are contributors to obesity and overweight. However, they are also quick to highlight the various community assets and resources to address these issues. These assets include religion, spirituality and the passing of information via word of mouth. The latter asset is applied to obesity and overweight reduction and overall health promotion in the next phase of this work when we implement the intervention utilizing Motivational Interviewing Counseling and CHWs.

The primary limitations of the present study are the small population of participants who are drawn from a specific geographic area. The women in this sample were likely poorer than the general population of African American women in the US. As such, some of their comments are not generalizable to the population of African American women as they represent the thoughts and ideas of this particular group.

Based on our observations, interventions to reduce obesity should not only target and take into account the sociocultural constructions of obesity and overweight, but should also take advantage of the community resources and assets such as passing knowledge via "word of mouth" and the influence of religion and spirituality.

## References

Adams-Campbell, Lucile, Lynn Rosenberg, Richard Washburn, R. Sowmya Rao, Kyung Sook Kim and Julie Palmer. 2000. "Descriptive Epidemiology of Physical Activity in African-American Women." *Preventive Medicine* 30: 43–50.

Allen, Janet D., Kelly Mayo and Yvonne Michel. 1993. "Body Size Values of White and Black Women." *Research in Nursing and Health* 16(5): 323–33.

Altabe, Madeline. 1998. "Ethnicity and Body Image: Quantitative and Qualitative Analysis." *International Journal of Eating Disorders* 23(2): 153–9.

Andreyeva, Tatiana, Daniel M. Blumenthal, Marlene B. Schwartz, Michael W. Long and Kelly D. Brownell. 2008. "Availability and Prices of Foods across Stores and Neighborhoods: The Case Of New Haven, Connecticut." *Health Affairs* 27(5): 1381–8.

Bakhshi, Savita. 2007. "Women's Body Image and the Role of Culture: A Review of the Literature." *Europe's Journal of Psychology* 7(2):374–394.

Banks, Ingrid. 2000. *Hair Matters: Beauty, Power, and Black Women's Consciousness*. New York: New York University Press.

Barnes, Patricia M. and Charlotte A. Schoenborn. 2003. *Physical Activity among Adults: United States, 2000. Advanced Data from Vital and Health Statistics No. 333*. Hyattsville, MD: National Center for Health Statistics.

Blumberg, Rhoda Lois. 1987. *Organizations in Contemporary Society*. Englewood Cliffs, NJ: Prentice-Hall, Inc.

Botta, Renee A. 1999. "Television Images and Adolescent Girls' Body Image Disturbance." *Journal of Communication* 49: 22–41.

———. 2000. "The Mirror of Television: A Comparison of Black and White Adolescents' Body Image." *Journal of Communication* 50: 144–59.

———. 2003. "For Your Health? The Relationship between Magazine Reading and Adolescents' Body Image and Eating Disturbances." *Sex Roles* 48(9/10): 389–99.

Brownstein, J. Nell, Talley Andrews, Hilary Wall and Qaiser Mukhtar. 2011. *Addressing Chronic Disease through Community Health Workers: A Policy and Systems-level Approach*. Atlanta, GA: Centers for Disease Control and Prevention. Retrieved November 15, 2013: http://www.cdc.gov/dhdsp/docs/chw_brief.pdf.

Burke, Gregory L., Diane E. Bild, Joan E. Hilner, Aaron R. Folsom, Lynne E. Wagenkencht and Stephen Sidney. 1996. "Differences in Weight Gain in Relation to Race, Gender, Age, and Education in Young Adults: The CARDIA Study." *Ethnicity and Health* 1: 327–35.

Bush, Helen M., Rory Williams, Mike Lean and Annie Anderson. 2001. "Body Image and Weight Consciousness among South Asian, Italian and General Population Women in Britain." *Appetite* 37(3): 207–15.

Byrd, Ayana and Lori Tharps. 2001. *Hair Story: Untangling the Roots of Black Hair in America*. New York: St. Martin's Press.

Cachelin, Fary M., Ramona M. Rebeck, Grace H. Chung and Elizabeth Pelayo. 2002. "Does Ethnicity Influence Body-size Preference? A Comparison of Body Image and Body Size." *Obesity Research* 10(3): 158–66.

———, Teresa K. Monreal, and Laura C. Juarez. 2006. "Body Image and Size Perceptions of Mexican American Women." *Body Image* 3(1): 67–75.

Centers for Disease Control and Prevention. 2012a. *Overweight and Obesity: Defining Overweight and Obesity*. Atlanta, GA: Centers for Disease Control and Prevention. Retrieved November 10, 2013: http://www.cdc.gov/obesity/adult/defining.html.

———. 2012b. *Overweight and Obesity: Wisconsin's Response to Obesity*. Atlanta, GA: Centers for Disease Control and Prevention. Retrieved November 11, 2013: http://www.cdc.gov/obesity/stateprograms/fundedstates/wisconsin.html.

———. 2013. *Overweight and Obesity: Adult Obesity Facts*. Atlanta, GA: Centers for Disease Control and Prevention. Retrieved November 10, 2013: http://www.cdc.gov/obesity/data/adult.html.

Chen, Han-Yang., Dennis J. Baumgardner, Loren W. Galvao, Jessica P. Rice, Geoffrey R. Swain and Ron A. Cisler. 2011. *Milwaukee Health Report 2011: Health Disparities in Milwaukee by Socioeconomic Status*. Milwaukee, WI: Center for Urban Population Health.

Cheney, Ann M. 2010. "Most Girls Want to be Skinny: Body (Dis)Satisfaction among Ethnically Diverse Women." *Qualitative Health Research* 21: 1347–59.

Collins, Patricia Hill. 2000. *Black Feminist Thought: Knowledge, Consciousness, and the Politics of Empowerment*. New York: Routledge.

———. 1995. "The Social Construction of Black Feminist Thought." in *Words of Fire: An Anthology of African-American Feminist Thought*, ed. B. Guy-Sheftall. New York: New York Press, pp. 338–57.

Conrad, Peter and Kristin Barker. 2010. "The Social Construction of Illness: Key Insights and Policy Implications." *Journal of Health and Social Behavior* 51: S67–S79.

Cowie, Catherine, Maureen I. Harris, Robert E. Silverman, Ernest W. Johnson and Keith Rust. 1993. "Effect of Multiple Risk Factors on Differences between Blacks and Whites in the Prevalence of Non-insulin-dependent Diabetes Mellitus in the United States." *American Journal of Epidemiology* 137(7): 719–32.

Crespo, Carlos J., Steven J. Keteyian, Gregory W. Heath, and Christopher T. Sempos. 1996. "Leisure-time Physical Activity among US Adults, Results from the Third National Health and Nutrition Examination Survey." *Archives of Internal Medicine* 156: 93–8.

Demarest, Jack and Rita Allen. 2000. "Body Image: Gender, Ethnic, and Age Differences." *The Journal of Social Psychology* 140(4): 465–72.

DeBate, Rita DiGioacchino, Marvette Topping and Roger G. Sargent. 2001. "Racial and Gender Differences in Weight Status and Dietary Practices among College Students." *Adolescence* 36: 819–33.

Di Noia, Jennifer, Gennifer Furst, Keumjae Park and Carol Byrd-Bredbenner. 2013. "Designing Culturally Sensitive Dietary Interventions for African Americans: Review and Recommendations." *Nutritional Reviews* 71(4): 224–38.

Drewnowski, Adam. 2003. "Fat and Sugar: an Economic Analysis." *Journal of Nutrition* 133(1): S838–S840.

—— and S.E. Specter. 2004. "Poverty and Obesity: The Role of Energy Density and Energy Costs." *American Journal of Clinical Nutrition* 79: 6–16.

Dutton, Gareth R., Pamela Davis Martin and Phillip J. Brantley. 2004a. "Ideal Weight Goals of African American Women Participating in a Weight Management Program." *Body Image* 1(3): 305–10.

——, Pamela Davis Martin, Paula C. Rhode and Phillip Brantley. 2004b. "Use of the Weight Efficacy Lifestyle Questionnaire with African American Women: Validation and Extension of Previous Findings." *Eating Behavior* 5(4): 375–84.

Elliot Brown, Karin A., Frances E. Jemmott, Holly J. Mitchell and Mary L. Walton. 1998. "The Well. A Neighborhood-based Health Promotion Model for Black Women." *Health & Social Work* 23(2): 146–52.

Fielding, Johnathan E. and Paul A. Simon. 2011. "Food Deserts or Food Swamps: Comment on Fast Food Restaurants and Food Stores." *Archive Internal Medicine* 171(13): 1171–2.

Fitzgibbon, Marian L., Lisa R. Blackman and Mary E. Avellone. 2000. "The Relationship between Body Image Discrepancy and Body Mass Index across Ethnic Groups." *Obesity Research* 8(8): 582–9.

Flynn, Kristin and Marian Fitzgibbon. 1996. "Body Image Ideals of Low-income African-American Mothers and their Preadolescent Daughters." *Journal of Youth and Adolescence* 25: 615–30.

Freund, Peter E.S. and Meredith McGuire. 1999. *Health, Illness, and the Social Body: A Critical Sociology.* Upper Saddle River, NJ: Prentice Hall.

Gore, Shirley V. 1999. "African-American Women's Perceptions of Weight: Paradigm Shift for Advanced Practice." *Holistic Nursing Practice* 13(4): 71–9.

Greene, Jessica and Judith H. Hibbard. 2012. "Why Does Patient Activation Matter? An Examination of the Relationships between Patient Activation and Health-related Outcomes." *Journal of General Internal Medicine* 27(5): 520–26.

Hunter, Margaret L. 2005. *Race, Gender, and the Politics of Skin Tone.* New York: Routledge-Taylor Francis.

Kahn, Henry S., David F. Williamson and Judy A. Stevens. 1991. "Race and Weight Change in US Women: The Roles of Socioeconomic and Marital Status." *American Journal of Public Health* 81: 319–23.

Karpyn, Allison and Sarah Treuhaft. 2009. *The Grocery Gap: Who Has Access to Healthy Food and Why It Matters*. Oakland, CA: Policy Link and The Food Trust. Retrieved November 10, 2011: http://www.policylink.org/atf/cf/%7B97C6D565-BB43-406D-A6D5-ECA3BBF35AF0%7D/FINALGroceryGap.pdf.

Kopelman, Peter G. 2007. "Health Risk Associated with Overweight and Obesity." *Obesity Reviews* 8(l): 13–17.

Kuczmarski, Robert J. and Katherine M. Flegal. 2000. "Criteria for Definition of Overweight in Transition: Background and Recommendations for the United States." *American Journal of Clinical Nutrition* 72(5): 1074–81.

Kumanyika, Shiriki, Judy Wilson and Marsha Guliford-Davenport. 1993. "Weight-related Attitudes and Behaviors of Black Women." *Journal of the American Dietetic Association* 93: 416–22.

Kushner, Robert F., Susan B. Racette, Karen Neil and Dale A. Schoeller. 1995. "Measurement of Physical Activity among African-American and Caucasian Women." *Obesity Research* 3: 261–5.

Levine, James A. 2011. "Poverty and Obesity in the U.S." *Diabetes* 60(11): 2667–8.

Lupton, Deborah. 2000. *Medicine as Culture: Illness, Disease and the Body in Western Societies*. Thousand Oaks, CA: Sage Publications, Inc.

Macera, Caroline A., Deborah A. Jones, Michelle Yore, Sandra Ham, Harold W. Kohl, C. Dexter Kimsey and David Buchner. 2003. "Prevalence of Physical Activity, Including Lifestyle Activities among Adults – United States, 2000–2001." *Morbidity Mortality Weekly Reports* 52(32): 764–69.

Martin, Pamela D., Gareth R. Dutton and Phillip J. Brantley. 2004. 'Self-efficacy as a Predictor of Weight Change in African-American Women." *Obesity Research* 12(4):646–51.

Moore, Latetia V., Ana V. Diez Roux, Kelly R. Evenson, Aileen P. McGinn and Shannon J. Brines. 2008. "Availability of Recreational Resources in Minority and Low Socioeconomic Status Areas." *American Journal of Preventative Medicine* 34: 16–22.

Nasser, Mervat. 1988. "Culture and Weight Consciousness." *Journal of Psychosomatic Research* 32(6): 573–77.

Nies, Mary A., Michael Vollman and Thomas Cook. 1999. "African American Women's Experiences with Physical Activity in their Daily Lives." *Public Health Nursing* 16(1): 23–31.

O'Connor, Anahad. 2011. "Surgeon General Calls for Health over Hair." New York Times [online] 25 August. Retrieved November 11, 2013: http://well.blogs.nytimes.com/2011/08/25/surgeon-general-calls-for-health-over-hair/.

Office of Minority Health. 2013. *Obesity and African Americans*. Washington, DC: The Office of Minority Health. Retrieved September 20, 2013: ****http://minorityhealth.hhs.gov/templates/content.aspx?ID=6456.

Ogden, Cynthia L., Margaret D. Carroll, Brian K. Kit and Katherine M. Flegal. 2013. *Prevalence of Obesity in the United States, 2011–2012. NCHS data brief, no. 131*. Hyattsville, MD: National Center for Health Statistics. Retrieved November 24, 2013: http://www.cdc.gov/nchs/data/databriefs/db131.pdf.

Parnell, Kathy, Roger G. Sargent, Sharon H. Thompson, Sonja Duhe, Robert F. Valois and Richard Kemper. 1996. "Black and White Adolescent Females' Perceptions of Ideal Body Size." *Journal of School Health* 66(3): 112–18.

Parrill, Rachel and Bernice Roberts Kennedy. 2011. "Partnerships for Health in the African American Community: Moving Toward Community-based Participatory Research." *Journal of Cultural Diversity* 18(4): 150–54.

Pompper, Donnalyn and Jesica Koenig. 2004. "Cross-cultural-generational Perceptions of Ideal Body Image: Hispanic Women and Magazine Standards." *Journalism and Mass Communication Quarterly* 81(1): 89–107.

Powell Lisa M., Sandy Slater, Frank J. Chaloupka and Deborah Harper. 2006. "Availability of Physical Activity Related Facilities and Neighborhood Demographic and Socioeconomic Characteristics: A National Study." *American Journal of Public Health* 96: 1676–80.

Pulvers. Kim M., Rebecca E. Lee, Harsohena Kaur, Matthew S. Mayo, Marian L. Fitzgibbon, Shawn K. Jeffries, James Butler, Qingjiang Hou and Jasjit S. Ahlwalia. 2004. "Development of a Culturally Relevant Body Image Instrument among Urban African-Americans." *Obesity Research* 12: 1641–51.

Rollnick Stephen, and William R. Miller. 1995. "What is Motivational Interviewing?" *Behavioural and Cognitive Psychotherapy* 23(4): 325–34.

Rooks, Noliwe. 2001. "Wearing Your Hair Wrong: Hair, Drama, and Politics of Representation for African American Women at Play on a Battlefield." in *Recovering the Black Female Body: Self-Representations by African American Women*, eds. M. Bennett and V.D. Dickerson. New Brunswick, NJ: Rutgers University Press, pp. 279–95.

Rose, Donald, J. Nicholas Bodor, Chris M. Swalm, Janet C. Rice, Thomas A. Farley and Paul L. Hutchinson. 2009. *Deserts in New Orleans? Illustrations of Urban Food Access and Implications for Policy.* Washington, DC: National Poverty Center. Retrieved November 11, 2013: http://www.npc.umich.edu/news/events/food-access/index.php.

Russell, Kathy, Midge Wilson and Ronald Hall. 1992. *The Color Complex: The Politics of Skin Color among African Americans.* New York: Harcourt Brace Jovanovich.

Sherwood, Nancy E., Mary Story, Bettina Beech, Lisa Klesges, Allison Mellin and Dianne Neumark-Sztainer. 2003. "Body Image Perceptions and Dieting among African-American Pre-adolescent Girls and Parents/Caregivers." *Ethnicity & Disease* 13: 200–207.

Sobal, Jeffrey. 1991. "Obesity and Socioeconomic Status: A Framework for Examining Relationships between Physical and Social Variables." *Medical Anthropology* 13: 231–47.

Spellers, Regina E. 2002. "Happy to be Nappy: Embracing an Afrocentric Aesthetic of Beauty." in *Readings in Intercultural Communication: Experiences and Contexts*, eds. Judith N. Martin, Thomas K. Nakayama and Lisa Flores. Boston, MA: McGraw Hill, pp. 52–9.

Stevens, June S., Shiriki K. Kumamyika and Julian E. Keil. 1994. "Attitudes toward Body Size and Dieting: Differences between Elderly Black and White Women." *American Journal of Public Health* 84: 1322–5.

Swartz, David. 1997. *Culture and Power: The Sociology of Pierre Bourdieu.* Chicago, IL: University of Chicago Press.

Wagner, Dale R. and Vivian H. Heyward. 2000. "Measures of Body Composition in Blacks and Whites: A Comparative Review." *American Journal of Clinical Nutrition* 71(6): 1392–402.

Walker, Renee E., Christopher R. Keane and Jessica G. Burke. 2010. "Disparities and Access to Healthy Food in the United States: A Review of Food Deserts Literature." *Health Place* 6(5): 876–84.

Washburn, Richard A., Gregory Kline, Daniel T. Lackland and Frances C. Wheeler. 1992. "Leisure Time Activity Physical Activity: Are there Black/White Differences?" *Preventative Medicine* 21(1): 127–35.

Weber, Tyler and David Frazer. 2012. *The Lindsay Heights Men's Wellness Council Report: 2012 Progress and Findings Report.* Milwaukee, WI: The Lindsay Heights Men's Wellness Council. Retrieved November 11, 2013: http://www.cuph.org/projects/global/material/5702/binary/.

Wilbur, JoEllen, Peggy Chandler, Barbara Dancy, JiWon Choi and Donna Plonczynski. 2002. "Environmental, Policy and Cultural Factors Related to Physical Activity in Urban, African American Women." *Women Health* 36(2): 17–28.

Wisconsin Department of Health Services, 2008. *Obesity, Nutrition, and Physical Activity in Wisconsin.* Madison, WI: Wisconsin Department of Health Services. Retrieved November 12, 2013: http://www.dhs.wisconsin.gov/publications/P0/P00009.pdf.

World Health Organization. 2007. *Community Health Workers: What do we know about them?: Evidence and Information for Policy.* Geneva, Switzerland: Department of Human Resources for Health. Retrieved November 13, 2013: http://www.who.int/hrh/documents/community_health_workers.pdf.

———. 2013. *Obesity and Overweight.* Geneva, Switzerland: World Health Organization. Retrieved July 1, 2013: http://www.who.int/mediacentre/factsheets/fs311/en/index.html.

# HIV: A Social Catastrophe

## Marye Bernard and Malinda R. Conrad

## HIV: The Beginning

The global Human Immunodeficiency Virus (HIV) epidemic currently impacts more than 34 million people worldwide. Although there has been a steady decline in the number of new HIV infections and HIV-related deaths around the world, this virus continues to burden many countries, especially those in sub-Saharan Africa where the incidences of HIV infections in that region exceeds other parts of the world (Joint United Nations Programme on HIV/AIDS 2010). In the United States, the South accounts for close to half of all new HIV infections and AIDS-related deaths for all age groups, with African American women and men who have sex with other men (MSM) representing the fastest growing group of newly infected persons (Centers for Disease Control and Prevention 2011a).

## History

Chimpanzees from sub-Saharan Africa are suspected to be the original source of HIV as they carry Simian immunodeficiency viruses (SIVcpz) which share nine components that are similar to those found in HIV-1 (Bailes et al. 2002). Another virus strain, Simian immunodeficiency viruses (SIVmm), have been known to mutate across species. The mutation from chimpanzees to humans is possible since both share more than 98 percent of their gene identity (Sharp et al. 2005). However, HIV infections in humans differs from SIV in chimpanzees in that SIV infections do not progress to immunodeficiency in chimpanzees or result in AIDS (Watanabe et al. 2004). Although it is uncertain that HIV is borne from transmissions from chimpanzees to humans, the most approximate theory to date suggests that humans became exposed to SIV through blood exchanges while either hunting, butchering or consuming chimpanzees for food.

The eating of chimpanzee meat (bushmeat) originated in Cameroon and has been practiced along the path of the Sangha River to Kinshasa (Rambaut et al. 2004). This is ironic since the earliest documented case of HIV, the virus that causes Acquired Immunodeficiency Syndrome (AIDS), was first diagnosed in 1959 in a man from Kinshasa, Democratic Republic of the Congo (Center for Disease Control and Prevention 2009b).

It is highly suggestive that HIV was introduced to the United States by heterosexual individuals born in West Africa and who later relocated to the United States prior to 1985 (Centers for Disease Control and Prevention 1989). Exposures in these cases were possibly through contact with sex workers in West Africa. During its early years the disease was mostly asymptomatic or included vague symptomology (ibid.). The first symptomatic cases of HIV in the United States came from three hospitals in Los Angeles, California where five similar cases of a poorly understood, yet aggressive, illness affected men with a history of having sex with men. This was cause for alarm among scientists, healthcare clinicians and the gay community as the disease was initially described as the "gay cancer," a disease thought to only plague MSM. Since the early cases were considered the consequence of lifestyle decisions the federal government did not appropriate resources for aggressive study and analysis. Additional cases of HIV were soon discovered in persons with hemophilia—a bleeding disorder that requires frequent blood transfusions. People with hemophilia contracted the virus largely through contaminated blood sources. Fortunately, current systems for screening blood have improved significantly and the risk of obtaining the virus via this method is essentially nil (Kessler 2007).

Comparing the frequency of HIV infection among groups in Africa and the United States, it is important to understand the culture of West Africa at the time HIV was first discovered. Sex between men was, and is still, considered taboo in Africa. This is why, unlike in the United States, the majority of reported infections from Africa were of heterosexual transmission (Gisselquist and Potterat 2003). Because the first cases of HIV in the United States were diagnosed in MSM, negative public perception and misconception of HIV transmission within populations were established and would continue to exist more than 30 years later (Centers for Disease Control and Prevention 2011b).

The early cases of HIV were found primarily within the populations of homosexual men, Haitians migrating to Florida, heroin addicts and hemophiliacs—known colloquially as the "Four H Club." This fact resulted in the immediate and negative assignment of stigma to these groups and their potential HIV status (Stone et al. 2010). The Four H Club became the *nom de guerre* for acquisition of HIV disease. Presumptively, in order to have HIV one was either Haitian (or of Black descent), a hemophiliac (blood disease), a homosexual or a heroin addict (intravenous drug use) (U.S. Department of Health and Human Services Health Resources and Services Administration 2011). Later, people who sold sex for money (Ho's) were also included in this club. The repugnant reputation associated with HIV acquisition birthed the onset of negative stigma surrounding this disease that continues to this day.

Social determinants of health represent an individual's inherent social system (i.e., economic, education and political beliefs that influence health perceptions) and include declining marriage participation, low literacy, substance abuse, violence, access to health care and female-headed and single-parent household structures (Stanhope and Lancaster 2008). Multiple social determinants of health influence HIV acquisition at disproportionately higher rates. Poverty has been identified as one of the most significant contributors to acquiring HIV because of inadequate access to appropriate health care and limited financial resources (Stone et al. 2010). Emergency rooms are frequently used as a source of primary health care for many within these communities and some emergency rooms do not perform routine testing or evaluation for HIV. Low health literacy also contributes to health disparities and impact HIV acquisition in impoverished communities.

Women in poorer communities continue to experience higher rates of HIV infection, with African American women in the South in the forefront of this epidemic (Center for Disease Control and Prevention 2009c). Although African Americans comprise only 12 percent of the United States population, a reported 64 percent of HIV infections were among African American women (Center for Disease Control and Prevention 2009a; Stone et al. 2010; Weiss et al. 2011). Unlike earlier disease transmissions involving Caucasian males (e.g., MSM), the vast majority of new cases are African American women who indicate their mode of infection as via heterosexual transmission (Neundorfer et al. 2005; Weiss et al. 2011). Many African American women are single heads of household who may desire companionship and/or support from men (Stanhope and Lancaster 2008). These women are less likely to negotiate safe sex practices and are more likely to participate in at-risk sexual behavior with inconsistent condom use.

Both men and women may minimize or underestimate their sexual behavior based on their knowledge or personal belief in their ability to recognize sexual partners who may or may not be at risk for HIV (ibid.). Many believe you can look at a person and determine their HIV status. Uninformed providers miss opportunities for early testing and diagnosis of HIV disease based on one's profile. Mistakenly, some providers believe that certain clients (i.e., those who are well dressed, well educated, have a high income and/or reside in a respectable neighborhood) do not "fit the model." Thus, some providers fail to test these clients and this can sometimes result in unfavorable conditions when the client learns they are HIV positive later and enter into care only after the symptoms are present (Stone et al. 2010).

According to the Centers for Disease Control and Prevention, one in five persons living in the United States is unaware of their HIV status. Risk behaviors such as inconsistent condom use, frequency of sexual intercourse with multiple sexual partners, substance abuse and those who participate in survival sex (i.e., prostitution) contribute to this fact (Center for Disease Control and Prevention 2009b). Other factors such as stigma contribute to a person's voluntary unwillingness to be tested for HIV.

## Stigma

Despite advancements in HIV treatment, disgust and disgrace continue to be exhibited toward people living with HIV/AIDS or PLWHA. Stigma is defined by Webster "as a mark of disgrace or infamy; a stain or reproach as on one's reputation." Moreover, stigma has been defined as "all unfavorable attitudes, beliefs and policies directed toward people who have HIV/AIDS as well as their loved ones and communities" (Brimlow et al. 2003). Stigma can be experienced from external or internal sources and can be experienced singularly or simultaneously (Florom-Smith and De Santis 2012). Internal stigma reflects what PLWHA think about themselves (Brimlow 2003). In clinical practice, internal stigma appears to be worse than the external stigma which reflects how others feel, think or perceive PLWHA. Sometimes stigma is even projected onto those who work with PLWHA or family members and friends of PLWHA. Agencies and services designed to help PLWHA have also been stigmatized (ibid.). Stigma is precipitated and driven by ignorance about HIV and often subjectively transferred via religious beliefs. HIV-related stigma is recognized as one of the major burdens that PLWHA experience (Ugarte et al. 2013).

There is no standardized method for measuring stigma although such attempts are underway. Meanwhile, definitions, new dynamics and cultural difference for stigma are constantly being redefined (Florom-Smith and De Santis 2012). The experience of stigma and its effect on public health can be postulated through reluctance to test for HIV, declination of treatment, poor adherence to treatment and failure to disclose status (Florom-Smith and De Santis 2012). Some people with the diagnosis of HIV may sever relationships in lieu of disclosure of their status (Dowshen et al. 2009). The shame and anticipated fear of rejection from family and friends sometimes results in PLWHA avoiding treatment, resulting in disease progression (ibid.).

## Depression

The ability to adjust to personal adversity is a useful indicator in determining how well people may respond to health changes. Some authors believe it is important for PLWHA to accept, acknowledge and manage life events for the successful treatment of HIV (Sherra et al. 2011). Depression is the most common mental health diagnosis among PLWHA and may result in social withdrawal and/or engagement in behaviors that subject them and others to unfavorable health outcomes (i.e., increased transmission of the virus) (Macapagal et al. 2012). Depressive disorders may not be expressed physically or overtly. However, depression can be demonstrated in behaviors which include poor medication adherence, cessation of social activities and severing relationships (MacDonell et al. 2011). Though depressive disorders may be experienced by persons prior to the diagnosis of HIV/AIDS, the diagnosis of HIV/AIDS may exacerbate the symptoms (Sherra et al. 2011). People who lack social support (real or perceived) frequently experience higher rates of depression compared to those who have positive support systems and thereby manage stressors associated with HIV/AIDS better (Grov et al. 2010; Vyavaharka et al. 2011).

Transgenders, MSM and African American women experience depressive disorders more frequently than other groups (Schackman et al. 2008; Clum et al. 2009). These groups may also engage in riskier behaviors as a result of depression (Moreno et al. 2007; Mustanki et al. 2010). Depression has also been linked to immune suppression in PLWHA and those who experience prolonged depressive symptomology are less likely to adhere to anti-retroviral treatment, contributing to advancement of AIDS and increased mortality (Cook et. al. 2004). Management of depressive disorders may result in improved HIV outcomes in PLWHA.

## Religion

Historically, religion and spirituality have been a source of strength amid trouble, despair and illness for African Americans. Religion and spirituality (R/S) often serve as coping mechanisms adopted by many to manage chronic illness like HIV. Some PLWHA assert that spirituality acts as a catalyst for positive changes in life (i.e., cessation of alcohol/drugs, diminished promiscuity, etc.). Other PLWHA attribute personal growth, decreased symptoms of depression, increased support, feelings of internal peace and increased adherence to HIV therapy. The perceived benefits of spirituality may account for the impression of life being better after the diagnosis of HIV (Biggar et al. 1999; Cotton et al. 2006a, 2006b; Parsons et al. 2006). Others find R/S a negative force that highlights the perceived sin involved in HIV acquisition or as punishment from God because his "wrath" is undisputable (Cotton et al. 2006b; Parsons et al. 2006). Therefore, religion and spirituality may have either a positive or negative impact on HIV acquisition and subsequent survival or demise.

## Demographics and Trends

The Centers for Disease Control and Prevention is a federal agency under the direction of the Department of Health and Human Services (DHHS) that was created to provide education through research, which promotes the public's health and safety against disease, injury and disability. Since 1991 HIV has been a reportable disease in all 50 states and U.S. territories. However, methods of surveillance vary among the states and, in some, data are not reported, which explains differences in the number of positive cases. While incidence reflects new cases, prevalence is the total number of cases of a disease in population at a specific time (Centers for Disease Control and Prevention 2011c). The Northeast and the South have the highest prevalence of HIV infections, yet the South has the greatest incidence. Due to rapid increases in new case of HIV in the South it is considered a "hotspot" for new infection (Center for Disease Control and Prevention 2007b). Of the adults and adolescents diagnosed with HIV infection in the United States and its territories, an estimated 62 percent were infected via MSM, 18 percent via heterosexual contact for females and 10 percent for males, 5 percent from injection drug use for males and 3 percent for females and 3 percent from a combination of MSM and injection drug use.

## Current Treatments: Evolution of Medication

HIV is classified as a retrovirus because it requires a host to survive and replicate. Human CD4 cells are the only cells that HIV can use as a host. Medications used to treat HIV are referred to as "Antiretroviral Therapy" (ART) and there are five classes of medications approved by the Food and Drug Administration (FDA) to treat HIV. Medications that fight HIV in the CD4 cells can interrupt viral replication and suppress the amount of virus in the blood until the levels of HIV drop so low they are undetectable. There are two basic goals of treating HIV: 1) revive the immune system by increasing the number of CD4 cells and 2) obstruct viral replication resulting in low or undetectable levels of HIV.

When HIV was first discovered in the 1980s, there were no pharmacological treatments available. Azidothymidine (AZT), an anti-cancer drug developed in the 1960s, was found to inhibit viral progression of HIV in mice and was later used in HIV-positive humans. Initial dosages of AZT were much higher than current regulated doses for HIV (Department of Health and Human Services 2011). Because of misinformation, lack of understanding and stigma, many delayed receiving AZT treatment. Urban legends suggesting that HIV medications were manmade and intended to eradicate Blacks also caused many to delay treatment. During the early 1980s, by the time many PLWHA entered into care, their renal (kidney) and/or hepatic (liver) functions were already compromised. Early treatment attempts with high doses of AZT were plagued with inflated side effects as well as many deaths; especially in those experiencing liver and renal damage. This served as superficial evidence for some to support the urban legend that "HIV Meds will kill you."

The FDA approved the first class of HIV drugs, Nucleoside Reverse Transcriptase Inhibitors (NRTIs), in 1987. NRTIs interfere with HIV DNA, thereby impairing HIV's ability to replicate. Practitioners haphazardly prescribed one or two drugs from this class for years. Much of what is known today regarding HIV treatment had not been conceptualized during early treatment attempts. Protease Inhibitors, the second class of HIV medications that debilitate the necessary protein (Protease) that HIV depends on for replication, were approved by the FDA in 1995. By this time scientists understood that HIV replicated quickly and that they should utilize a multi-drug therapy strategy. This combining of classes of medications was referred to as an HIV "cocktail," or HAART (Highly Active Antiretroviral Therapy). The addition of Protease Inhibitors to NNRTIs was a game changer in HIV treatment and resulted in noticeable declines in HIV-related deaths (Center for Disease Control and Prevention 2009a). By 1996 the third class of medications, Non-Nucleoside Reverse Transverse Inhibitors (NNRTIs), was approved by the FDA. These drugs impeded self-replication of HIV. In 1997 some of the NRTIs became available in fixed-dose combinations. This breakthrough offered the first attempt at medication simplification.

Despite advances in the care of HIV some PLWHA had to take up to 30 pills a day, with some experiencing such severe adverse reactions that they refused treatment (Gilead Sciences 2013). The new millennium would yield greater treatment options for clinicians and PLWHA. In 2003 entry inhibitors was the novel new class of medications credited with bridging treatment for PLWHA who had few treatment options left. The first one, Fusion Inhibitors, blocked HIV entry into CD4 cells by disallowing HIV to penetrate the CD4 cell. Fuzeon (efurvitide) was only drug with this mechanism of action that was approved by the FDA. Although this medication was effective it had some disadvantages. This drug was tedious to prepare and required mixing and intense shaking at least 30 minutes before injection. The injections had to be administered twice a day and left painful nodules at the site of entry. Few providers initiate therapy with Fuzeon today unless it is absolutely necessary.

Maraviroc is the other medication that disallows HIV to enter into CD4 cells. Maraviroc blocks HIV entry into cells by obstructing the CCR5 receptor site on the surface of the CD4 cell. Maraviroc is referred to by some as "CCR5 Inhibitor." The other receptor site on CD4 cell surface is CCRX4. A tropism test is necessary in order to identify the receptor site. Although Maraviroc and Fuzeon function differently, they both prevent HIV cell entry into CD4 cells and comprise the class of Entry Inhibitors. Integrase Inhibitors, the fifth and final class of HIV medications to be approved by the FDA, offer the newest medications. These medications cripple the protein used by HIV to infect CD4 cells. Taken altogether, these newer medications are powerful in the treatment of HIV.

Antiretroviral therapy with at least three drugs from two different classes are recommended for effective treatment of HIV (Department of Health and Human Services 2011). Successful treatment of HIV permits PLWHA to live life free of HIV-related illnesses and death. Untreated HIV has been associated with heart disease, renal disease, dementia and cancer (Doepel 2006; Stone et al. 2010). School, work, marriage, relationships and even children are possible for effectively treated PLWHA. Nevertheless, it is imperative to note that even when the immune system is healthy with a large number of CD4 cells and HIV levels are low or undetectable, HIV can still be transmitted if exposures occur.

## Summary

Through the diligence of scientist and medical leaders, the life expectancy of PLWHA has far surpassed initial projections. The evolution of treatment regimens continue to offer positive outcomes for PLWHA. Public understanding and perception remain a challenge and a potential threat to overcoming the HIV pandemic. However, through continued education, testing and objective and honest conversations about HIV, the hope that there will be "generations without HIV" could actually become reality.

## References

Bailes, Elizabeth, Roy Chaudhuri, Mario Santiago, Frederic Bibollet-Ruche, Beatrice Hahn and Paul Sharp. 2002. "The Evolution of Primate Lentiviruses and the Origins of AIDS." in *The Molecular Epidemiology of Human Viruses*, ed. T.A. Leitner. Boston, MA: Kluwer Academic Publishers, pp. 65–96.

Biggar, H., R. Forehand, D. Devine, G. Brody, L. Armistead, E. Morse, and P. Simon. 1999. "Women Who are HIV Infected: The Role of Religious Activity in Psychosocial Adjustment." *AIDS Care* 11(2): 195–9.

Brimlow, Deborah, Jennifer Cook and Richard Seaton. 2003. "Stigma and HIV/AIDS: A Review of the Literature. Rockville" Retrieved April 23, 2015: http://archive.org/stream/hivaidsstigmathe00hiva/hivaidsstigmathe00hiva_djvu.txt.

Centers for Disease Control and Prevention. 1989. "Current Trends Update: HIV-2 Infection—United States." *Mortality and Morbidity Weekly Report* 38: 572–80.

———. 2007. "AIDS in the United States by Geographical Distribution." Retrieved August 29, 2011: http://www.cdc.gov/hiv/resources/factsheets/geographic.htm.

———. 2009a. "HIV in the United States: At A Glance" Retrieved September 3, 2011: http://www.cdc.gov/hiv/resources/qa/definitions.htm.

———. 2009b. "HIV/AIDS Surveillance Report, 2007" 19: 1–63. Atlanta, GA: US Department of Health and Human Services, Centers for Disease Control and Prevention.

———. 2009c. "HIV among Women." Retrieved September 3, 2011: http://www.cdc.gov/hiv/topics/women.

———. 2011a. "Disparities in Diagnosis of HIV Infections between Black/African American and Other Racial/Ethnic Populations 37 States 2005–2008." *Morbidity and Mortality Weekly Report* 6: 25–30.

———. 2011b. "AIDS: the Early Years and CDC's Response." *Mortality and Morbidity Weekly Report* 60: 64–9.

———. 2011c. "Diagnoses of HIV Infection in the United States and Dependent Areas, 2011." Vol. 23 Atlanta, GA: US Department of Health and Human Services, Centers for Disease Control and Prevention

Clum, Gretchen, Shang-En Chung, Jonathan Ellen and Adolescent Medicine Trials Network for HIV/AIDS Interventions. 2009. "Mediators of HIV-related Stigma and Risk Behavior in HIV Infected Young Women." *AIDS Care* 21(11): 1455–62.

Cotton, Sian, Christina Puchalski, Susan Sherman, Joseph Mrus, Amy Peterman, Judith Feinburg and Joel Tsevat. 2006a. "Spirituality and Religion in Patients with HIV/AIDS." *Journal of General Internal Medicine* 21: S5–S13.

———. 2006b. "Changes in Religiousness and Spirituality Attributed to HIV/AIDS: Are There Sex and Race Differences?" *Journal of General Internal Medicine* 21: S14–S20.

Department of Health and Human Services. 2011. *Guidelines for the Use of Antiretroviral Agents in HIV-1 Infected Adults and Adolescents.* Department of Health and Human Services: http://www.cdc.gov/hiv/topics/treatment/guidelines.htm.

Doepel, Laurie 2006. *International HIV/AIDS Trial Finds Continuous Antiretroviral Therapy Superior to Episodic Therapy.* National Institute of Allergy and Infectious Diseases.

Dowshen, Nadia, Helen Binns and Robert Garofalo. 2009. "Experiences of HIV-related Stigma among Young Men Who have Sex with Men." *AIDS Patient Care and STDs* 23(5): 371–6.

Florom-Smith, Al and James De Santis 2012. "Exploring the Concept of HIV-Related Stigma." *Nursing Forum* 47(3): 153–65

Garofalo, Robert, Brian Mustanski, Amy Johnson and Erin Emerson. 2010. "Exploring Factors that Underlie Racial/Ethnic Disparities in HIV Risk among Young Men Who Have Sex with Men." *Journal of Urban Health* 87(2): 318–23.

Gilead Sciences. 2013. *Evolution of HIV Treatment: Adapted from the Panel on Antiretroviral Guidelines for Adults and Adolescents. Guidelines for the Use of Antiretroviral Agents in HIV-1-Infected Adults and Adolescents.* US Department of Health and Human Services; 1998–2014.

Gisselquist, David and John Potterat. 2003. "Heterosexual Transmission of HIV in Africa: An Empiric Estimate." *International Journal of STD AIDS* 14: 162–73.

Grov, Christian, Sarit A. Golub, Jeffrey T. Parsons, Mark Brennan and Stephen E. Karpiak. 2010. "Loneliness and HIV-Related Stigma Explain Depression among Older HIV-Positive Adults." *AIDS Care* 22(5):630-39

Joint United Nations Programme on HIV/AIDS. 2010. *UNAIDS Report on the Global AIDS Epidemic*. Retrieved April 23, 2015: http://www.unaids.org/globalreport/Global_report.htm.

Kessler, Craig. 2007. "Hemorrhagic Disorders: Coagulation Factor Deficiencies." in *Cecil Medicine*, eds. L. Goldman and D. Ausiello D. Philadelphia, PA: Elsevier, pp. 180.

Macapagal, Kathryn, Jamie Ringer, Shannon Woller and Paul Lysaker. 2012. "Personal Narratives, Coping, and Quality of Life in Persons Living with HIV." *Journal of Association of Nurses in AIDS Care* 23(4): 361–5.

MacDonell Karen, Sylvie Naar-King, Debra Murphy, Jeffery Parsons and Heather Huszti 2011. "Situational Temptation for HIV Medication Adherence in High-Risk Youth." *AIDS Patient Care and STDs* 25(1): 47.

Moreno, Claudia L., Nabila El-Bassel and Allison. C. Morrill. 2007. "Heterosexual Women of Color and HIV Risk: Sexual Risk Factors for HIV among Latina and African American Women." *Women and Health* 45: 1–15

Neundorfer, Marcia, Phyllis Harris, Paula Britton and Delores Lynch. 2005. "HIV-Risk Factors for Midlife and Older Women." *The Gerontologist* 45(5): 617–25.

Parsons, Sharon, Peter Cruise, Walisa Davenport and Vanessa Jones. 2006. "Religious Beliefs, Practices, and Treatment Adherence among Individuals with HIV in the Southern United States." *AIDS Patient Care and STDs* 20(2): 97–111.

Rambaut, Andrew, David Posada, Keith A. Crandall and Edward C. Holmes. 2004. "The Causes and Consequences of HIV Evolution." *Nature* 5: 52–61.

Schackman, Bruce, Zubin Dastur, Quanhong Ni, Mark Callahan, Judith Berger and David Rubin. 2008. "Sexually Active HIV-Positive Patients Frequently Report Never Using Condoms in Audio Computer-Assisted Self-Interviews Conducted at Routine Clinical Visits." *AIDS Patient Care and STDS* 22(2): 123–9.

Sharp, Paul, George M. Shaw and Beatrice H. Hahn. 2005. "Simian Immunodeficiency Virus Infection of Chimpanzees." *Journal of Virology* 79(7): 3891–902.

Sherra, Lorraine, C. Clucas, Richard Harding, Elissa Sibley, Jose Catalan and Natasha Croome. 2011. "HIV Infection and Mental Health: Suicidal Behaviour—Systematic Review." *Psychology Health Medicine* 16(5): 588–611

Stanhope, Marcia and Jeanette Lancaster, eds. 2008. *Public Health Nursing: Population-Centered Nursing Care in the Community*. New York: Mosby Elsevier.

Stone, Valerie, Bisola Ojikutu, Marsden Rawlings and Ken Smith, eds. 2010. *HIV/AIDS in U.S. Communities of Color*. New York: Springer.

Ugarte, William J., Ulf Högberg, Eliette C. Valladares and Birgitta Essén. 2013. "Measuring HIV and AIDS-Related Stigma and Discrimination In Nicaragua: Results from a Community-Based Study." *AIDS Education and Prevention* 25(2): 164–78.

US Department of Health and Human Services Health Resources and Services Administration. 2011. "Addressing HIV among African-Americans," pp. 4–5. Retrieved from http://hab.hrsa.gov/livinghistory/issues/aframerican_5.htm.

Vyavaharkar, Medha, Linda Moneyham, Abbas Tavakoli, Kenneth Phillips, Carolyn Murdaugh, Kirby Jackson and Gene Meding. 2007. "Social Support, Coping, and Medication adherence among HIV-Positive Women with Depression Living in the Rural Areas of the Southeastern United States." *Aids Patient Care and STDs* 21(9): 667–80.

Weiss, Stephen, Jonathan Tobin, Michael Antoni, Gail Ironson, Mary Ishii, Anita Vaughn and J. Bryan Page. 2011. "Enhancing the Health of Women Living with HIV: The SMARTEST Women's Project." *International Journal of Women's Health* 3: 63–77.

# PART V
# Health Disparity Solutions

# Gaining Equity in Health Care: Building the Pipeline of Black Nurse Leaders

Yvonne Wesley

The existing health-care paradigm remains largely focused on the treatment of diseases and the discovery of cures. Unfortunately, the notion of providing illness care limits opportunities for promoting wellness. While an illness care system is good for restoring health, the opportunity to prevent disease and illness is also deserving of increased attention. Basic nursing education includes some discussion of wellness promotion, but the primary focus in this substantive area is on ascertaining the signs and symptoms of disease. Regrettably, most nurses function at this biophysical level as they work in hospitals. However, it is proposed here that a pipeline of Black nurse leaders who are grounded in the notion of wellness promotion are needed to help prevent or limit illness. To that end, the objectives of this query are to: 1) identify several factors that may contribute to a healthy community, 2) offer a list of current health indicators and 3) describe how Black nurse leaders can facilitate health equity in the U.S. and Ghana.

## Un-skewing the View of Health

It is proposed herein that much of what we call health care in America and Ghana is more accurately defined as illness care. If health can be viewed as a continuum where one end represents total wellness and the other death, one can clearly see that health care in America and Ghana are designed to prevent death and disease progression rather than provide a thorough wellness promotion campaign. Health-care systems and hospitals are intended to provide treatment and, at times, cures for specific illnesses and diseases. I argue that the promotion of wellness has been largely missing from society's models of health care. Unfortunately, the ability to embrace the notion that health is more than the absence of injury or disease continues to elude many health leaders. According to the World Health Organization (WHO 1978), health encompasses one's physical, mental and social well-being. Evans and Stoddart (2003) describe health as a state of not suffering from any designed undesirable condition. These descriptions of health cover a lot of ground. The image of health as a phenomenon where a person is not afflicted with any designed undesirable condition includes multiple factors. Updating their 1990 conceptual framework which highlights the determinants of health, Canadian authors Evans and Stoddart make it clear that death is an incomplete measure of health. Based on a collection of their work and experience, Evans and Stoddart (ibid.) developed a model showing the relationship between well-being and 1) individual behavior and biology; 2) social, physical and genetic environments; 3) health and function; 4) disease; 5) health care and 6) propensity. They note that variations in mortality rates are a function of incomplete measures of health. Drawing on literature from various disciplines, Evans and Stoddart's framework accepts death as a measure of health but explains the need for a broader definition of health and its determinants.

Heath indicators for the U.S. have evolved over time from rates of death due to illnesses (e.g., stoke, cardiovascular disease, HIV, etc.) to indicators such as the amount of physical activity, substance use, violence exposure, etc. The evolution of health indicators suggests that the treatment of illness is a small factor contributing to a society's health. In fact, current health indicators in the U.S. are becoming more similar to those outlined by the World Health Organization (2009). These include peace, shelter, income, sustainable resources, food, education, a stable ecosystem, social justice and equity.

Sickness care may be the mainstay of health care for now, but it is becoming more obvious that the sickness care system permits individuals to slide closer, and at a much faster rate, to the death end of the health continuum. It is suggested here that health-care systems, primarily doctors and nurses, should rethink the determinants of health and be amenable to embracing broader definitions that may un-skew their potentially biased view of health.

## Sickness Care System

Short of understanding that health is a resource for everyday living and not the goal of living as put forward by WHO, prerequisites for health include a list of fundamental conditions that reach far beyond sickness care provided in many health-care systems. With the ability to favor or harm one's health, socio-political, economic, cultural and environmental factors have an impact on behavior and biology. The WHO's (2009) view of health highlights the notion that the health-care sector alone is not the prerequisite to health. While sickness care systems may prevent death, alleviate some suffering and in some cases restore a measure of one's health, the current health-care system fails to adequately answer the question, "What is required to build a healthy community?" According to a lecture provided by Norris and Clough (2003) at the Health Forum Fellowship, factors that contribute to health include medical care (10 percent), human biology (20 percent), environment (20 percent) and lifestyle/behavior (50 percent). This view of health appears similar to the WHO's and credits daily living as a major component in the formula for health. This, again, is where the emphasis on health care should be focused: lifestyle behavior wellness care.

Fortunately, nursing programs include educational requirements whereby students are exposed to multiple factors, such as those identified above, which impact one's health. From an illness-care model, nurses are trained at the entry level of nursing practice to identify the following: 1) adverse effects, contraindications, side effects and/or interactions of medications; 2) expected actions/outcomes of treatments; 3) the administration of medication; 4) blood/blood products; 5) how to start and maintain parenteral/intravenous therapies; 6) how to care for central venous access devices; 7) ways to manage the of pain via pharmacological interventions and 8) how to calculate medication dosages, including the maintenance of total parenteral nutrition. This list of nursing activities was discovered when, in 2009, the National Council of State Boards of Nursing (NCSBN) conducted a survey of newly licensed nurses. The purpose of this survey was to develop some recommendations for changing the licensure examination for nurses. Missing from this list of activities for entry-level nursing was health and wellness promotion. The NCSBN report indicates that less than 12 percent of a new nurse's time is spent providing health wellness promotion activities. The majority of their time centers on providing physiological care. It appears that most entry-level nurses miss the WHO's specific view of health and are in need of a paradigm shift. Again, it is my contention that a wellness-centered model adopted within this profession, but more specifically to Black and minority nurses given the changing demographic projections, will lead to a more efficient and positive health-care outcome.

## Health-care Paradigm Shift in Nursing

According to Covey (2004), if one wants to make minor or incremental changes and improvements in health care, they should work on practices, behaviors and/or attitudes. However, in order to impact those areas a nearly complete paradigm shift must be made. Nursing's health paradigm, if it is to truly become more effective, should be revised since, as currently practiced, it is closely related to the medical model of sickness care. As shown by data provided by the NCSBN's survey, the activities currently performed by entry-level nurses are important but more emphasis on wellness is needed in order to build healthy communities.

Lucey (2007) notes that disease reflects the cumulative lifetime exposure to damaging physical and social environments. I call for a new health-care paradigm that recognizes societal factors as primary pathogenic forces facing the American population. This can be said for Ghana as well as socio-economic factors contribute greatly to the wellness of that population also. Root causes of illness, such as poverty, make it difficult to pinpoint the moment that a series of risk factors will impact a person's health. The cumulative lifetime exposure model acknowledges that the number and length of times exposed to a risk factor increases a person's likelihood of sickness and disease. This perspective informs nurses that it will take more than sickness care to bring about a healthy community. As nurses advance in their career they should move beyond traditional hospital care and toward the wellness paradigm. Re-thinking what nurses "see" as health and "being" healthy are beginning to extend far beyond death and illness.

## Old Health Indicators

In the past, major U.S. health indicators included infant mortality per 1,000 live births, total death per 100,000 people, motor vehicle death crashes per 100,000 people, work-related injury deaths per 100,000 people, suicide per 100,000 people, homicide per 100,000 people and lung cancer per 100,000 people. Ghanaian health indicators are similar to those used in the United States. The rationale for counting the number of deaths is to provide statistical markers that can be used to signal unacceptable confirmations of death thereby, in theory, impacting behavior in such a manner as to decrease reported incidents of death in future reports. It is suggested within this paradigm that less death means improved or stagnant health for American and Ghanaian residents. In previous years, the primary goal was to decrease the number of illnesses leading to one's death. By monitoring the rate of deaths per a given population, the focus is on avoiding death as opposed to engaging in wellness promotion. The old paradigm of health care, as opposed to wellness promotion, promotes an emphasis on curing the illness on the back end as opposed to preventing the illness on the front end. While seeking a remedy for sickness and disease is certainly admirable and part of the Hippocratic Oath, understanding the causes of illness combined with the aggressive promotion of prevention awareness may be far more efficacious.

The call for a paradigm shift in this profession has been embraced by some. While the emphasis on curing disease remains the dominant health-care paradigm, prevention and wellness promotion are now becoming more central to this discussion. The days of counting the leading causes of death have been replaced in the U.S. with modern indicators such as physical activity, overweight and obesity, tobacco use, substance abuse, responsible sexual behavior, mental health, injury and violence, environmental quality, immunizations and access to health care. The Ghana Health Service 2011 annual report also shows that modern-day practices include immunizations. There are also data showing that for an investment of $10 per person per year in proven community-based programs, there is an increase in physical activity, improved nutrition and smoking prevention that saves the country more than $16 billion annually within five years. This is a return on an investment of $5.60 for every $1 spent (Levi et al. 2009)

## Black Nurse Leaders Embracing a Paradigm Shift

Nursing has always played a role in health promotion. However, much of nursing's activities in health promotion have been relegated to the hospital and focused on patient education to prevent disease progression. Studies from Great Britain show that the role of health promotion activities within the primary health-care setting have been a struggle for nurses in general. As outlined by Nies and McEwen (2007), tertiary prevention activities can prevent or correct deterioration due to disease. For example, insulin administration in the home for the diabetic patient helps avoid comorbidities as such kidney failure, cardiovascular disease and/or stoke. Secondary prevention includes early detection and prompt intervention of disease pathogenesis. This type of health promotion is common among Black Nurse Association members as they conduct community health fairs where information is offered and blood pressure screening provided to ensure early detection and entry into the health-care system. Primary prevention activities that include the promotion of good nutrition, exercise and healthy lifestyle behavior, such as condom use to prevent sexually transmitted infections or HIV, is an area that needs greater attention.

Aside from primary prevention-type health promotion activities as defined by Nies and McEwen (2007), Black nurses moving forward in their careers have begun to address socio-political, economic and cultural factors that help build healthy communities through research and publications. With a broader definition of health and wellness, this author's experiences note how career-minded Black nurses are beginning to embrace the paradigm shift from sickness care to wellness promotion. Addressing the impact of social oppression, Black nurses acknowledge the influence of social determinates of health and base their practice on scientific evidence when providing patients with information in the hospital or conducting health fairs to promote healthy lifestyles. Similar to Wright and Calhoun (2006), Black nurses in the U.S. and abroad struggle to gain power to influence social environments that impact a population's health (Wesley and Dobal 2009).

Although nurses are best known for their bedside care in hospital settings, nursing's leadership role reaches far beyond a health center or hospital bed. The role of a nurse leader involves the use of technology and interpersonal, analytical and organizational skills to address problems of health as they impact the community. Specific to Black nurses, there is still the problem of marginalization. Moreover, an argument can be made that many non-Black nurses lack interest in embracing a new paradigm and understanding of health care that provides optimal outcomes for the increasingly majority minority population of the United States. Unfortunately, there is a dearth of scientific evidence explaining health belief behaviors among Blacks. Whether in the U.S. or in Africa, nurse leaders who design, implement and evaluate health promotion programs need scientific evidence to achieve health equity. While in America, racial health disparities go unabated, in Ghana, rural versus urban health disparities exist (Owens 2011). Owens notes that Ghanaians living in urban areas have greater access to sickness care and information. Conversely, Ghanaians living in rural regions lack education and an understanding of how their behaviors impact their health (ibid.). In either case, scientific attention to the problem of marginalization and the meaning of health to Black people is oftentimes overlooked. It is safe to say that Black nurses, who are increasingly transitioning into positions in nursing leadership, have begun to embrace a new paradigm of health and health care (Wesley and Dobal 2009). Nevertheless, there is sparse evidence in the existing literature to support health promotion activities among Black populations that focus primarily on prevention. Black nurse leaders understand that lifestyle behaviors are thought to be major contributors to wellness and well-being (Wesley and Dobal 2009).

## Wellness/Well-being

The designing of population-based interventions to educate people via electronic media has become very popular in recent years. According to the World Bank, mobile phones were an anomaly in developing countries prior to 2000. However, by 2012 mobile phones facilitated the dissemination of important information concerning wellness and well-being. The ability to share basic health information or education with the masses enables nursing leaders who understand the value of mobile health (mHealth) to improve the delivery of primary and secondary health-care services. This new global wave of technology provides the patient greater personal responsibility for managing their health choices and shifts control over health care from the provider to the patient, who is now considered a consumer. An example of how primary prevention efforts can make an impact is captured by nurse researchers Jones, Hoover and Lacroix (2013) who discovered that Black women (mean age 22 years) watching 20-minute videos on their smartphones significantly ($p < .001$) decreased their episodes of unprotected anal and vaginal sex. Notwithstanding the cost of a smartphone, the study shows that today's technology is useful in changing young Black women's attitudes and behaviors towards sex.

Black nurse leaders must be ready to embrace mHealth to provide improved health services to consumers and to promote positive public health messages. Mobile phone applications designed to deliver health information in the form of a quiz or game are becoming more common in developing countries. In fact, mHealth educational campaigns and health prevention messages have been successfully launched in Uganda (Vital Wave Consulting 2011). Furthermore, short message service (SMS), known by most as texting, is now a prominent mode of sharing health messages globally (Gombachika and Monawe 2011).

In addition to using technology to improve the health of consumers, some Black nurse leaders have taken ownership of community outreach projects that support primary prevention activities such as consumer education seminars that change knowledge, attitude and behavior in order to prevent the spread of HIV. For example, Black nurse leader Dr. Loretta Sweet Jemmott developed the "Be Proud Be Responsible Program" to alter lifestyle behaviors.

In a study of Black women's descriptions of health beliefs, nurse scientist and educator Dr. Minnie Campbell's (2009) research shows that Black women hold traditional African cultural beliefs. Concepts such as balance among social, mental, emotional and physical aspects of the person's life are important to achieve positive health. Consistent with the West

207

African notion that health is a matter of being in harmony with nature and illness evidence of disharmony, this Black nurse leader's findings show the need for nurses to understand the meaning of health according to Black women. This definition of health, wellness and well-being is similar to that of the WHO's definition which extends far beyond simply the absence of death.

Attitudes and beliefs among Black populations warrant more attention as there are some authors who suggest these beliefs may be a deterrent to life-sustaining behaviors. For example, Johnson and Wesley (2013) report that Black women think Black men prefer full-figured women and that this belief can become a deterrent to weight-loss behaviors such as exercise and proper nutrition. Bradley (2013) also notes that Black women may avoid early breast cancer detection due to fatalistic beliefs about cancer such as they will die due to a diagnosis with cancer. Moreover, based on a review of the literature, Underwood, Jones and Rivers (2006) report that attitudes and perceptions regarding prostate screening interfered with early cancer detection among Black men in the U.S. and abroad.

With an understanding that modern technology can help prevent illness, that health beliefs within the Black community can and have been a deterrent to healthy lifestyle behaviors and that health beliefs among Blacks are not limited to physical ailments, Black nurse leaders are positioned to play a role in the establishment of health-care equity.

## Black Nurses' Leadership Training and Health-care Equity

First and foremost, Black nurse leaders must be educated and equipped with competencies that strengthen public health while they make every effort to prevent illness with a clear understanding that determinants of health span far beyond medical care in a hospital. The impact of socio-political-economic-cultural and environmental factors must be highlighted in leadership training for Black nurses interested in health-care equity. Introducing a paradigm shift that acknowledges bio-physical aspects of health is acceptable. However, the influence of lifestyle is key to the prevention of illness and disease. While it is imperative that Black nurse leadership training include the skills listed below, there is also the need for Black nurse leaders to acknowledge racial barriers to career advancement: analytic assessment skills, policy development/program-planning skills, communication skills, cultural competency skills, public health science skills, financial management skills and systems-thinking skills.

Aside from competencies in analytic and systems thinking, Wesley and Dobal (2009) note that interactive leadership training helps Black nurse leaders address issues of racism, sexism, discrimination and power differentials within health-care systems. With an understanding of what it means to be Black, nurse leaders are better prepared to reflect upon the impact of racialization and the extent to which they make attempts to circumvent racialization.

Key to the elimination of health disparities, the IOM (Institute for Medicine 2008) and U.S. Department of Health and Human Services (2011) suggest an increase in the number of minority health professionals. These recommendations are built on Smedley, Stith and Nelson's (2003) work which shows that racism is alive and well in the health-care system. Moreover, Smedley and colleagues show that practitioners are biased and that Black patients suffer as a result. An example illustrated in their report includes physicians not recommending smoking cessation to Blacks due to the doctor's belief that their instructions would not be followed. Additionally, the report linked a patient's experiences of discrimination in the broader society to clinical encounters in the health-care system.

This suggests that both the patient and provider may be influenced by the larger society's behavior towards Blacks. In other words, the legacy of a segregated health-care system from the early 1900s, the passage of Jim Crow laws and the 1964 civil rights legislation mandating racial integration shaped both patient and provider attitudes in the twenty-first century. Whether the influence of social oppression outside the health-care system or a biased provider within the health-care system, a pipeline of Black nurse leaders is needed today to raise society's levels of awareness of systematic biases that contribute to health disparities and prevent health-care equity.

With a specific focus on the intersection of leadership, health-care disparities and career advancement, both U.S. and Ghanaian nurses must engage in leadership training to enlarge the pipeline of new health-care providers in their respective countries. Both U.S. Black and Ghanaian nurses benefit from training that addresses self-worth and promotes self-reflection exercises. As leaders, Black nurses are expected to have a self-awareness that acknowledges culture, environment and community. The old paradigm limiting health care to the hospital should be challenged by Black nurse leaders who must embrace a paradigm shift and make disease prevention a priority. Modern technology should be a part of today's Black nurse leaders' arsenal to promote wellness. Whether by text or video, health education is key to health promotion. Enlarging the pipeline of Black nurse leaders ensures that the next generation of Black nurses are prepared to address lifestyle issues that contribute to premature death and illness in the Black community.

# Conclusion

One of the most important and basic steps to building a pipeline of Black nurse leaders is to subscribe to the thinking of W.E.B. Du Bois, who encouraged Blacks to add to the body of knowledge, such that changes to the social, economic and physical condition of Black people can be made. While nurses mainly work in hospitals to improve the health of the Black community and create health equity, it is imperative that Black nurse leaders make the connection between wellness promotion and factors that contribute to a healthy community beyond the hospital walls. Leadership training that contains content similar to Du Bois's (1903) two-ness concept of racialization is needed as racism, discrimination and oppression continue to be an issue. Because basic nursing education gives minimal attention to wellness and health promotion, Black nurse leaders must embrace a paradigm shift to improve the community's health.

Un-skewing one's perception of health involves the awareness of health as a continuum. In a new paradigm health is more than the absence of disease and death; it's a balance of numerous factors. Furthermore, value is placed on lifestyle behaviors as they are major contributors to health and wellness in the new paradigm. Moreover, in a new paradigm the nurse leader helps re-shape health-care systems to do more than administer treatment to the physical body. Socio-political-economic-cultural and environmental factors are taken into account as a Black nurse leader works to establish health equity. Leadership training that omits the impact of a past filled with discrimination and oppression fuels health disparities in both the U.S. and Ghana. The burden of illness, injury, disability or mortality when comparing racial or geographic groups in the case of Ghana, requires a pipeline of Black nurse leaders. As such, similar to posits outlined by Wright and Calhoun (2006), it is the responsibility of marginalized professionals—the talented tenth—to find answers to issues among marginalized persons.

# References

Bradley, Patricia K. 2013. "African American Women and Breast Cancer Issues." in *African American Women's Life Issues Today: Vital Health and Social Matters*, ed. C.F. Collins. Santa Barbara, CA: Praeger, pp. 63–84.

Campbell, Minnie. 2009. "Perceptions of Personal Health of Contemporary Black Women." in *Black Women's Health: Challenges and Opportunities*, ed. Yvonne. Wesley, NY: Nova Science Publishers, Inc., pp. 131–46.

Covey, Stephen, R. 2004. *The 8th Habit. From Effectiveness to Greatness*. New York: Free Press.

Du Bois, William E.B. 1903 (1969). *The Souls of Black Folk*. New York: Signet Classic.

Evans, Robert G., and Stoddart, Greg L. 2003. "Consuming Research, Producing Policy?" *American Journal of Public Health* 93(3): 371–9.

Gombachika, Harry, and Monawe, Maganizo. 2011. "Correlation Analysis of Attitudes towards SMS Technology and Blood Donation Behavior in Malawi." *Journal of Health Informatics in Developing Countries* 5(2): 259–72.

Institute of Medicine 2008. *Challenges and Successes in Reducing Health Disparities*. Workshop Summary. Washington, DC: National Academy Press.

Johnson, Portia and Wesley, Yvonne. 2013. "The Skinny on Fat and Exercise: Truth about Obesity among Black Women." in *African American Women's Life Issues Today: Vital Health and Social Matters* ed. C.F. Collins. Santa Barbara, CA: Praeger, pp. 85–100.

Jones, Rachel, Hoover, Donald R. and Lacroix, Lorraine J. 2013. "A Randomized Controlled Trial of Soap Opera Videos Streamed to Smartphones to Reduce Risk of Sexually Transmitted Human Immunodeficiency Virus (HIV) in Young Urban African American Women." *Nursing Outlook* 61(4): 205–15.

Levi, Jeffery, Segal, Laura M. and Juliano, Chrissie, 2009. *Prevention for a Healthier America: Investments in Disease Prevention yield Significant Savings, Stronger Communities*. Washington, DC: Trust for America's Health.

Lucey, Paula. 2007. "Social Determinants of Health." *Nursing Economics* 25(2): 103–9.

Nies, Mary A., and McEwen, Melanie. 2007. *Community/Public Health Nursing: Promoting the Health of Populations*, 4th edn. St. Louis, MO: Saunders.

Norris, Tyler, and Clough, Gruffie. 2003. "Creating Healthier Communities Fellowship," at the Health Forum Leadership Summit held in Berkeley and San Francisco, CA.

Owens, Rudy. 2011. *Ghana's Health Challenges Are Exacerbated by Poverty, Rural-Urban Divisions, and the Inequitable Distribution of Health Care Resources to Underserved Areas*. Retrieved March 1, 2014: http://iwonderandwander.rudyfoto.com/public-health-research/.

Smedley, Brian D., Stith, Adrienne Y. and Nelson, Alan R. 2003. *Unequal Treatment: Confronting Racial and Ethnic Disparities in Health Care*. Washington, DC: Institute of Medicine, The National Academies Press.

Underwood, Sandra, Jones, Randy and Rivers, Brian. 2006. "Prostate Cancer in African American Men: Review of the Science." *JOCEPS: The Journal Of Chi Eta Phi Sorority* 52(1): 1–9.

US Department of Health and Human Services. 2011. *HHS Action Plan to Reduce Racial and Ethnic Disparities: A Nation Free of Disparities in Health and Health Care*. Washington, DC: US Department of Health and Human Services.

Vital Wave Consulting. 2011. "Mobile Applications Laboratories Business Plan." *infoDev*. Retrieved November 14, 2013: http://www.infodev.org/en/Publication.1087 .html.

Wesley, Yvonne and Dobal, May. (2009). "Nurses of African Descent & Career Advancement. *The Journal of Professional Nursing* 25(2): 122–6.

World Bank. 2012. *Information and Communications for Development 2012: Maximizing Mobile*. Washington, DC: World Bank. DOI: 10.1596/978-0-8213-8991-1; retrieved November

14, 2013 from http://www.worldbank.org/ict/IC4D2012. License: Creative Commons Attribution CC BY 3.0

World Health Organization (WHO). 1978. *Primary Health Care. Report of the International Conference on Primary Health Care Alma-Ata, USSR, Declaration of Alma-Ata*. Geneva, Switzerland.

———. 2009. *Milestones in Health Promotion Statements from Global Conferences*. Geneva, Switzerland.

Wright, Earl and Calhoun, Thomas C. 2006. "Jim Crow Sociology: Toward an Understanding of the Origin and Principles of Black Sociology via the Atlanta Sociological Laboratory." Sociological Focus 39(1): 1–18.

# Increasing Community Engagement to Meet the Challenges of Mental Health Disparities In African American Communities

Edward V. Wallace

## Introduction

It is estimated that by 2053 nearly half of the US population will be composed of people of color (Carrington 2006). With this growing rate of diverse groups public health practitioners, health educators and researchers need to understand that Eurocentric views may, at best, not be relevant or, at worst, not be adequate to address the mental health needs of people of color. The Centers for Disease Control and Prevention (CDC) encourages mental health agencies to utilize community-based approaches to eliminate health disparities (Martin et. al. 2009). Community-based approaches include measuring knowledge and attitudes toward depression, identifying possible signs of depression and seeking help for depression from friends and family—these are effective in reducing mental health disparities in the United States (National Mental Health Association 2000). According to the CDC, community-based interventions build upon the collective strength and resources of communities in the fight against depression. The result is a greater potential for success because interventions are centered on cultural competency and are appropriate for individuals living in those communities (Goodman et. al. 1998).

A careful literature review of community-based mental health programs for underserved populations reveals that traditional treatment methods (e.g., antidepressant drugs) show very little evidence of reducing disparities (Fagan et. al. 2004). For example, one study indicates that most African Americans prefer counseling and are less inclined to use medications prescribed by primary care physicians (Miranda and Cooper 2004). Another study finds that African Americans are more likely than Caucasians to believe that antidepressants are addictive; thus, making antidepressant medications less likely to be acceptable for treatment for African Americans (Cooper et. al. 2004). Despite an increasing body of research on coalitions fighting mental health disorders there is little in the literature that provides adequate guidance for public health practitioners to reduce disparities.

Community engagement, the ability of communities to mobilize, identify and address social and health problems, is essential to community-based initiatives (Goodman et. al. 1998). There is substantial evidence suggesting that leadership is the most important factor in community building and engagement. Goodman (2008) finds that community engagement is associated with activism, leadership and the ability to organize a campaign. Additionally, there is evidence to suggest that mental health care in underserved communities is associated with leadership, collaboration and having an understanding of the communities (Baezconde-Garbantai et al. 2007).

Availability and access to mental health care can play a significant role in the treatment of mental illness for African Americans who are less likely to seek psychiatric care than Caucasians and more likely to receive health care services in emergency care settings (US Department of Health and Human Services 2001). The problem with these facilities is that, by definition, they are not designed to provide good long -term mental health care. In 2000 nearly 25 percent of African Americans were uninsured, a rate almost two times greater than that of Caucasians (Brown et. al. 2000). (As of 2015, since the implementation of the Affordable Care Act, the percentage had decreased to 15–17 per cent.) Additionally, only 53 percent of African Americans have employer-based health insurance versus 73 percent of Caucasians (Adler 2010). Given the mental health disparities that exist among African Americans there is a need to understand the significance of community-based engagement efforts and their role in reducing these problems within racial and ethnic minority communities (Fagan et. al. 2004). To successfully accomplish this goal the planning and implementation of a community engagement protocol is imperative. Accordingly, the objective of this study is to develop a model of community-based health care that increases participation of African Americans and minorities in addressing mental health disparities. It is believed that this grounded theory study will help improve health-care engagement and distribution within the African American and minority communities by providing a framework to design and implement innovative community partnerships.

# Methods

## Design and Sample

A constructivist grounded theory approach was used to obtain descriptions of the process of developing and implementing mental health treatment interventions in African American communities. A constructivist grounded theory assumes there is no single truth or objective reality awaiting discovery, but that multiple realities exist based on an individual's culture, history and life. In this approach, realities are created as individuals seek to make sense of what is going on within a situation (Charmaz 2006). A constructivist perspective acknowledges the multiple viewpoints and realities of partnerships and does not seek to find one reality. Grounded theory was chosen because it provides a framework to understand the action that is occurring within a situation. An underlining assumption in this study is that leaders and administrators of mental health agencies conceptualize and implement interventions based on life experiences, interactions and mental health practices.

Most mental health treatment studies have not tailored interventions to reach vulnerable populations (Sorenson et al. 1998). As a result, some mental health centers have received funding to develop effective mental health treatment interventions for African American and minority communities. This study sample was limited to African American participants because we wanted to develop a framework for conducting mental health initiatives from the perspective of African American mental health supporters and advocates. An African American mental health organization is defined as an organization that addresses mental health issues, serves the African American community and has an African American in a leadership position to share information about the organization's mental health efforts.

A person in a leadership position is operationalized as being an individual, 21 years or older, in a key decision-making position within the mental health organization for at least one year.

Mental health organizations were identified based on the researcher's knowledge and experience working with mental health organizations and via an internet search for organizations. Since a complete database of African American organizations does not exist the researcher asked participants for the names of other organizations working in the area of mental health at the completion of each interview. Local, state and national mental health organizations were included in the sample since our primary objective was to understand the process of working in African American communities on the topical area of mental health disparities. By conducting a study that allowed for local, state and national organizations to participate, this allowed for an analysis as to whether processes varied by region or level of organizational focus.

An email invitation was sent to 20 participants asking them to respond only if they were not interested in participating in the study. The researcher waited 7–14 days after the original invitation to allow participants time to indicate their desire for no additional contact. The majority of participants who were sent an email invitation responded within 7–14 days. After the closing date participants who had not responded to the invitation were contacted by telephone or e-mail to determine their interest in participating in the study. Fourteen leaders agreed to participate in the study and six leaders declined. Interviews were conducted with the leaders of five national, six state and three local organizations. Participants represented organizations located in the Northeast, Southeast, Northwest and Southwest geographic regions of the United States, as well as local, state and national, mental health organizations. The Committee for the Protection of Human Subjects approved the study and the use of informed consent.

## Measures

The research team conducted 14 interviews between September 2008 and October 2009 using an open-ended questionnaire. Participants had the opportunity to have an in-person or telephone interview. Each participant was interviewed once with each interview lasting approximately 35–60 minutes. We asked questions about their organization's priorities, activities and strategies, for example, "What are some of your strategies for gaining trust in the African American community?", "How has collaborating with other organizations help you reach your goal?" and "Why is it important to never give up your mission to address mental health disparities in the African American community?" These questions were designed to elicit information about what guides the organization's work.

## Analytic Strategy

Interviews were audio taped and transcribed by graduate students. The transcripts were then crossed-checked for accuracy. Since a grounded theory methodology was used data collection and analysis were simultaneously conducted. First, data were analyzed by examining the text line by line searching for thematic codes. After the data were coded they were sorted into appropriate categories. Data collection ended with the recurrence of identified themes and when sufficient data were gathered to fully explain the phenomena of addressing mental health disparities. Scientific rigor was maintained by writing memos immediately after conducting interviews to identify personal biases and differentiate personal experiences from actual data.

# Results

## Understanding Cultural Competency

Findings show that African American mental health organizations increase community engagement by understanding cultural competency to address mental health issues. This understanding of mental health involves two strategies: (a) developing relationships and partnerships and (b) creating collective power (see Figure 15.1).

Implementing strategies to address mental health disparities in a culturally competent manner is a vital part of strategizing to involve African American communities in mental health. Cultural competency is a framework that includes local culture and context, history and geography to develop community-level culturally relevant interventions (Robinson 2005). Participants view their organization's work as being culturally specific rather than using identifiable culturally-specific approaches such as photos of famous African Americans, African colors such as red, black and green and language. For the participants, being culturally specific means that the organization must have a critical analysis and understanding of how cultural factors such as ethnicity, race, historical events and (mis) trust of the medical profession influence African Americans' decisions to seek, or not seek, mental health treatment. According to participants, an organization must have a knowledge and understanding of people of African descent in order to garner capital within that community. Leaders describe a need for culturally relevant topics to "personify mental health" to African American communities:

> You want to pull in some of that cultural aspect ... the impact of discrimination and oppression. During slavery many Blacks were oppressed and discriminated against. Today when someone is looked over for a job even when they are qualified, it can become more than just try harder next time. It can generate economic hardship, depression, social isolation and suicide. Most people don't understand the connection between oppression and mental illness. (Participant #5)

Cultural competency helps to engage communities and develop sustainable partnerships and community relationships.

## Developing Partnerships and Relationships

The primary outcome for each organization's leader is to establish partnerships and relationships that foster the creation of a network of individuals and groups knowledgeable about mental illness and the development of a staff dedicated to eliminating mental health disparities among African Americans. Participants believe that a core network of partners results in a multi-level response to mental illness, which includes community-based organizations, Black churches and African American fraternities and sororities. Participants understand that working with other organizations to address serious mental health problems (e.g., schizophrenia, depression and suicide) strengthens their partnerships. This

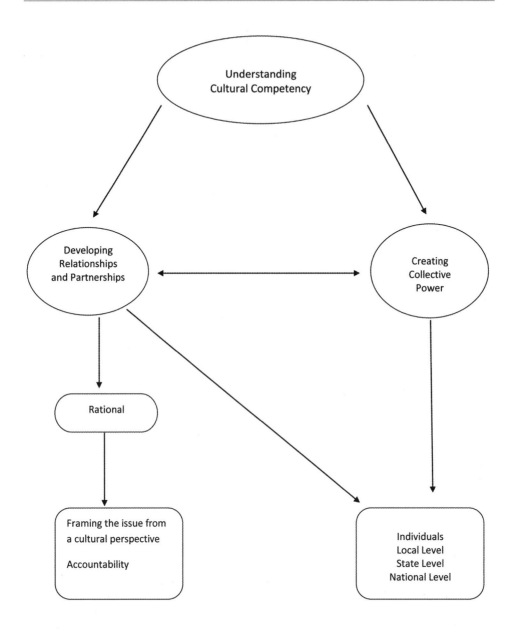

**Figure 15.1    Understanding Cultural Competency for Community Engagement to Address Mental Health Disparities**

is expressed by several participants in the quotes below: "Making the connection for their particular issue … how does mental health disparities fit in to what is important to them? And until you do that … people will continue to be disinterested" (Participant # 10).

The process of developing partnerships and relationships also helps to minimize competition among organizations. One participant states: "We're going to the same watering hole to try and get assistance to make our programs effective … So I think that regardless of whether its mental health or heart disease … that is where a majority of the competition is" (Participant # 2).

Many participants indicate that in order to develop true relationships with other community organizations one must never give up; they must continue to persevere. Perseverance is demanded because the same communities are often repeatedly approached about collaborating when it comes to dealing with health issues in the African American community. Often new partnerships tend to fade over time when communication about mental health and the African American community decreases. Participants understand that many community groups do not want to deal with mental health issues even after receiving oral and written follow-ups. One participant states:

> *You take the first step by initiating conversation about addressing mental health in the Black community and people are interested, you send them information, and they say "yes, it sounds like a good idea. Yes this would help eliminate the stigma around mental health." When you call back, they don't remember you, or don't remember receiving the information. You send it to them again, and then they stop taking your call. (Participant # 7)*

In these situations organizations try a different approach to gain access to members of the community. When organizations previously discussed mental illness in the African American community with national organizations they were met with resistance. However, when the organizations learned there were several local chapters willing to cooperate and discuss mental health in the Black community they were much more successful. The statement below is representative of the organization's strategy:

> *I felt I needed to deal with some of the local groups here who have a national [office], because the national [office] can't just ignore their local chapters because they are the eyes and ears for the national [office]. This gives me an opportunity to build a true partnership with the local group and expand out, rather than trying to deal with someone who I can only talk with on the phone … and doesn't have to look at me. (Participant # 3)*

## Creating Collective Power

The second process that organizations use to get communities involved in addressing mental health disparities is called "creating collective power." This involves bringing together new and existing organizations as a collective body to leverage their power to confront mental illness in African American communities. The statement below highlights how an organization can gain access to an African American community through existing relationships in the community:

> *You got to first look at those groups that you have established a relationship with initially. Then the buy-in on that level is going to be a high-end buy-in … because you already established mutual admiration, mutual trust, and shared effort to address mental health in the Black community. You don't take them for granted, but you solidify that right away. Because by doing that, now those organizations that did not*

*know of your work, other organizations may have relationships with. They buy into
what you are doing when you come to the door. (Participant # 8)*

Collective power networks help address mental health disparities in the African American communities by combining their strengths, assets, knowledge, resources and expertise with other organizations into one collective movement. The leaders identified herein know that collective power is useful in terms of changing social norms, disseminating information and educating policy makers on mental health issues. The following statement shows how a government agency and an African American community-based organization combines resources for maximum impact in a local community:

*The state wanted to get the word out to the African American community. We had
the marketing skills and the vehicle that could get the word out. They had a plan and
had a strategy ... but in terms of reaching the grassroots community ... they didn't
have that sort of network set up. So they talked to us about it and it seemed like a
good marriage. So we didn't know if educating the public about mental health would
be a great idea for us to do ... We said this would be a good thing to do and make a
difference in our community. (Participant # 12)*

The interactions between understanding cultural competency, developing partnerships and relationships, and creating collective power results in a critical mass of committed community organizations and individuals focused on addressing mental health disparities in African America communities.

# Discussion

The findings of this study help improve our understanding of how mental health organizations use culturally competent strategies to address mental health disparities in African American communities. Traditionally, mental health interventions in minority communities have focused on raising the awareness of mental illness; however, the need to develop partnerships and community power are often overlooked in capacity building (Baezconde-Garanati et al. 2007). We found that understanding cultural competency to address mental health disparities in African American communities consists of developing relationships and creating collective power. Participants suggest that seeking the truth and understanding historical events are essential in building relationships to address mental health disparities. This approach allows for an understanding of cultural factors (i.e., ethnicity and race) that must be taken into consideration when addressing mental health in the Black community. The results of this study indicate that cultural competency helps engage communities in partnerships which could eventually impact the lives of people in the community.

Community health educators are essential advocates for and provide leadership in developing and implementing health promotion and prevention strategies for minority populations (American Public Health Association 2009). As providers, community health educators play a major role in educating the public about depression, suicide and the feeling of hopelessness as risk factors of mental illness (Cunningham et al. 2006). Community health educators and other public health officials should use the two culturally relevant methods suggested herein as a basis for planning interventions. Public health professionals of all disciplines should use culturally appropriate strategies to build relationships to address mental illness.

Public health professionals and community health educators should also advocate for state and federal policies to fund organizations with a commitment to address mental illness in racial and ethnic communities. These policies can level the playing field and help to reduce mental health disparities. Additional funding to these organizations will allow them to continue the process of developing new leaders who are interested in developing partnerships and creating collective power.

Despite the many strengths of addressing mental illness in the African American community the study itself has some limitations that must be considered for future research purposes. First, only one interview was conducted per organization. Conducting an interview with more than one member of each organization would have provided additional and useful data to better understand how mental health organizations conduct their work to address mental health in African American communities. Second, it was extremely difficult to determine the actual number of mental health organizations that exist in the United States because many of these organizations are not sustainable since they depend heavily on government funding and policy makers' agendas. Despite these limitations the key finding of this study contributes to the literature by documenting how African American mental health organizations use community engagement to address mental health disparities in African American communities.

## Implications for Future Research

Most of the research on mental health and African Americans has focused on standard practices such as hospitalization or medication. Unfortunately, there is no scientific evidence to suggest that this practice prevents immediate or eventually long-term mental illness. Accordingly, there is a need to go beyond the traditional practices concerning African Americans such as prescribing higher dosages of antipsychotic drugs and placing them in seclusion while in psychiatric hospitals (Jeste et al. 1996).

Future studies should focus on cultural competency and how organizations build community relationships to address mental health disparities. Empirical research of organizations working to address mental health issues are required to provide the solutions necessary to address mental health disparities in African American communities. Finally, community health educators and public health professionals should collaborate to perform culturally centered community-based interventions to determine what works, what might work and what does not work, in reducing mental health disparities within vulnerable populations.

## References

Adler, Nancy. 2010. "Socioeconomic Status and Health in Industrial Nations." *Annals of New York Academy of Sciences* 869: 427–30.

American Public Health Association. 2009. "The Role of Public Health Nurses": http://www.apha.org./membergroups/sections/aphasections/phn/abiut/phnroles.htm.

Baezconde-Garanati, Lordes, Laura Beebe and Elisio J. Perez-Stable. 2007. "Building Capacity to Address Disparities among American Indian Communities: Conceptual and Systematic Considerations." *Addiction* 102(Suppl. 2): 112–22.

Brown, Richard, Victoria D. Ojeda, Roberta Wyn and Rebecca Levan. 2000. *Racial and Ethnic Disparities in Access to Health Insurance and Health Care*. Los Angeles, CA: University of Los Angeles Center for Health Policy Research and the Henry J. Kaiser Family Foundation.

Carrington, Christine. H. (2006). "Clinical Depression in African American Women: Diagnoses, Treatment, and Research." *Journal of Clinical Psychology* 62(7): 779–91.

Centers for Disease Control and Prevention. 2007. "Best Practices of Mental Health Programs—Report." Atlanta, GA: US Department of Health and Human Services, Centers for Disease Control and Prevention and Health Promotion.

Charmaz, Kathy. 2006. "Grounded Theory: Objectivist and Constructivist Methods." in *Handbook of Qualitative Research*, eds. N.K.I. Denzin and Y.S. Lincoln. Thousand Oaks, CA: Sage Publications, pp. 509–35.

Cooper, Lisa. A., Junios. J. Gonzales, Joseph J. Gallo, Katherine Rost, Lisa S. Meredeth and Nah-Yuh Rubenstein. 2004. "The Acceptability of Treatment for Depression among African Americans, Hispanic, and White Primary Care Givers." *Medical Care* 41: 479–89.

Cunningham, Peter, Kellan McKenzie and Erin Taylor. 2006. "The Struggle to Provide Community-Based Care to Low-Income People with Serious Mental Illnesses." *Health Affairs* 25(3): 694–705.

Fagan, Pebbles, Gary King, Deirdre Lawrence, Sally-Anne Petrucci, and Robert Banks. 2004. "Eliminating Health Disparities: Directions for Future Research." *American Journal of Public Health* 94(2): 211–17.

Goodman, Robert M. 2008. "A Construct for Building Community-Based Initiatives in Racial and Ethnic Communities. A Qualitative Cross-Case Analysis." *Journal of Public Health Management and Practice* 14(6): 18–25.

———, Marjorie Speers, Kenneth McLeroy and Stephen Fawcett. 1998. "Identifying and Defining the Dimensions of Community Capacity to Provide a Basis for Measurement." *Health Education and Behavior* 25(3): 258–78.

Jeste, Dilip D.V., Laurie A. Lindamer, Jovier Evans and Johnothan P. Larco. 1996. "Relationship of Ethnicity and Gender to Schizophrenia and Pharmacology of Neuroleptics." *Psychopharmacology Bulletin* 32(2): 243–51.

Martin, Sarah I., Dorean Maines, Maurice Martin, Pamela McDonald, Michele Polackseck and Debra Wigand. 2009. "Healthy Maine Partnerships: Policy and Environmental Changes." *Preventing Chronic Diseases* 6(2): 1–8.

Miranda, Jeanne and Lisa Cooper. 2004. "Disparities in Care for Depression among Primary Care Patients." *Journal of General Internal Medicine* 19: 120–26.

National Mental Health Association. 2000. "Depression and African Americans" (factsheet). Verona, VA: National Mental Health Association.

Robinson, Robert G. 2005. "Community Development Model for Public Health Applications: Overview of a Model to Eliminate Population Disparities." *Health Promotion Practice* 6(3): 338–46.

Sorenson, Glorean, Karen Emmons, Mary W. Hunt and Douglas Johnson. 1998. "Implications of Results of Community-Based Trials." *Annual Review of Public Health* 19: 379–416.

US Department of Health and Human Services. 2001. "Mental Health: Culture, Race, and Ethnicity—A Supplement to Mental Health." Rockville, MD: US Department of Health and Human Services.

# As Seen on TV?: Hip Hop Images and Health Consequences in the Black Community

Omotayo O. Banjo, Guy-Lucien Whembolua,
Shewanee Howard-Baptiste, Nathaniel Frederick II
and Jerod D. Lindsey

From its origins in the Black communities of New York City, hip hop has been known as a form of cultural expression and empowerment for disenfranchised groups. Over thirty years since its inception hip hop has seeped into the fabric of American culture through advertisements, film and television. This form of popular culture has transcended cultural boundaries as far as Japan and China and continues to be one of the most popular and profitable cultural commodities in the world (Kitwana 2002). In the United States hip hop remains a cultural product heavily produced and populated by Black Americans (Stapleton 1998). As such, scholars have continued to explore and critique the relationship between the cultural production of hip hop music and the lived experiences of Blacks. While the music is featured in marketing campaigns from cars to cereals, community members from whom the music is derived continue to be impacted in ways that are arguably not as profitable.

Some critics argue that contemporary and popular rap music has strayed from its history of anti-systemic and counter-cultural messages. A litany of critiques includes questions of representation, the amount of violent and misogynistic lyrics and materialism as motivated by commercial interests. Such messages are deemed problematic when considering its potential impact on mainstream perceptions of Black culture as well as its impact on members of the Black community. Although a host of rappers have claimed the lavish lifestyle they portray in their videos motivates young boys and girls to pursue and achieve social mobility, there is currently no empirical evidence directly linking upward mobility of Blacks to hip hop exposure. Instead, there seems to be a number of irreconcilable inconsistencies between messages in hip hop music compared to the actual lived experiences of their Black consumers as well as data to support such correlations.

This chapter addresses the relationship between messages in hip hop music and actual health consequences in the Black community. This chapter also problematizes post-identity rhetoric which claims to empower audiences but may in fact help to perpetuate poor decisions that impact Black men and women's wellness. First, we employ social learning as a theoretical framework then discuss the relationship between hip hop messages and sexual health. Last, we propose a media literacy approach to hip hop music consumption to address the inconsistencies between the messages in hip hop music and the wellness of the Black community.

## Media, Culture and Social Learning

Although culture, family and friends help to shape our perceptions, attitudes and behaviors, much of our understanding about our social world is influenced by visual cues and messages embedded in our media. From a critical cultural perspective, the concept of ideological hegemony—a dominant system of beliefs—helps to explain the media's pervasive influence on our lives. Adorno and Horkheimer posit that culture industries prevent any potential for radical change in depictions of race, class and gender; thus, media convey and normalize ideologies that support the status quo. Critical scholars maintain that it is not possible for artistic products created under a capitalistic system to have liberating potential (Adorno and Horkheimer 1993; Stokes 2002). Gitlin (1979: 253) asserts, "Commercial culture does not *manufacture* ideology; it *relays* and *reproduces* and *processes* and *packages* and *focuses* ideology that is constantly arising both from social elites and from active social groups and movements throughout society (as well as within media organizations and practices)" (original emphasis). Because the industry favors profit over risk, media producers avoid innovation and novelty; thus, hegemonic ideology becomes reproduced within these systems over long periods despite significant industry shifts (Butsch 2003). This is especially true when examining representations of race, class and gender. While hip hop has traditionally existed as a countercultural voice, in the hands of corporations its current iteration reinforces a dominant ideology which reproduces social relations of domination and subordination (Kellner 2003).

Media effect scholars maintain that repeated exposure to ideologically laden messages work to inform social identity and behaviors associated with a social group. Bandura's social learning theory (1977) helps explain how viewers' behaviors are impacted by what they see onscreen. Viewers learn by attending to messages in the media and reproducing or performing observed behaviors which are culturally rewarded. For example, when rappers boast about having multiple sexual partners in their music and gain status instead of sexually transmitted diseases, such behaviors may motivate viewers to model the observed behavior without concern for real-life consequences. Taking into consideration the role of ideological hegemony in influencing the cultural production of hip hop music and the psychological impact of messages in hip hop music, we explore the relationship between hip hop music and sexual health. In order to understand this relationship it is valuable to first unpack the ways that hip hop video culture construes gender identity and gender performance and, thus, influences gender relations and sexual health.

## Hip Hop and Gender Performance

Gender identity and gender performance are crucial to the production and popularity of hip hop music in the United States. Hip hop continues to be a cultural site through which traditional narratives about masculinity persist and, with time, has also become a space where scripts about femininity are somewhat disrupted. Some scholars contend that this multi-billion-dollar industry is perceived to have negatively transformed gender identity and gender relations (Hunter 2011; Hurt 2006), which has implications for health choices.

## Men and hip hop

The role played by men in hip hop has been explained through different lenses. Using the lens of consumption, Hunter examined rap videos and attempted to explain "the rap lifestyle" (Hunter 2011). Her data revealed several compelling patterns about the relationship between conspicuous consumption and gender relations in popular rap music videos. Despite her focus on females and their representations, her work clearly identified themes about manhood as well. An association between manhood and financial means was seen as central as it allowed male characters to order females to "shake it" and expressions such as "making it rain," taken from the strip club culture, were found significant to the misogynist norms that permeated a number of hip hop songs in which men expressed their manhood. Such representations of masculinity arguably have significant implications for young men's attitudes towards women and sex.

In addition, hip hop videos portray underclass Black males as ritualizing and perpetually pursuing America's obsession with achieving status through material acquisition (Dyson 1996; Kitwana 2002). Recently, Gordon, Maiben and Wright (2010) posited that many hip hop artists articulate the implications of aspirations to live the "American Dream" juxtaposed with their current lived experiences. Johnson and colleagues (1995) found that men who were exposed to rap videos tended to value material acquisition over academic achievement. In his award-winning documentary, "Hip Hop: Beyond Beats and Rhymes," Hurt examined these realities and identified similar dominating patterns, stating that images of status, wealth and materialism presented a masculine energy. Such images contribute to the dehumanizing representations of Black men and, as Hall (2006) argues, results in a meta-minstrelsy by which Black characters fit White audiences' voyeuristic needs and expectations. In other words, hip hop is often a stage upon which Black men perform ideas of Black masculinity consistent with Whites' perceptions.

Moreover, an important facet of manhood exposed by hip hop is the presentation of "the streets" as the central socialization institution for Black males. Defined by Oliver (2006) as the network of public and semi-public social settings (e.g., street corners, recreational places, etc.) in which primarily lower- and working-class Black males tend to congregate (ibid.), one can see the omnipresence of "the streets" particularly in gangsta rap hip hop lyrics as problematic as it overexposed a stage where marginalized Black males embrace street-related values, norms and roles (Madhubuti 1990; Perkins 1975; Wilson 1996). In addition, Oliver (2006) suggests that three roles—the "Tough Guy/Gangsta," the "Player of Women" and the "Hustler/Balla"—are over-represented in hip hop imagery and work together to constitute the hierarchy of manhood valued by Black males in the streets. Exposure to this type of material has been shown to greatly influence the social construction of gender identity among both poor and non-poor Black American males (Kitwana 2002). For example Johnson and colleagues (1995) found that males exposed to violent music videos were more likely to be accepting of violent acts, especially toward women. Therefore, consumption of "the street" scripting of Black masculinity may also be associated with listeners' substance use, abuse behavior and sexual attitudes.

Hip hop culture appeals to young male audiences because its chief storytellers look like them; young, Black and Brown. Hip hop video images in which mostly young Black men are portrayed as gangsters, players and/or ballers are problematic because such limiting portrayals only glorify a narrow view of manhood, where exploiting others to achieve material success, resorting to violence as a means of resolving disputes and indiscriminate pursuit of sexual relationships with women is the only way to achieve real manhood (Kitwana 2002). Despite this, hip hop cannot take all the credit or blame for shaping one's masculinity (Hurt 2006). While many educators have already acknowledged the importance of understanding the impact of hip hop on American culture (Chang 2005), it is as equally important to highlight the impact American culture has on hip hop. Any vested interest in transforming manhood within hip hop and some of its negative consequences will not be possible without an understanding of male identity construction within the larger culture (Houston 2010). This supports Ratcliff's (2010) argument that those who appreciate, produce and live hip hop culture must develop a unified hip hop intelligentsia that will critique and challenge the sexism, violence and the anti-intellectualism permeating much of mainstream rap.

## Women and Hip Hop

Hip hop lyrics and video culture has also informed traditional scripts of womanhood, which have significant implications for women's self-identity and their sexual health choices. In the mainstream media, Black women's sexuality is often depicted as animalistic or associated with nature (Railton and Watson 2005). In sum, Lamb and Brown (2006) suggest that Black women are primarily reduced to "jiggling butts and cleavages." Historically, images of Black women in popular media included the Mammy—an asexual nurturing figure, the Jezebel—a hypersexual deviant or the Sapphire—an aggressive untamed woman (Collins 2006; West 1995). Such characterizations are also prominent in hip hop where women tend to be featured as an earthy mother figure, money-hungry gold digger, ride-or-die gangster bitch or the promiscuous freak, to name a few (Stephens and Phillips 2003). Turner's (2011) content analysis confirms that Black-oriented music videos (r&b and hip hop) portray greater hypersexual images of Black women than other genres portray White women.

As a result, hip hop artists have been accused of being misogynistic and the music critiqued as being oppressive to women, problematizing female participation in the creation of both hip hop music and videos. According to Peoples (2008: 21), however, hip hop permits young Black women "… [t]o build or further develop their own gender critique and feminist identity which they can then turn toward the misogyny of rap music." Through the lens of hip hop feminism, feminist scholars such as Joan Morgan (1999) and Shani Jamilla (2002) argue for a reframing and celebration of women's participation in hip hop while critiquing limiting roles of women in hip hop music videos. Hip hop feminism seeks to empower and liberate young Black women from constraints on their sexual expressiveness by participating in the creation process, appropriating a traditional masculine space and reclaiming traditionally derogatory labels for women (i.e., bitch). For example, Pough's (2004) analysis of rapper Lil' Kim reveals an appropriation, dominance and command for respect as the rapper referred to herself as "Queen Bitch," complicating the tensions between what Durham, Cooper and Morris (2013) refer to as a "queen-subject/ho-object" dichotomy.

Female empowerment is also associated with sexual permissiveness. Hip hop feminism finds itself located within a sex-positive discourse as it also argues that a woman within a predominantly male space such as hip hop can assert her power with her body, an often objectified entity in the hip hop music and video culture. Instead of being objectified by men, however, women in hip hop have control over the form and function of their sexuality and are considered the subjects. A clear illustration of this ideological shift is the backlash rapper Nelly received for a lewd act in his "Tip Drill" video. Although Nelly was lambasted for swiping a credit card between the buttocks of a female dancer, he emphatically counters in his *Behind the Music* bio-documentary, "It was her idea!"

Women's active participation in the reinforcement of gender identity and gender performance complicate early criticisms of hip hop music's impact on young women's self-identity and their sexual health choices. Although a proponent for discussions surrounding healthy sexuality, Lamb (2010) questions how scholars and young teen girls are able to discern between subjectivity and pressure to appeal to the male pornographic gaze. In the same vein, Banjo (2014) questions the distinctions, if any, between consequences for sexually expressive Black female artists compared to the everyday Black adolescent who is still exploring her sexuality. Petersen (2013) problematizes Beyonce Knowles's *GQ* interview where she addresses financial gender inequities and male-dominated constructions of sexiness while doing several scantily clad photo shoots. The tensions between subjectivity and objectivity remain and are perhaps most noticeable in a time where there are few popular female hip hop artists and such representations are more persuasive in the absence of competing images. In such cases, it is critical to explore the impact that hip hop music and its videos has on not only Black girls, but Black boys' health choices. The next section discusses health issues among Black men and women in more detail.

## Nicki Minaj: A Case Study

Trinidadian American rapper Nicki Minaj is one of the leading hip hop artists and it is most notable that she is female. Gaining platinum certification for both her debut and sophomore albums, Minaj has sold millions of albums in the United States and worldwide, positioning her in stiff competition with her male contemporaries; namely, Jay-Z, Kanye West and Lil Wayne. In fact, Minaj's debut album outsold veteran Kanye West's fifth studio album. Her recent album, *Pink Friday: Roman Reloaded*, was the sixth top-selling record in 2012. In 2012 Nicki Minaj was ranked tenth for receiving the most airplay and was also the only hip hop artist on this list (RIAA 2012). Minaj's commercial success sets her apart from her female predecessors like Queen Latifah, Lil' Kim and Foxy Brown in that, while she has achieved fame in the hip hop community, she has also been able to reach a wider audience and transcend into popular culture spaces.

Born Onika Maraj, Nicki Minaj's name began to buzz around larger communities in 2009 when she was being featured on a number of male artists' records. She is known for her outrageous outfits and colorful wigs. Minaj is probably most known for her over-sexualized image as her increasingly expanding buttocks have often been on display in music videos and in her live performances. Likening herself to what she calls a "Harajuku Barbie," Minaj embodies and promotes fashion, fantasy and feminism. The term "Harajuku" references a district in Tokyo, Japan that is known for its popular fashion shops. Whitney (2012) notes that women's sexuality has increasingly become tied to fashion and, thus, Black women in popular cultures display their sexuality with style in order to contend with their male counterparts. Her association with Barbie has also been critiqued as affording her opportunities to perform with many personalities. Challenging notions of static identity, Minaj embodies a postmodern perspective where identity is fluid, idiosyncratic and mutable. Minaj has spoken of a few of her alter egos, the most popular of them being Roman Zolanski. Accordingly, she vacillates between these different persona manipulating her voice, attire and body. Just as Barbie is able to wear many hats and dress in a wide range of outfits, Minaj has a range of outfits with extravagant accessories including a skirt with stuffed animals attached and an oversized multi-colored popsicle.

In addition, Minaj is well aware of the presence and power of her femininity. In several interviews she has expressed her desire to be a role model for young girls. Upon hearing the news of the success of her first album, Minaj is quoted as proclaiming "Girl Power!" Her lyrics and personal video blogs attest to her acknowledgement of gender disparity in the industry and her identification as a female artist in a male-dominated space.

Minaj has continuously problematized the double standard in hip hop where it is acceptable for men to be in control in pursuit of wealth, but where women who are in control are labeled "bitch." Nicki reclaims the historically pejorative term and refers to herself as a bitch, redefining it in terms of one's ability to achieve success. Perhaps a most marked expression and recognition of her gender position in relation to her status in the industry is her remark at the end of her "Stupid Hoe" video that "I am the female Weezy!" In her interview with ABC News' JuJu Chang, Minaj shared her desire to empower and encourage women to be successful without a man. Minaj has also been noted for queering her sexuality through her images, lyrics and identification as bisexual. As such, her fan base is quite varied as she appeals to men, women and transgendered individuals; she makes room for each of her audience groups, referring to her female followers as Barbies/Barbz, her male fans as Boyz and her gay fans as Ken Barbz.

However, Nicki's queer identity is sometimes questioned because it seems to be more of a branding strategy than an authentic standpoint. One of the reasons Minaj's sexuality has been questioned is because of her resistance to explicitly commit to a sexual identity despite mentioning her bisexuality in interviews. Perhaps Minaj's reluctance to openly ascribe to a sexual identity can be explained by commercial hip hop's resistance to lesbians as lesbianism does not provide space for male pleasure. Durham, Cooper and Morris (2013) point out the overwhelming support hip hop artist Frank Ocean has received from the hip hop community compared to Nicki Minaj, suggesting a longstanding preference toward males—even gay men—before lesbians. It may also be difficult to categorize Nicki because she performs typical scripts of black women in hip hop, playing with queer desire just enough to invite the male gaze and question her sexuality.

## Method and Analysis

For this chapter's analysis, songs and videos were taken from Nikki Minaj's first two albums. Sample selection was guided by four criteria. First, we selected songs for which there was a video. From this list, we reviewed the videos on the artist's VEVO channel on YouTube and selected songs that had the highest number of views. Last, we selected songs whose lyrics had feminist leanings. For example, the track "Starships" made the list after the first three criteria. However, after reviewing the lyrics and navigating the verification process the researchers decided that the song's party theme overshadowed any messages about the artist's position as a woman in the industry. Based on these criteria, the sample included "Super Bass" (from the album *Pink Friday*) and "Beez in the Trap" (from *Roman Reloaded*).

## Lyrical Representation

In the songs analyzed for this case study Minaj positions herself as having authority over other female rappers by virtue of her career success. Her popular line "all you bitches is my sons" ("Beez in the Trap") is a self-proclamation of her position as the new queen of hip hop. In the track "Super Bass," Minaj reveals a bold character who is unafraid of picking up men. To the idea that she would subvert a traditional script of male roles, Minaj replies, "Yes, I did. Yes I did, somebody please tell him who the F I is." In her lyrics, Minaj represents an independent, ambitious and confident woman who is aware of her status and sexual prowess which are threats to both men and women. Yet, she is unafraid of expressing a submissive side, one that is willing to take "her panties off" if a guy that she selects looks at her the right way.

## Visual Representation

Minaj's visual representation contrasts with her lyrical presence and, as such, the notion of power by virtue of womanhood is reinterpreted by means of her body in place of her words. Though her lyrics reflect dominance, confidence and authority, the rapper seems to reproduce images often associated with a paradox of Black female sexuality—undomesticated, yet restrained; available, yet threatening. On the surface, these images are problematic and can sometimes be seen as harmful. However, it is arguable that through the lens of hip hop feminism, Minaj is reclaiming the White imagination or interpretation of the Black body. Across three videos, themes of power through subjectivity and financial wealth emerge and are mediated through her body.

# Emergent Themes

## Control through Subjectification and Sexual Dominance

Sex-positive-oriented feminism contends that the contemporary woman is able to control her own sexuality and, thus, willfully chooses to display her body in a sexual nature for male and female pleasure. Not only is she in control of her own body, but the sex-positive woman is also able to exert control over her male and female gazers. The notion of subjectivity is prominent in Minaj's videos where she is often positioned as an empowered female whose source of control and dominance is mainly sexual. In addition, Minaj's persona fluctuates between playful and innocent to powerful and sexually dominant.

For example, in the music video for the song "Super Bass" the men in the video are depicted as objects that are mesmerized by her. An early scene focuses on a male's muscular torso, eyes and lips. When Minaj enters the scene she interacts with two men by groping and caressing their skin or playing with their ties while they stand still. The men look at her passively, yet permissively, allowing her to do as she wishes with their bodies. In another scene Minaj walks by a pink swimming pool wearing stiletto high-laced boots and a colorful bathing suit with a deep plunge neckline, revealing the inner curves of her breasts. We are shown her side profile and the curves of her buttocks are highlighted. The men in the background are positioned as props as they are sitting or standing nearby wearing no shirts and gaping at Minaj as she passes by. Minaj is later seen dancing in the pool with one of the men. With her champagne glass in hand, Minaj slowly pours the pink liquid over her breasts as the men watch. She playfully douses the man in the pool with the glass of water and he responds with shock while the men in the background grin. In the final sequences of "Super Bass" Minaj and other women dance for their male onlookers, but are still able to maintain control. With her in the center, Minaj and the dancers straddle the men as they sit passively, seemingly spellbound by the women's bodies. The men provide no eye contact. Instead, their eyes are focused on various parts of the women's bodies as they dance around them. Their hands are at their sides except when their role is to literally serve as props to support women's bodies during the dance routine. These scenes simultaneously present the men as objects of her desire and subjects of her sexuality. In a role-reversal, the men are purely

229

present for her to fondle. They are also stunned or subdued by her body and her "pink liquid" so much so that they cannot help but stare. While Minaj's body is on display for both the viewer and the other video actors, she rejects the one man who dares to approach her. By doing so, Minaj is portrayed as being aware of her sexual influence and her power to select or reject a male voyeur.

Minaj's subjectivity and sexual dominance over men is also demonstrated in the video "Beez in the Trap." In Minaj's scenes with rapper 2 Chainz she situates herself as the object and controller of her own will. Both Minaj and 2 Chainz wear animal-patterned clothing, thus, exuding symbolic connotations of instinctive sexual attraction. She wears a leopard-print leotard showcasing her back and buttocks while his shoes feature a leopard pattern. As Minaj gyrates with her back toward the camera she gives the audience a view of her posterior. She presents herself as an object of desire for both 2 Chainz as well as the audience. However, Minaj is shown as having the power to decide where the line is drawn. In the last scene, 2 Chainz dances with Minaj while playfully imitating sexual movements toward her. However, these movements never progress to actual touching. Minaj is not facing 2 Chainz, yet she stands confident and permissive of his actions. Having willfully subjected herself to being an object, Minaj then looks at the camera and smiles all the while fully aware of what has taken place behind her. Her body is certainly an object of his sexual desire, but under her conditions. Minaj's subjectivity emerges through this posturing and is meant to demonstrate new configurations of female power. That is, she is not only able to lay her body down for public musing, she also has the power to raise it up again.

Minaj is also seen exerting her influence over women. In "Super Bass," the dancers show solidarity with her by wearing matching cu-off shorts and pink wigs. They wear color-contrasting boots as their only distinguishing characteristic. Thus, the dancers have embodied Minaj's influence by appropriating her image. Unlike how the men have been portrayed, these females are not objects but participate with Minaj in their control of the men. In the video "Beez in the Trap," this construction is quite the opposite. Here, female actors are the objects and are depicted as lusting after and desiring attention from Minaj. In a few scenes, Minaj plays sexually with the women; whether through flirtation or physical touch. Subdued by her, the women yield to her beckoning and accept her fondling just as the men in "Super Bass." Not only is Minaj able to situate herself as an object for the male pornographic gaze, Minaj also participates as an objectivist, using her body to control women. We theorize more about the reasons for Minaj's influence over women below.

## Money, Power, Respect: The Great Equalizers

Hip hop feminists also seek to claim traditionally male-dominated spaces and use their bodies as modes for access. In "Beez in The Trap" Minaj is featured in a strip club alongside male rapper, 2 Chainz. Though Minaj is dressed similarly to the women in the club, what differentiates her from them is her financial status. This status is solidified through a conspicuous display of cash and material acquisitions. We are shown close-ups of Minaj's hand fanning a stack of money as if she is a patron; then the video cuts to a close-up of a man's hand fanning a similar stack of money. The sequence reinforces her position as the dominant person in the scene, propelling her to a typically male space/position in the club and thus making her desired and respected. We also see this in the video for "Super Bass." The beginning scenes in the video include a model Ferrari, stacks of money, champagne and a model airplane. All are conspicuous symbols of wealth with which she desires to be associated. These images establish her status for the viewer and legitimize the counterhegemonic depiction of passive men and aggressive women in the video. In a later scene, two women flank Minaj but she is not dancing with them because she does not identify with them. As she makes sexual advances toward them her hand moves down as she rubs the back of the woman with the largest buttocks. The women are there for her to objectify.

Minaj crosses physical boundaries with the women early in the video; however, the power dynamic changes when she is in a scene with 2 Chainz. As he motions toward her he does not touch her, as mentioned previously. There is a boundary that 2 Chainz recognizes, which differentiates Minaj from the strippers/dancers in this video. She does not undress for money; instead, her money allows her to undress and still be respected. She will allow him to play with her in a sexual way and he will respect her for it. At the end of the video they stand back to back implying equality and respect. However, they are not equal in that she possesses a body that he could only enjoy should she allow him to. She is always aware of her power as a female and her willingness to accept this is profitable and makes her an equal.

Although "Beez in the Trap" illustrates Minaj's shared status with men, a frequent and conspicuous presence in Minaj's video is her hypeman/boyfriend Safree. While gendered notions of power are themes in the aforementioned videos, Safree seems to be inoculated from her influence. Often clad with chains or standing next to luxury cars, his role serves to display symbols of monetary and material wealth. Safree is rarely featured in scenes without Minaj and he usually stands behind or beside her. Following the lap dance scene in "Super Bass" we see a close up of Nicki's stilettoes and Safree's sneakers. As the image pans up they are both on a platform. Safree has a chain around his neck with the initials "SB," which stand for his nickname, Scaff Breezy. As he leans down toward Nicki she holds up his chain. In "Beez in the Trap" Safree is again with Minaj, standing behind her, lip-syncing her lyrics while counting what is presumably her money. In both videos Safree is a prop whose purpose is not to demonstrate Minaj's sexual dominance but to display her financial status.

From a sex-positive perspective, Minaj embodies sex-positive principles both through her ability to capture and play with male attention and sexual desire and through her financial success. All of this is navigated and controlled through the medium of her body. Although her lyrics convey confidence, her visual representation clearly emphasizes her reliance on her sexuality to access and thrive in a male-dominated space. In concordance with Lamb's (2010) critique, it is unclear first whether Minaj's lyrical message overshadows her visual message, and, second, whether young girls are able to navigate the sex-positive space Minaj celebrates in her videos. As such, sociological, psychological and communication research should investigate the impact of these messages on young girls' negotiations of their racial and sexual identity as well as their sexual health practices.

## Hip Hop and Health Impacts

Scholarship on health and media messages continues to identify the abundance of unhealthy messages within hip hop music. For example, Anderson and colleagues (2014) found that compared to other genres, R&B and hip hop music were more likely to contain substance abuse and sexually deviant content. Although more than half of all the songs analyzed across genres involved casual sex, an overwhelming majority of the rap songs involved casual sex without consequences. Such findings are disturbing as a number of public health research studies show correlations between lyrical content in hip hop and risk behaviors for Black boys and girls, even as other factors are controlled. For example, Peterson and colleagues (2007) reported that the more hours of rap music videos Black American girls watch the more they were likely to binge drink, smoke marijuana, have multiple sexual partners or have a negative body image. Wingood and colleagues (2003) reported similar findings with negative outcomes such as getting arrested, hitting a teacher and contracting a sexually transmitted infection. These findings demonstrate the importance of examining the inconsistencies between the celebrations of substance use, abuse and sexual promiscuity in hip hop music and the health consequences plaguing the Black community. However, a plethora of studies have focused primarily on sexual identity and, therefore, we address the relationship between hip hop and sexual health.

Sexual health comprises more than determining whether or not to wear a condom or asking your partner to wear a condom. Sexual health is understanding the emotional, social and physical choices and consequences associated with sexual behavior. According to Insel and Roth (2011), sexuality is more than just sexual behavior. It is a complex interacting group of biological characteristics and acquired behaviors that people learn while growing up in a particular family, community and society. Sexuality includes biological sex (being biologically male or female), gender (masculine and feminine behaviors), sexual anatomy and physiology, sexual functioning and practices and social and sexual interactions with others. Our individual sense of identity is powerfully influenced by our sexuality. We think of ourselves in fundamental ways as male or female, heterosexual or homosexual and single, attached, married or divorced. However, developing a more comprehensive definition of sexuality should allow for a greater discussion about the needs of teens and adults in making more informed decisions about sexual health.

Sexually transmitted diseases (STDs) are infections that come from contact with blood, semen, vaginal fluid and other body fluids. Though the number of Blacks diagnosed with AIDS has remained steady since 2007, the Centers for Disease Control and Prevention (CDC) estimates that 1 in 16 Black men and 1 in 32 Black women will test positive for HIV infection (CDC 2013). Sexually transmitted infections like gonorrhea, chlamydia and syphilis affect African Americans disproportionately higher than any other population in the US: "Blacks represent just 14 percent of the U.S. population, yet account for one-third of all reported chlamydia cases, almost half of all syphilis cases, and two-thirds of all reported gonorrhea cases" (CDC 2011). Women who are Black, unmarried and have less income and education are at greatest risk for an unintended pregnancy (Nettleman et al. 2007). Mosher and colleagues (2012: 14) stated that "most births to teenagers and to unmarried adult women are unintended. Underestimating the risk of pregnancy is the most common reason for not using contraception that leads to unintended pregnancy." If teenagers and young men and women are not armed with accurate information that includes, but is not limited to, assessing their own risky behaviors, wearing condoms and knowing the sexual history of their partners, they are putting themselves in harm's way for any number of negative health consequences.

In order to assess how individuals make decisions about their sexual health it is essential to include additional factors like physical environment, socioeconomic status, poverty level and access to health insurance. These social determinants of health directly impact how people live, work, socialize, meet people and ultimately with whom they have intimate relationships, regardless of age. Teenagers and adults are not only influenced by their physical environment, peers and parents, but also media outlets.

Media has the ability to influence social norms, behaviors, decision-making skills and self-esteem. In a study by Wingood and colleagues, researchers determined the relationships between exposure to rap music videos and the incidence of risky health behaviors and sexually transmitted infections amongst 522 African American females between the ages of 14 and 18, living in lower socioeconomic-status neighborhoods. According to the findings, young women who had higher exposure to rap music videos were "… 2 times as likely to have had multiple sexual partners; and more than 1.5 times as likely to have acquired a new sexually transmitted disease … over the 12-month follow-up period" (Wingwood et al. 2003: 2). Peterson and colleagues (2007) also examined effects of exposure to rap music videos but with an emphasis on content. Researchers found that young women who were exposed to sexual stereotypes in rap music videos were more likely to have poor body image and were sexually promiscuous. Martino and colleagues (2006: 430) conducted a national longitudinal telephone survey of 1,461 adolescents over a two-year period and determined that adolescents who listened to more demeaning sexual content were more likely to initiate sexual intercourse and "progress to more advanced levels of non-coital sexual activity." They argued that "musicians who incorporate this type of sexual imagery in their songs are not simply modeling an interest in healthy sexual behavior for their listeners; they are communicating something specific about what are appropriate sexual roles for men and women" (ibid.: 438). As social learning suggests, media consumers observe and model behaviors which are seemingly culturally rewarded by wealth status and "respect." These findings are disconcerting in light of Stephens and Few's (2007) findings that Black boys and girls rely on images in hip hop to learn about sexual behavior when compared to the prevalence of sexually transmitted diseases that plague the Black community.

## Conclusion and Future Directions

Hip hop, a predominantly non-White space in the United States, celebrates consumerism and glorifies wealth status and material acquisition as a reiteration of the American Dream. However, while African Americans are one of the largest consumers, African American households reportedly have the lowest net worth compared to Latinos, Asians and Whites. These are among the obvious disconnects between the representations of urban life, Black masculinity, Black femininity in hip hop and the lived experiences of Black people; especially related to health. Although the health disparities in the African American community cannot fully be blamed on hip hop, it is arguable that the political and economic factors that define contemporary hip hop work to encourage and sustain poor and irresponsible health choices.

Other disconnects lie in the promotion and celebration of errant sexual behavior in music videos and the proliferation of sexual disease in the Black community. Hip hop encourages a masculinity that pursues sexual experiences with women, sometimes at any cost. Recently, a more aggressive articulation of manhood has emerged where Black male rappers brag about sexual assault/rape, which ultimately has the same silencing effect on women as sexual lyrics (Rebello-Gil and Moras 2013). Rick Ross, for example, was recently chastised for a lyric that explicitly indicated that he would slip ecstasy into a woman's drink so that he could rape her. For female artists in this traditionally male-dominated space, hip hop requires a woman's permission to be pursued, but on her terms. It should also be noted, however, that sexual pursuit is really her only option. Given the rates at which Black men and women are contracting sexually transmitted diseases and having unwanted pregnancies, it does not seem that young people are sexually competent, much less empowered when it comes to making informed health choices.

Future research should expound upon Stephens and Few's (2007) research and examine how young people utilize hip hop to develop sexual competencies. Recently, the link between health and hip hop music has been the focus of work using hip hop as a relevant pedagogical tool to broaden health awareness in underserved populations such as African American males (Whembolua et al. 2014). For example, in 2012, Nicki Minaj was the source of controversy when she announced in an interview in the United Kingdom that more than 10 per cent of the Republic of Trinidad and Tobago is suffering with the deadly Acquired Immune Deficiency Syndrome (AIDS), thus, forcing the Trinidadian ministry of tourism to embark on a public relations campaign to "correct" that statement (Caribbean 360, n.d.)—a testament to the influence hip hop artists could have on the overall health of minority communities

In addition, organizations serving this population must consider ways to use hip hop as an empowering agent. For example, Turner-Musa and colleagues employed a hip hop-based curriculum to educate Black teens about STD prevention. The program "H2P" is "based on cultural competence perspective, risk and protective framework, social learning theory, and uses social learning strategies as the foundation to promote effective behavioral change" (Turner et al. 2008: 357). The researchers report that participants' knowledge of sexual prevention increased after the intervention. In 2011, rapper Doug E. Fresh collaborated with neurologist Olajide Williams to create an intervention program, "Hip Hop Public Health," to address health illiteracy. Joining Michelle Obama's "Let's Move" campaign, the program has produced music to promote healthy decision making.

Another approach to empowering hip hop listeners is to train them to become critical listeners and developing a keen eye for media consumption. This is also referred to as "media literacy." Media literacy involves an evolving continuum of skills, knowledge, attitudes and actions (Bergsman et al. 2000). Learning how to read, criticize and resist sociocultural manipulation can empower Black Americans in relation to dominant forms of media and culture (Kellner 2003). By acquiring and consciously applying skills of analysis and evaluation to media texts, Black Americans can make the shift from media consumer to media citizen. Media literacy, or hip hop literacy workshops, help to develop critical thinking skills whereby students can identify these disconnects for themselves and draw independent conclusions.

Music video culture also complicates the evaluations of Black sexual bodies compared to White sexual bodies. Scholars contend that Black women are subjugated to sexual politics and are likely to experience more harmful ramifications. For example, Banjo (2014) found that popular Black female artists, including Nicki Minaj, were more likely to be addressed as sexual objects or passive receivers, whereas White female artists were more likely to be addressed as sexual subjects and active creators of sexual pleasure. Surely, it is more challenging for Black women to participate as agents of their own sexuality when they are more likely read as bodies to be "done to," versus those who are "doing." For example, Watson and colleagues (2012) found that Black women experience objectification and suffer the consequences including emotional stress and unhealthy relationships with men. Future scholarship should engage this dilemma, explore its consequences and develop useful campaigns or workshops that encourage Black women to be both comfortable with their sexuality and responsible with their bodies.

Because hip hop is a global phenomenon and a profitable product it is important to consider its role on health choices for marginalized Others across the globe. Future research should investigate the social and cultural consequences of gender performance on individuals of African descent in other parts of the world such as Europe, Latin America and Africa. It would be valuable to identify whether these disconnects are unique to the United States so that we can further investigate other structural factors that interact with hip hop's relationship with African Americans.

# Bibliography

Adorno, Theodore and Max Horkheimer. 1993. "The Culture Industry: Enlightenment as Mass Deception." in *The Cultural Studies Reader*, ed. Simon During. London: Routledge, pp. 31–41.

Anderson, Christina, Kyle J Holody, Mark Flynn and Clay Craig. 2014. "Drunk in Love: The Portrayal of Risk Behavior in Music Lyrics." Paper presented at the Association for Education in Journalism and Mass Communication Conference, Montreal, Ontario.

Bandura, Albert. 1977. *Social Learning Theory*. New York: General Learning Corporation

Banjo, Omotayo O. 2014. "Can Black Women Be Sex-Positive? Examining Audience Responses to Female Music Artists." Conference Paper. International Communication Association.

Bergsma, Lynda, David Considine, Sherri Hope Culver, Renee Hobbs, Amy Jensen, Faith Rogow, Elana Yonah Rosen, Cyndy Scheibe, Sharon Sellers-Clark and Elizabeth Thoman. 2000. *Core Principle of Media Literacy Education in the United States*: http://namle. net/publications/core-principles/.

Butsch, Richard. 2003. "Ralph, Fred, Archie, Homer, and the King of Queens: Why Television Keeps Re-Creating the Male Working-Class Buffoon." in *Gender, Race, and Class in Media*, eds. Gail Dines and Jean M. Humez. Thousand Oaks, CA: Sage, pp. 575–85.

Caribbean 360. n.d. "Nicki Minaj Increases AIDS Figures for TT Tenfold." Retrieved April 16, 2015: http://www.caribbean360.com/news/trinidad_tobago_news/nicki-minaj-increases-aids-figures-for-tt-tenfold#ixzz3XZHRIA2I.

Centers for Disease Control and Prevention. 2011. "CDC Fact Sheet: African Americans and Sexually Transmitted Diseases." Retrieved November 16, 2013: http://www.cdc.gov/nchhstp/newsroom/docs/AAs-and-STD-Fact-Sheet-042011.pdf.

———. 2013. *HIV Among African Americans. National Center for HIV/AIDS, Viral Hepatitis, STD, and TB Prevention: Division of HIV/AIDS Prevention*. Retrieved November 16, 2013. http://www.cdc.gov/hiv/pdf/risk_HIV_AAA.pdf.

Chang, Jeff. 2005. *Can't Stop, Won't Stop: A History of the Hip-Hop Generation*. New York: St. Martin's Press.

Collins, Patricia Hill. 2006. "New Commodities. New Consumers: Selling Blackness in a Global Market Place." *Ethnicities* 6(3): 297–317.

Durham, Aisha, Britney C. Cooper, and Susana M. Morris. 2013. "The Stage Hip Hop Feminism Built: A New Directions Essay." *Signs* 38(3): 721–37.

Dyson, Michael. E. 1996. *Between God and Gangsta Rap: Bearing Witness to Black Culture*. New York: Oxford University Press.

Gitlin, Todd. 1979. "Prime Time Ideology: The Hegemonic Process in Television Entertainment." *Social Problems* 26(3):251–66.

Gordon, Jr., Clearance. L., Andonnia Maiben and Earl Wright II. 2010. "The Damnation of Hip Hop: A Critique of Hip Hop Through the Lens of W. E. B. Du Bois." *International Journal of Africana Studies* 16(1): 62–76.

Hall, Stuart. 2006. "Popular Culture and the State." in *The Anthropology of the State: A Reader*, eds. Aradhana Sharma and Anil Gupta. Maiden, MA: Blackwell Publishing, pp. 360–80.

Houston, Akil. 2010. "The Art of Shadowboxing: Teaching about Gender Performance Using Hip Hop Culture as Pedagogy." *International Journal of Africana Studies* 16(1): 62–76.

Hunter, Margaret 2011. "Shake It, Baby, Shake It: Consumption and the New Gender Relation in Hip-Hop." *Sociological Perspectives* 54(1): 15–36.

Hurt, Byron. 2006. *Hip Hop: Beyond Beats and Rhymes* [documentary]. United States: God Bless the Child Productions.

Insel, Paul M., and Walton T. Roth. 2011. *Core Concepts in Health*. London: McGraw Hill.

Jamila, Shani. 2002. "Can I Get a Witness? Testimony from a Hip-Hop Feminist." in *Colonize This! Young Women of Color on Today's Feminism*, eds. Daisy Hernandez and Bushra Rehman. Berkeley, CA: Seal Press, pp. 382–94.

Johnson, James D., Lee Anderson Jackson and Leslie Gatto. 1995. "Violent Attitudes and Deferred Academic Aspirations: Deleterious Effects of Exposure to Rap Music." *Basic and Applied Social Psychology* 16(1-2): 27–41.

Kellner, Douglass. 2003. "Cultural Studies, Multiculturalism, and Media and Media Culture." in *Gender Race and Class: A Text Reader*, eds. Gale Dines and Jane M. Humez. Thousand Oaks, CA: Sage Publications, pp. 9–20.

Kitwana, Bakari. 2002. *The Hip Hop Generation: Young Blacks and the Crisis in African American Culture*. New York: Basic Civitas Books.

Lamb, Sharon. 2010. "Feminist Ideals for a Healthy Female Adolescent Sexuality: A Critique." *Sex Roles*, 62(5-6): 94–306.

Lamb, Sharon and Lyn Mikel Brown. 2006. *Packaging Girlhood*. New York: St. Martin's.

Madhubuti, Haki (1990). *Black Men: Single, Dangerous and Obsolete*. Chicago, IL: Third World Press.

Martino, Stephen C., Rebecca L. Collins, Marc N. Elliot, Amy Strachman, David E. Kanouse and Sandra H. Berry. 2006. "Exposure to Degrading Versus Nondegrading Music Lyrics and Sexual Behavior Among Youth." *Pediatrics* 118: 430. Retrieved April 24, 2015: http://pediatrics.aappublications.org/content/118/2/e430.full.html

Morgan, Joan. 1999. *When Chickenheads Come Home to Roost: A Hip-Hop Feminist Breaks It Down*. New York: Simon & Schuster.

Mosher, William D., Jo Jones and Joyce C. Abma. 2012. "Intended and Unintended Births in the United States: 1982–2010." *National Health Statistics* 55: 1–28 Retrieved November 16, 2013: http://www.cdc.gov/nchs/data/nhsr/nhsr055.pdf.

Nettleman, Mary D., Hwan Chung, Jennifer Brewer, Adejoke Ayoola and Phillip L. Reed. 2007. "Reasons for Unprotected Intercourse: Analysis of the PRAMS Survey." *Contraception* 75(5): 361–6.

Oliver, William. 2006. "'The Streets': An Alternative Black Male Socialization Institution." *Journal of Black Studies* 36: 918–37.

Peoples, Whitney. 2008. "'Under Construction' Identifying Foundations of Hip-Hop Feminism and Exploring Bridges between Black Second-Wave and Hip-Hop Feminisms." *Meridians: Feminism, Race, Transnationalism* 8(1): 19–52.

Perkins, Eugene 1975. *Home is a Dirty Street: The Social Oppression of Black Children*. Chicago, IL: Third World Press.

Petersen, Anne Helen 2013. "Beyonce, Feminism, Ambivalence." *Celebrity Gossip, Academic Style*. Retrieved April 24, 2015: http://www.annehelenpetersen.com/?p=3177.

Peterson, Shani H., Gina M. Wingood, Ralph J. DiClemente, Kathy Harrington and Susan Davies. 2007. "Images of Sexual Stereotypes in Rap Videos and the Health of African American Female Adolescents." *Journal of Women's Health* 16(8): 1157–64.

Pough, Gwendolyn D. 2004. *Check it While I Wreck it: Black Womanhood, Hip-Hop Culture, and the Public Sphere*. Boston, MA: Northeastern University Press

Railton, Diane and Watson, Paul. 2005. "Naughty Girls and Red Blooded Women: Representations of Female Heterosexuality in Music Video." *Feminist Media Studies* 5(1): 51–63.

Ratcliff, Anthony 2010. "The Crisis of the Hip Hop Intellectual." *International Journal of Africana Studies* 16(1): 62–76.

Rebello-Gil, Guillermo and Amanda Moras. 2012. "Black Women and Black Men in Hip Hop Music: Misogyny, Violence and the Negotiation of (White-Owned) Space." *Journal of Popular Culture* 45(1): 118–32

RIAA (Recording Industry Association of America) 2012. Retrieved April 24, 2015: https://www.riaa.com/newsitem.php?content_selector=riaa-news-gold-and-platinum&news_month_filter=1&news_year_filter=2013&id=47E019AC-8975-3E8E-7D93-D4736B7D9BCF.

Stapleton, Katina R. 1998. "From the Margins to Mainstream: The Political Power of Hip-Hop." *Media, Culture & Society* 20(2): 219–34.

Stephens, Dionne P. and April L. Few. 2007. "The Effects of Images of African American Women in Hip Hop on Early Adolescents' Attitudes Toward Physical Attractiveness and Interpersonal Relationships." *Sex Roles* 56(3-4): 251–64.

———, and Layli D. Phillips. 2003. "Freaks, Gold Diggers, Divas, and Dykes: The Sociohistorical Development of Adolescent African American Women's Sexual Scripts." *Sexuality and Culture* 7(1): 3–49.

Stokes, Martin. 2002. "Marx, Money, and Musicians." in *Music and Marx: Ideas, Practice, Politics*, ed. Regula Qureshi. New York and London: Routledge, pp. 139–66.

Turner, Jacob S. 2011. "Sex and the Spectacle of Music Videos: An Examination of the Portrayal of Race and Sexuality in Music Videos." *Sex Roles* 64(3–4): 173–91.

Turner-Musa, Jocelyn O., Warren A. Rhodes, P. Thandi Hicks Harper and Sylvia L. Quinton. 2008. "Hip-Hop to Prevent Substance Use and HIV Among African-American Youth: A Preliminary Investigation." *Journal of Drug Education* 38(4): 351–65.

Watson, Laurel B., Dawn Robinson, Franco Dispenza and Negar Nazari. 2012. "African American Women's Sexual Objectification Experiences: A Qualitative Study." *Psychology of Women Quarterly* 36(4): 458–75.

West, Carolyn M. 1995. "Mammy, Sapphire, and Jezebel: Historical Images of Black Women and their Implications for Psychotherapy." *Psychotherapy: Theory, Research, Practice, Training* 32: 458.

Whembolua, Guy-Lucien, Edward V. Wallace, Derrick Jenkins and Kenneth Ghee. Forthcoming. "Black Men's Health and Manhood: A Hip- Hop Approach." in *Droppin Knowledge : Hip Hop Pedagogy in the Academy*, eds. Karin L. Stanford and Charles E. Jones. Baltimore, MD: Black Classic Press.

Whitney, Jennifer Dawn. 2012. "Some Assembly Required: Black Barbie and the Fabrication of Nicki Minaj." *Girlhood Studies* 5: 141–59.

Wilson, William J. 1996. *When Work Disappears: The World of the New Urban Poor*. New York: Alfred P. Knopf.

Wingood, Gina M., Ralph J. DiClemente, Jay M. Bernhardt, Kathy Harrington, Susan L. Davies, Alyssa Robillard and Edward W. Hook, III. 2003. "A Prospective Study of Exposure to Rap Music Videos and African American Female Adolescents' Health." *American Journal of Public Health* 93(3): 437–9.

# PART VI
# Agency and the Black Community

# Music as Identity: Cultural Meaning, Social Hybridity and Musical Sonority In Indigenous Caribbean Music

Meagan Sylvester

## Introduction

Popular music is an interdisciplinary area of study. Tagg (1982) asserts that no analysis of musical discourse can be considered complete without consideration of the social, psychological, visual, gestural, ritual, technical, historical, economic and linguistic aspects relevant to the genre, function, style, (re)performance situation and listening attitude connected with the sound event being studied. According to Tagg (ibid.), musicology as a discipline still lags behind other areas of specialization in the field of sociology. The musicologist is, thus, positioned in an advantageous position as it relates to their research possibilities. The advantage is that they can draw on sociological research to provide the proper analytical perspective of the subject. The empirical sociology of music approach assists musicologists in (re)configuring their approach from culture-centricity and ethno-centricity towards a focus on the musical habits among the population at large. This can provide valuable information about the functions, uses and, with the help of psychology, effects of the genre, performance or musical object under analysis. In this way, results from perceptual investigation and other data about musical habits can be used for cross-checking analytical conclusions and for putting the whole analysis in its proper sociological and psychological perspectives. In that regard, this work begins with the premise that the approach to the study of music will be sociological in nature yet there will be elements of other disciplines infused into the analysis. The benefit of the sociological approach, however, allows for a dedicated focus on issues of identity within music as sociological stratified levels within society such as race, class, status, color and gender are extrapolated from the lyrical content and musical resonance of the indigenous music. As a result, there would be a heightened sense of understanding of the musical text and its meaning within the analysis. Through an examination of popular Carnival music in Trinidad and Tobago, this study charts identity formation of Trinbagonians. I posit that the lyrics of the songs written and produced for the Carnival season project specific themes which can be used as a lyrical lens through which an analysis of various island identities are understood within this multi-ethnic space.

# A Brief History of Trinidad and Tobago

The Republic of Trinidad and Tobago is a twin-island economy that displays characteristics of aesthetic cosmopolitanism in the production of its music (Szerszynski and Urry 2002, 2006; Beck 2000; Cheah and Robbins 1998; Hannerz 1990, 2004; Vertovec and Cohen 2002; Tomlinson 1999). According to some theorists, aesthetic cosmopolitanism reflects, at the individual level, a taste for art, culture and music of other nations and groups external to one's own. When completed, the finished product possesses components of a global sound which contains stylistic traces and influences from both external and local spaces. Further, the incorporation of these influences naturalizes elements of otherness into the current sense of national uniqueness. As Regev argues (2007), aesthetic cosmopolitanism comes into being not only through consumption of art works and cultural products from the wider shores of cultural experience, but also more intensively through the creation and consumption of much of the local art, culture and music that can be further described as ethno-national uniqueness.

Trinidad and Tobago produces a vast array of musical genres by diverse ethnic groups attempting to hold on to specific parts of their Trinbagonian-ness. Yet with the multiplicity of sounds in the area, a combining of the local with the global is revealed. Calypso, together with derivatives of soca such as chutney soca, ragga soca, parang soca and groovy soca, all utilize sound, beat and tone from music external to the Trinbagonian space. The chutney element is derived from Asian/East Indian sources and the ragga sound in ragga soca is culled from Jamaican dancehall influences. The groovy aspect in groovy soca is borrowed from rhythm and blues of American music while parang soca is influenced by Span, Brazil and Puerto Rico. It is a popular folk music originating out of the islands' Hispanic heritage that originated from over 400 years ago during Spanish rule via Venezuela.

The historical, demographic, social and cultural milieu in which Trinidad and Tobago is situated is key to understanding the interconnections between music identity and how music is actualized. The European influence on the culture of Trinidad and Tobago primarily comes from Spain, France and Great Britain as all three countries claimed the islands at various times during the nation's colonial history. Spanish rule began when Columbus "discovered" Trinidad—that rule lasted nearly 300 years. During the latter part of Spain's occupation, French immigrants began to control the island's political operations. Resultantly, Trinidadians began to adopt French customs and language. Later, influences from East India, China, Portugal, Syria and Lebanon, all of whom accounted for a large number of migrants to the Caribbean, impacted the island's unique culture, musical backgrounds and sounds.

As indicated earlier, the objective of this chapter is to chart identity formation of Trinbagonians through Carnival music. Specifically, we argue that the traditional/ indigenous forms of sound and music which emanate from a cultural space reflect the identity of a people. Given the rich diversity of the island, the group identity of and loyalty for each musical sub-genre analyzed is at times static, fixed and expected. At other times, the Carnival based following is varied, wide reaching and unpredictable. This conundrum gives impetus to the notion that there is at once a current of national cultural uniqueness inherent in the varying styles of music. To better understand the cultural richness of the impact of music on identity formation, three arguments are offered. First, that it is necessary to build on the theoretical and conceptual use of genre to better understand the dynamics of symbolic classification and change in order to identify recurrent sociocultural forms of music genres. In this regard, this work builds on that of Garofalo (2002) and Toynbee (2000) which focus on charismatic performers only and seek to identify the cultural factors which promote the growth of music genres. Second, that there must be an identification of both the developmental sequences of the genre of calypso music, the sub-genre soca music and its subsequent hybrids chutney soca music and ragga soca music. Third, a focus on the mechanisms that allow for the transition from one genre to the next. Accordingly, what follows is an examination of the significance and impact of Carnival music on Trinbagonians. However, before this task is performed, a brief note on the methods of research is presented.

## Research Methods

This project employs a qualitative framework of analysis. In the main, phenomenology is utilized where the lived experiences of the interviewees are the main analytical tool. Subjects were identified through snowball sampling and each participant completed a loosely structured questionnaire from which first-hand accounts were collected. Content analysis is used to extract secondary data via texts, articles and newspaper clippings on the subjects included in this investigation. Ultimately, the interviewees, through their experiences as performers of traditional and indigenous music in Trinidad and Tobago, provide insightful data on identity formation of Trinbagonians through Carnival music.

## Multi-ethnic and Multicultural Realities

Musicians and theorists of all schools and styles agree that music has meaning that is communicated amongst participants, listeners and creators. What constitutes musical meaning and by what processes it is communicated has been the subject of much debate. In the main, there are two schools of thought. First, that musical meaning lies within the context of the work itself and in the perception of the relationships set forth within the musical work of art. On the other hand, in addition to the intellectual meanings, music also communicates meanings in the extra musical way of concepts, actions, emotional states and character. The first group has been termed "absolutists" and the second "referentialists."

The emergence of musical theory and musical practice in different cultures and epochs strongly suggest that music can possess referential meaning. The music cosmologies of Asia, Latin America, the United States and the Caribbean are locales where tempi, pitches, rhythms and modes are linked to express concepts, emotions and moral qualities. Musical symbolisms and interpretations utilized by composers, arrangers and musicians corroborates the view that music is referential in nature and can communicate meanings based on space and time global and local references (Meyer 1961). Following the tenets espoused by Meyer, this work centers on the perspective of referentialists as we seek to interrogate the extra musical way in which the concepts, actions, emotional states and character are exemplified through musical expression.

It is essential here to focus on the theme of the cultural encounter between Europeans and Indigenous populations while acknowledging that *the societies of the Americas have been established through a fundamental process of transculturation resulting in cultural hybridity*. This cultural hybridity comes not only from the impossibility to reproduce, exactly, European cultures and their later borrowings (implicit and/or explicit) from native cultures on American soil, but also from the impossibility of keeping these native cultures intact. The signs of this fundamental cultural hybridity are more or less pronounced depending on additional contexts such as the mixed composition of populations, dietary practices, material culture, later migratory phenomenon, transformations in gender relations, recognition of supra-ethnic and supra-national Native affiliations and interests extending beyond traditionally recognized borders. Trinidad and Tobago's multi-ethnic and multicultural realities lend to the existence of social and cultural hybridity in the society's mores and further in its musical development and expression.

## Music as Identity

Identity is presented through a focus on themes of national, ethnic and reference group affiliation. National identity is the individual's identity and sense of belonging to one's country or nation. National identity is not an inborn trait, but one that it fostered over time by emblems of national consciousness. Ethnic identity refers to behavior patterns specific to an ethnic group. Reference group identity refers to the categorizing of oneself by aspects of groups to which one aspires to belong (e.g., professional groups, social groups, etc.) as identity within such a group is a legitimate substitution for persons for whom ethnicity is not salient.

Over the last decade or so, some important works on music, place and identity have been published. For example, Stokes (1994) assembled a collection of work examining the significance of music in the construction of identities and ethnicities and the ways these issues relate to those of place. Connell and Gibson (2003) explored the links of places, popular music and identities, where a range of spatial scales—local, national and global—were explored. In effect, musical genres are created, produced, arranged and listened to by individuals, groups and nations of people who have been responsive to a beat, a sound and a nuance that speaks to them on a level with which they can identify.

Given the multi-ethnic nature of Trinidad and Tobago, musical hybridization, fusion and the mixing of various musical traditions are to be expected. However, theorists like Connell and Gibson (ibid.) assert that fusion music leads to an unauthentic sound not indigenous to the locale, but representative of a sort of world music which renders impossible the tracing of authenticity. Refuting this view, however, Hudson (2006) posits that these processes create new identities that fuse local and global, traditional and modern, while at the same time de-territorializing culture, though paradoxically, only as a result of the construction and contestation of discourses of Otherness and place. Soca music, in the case of Trinidad and Tobago, exemplifies the latter by the distinction that emerges out of the separate elements: *groovy soca* (rhythm and blues strain), chutney soca (Asian/East Indian strain) and ragga soca (Jamaican dancehall strain). Part of the essence of being a Trinbagonian is the understanding of self as having various parts which make up the whole. Miscegenation and interracial relations have allowed for the blurring of race distinctions and the blurring of the sound and beat of the music emanating out of such spaces. Further, this fusion sound possesses its own authenticity and identity by way of the blend of cultures and local, regional, national and global musical traditions.

Calypso music embodies a wide variety of fusion sounds including calypso swing, calypso fox trot, Trinidad Carnival paseo, Grenada paseo and Tobago paseo. Creole calypso, circa the 1930s, began graduating to the use of rhythmic patterns on the high hat, musical riffs on the keyboard and the bass lines from the African American disco era of the 1970s (Guilbault 2007). The presence of American sailors and other military personnel at the US military base in Trinidad during wartime set the groundwork for a constant audience for calypso music and also affected the speed and tenor of the songs sung for tourists. Satirical skill and creativity were used to deliver the message, yet the tempo of the songs on display were always at a pace at which the foreigner could grasp the full meaning. The calypso ballad was birthed out of this practice. The loss of authenticity that Connell and Gibson (2002) allude to in their work is not borne out here as the history of the Calypso art form demonstrated. Instead, it speaks to the creation of a fusion music that laid claim to the delivery of the creation of a new genre which exemplified the local, regional and global elements which it embodied.

## The Makings of Calypso Music

Calypso music dates back to the mid-1800s and signifies the importance of place and space of national, social and political realities within the Trinbagonian music landscape. In Trinidad and Tobago, during Carnival season, which is the week directly before the Catholic Lenten season commences, calypso is performed and can be heard nearly everywhere. Most of the performances take place in calypso tents and the highlight of that genre's festivities occur in the final competition on the Sunday before Carnival days known as *Dimanche Gras* (Big Sunday), as this symbolizes the end of another successful calypso season where the merry monarch is crowned. Traditionally, calypso encompasses three or four verses and a chorus. The lyrics typically focus on the social, political and economic realities of Trinbagonian life. In terms of location, the island of Trinidad is the most southerly isle of the tropical Caribbean and, given its proximity to South America, has had the fortune to have inherited many of the natural oil and gas resources of the adjoining continent. In that regard, Trinidad became a hub of migratory activity as Caribbean citizens came in search of work. One of the main implications of having a fruitful oil and gas economy was thriving commercial economic opportunities. As such, migrants from adjoining West Indian territories came to Trinidad to find work and to become involved in calypso music. In its embryonic stages the calypso art form resulted in a melding pot of local folk tunes from the islands. In addition to such a strong history of collaborative styles, the music genre went through yet another sound iteration with the appearance of the US military presence, mentioned above, which also affected the speed and tenor of the songs sung for the tourists. The use of double entendre, where one word is related to the erotic meaning and the other was related to the neutral meaning, was one of the main displays of satire and lyrical genius used to deliver messages.

According to traditional music pundits, calypso is believed to have started its decline in popularity circa 1983 with the ascendance of soca. In the 1990s, other musical offshoots of soca were born such as chutney soca and groovy soca; which gained prominence as the preferred party music to the original upbeat versions of some calypso.

Calypso's rich history of imploring witty lyrical content with vibrant and controversial social commentary has lent itself to the patterns and specific characteristics of both the performer of the art form and its audience. The role of the calypsonian was and is seen as the leader of the societal lobby group that keeps the government, opposition party and society at large in check. In so doing, calypso has enjoyed primacy of place and space to be representative of national, social and political realities within the Trinidadian music landscape. In a similar vein, this art form has garnered a mass following who enjoy the check-and-balance role that the songs' lyrics provide as they seek to realize their national pride and love for country. People who identify with this music are often avid supporters of change and publicly vocalize their views on radio talk shows and public television programs and in the print media. The culture of Trinidad and Tobago is such that people exercise their freedom of speech rights freely. In this regard, calypso is the ultimate expression of the lobby group.

In the following example of calypso, colloquially known as "Kaiso," Kurt Allen alludes to days gone by when the personality of the calypsonian spoke to the caricature of the local term "Badjohn," which means a bully with a sharpened tongue, who could hold his own in any fist fight. In a song titled "Last Badjohn of Calypso," he sings:

*In Kaiso so long ago, In dem days de kaiso would attract drunkards and ghetto rats*
*Ah dash of Chinese, Some middle class, Ah whole heap of jagga-bats,*
*In dem days de Calypsonian he carried a bad-john reputation*
*A gentleman in disguise, But his razor sharper than any knife*
*Chorus*
*We eh have no bad-johns again, Kaiso have no bad-johns again*
*Since we put down de bottle of rum for champagne, Kaiso have no bad-johns again*
*Since we get caught up with political campaigns, No bad-johns again*

In the excerpt below, Brian London is speaking to the political situation in Trinidad and Tobago in 2011. Specifically, a new political party had been elected but the racial, social and political atmosphere had become extremely tense since their arrival in office. Further, the new administration seemed to be pitting one racial group against the next and, resultantly, there was social unrest and political protests of the uneven policy changes administered. This is the cry from a voice of the calypsonian who acts as an agent of the people, who expresses to the government that the people are fed up with their emphasis on peripheral issues without concentrating on the needs of the people. Brian London, in the song "We Fed Up," sings:

*Chorus*
*We fed up of the SIA, SIA, SIA, SIA,*
*While poor people suffering, suffering, suffering everyday*
*We fed up hearing about the Piano, Piano, Piano, Piano*
*While poor people struggling, struggling, struggling, struggling in de ghetto*
*Verse*
*Driver people singing de blues, Dem ting eh making de front page news*
*Is time yuh listen to the people's views, Get up and deal with the real issues*

## The "Soul of Calypso": Soca Music

Soca is stylistically different from calypso in its tempo, lyrics and beat. Calypso is mostly associated with social satire, political satire and wit, with lyrics that challenge the status quo. It also includes a slow repetitive beat and continuous, steady tempo. This music, however, seems to have lost its hegemonic role as the dominant Carnival music and has been replaced by a high-tempo genre with lighter lyrics that create and foster wild abandon in its patrons while providing music simply for dancing and pleasure; not for political purposes.

Soca is the "soul calypso" offspring of calypso proper and the dominant carnival music of the past two decades. This musical form is widely acknowledged to be a melding of calypso and Indian forms. The birth of soca occurred during the oil-boom period and is most often credited to Calysonian Lord Shorty, but it was not invented by him. Soca is mainly known to have been a melding of African and East Indian rhythms. However, upon deeper reflection, the cross-fertilization of the variants of indigenous and fusion music extant at the time in Trinidad and Tobago and the region, coupled with the myriad of composers, arrangers and musicians who were inimical to the development of soca, has sought to explain the genesis of this musical form. Key practitioners in the art form were Ed Watson, Lord Kitchener, Leston Paul, Pelham Goddard, Joey Lewis and Byron Lee and the Dragonnaires of Jamaica, Arrow of Montserrat and Lyle Taitt. Taitt is a Trinidadian who migrated to Jamaica and experimented with various new and emerging beats and influenced mento, ska and rock steady. This regional musical and sonic fusion of art forms is testament to the fact that soca became a movement of the people and cannot be said to have been created by any one artist. Regis (1999) argues that when one listens to soca the dominant sound they hear is a combination of Indian rhythms to a sped-up mix of calypso. In this way the music would have been representative of nation-within-a-nation ethnic group affiliation and national identity, being a new musical form both emerging out of Trinidad and Tobago and later being seen at once as a global sound distinctly highlighting sounds and beats of Asian (East Indian) heritage and also as a signifier of Trinidadian music, that is, not being either African nor Indian.

In recent times, the music of artistes like JW and Blaze together with Destra and Machel reflect a different kind of understanding of national identity. Most of their content is reflective of "jam and wine" lyrics coupled with directives on varying ways of enjoying Carnival. The question this provokes is "Does this content represent the new lifestyle of Trinidadians since almost all soca songs have this theme?" Is it an understood subtext that this is only "advice" for the season as to how to enjoy oneself as a Trini? Or still, do the lyrics take into consideration that a large part of the populace of Trinidad and Tobago do not become involved in Carnival nor do they prescribe to the tenets of gay abandon as a way of life for any time of year? And if this is so, this seemingly national festival with its attendant all-encompassing appeal may only speak to the nation of those who understand its rules and socially exclude those who do not prescribe to its norms and values. Does soca music then reveal the presence and primacy of one nation or group over the other? And if so, which nation of peoples in Trinidad and Tobago?

The main themes of identity in soca are wine and jam, total abandon, party fuh so, endless fun, non-stop action, frenetic pace and bacchanal. The lyrics of the song below illustrate the wild abandon theme that is soca music.

> *"Consider It Done" by Faye-Ann Lyons*
> *Ay, Ay, Alright, Alright*
> *What they want, They want mih to Mash up, mash up, mash up anything, everything,*
> *anything. Consider It Done*
> *Verse*
> *This cyah be good, nobody jumping, No hands eh waving, de party stand still*
> *Ah in the mood to create something, achieving something*
> *Yuh done know when yuh see de waist dem moving*
> *When yuh see the hands dem waving, de party jumping,*
> *Everybody misbehaving, Ah reach, Ah reach*

Destra Garcia and Machel Montano are commonly known as the queen and king of soca music in Trinidad and Tobago. In the following lyrics, the essence of and the passion for Carnival are described.

> *"It's Carnival" by Destra and Machel*
> *Yeah, baby you know how we do, You, me*
> *You tell your friends, I'll tell mine, It's dat time again*
> *verse 1: Destra*
> *Carnival in T and T, Is so special to all ah we, Like we need blood in we vein*
> *Dats how we feel about Port-of-Spain*
> *When de posse dem come in town, Beating pan and ah bongo drum*
> *Is madness everywhere, Carnival is ah true freedom*
> *Make ah noise or ah joyful sound, And jump up in de air, So ...*
> *Chorus:*
> *Everybody take ah jump, take ah jump, take ah jump up now*

> *Start to wave, start to wave, start to wave up now*
> *Start to wine, start to wine, start to wine up now*
> *Because, it's Carnival*

In the excerpt below the writer attempts to capture national pride in a groovy beat! A different sentiment is being championed here from the national sentiment displayed in calypso lyrics. However, the sense of national identity is high on the agenda in both calypso and soca music:

> *"Trini" by Benjai*
> *Verse 1*
> *Ah partying till it rain nah, nah, nah*
> *Ah dressing in up in mih Red, White and Black*
> *I doh care what nobody say, Every carnival ah done dey*
> *Dem say ah mad and ah bad, ah telling yuh*
> *Whey yuh from, ah from Trinidad and Tobago*
> *Ah is a Trini, Ah Trini, Talk 'bout Trini*
> *Chorus*
> *Cause they love how Trini does look, look, look*
> *They love how Trini does cook, cook, cook,*
> *They love to hear Trini talk, talk, talk*
> *And they love Trini woman wuk, wuk, wuk*
> *And we make good company, and we make good company*
> *We does represent for we Soca … .*

## Blending in the Chutney Soca Music

Since the Indian cultural revival of the 1990s, regular soca has been joined by the much more self-consciously Indian form of chutney soca which exploded onto the Carnival scene in 1996. The development of chutney soca came on the heels of pitchakaree which emerged in 1990. It has been termed a sort of Indian calypso. The advent of chutney soca came not long after the establishment of the first all-Indian national radio station in 1994 named Radio Masala. Prior to this, Indian music, traditionally sung in Hindi only, was often relegated to the occasional time slot for ethnic music on regular radio stations. However, as its popularity grew and as it became more of a participatory style of music, English phrases were mixed with the Hindi and today it is now a hybrid of both language forms in one musical genre. Popular artists who perform within this genre are Triveni, Rikki Jai, Hunter and Dil E Nadan.

From a music standpoint, chutney refers to music that is as hot as chutney, in reference to the sauce, where in later times its characteristics became associated with a set of melodic structures in combination with a fast, hot tempo, inciting dancers to break away. Interestingly, we notice a similar theme to soca music in the wild abandon of its lyrics. And this is even before the actual merging of chutney with soca as a musical genre. This begs the question, 'Was the eventual melding of chutney with soca an eventual hybrid due to music similarity or was there a deeper national or ethnic significance that lay beneath the surface?'

According to Mungal Patasar, a prolific sitar player of Indian classical music, the arrival of chutney and the fusion with soca was inevitable as Trinidadians have always sought ways to improve Afro-Indian integration. To East Indians he says what has occurred is the authentication of their group—a nation within a nation. Alternatively other scholars have argued that East Indians have sought to use the traditional music of their ethnic group to leverage more recognition and power in the national sphere in terms of the presence of a music specific to the needs of their community.

The main themes of identity in chutney soca are alcohol abuse, the use of alcohol to boost sexual prowess, male assertion of masculinity, change in cultural norms (e.g., no dowry or bride price for daughter's hand in marriage) and domination of Indian females by their males. An excerpt from the 2011 Chutney Soca Monarch Rikki Jai's song, "White Oak and Water," tells of the traditional "wine and woman" song that is one of the central themes in Chutney Soca Music:

> Barman, ah want something white and smooth
> When I see de guyl, I bazodee, When I see she waist, I bazodee
> When she walk my way, I tootoolbey, When she smile with me, right away, right away
> Ah see she, Ah like she, Ah wanted to get married, She father he tell me Rikki
> I doh have money, for the dhourie, White Oak and Water x2
> Is all I have to offer, If yuh want mih daughter

The 2010 Chutney Soca Monarch Ravi B delivers a stirring rendition in the song "Ah Drinka," that includes themes of alcohol abuse, male assertion of masculinity and domination of Indian females by their male counterparts:

> Yuh cyah change mih, No way, Gyul yuh know I was a Drinka
> Yuh always know I was a Drinka 2x
> Yuh only telling mih, What I should do or say 2x
> Just how yuh mudda have yuh fadda, Girl yuh know I was ah Drinka
> Verse
> Every time I liming, Cell phone only ringing,
> Mih pardoners laughing, They know is you who calling
> Saying that yuh miss me, And to come home early
> Come leh we hug up and watch ah Indian movie, Why yuh trying to change mih
> Gyul you too blind to see, Yuh always know I was ah Drinka …

## Conclusion

Lyrically the songs analyzed in this chapter reflect a combination of two forces at work at the same time—globalization and localization—which combine into what Robertson (1995) calls "glocalization." Local music themes reflect the identity of the various multifaceted populations within Trinidad and Tobago. The East Indians and their chutney soca beat and lyrics reflect patterns of behavior specific to their group and their ways of conjugal life. The groovy soca exemplifies both in beat and lyrics the laid-back groove of a people committed to national pride in simply being "Trini." Soca highlights the wild abandon lyrics which are truly reminiscent of a "True Trini" whose carnivalesque-ness reaches its peak during Carnival season. Calypso has its place of primacy during Carnival and still attracts the consciously minded nationals. Globally, sounds and beats take on international significance as chutney soca culls from Asian (East Indian) culture and is fused with local soca rhythms. Groovy soca plays on the R&B tradition which has its roots in American pop culture. Soca is a fusion of music from Africa and India, and Calypso originated from African slave rhythms. Therein lies the genesis and zenith of the multiple identities of the Trinbagonian as demonstrated through lyrics, sounds and beats. In sum, in this musically expressive culture traditional music has been hybridized with global sounds to develop its ethno-national style of Trinidadian music. In so doing, musical content emerging from the twin-island nation will at once reflect indigenized sounds, especially in lyrics and beats, while continuing to absorb influences from traditions of the music of the world.

In this chapter, identity was operationalized as ethnic identity, sociocultural identity and reference group identity. In an attempt to understand Caribbean identity it behoves one to examine the post-colonial formations in multi-ethnic areas like Trinidad and Tobago and Guyana where ethnic nations are in search of homes. As such, it becomes possible to understand the role of the collective conscious agreement by a group to adhere to nuances and peculiarities which give them a sense of belonging and ownership of a particular aspect of their home, food, language forms and cultural practices, namely music in this case. Hybridization of the musical culture, namely all of the soca music variants—chutney music, groovy soca, parang soca, ragga soca—and strains developed within the Trinidad and Tobago musical landscape becomes one of the ways in which each ethnic group asserts their musical identity and by extension their ethnic, sociocultural and reference group identity.

# Bibliography

Beck, Ulrich. 2000. "The Cosmopolitan Perspective: Sociology of the Second Age of Modernity." *British Journal of Sociology* 51(1): 79–106.

———. 2003. "Rooted Cosmopolitanism: Emerging from a Rivalry of Distinctions." in *Global America?* ed. U. Beck, N. Sznaider and R. Winter. Liverpool: Liverpool University Press, pp. 15–29.

——— and N. Sznaider. 2006. "Unpacking Cosmopolitanism for the Social Sciences." *British Journal of Sociology* 57(1): 3–23.

Bourdieu, Pierre. 1992. *The Rules of Art*. Stanford, CA: Stanford University Press.

———. 1993a. *The Field of Cultural Production*. Cambridge: Polity.

———. 1993b. *Sociology in Question*. London: Sage.

Cheah, Pheng and Bruce Robbins, eds. 1998. *Cosmopolitics*. Minneapolis: University of Minnesota Press.

Connell, John and Chris Gibson. 2003. *Sound Tracks: Popular Music, Identity and Place*. New York: Routledge.

Garofalo, Reebee. 2002. "Crossing Over: From Black Rhythm & Blues to White Rock 'n' Roll." in *Rhythm and Business: The Political Economy of Black Music*, ed. N. Kelley. New York: Akashit Books, pp. 112–37.

GIRA Inter-disciplinary Research Group on the Americas: http://www.gira.info/en/about-us/research-questions-and-key-notions/transculturation-and-cultural-hybridity

Guilbault, Jocelyne. 2007. *Governing Sound: The Cultural politics of Trinidad's Carnival Musics*. Chicago, IL: University of Chicago Press.

Hannerz, Ulf. 1990. "Cosmopolitans and Locals in World Culture." in *Global Culture*, ed. M. Featherstone. London: Sage, pp. 237–52.

———. 2004. "Cosmopolitanism." in *Companion to the Anthropology of Politics*, eds. D. Nugent and J. Vincent. Oxford: Blackwell, pp. 69–85.

Hudson, Ray. 2006. "Regions and Place: Music, Identity and Place." *Progress in Human Geography* 30(5): 626–34.

Online English Dictionary http://www.definition-of.net/sonority

Meyer, Leonard B. 1961. *Emotion and Meaning in Music*. Chicago, IL: University of Chicago Press.

Regev, Motti. 1992. "Israeli Rock or: A Study in the Politics of 'Local Authenticity.'" *Popular Music* 11(1): 1–14.

———. 1994. "Producing Artistic Value: The Case of Rock Music." *The Sociological Quarterly* 35(1): 85–102.

———. 1996. "*Musica Mizrakhit*: Israeli Rock and National Culture in Israel." *Popular Music* 15(3): 275–84.

———. 1997. "Organizational Fluency, Organizational Blocks, Cultural Relevance: The Case of the Music Industry in Israel." *Teoria ve-Bikoret* 10: 115–32 [in Hebrew].

———. 2000. 'To Have a Culture of our Own: On Israeliness and its Variants." *Ethnic and Racial Studies* 23(2): 223–47.

———. 2002. "The 'Pop-Rockization' of Popular Music." in *Studies in Popular Music*, eds. D. Hesmondhalgh and K. Negus. London: Arnold, pp. 251–64.

———. 2007. "Cultural Uniqueness and Aesthetic Cosmopolitanism." *European Journal of Social Theory* 10(1): 123–38.

——— and Eyal Seroussi. 2004. *Popular Music and National Culture in Israel*. Berkeley: University of California Press.

Regis, Louis. 1999. *The Political Calypso: True Opposition in Trinidad and Tobago, 1962–1987*. Mona, Jamaica: The University of the West Indies Press.

Robbins, Bruce. 1998. "Actually Existing Cosmopolitanism." in *Cosmopolitics*, eds. P. Cheah and B. Robbins. Minneapolis: University of Minnesota Press, pp. 1–19.

Robertson, Roland. 1995. "Glocalization: Time-space and Homogeneity-Heterogeneity." in *Global Modernities*, ed. M. Featherstone. London: Sage, pp. 23–44.

Robertson, Roland and David Inglis. 2005. "World Music and the Globalisation of Sound." in *Sociology of Art: Ways of Seeing*, eds. D. Inglis and J. Hughson. Houndmills: Palgrave Macmillan, pp. 156–70.

Stokes, Martin. 1994. *Ethnicity, Identity, and Music: The Musical Construction of Place*. London: Berg Publishing Limited.

———. 2004. "Music and Global Order." *Annual Review of Anthropology* 33: 47–72.

——— and John Urry. 2002. "Cultures of Cosmopolitanism." *Sociological Review* 50(4): 461–81.

——— and John Urry. 2006. "Visuality, Mobility and the Cosmopolitan: Inhabiting the World from Afar." *British Journal of Sociology* 57(1): 113–31.

Tagg, Phillip. 1982. "Analysing Popular Music: Theory, Method and Practice." *Popular Music* 2: 37–65.

Tomlinson, John. 1999. *Globalization and Culture*. Chicago, IL: The University of Chicago Press.

Toynbee, Jason. 2000. *Making Popular Music*. London: Arnold.

Urry, John. 1995. *Consuming Places*. London: Routledge.

Vertovec, Steven and Robin Cohen. 2002. *Conceiving Cosmopolitanism: Theory, Context and Practice*. Oxford: Oxford University Press.

# Give Us the Ballot! Gaining Enfranchisement in Mobile, Alabama: 1944–50

## Timothy Broughton and Komanduri S. Murty

*There are four ways in which one can deal with an injustice: (a) One can accept it without protest; (b) One can seek to avoid it; (c) One can resist the injustice non-violently; (d) One can resist by violence. To use violence is to increase injustice. To accept it is to perpetuate it. To avoid it is impossible. To resist by intelligent means and with an attitude of mutual responsibility and respect ... much the better choice, since attitudes simply cannot be challenged by avoidance, by complete or continuous acceptance, or by stupidity and violence.*

– Bayard Rustin (Long 2012: 16)

## Introduction

The black community's desire and commitment for racial equality in America began when they were brought to North America as indentured servants. For over 200 years blacks in America were either slaves with no rights or free people of color with minimal rights. It was not until 1863 that a limited, yet deliberate, proclamation signed by President Abraham Lincoln gave a semblance of universal freedom to millions of blacks in America. Lincoln's Emancipation Proclamation was reinforced in 1865 with the 13th Amendment which legally abolished slavery in the United States and the 14th Amendment which gave blacks in America citizenship rights.

Thus, after the American Civil War African American participation in the nation's political arena caused immense controversy. Whites were intimidated by African Americans' increasing roles in politics and, unfortunately, some blacks believed their peers were unqualified to participate in the political process. However, overall, the black community was united and its leaders sought equal rights for all African Americans under the law. With much of the nation focused on the issue of voting rights in the black community, by 1867 southern states began witnessing blacks entering public office in unprecedented numbers. Eventually some 600 blacks would serve in state legislatures. Specifically, the state of South Carolina boasted of having a black majority in its new state government. To prevent the increasing numbers of blacks from participating in the political system, southern states began to implement de jure and de facto policies to help restore white men to the political dominance they held prior to the Civil War. The measures resulted in blatant intimidation and the violation of the voting rights of African Americans. To address this matter the nation enacted the 15th Amendment in 1870. The 15th Amendment insisted that states could not use "race, color and servitude" to disenfranchise persons who were otherwise eligible to vote. Although the goal of this amendment was to provide African Americans with equal voting rights, leaders in all southern states manipulated it and passed subtle local and statewide ordinances that limited the voting rights of blacks. Thus, intimidation and the blatant disregard of the voting rights of blacks became the "order of the day." Historical data, especially in the new South, discloses how states and local governments implemented various tactics to block blacks (and other minorities) from voting (e.g., grandfather clause, literacy tests, poll taxes, intimidation, understanding clause and violence.) Active black voter registration activities resulted in arrests, firings, beatings, death threats and possibly death itself, although constitutionally blacks were part of the political framework.

The Reconstruction period, which blacks believed would bring about social equality, all but failed by the late 1870s. What followed was a barrage of local, state and national laws, as well as judicial rulings, which promulgated a separate and unequal society that in many ways paralleled slavery itself. Coupled with the insensitivity and inactivity of leaders occupying the Oval Office on matters of racial equality, most blacks remained in almost a perpetual state of poverty and illiteracy. Millions remained disenfranchised, suffered from poor health care and were psychologically impaired by a system that supported black inferiority. It has taken almost a century for the ideal of the 15th Amendment to come into practice. However, sustained movements in southern cities for voting equality that broke political barriers and reshaped American politics in the twentieth century began burgeoning in the 1940s. Although not viewed as important as the later movements for political equality, these movements gave birth to the more salient political actions of the 1950s and 1960s and are significant to understanding the struggle that African Americans and other minorities continue to face in the electoral process today. One such movement began in Mobile, Alabama, in the early 1940s.

## Mobile, Alabama: 1944–50

From 1944 to 1950, Mobile's African American leadership led an intense political struggle that permanently changed voting rights in Alabama. One major impetus to the Mobile civil rights movement was its bus protest efforts in 1942. The protest was the African American community's response to the shooting and killing of a black soldier by a white bus driver that year. The African American community threatened to boycott the city bus system if its listed recommendations (seven in all) were not met. The recommendations included, but was not limited to, disarming all bus drivers, hiring African American bus drivers and firing the bus driver who killed the African American soldier. The city bus line system agreed to five of the seven recommendations and the protest was called off. The boycott protest movement galvanized the African American community in an unprecedented manner not seen since the turn of the century. Because of this movement Mobile's NAACP grew remarkably and the African American community, including its growing working class, and the city's African American leadership, which had traditionally been divided, came together to form one of the most effective civil rights movements in the South.

With an increased political awareness in the aftermath of the bus protest, local African Americans stepped up their efforts to win enfranchisement for themselves. However, much of the political fate of the African American community in Mobile depended on the outcome of an ongoing battle by southern blacks to abolish the Democratic Primary. The tide would turn in their favor in 1944 when the United States Supreme Court abolished a similar Democratic Primary in Texas in the *Smith v. Allwright* case, the cornerstone of African American enfranchisement in the South was thus built.

The Democratic Primary in Alabama was based on a long history of political discrimination in the South. Wiley L. Bolden, a Mobile civil rights activist, noted that the Democratic Party of Alabama (as in other places of the South) operated as an all-white party:

> [In May 1944], it must be remembered that the Democratic Party of Alabama had been operating under the caption that were a white party, and that they were the white Democratic Party, a private party, so that the action of the committee was in keeping with what they had held for years. (McLaurin, n.d., Para 6).

These Democratic Party members were socially, racially and politically conservative southern whites who formed the private Democratic Party as a political strategy to eliminate the African American vote. They believed their homogenous political party could not be challenged by the state government. The result of such a prejudicial selection process led to an all-white party that silenced the voice of African Americans in Alabama (Grafton and Permaloff 1985). As an all-white party it initiated measures such as the cumulative poll tax, literacy exams and other means to disenfranchise individuals they considered to be potentially dangerous to the status quo. While these measures sometimes disenfranchised poor whites their key purpose was to keep African Americans from voting. The cumulative poll tax was a hefty $1.50 per year and it was collected every year from everyone between the ages of 21 and 45 years.

The NAACP leadership challenged this discriminatory voting procedure. John LeFlore, one of Mobile's most courageous civil rights leaders, led the fight. For over fifty years LeFlore was the most salient civil rights leader in Mobile (Thomason 2001). He led efforts to reorganize the dying Mobile NAACP in 1926 and it became Alabama's most potent civil rights organization during the first half of the century (Bracey and Meier 1991; LeFlore Papers 1944–48; Verney 2013). LeFlore rose quickly through the ranks of the organization. He served as Executive Secretary of the branch for thirty years. He chaired the Regional Conference of Southern Branches during the critical years 1936–45 and functioned as vice president of the Alabama Conference from 1945 to 1951. When the NAACP was outlawed in Alabama in 1956 LeFlore led efforts to shift their civil rights work to the Non-Partisan Voters League (NPVL), the city's most important civil rights organization after the abolition of the NAACP. LeFlore also actively participated in other organizations for social change such as Brotherhood of Sleeping Car Porters and the Mobile Committee for the Support of Public Education. He was the first African American appointed to the Housing Board and, in 1974, was the first African American elected to the Alabama House of Representatives for District 99 of Mobile County.

LeFlore also believed the Democratic Primary was an oppressive and demeaning political instrument used against African Americans. One particular abuse of the Primary was the poll tax, which he fought vehemently to abolish through his work with the National Committee to Abolish the Poll Tax. The purpose of this tax was to preclude African Americans from voting in the white Primary. In many instances African Americans in Mobile could not pay the poll tax (Mobile Press Register 1990). LeFlore recounted:

> If you waited until you were forty or fifty [years] to get registered to vote, you had to pay a retroactive poll tax back to your twenty-first birthday, although between twenty-one and forty-eight or fifty years of age you made no attempt to vote. All of this was a remaining part of the so called Black Codes that had been adopted by most of the southern states after Reconstruction for the purpose of almost re-enslaving blacks. (McLaurin 1972a: Para 13)

In 1944 the Democratic Party of Alabama consisted of 72 state members, 2,500 county members and 14,000 general election officials (*Davis v. Schnell* 1949). The chairman of the party was ultra-conservative attorney Gessner McCorvey of Mobile who insisted that white leaders in Alabama knew what was best for the party (McLaurin 1973). As a key player on Mobile's Board of Registrars he helped to set the agenda for voting in the city. With unlimited power over voter eligibility the Board used the poll tax, literacy test and understanding clause to disenfranchise African American voters.

The opportunity to successfully challenge the Democratic Primary became a reality with the US Supreme Court's decision in *Smith v. Allwright* (321 US 649) in 1944. In this decision the Court held that the Texas Democratic Party's policy of prohibiting blacks from voting in Primary elections violated the 14th and 15th Amendments. The Supreme Court further explained that:

> *The United States is a constitutional democracy. Its organic law grants to all citizens a right to participate in the choice of elected officials without restriction by any state because of race. This grant to the people of the opportunity for choice is not to be nullified by a state through casting its electoral process in a form which permits a private organization to practice racial discrimination in the election. (US Supreme Court, Smith v. Allwright, 1944, 321 US 664)*

Traditionally, the NAACP built upon locally initiated movements. However, it was the efforts of the national office that led local leadership in Mobile to organize for greater enfranchisement rights (Thornton 2002). Thus, the political bearing of the *Smith v. Allwright* decision was driven home to African American leadership in the South by the efforts of Thurgood Marshall, then special counsel for the NAACP. Marshall was convinced that this ruling authorized blacks to vote and he encouraged black leaders to ensure that qualified blacks register and vote in the Primary election. He appealed to black leaders to have any applicant denied this right to file affidavits and send them to his office.

Thurgood Marshall's frequent correspondence with the Mobile branch resulted in a close working relationship between Marshall and LeFlore. Marshall provided necessary guidance and kept the Mobile branch informed of national civil rights issues. He also contacted the Mobile branch about preparing a strategy for that city (LeFlore Papers 1945, 1948; McLaurin 1972a). LeFlore led the NAACP's efforts to abolish the state's Democratic Primary (McLaurin n.d). The Mobile NAACP appealed to local, state and national representatives through numerous letters emphasizing the need to end discrimination in the electoral process in Alabama and the importance of gaining voting rights for the African American community. They stressed that the rights of over 900,000 African Americans in the state were being jeopardized when they were barred from casting ballots; that investigators working on behalf of the NAACP discovered at least 19 cases of voter discrimination and that the community needed to provide financial support to end discrimination in government. LeFlore added:

> *It will take money, and quite a bit of it, to carry through the courts these fights for you and all other Negroes of our State and Country. We must have no slackers! The fight is too important to lose because of an attitude of indifference toward the principles of the cases. We claim we want liberty, fairness and justice, so let us prove to the world that we are willing to give for these causes. (LeFlore Papers 1944, Box 2, Folder 6, Series 1)*

Several weeks before the first Democratic Primary, and following the *Smith v. Allwright* decision, local leadership met to discuss viable ways of bringing their struggle to national attention. First, with the help of Thurgood Marshall they decided that on Election Day, May 2, 1944, 12 qualified African Americans would attempt to vote. Next, they invited *Life* and *Time* magazines to the city to cover the event. As Martin Luther King, Jr. and other civil rights leaders would do in the 1950s and 1960s, Mobile's local NAACP strategically used the press to champion their cause. As a correspondent for the *Chicago Defender* and the *Pittsburgh Courier*, LeFlore had seen first-hand the potential power of the media to shape public opinion. Carefully planned by the NAACP, the publishers agreed to cover the event (McLaurin 1972a).

On the day of the election twelve registered African American voters made their way to the polls to vote. All were summarily denied access by the Mobile Board of Registrars. In the case of James B. Battle, Deputy Sheriff Frank Pryor stood in the doorway leading to the canvassing room and informed Battle that he could not enter because the Democratic Primary election was being held for white voters only. An African American bystander voiced his frustration at the Board's actions by suggesting that a black person doesn't get to vote (McLaurin 1972b).

*Life* deployed a cadre of photographers to cover the event. Several photographs showed the Mobile Board denying blacks the right to vote. In 1944 *Time* made the incident its cover story. These images captured the attention of African Americans stationed in the armed forces throughout the United States, Europe and the Pacific. Through these images, LeFlore and the NAACP demonstrated how African Americans had to fight for democracy abroad while being denied the right to vote at home (McLaurin 1972b). In a 1970 interview, LeFlore emphasized the point that the press coverage was probably one of the most important reasons for the Department of Justice (DOJ) challenging the Democratic Primary in Alabama:

> *Life Magazine was distributed to men in the armed forces throughout the world in the European theater of war as well as the theater war in the Pacific. We believed that it may have been an important factor in having the Department of Justice take such prompt steps to challenge this sort of situation which proscribed the rights of black Americans to participate in a primary for the election of the officials who would control the destiny of all the people. (McLaurin n.d. Para 7)*

In addition, the NAACP had all 12 of the people who had been denied ballots to file petitions of discrimination with the DOJ. The affidavits were filed through the office of Attorney General Francis Biddle who promised to take action against the state for violating the federal rights of American citizens (McLaurin 1970). Biddle's announcement brought a sigh of relief to Mobile's NAACP as African American leaders anticipated a milestone in voting rights for African Americans in Alabama.

However, the relief was short-lived. In April 1944 President Franklin Roosevelt died and Biddle, who had vowed to challenge states' rights in discrimination cases, was replaced by Tom Clark. A Southerner from Texas, Clark promised to eliminate the Primary but allowed the southern states to do so at their own speed (LeFlore Papers 1945). Without pressure from the attorney general's office to act expeditiously, Alabama's legislators, recognizing change as inevitable, moved at a pace to give themselves time to come up with a piece of counter-legislation.

Disappointed by the dilatory process, the NAACP submitted several letters to federal officials and to Marshall complaining about the halt of assistance from the DOJ. Marshall was informed that African American voters were still being denied the right to vote and that several African American voters had filed suits against the Board. LeFlore added that the DOJ was indifferent to their request to end the all-white Democratic Primary and that the African American community was ready to take more drastic measures (LeFlore Papers 1945, 1946). At this point, LeFlore and others moved beyond negotiating with local white leadership and began the process of organizing a mass protest by the African American community in Mobile.

With the pressure mounting, McCovery introduced several bills designed to circumvent the negative impact of eliminating the Democratic Primary. The most formidable of these was the Boswell Amendment, drafted by State Senator E.C. "Bud" Boswell and supported by Governor Chauncey Sparks, former Governor Frank Dixon, former Senator Tom Heflin, Horace Wilkerson, a Birmingham lawyer who was a long-time supporter of white supremacy, the big mules of the industrial belt, the big planters of the Black Belt and, of course, the Ku Klux Klan. Sparks campaigned hard for the amendment and cautioned the Democratic Party to battle vehemently to prevent blacks from joining (Egerton 1995). McCorvey presented the amendment to the state legislature for approval in November 1945. He and other Democratic leaders were convinced the Boswell Amendment would have an even more debilitating impact on African American enfranchisement rights than the Democratic Primary (Foster 1949).

The NAACP leadership realized that the Boswell Amendment was devised by white racists and, if adopted, would be the ultimate strategy put forth by the Democratic Party in Alabama to defy the *Smith v. Allwright* ruling on the Democratic Primary (McLaurin 1972a). The basic tenets of the proposed amendment expanded the already discriminatory voting rights legislation utilized by the state through its Democratic Primary. A common ploy throughout the South, the Boswell Amendment was designed to restore ultimate authority of the electoral process to local registrars which, to many African Americans, was a covert way of permanently "fixing" the registration process.

Whereas the Democratic Primary had enforced the cumulative poll tax and literacy test, the Boswell Amendment placed African Americans at the complete discretion of biased voting boards (McLaurin 1972a). It read in part:

> *After the first day of January, nineteen hundred and forty-six, the following persons, and no others, who, if their place of residence shall remain unchanged, will have, at the date of the next general election, the qualifications as to residence prescribed in Section 178 of this article, shall be qualified to register as electors provided they shall not be disqualified under Section 182 of the this Constitution: those who can read and write, understand and explain any article of the Constitution of the United States in English language. (Mobile Press Register 1946b: 3)*

The Boswell Amendment not only required potential voters to understand and explain any section of the US Constitution in English, it also indicated that such an explanation should meet the satisfaction of a county registrar before being allowed to register. That means if the person's answer did not satisfy the registrar then the application was denied. In essence, local registrars were granted wide discretionary powers enabling them to lawfully refuse (without violating *Smith v. Allwright* ruling) the applications of blacks, poor whites and other undesirable potential voters.

The NAACP concluded that Boswell would create a permanent caste for African American voters. LeFlore maintained that the requirements were purely hypocritical and that if the amendment was passed the voters of Alabama would have to possess more knowledge than most Americans citizens, including those who sat on the Supreme Court. He also believed an amendment with such rigid educational requirements and the tactic to place the final decision in the hands of a racist Board of Registrars was fundamentally unjust (McLaurin n.d.). Members of the Board publicly admitted to asking African Americans almost every conceivable question before turning them away because of some trivial technicality (*Davis v. Schnell* 1949; McLaurin n.d.). This scene was common throughout the state. In some instances Boards required blacks to have white supporters and property holdings before being allowed to register (Thornton 2002).

The NAACP emphasized that Boswell himself could not adequately answer questions to the satisfaction of a group of constitutional experts. The sentiments of these jurists were later echoed by several of Alabama's court justices who maintained that to understand and to explain the constitution was legally ambiguous, uncertain and indefinite in meaning. The amendment failed to specify the level of satisfaction the applicant had to meet or whether the constitution be explained partially, fully, plainly, precisely, correctly, fairly or reasonably. Nor did the amendment indicate whose standards the applicant had to meet and set no standardized criteria whereby an objective Board could determine if the applicant's rights had been honored. Even the framers of the constitution and Supreme Court justices had disagreed over the meaning of the constitution (*Davis v. Schnell* 1949).

Despite opposition, the Alabama legislature adopted the Boswell Amendment in November 1945. Alabama voters would make their final decision in the general election on November 7, 1946. Still, the impact was immediate. By January 1946 over 19,000 Mobilians had registered to vote, of which only 275 were African Americans. Convinced of the eventual passage of the Boswell Amendment, which was already passed unanimously in the House of Representatives and was opposed by only three members of the Senate, the Alabama Democratic Executive Committee agreed to abolish the Primary and open its doors to all "qualified voters." On January 12, 1946 McCorvey met with the committee in Montgomery to declare that all racial barriers against blacks in the Alabama Democratic Primary be dropped immediately (McLaurin 1972a).

The adoption of the amendment served as a strong reminder to the African American community in Mobile and throughout the state that voting on an equal basis with whites would continue to be an uphill battle. Moreover, because most African Americans favored labor unions, Emory O. Jackson, the editor of the *Birmingham World*, believed there was collusion between politicians and labor adversaries to prevent African Americans from voting. Jackson likened the amendment to the Bradford Act which prohibited the closed shop in labor unions. According to Jackson, the two bills made a two-edged sword that the enemies of trade unions, working under the smoke screen of "white supremacy," would use to crush the labor movement in Alabama (Jackson 1945).

As the Mobile NAACP launched a campaign against the ratification of Boswell at the state level, members continued to protest the unfair treatment of local African Americans by the Mobile Board of Registrars. Again, Mobile NAACP notified the DOJ about the constitutional violations on the part of the Mobile Board of Registrars. This time, though, they requested that prompt action be taken against the various cases of voter discrimination. The NAACP wrote:

> The action of the Mobile County Board of Registrars in imposing unlawful requirements upon Negro citizens who desire to become qualified electors is, in our opinion, in violation of the Constitution of the United States. We urge the Department of Justice to promptly investigate the charges referred to in this message, which we have found evidence to substantiate. (LeFlore Papers, 1946, Box 8, Folder 13, Series 1)

Additionally, LeFlore complained to the DOJ via telephone that white leaders in Mobile had failed to make any efforts to correct the problem of discrimination in voter registration. On January 29, 1946 the Mobile NAACP informed the DOJ of additional cases where whites were allowed to complete registration forms but African Americans were rejected for failing to read certain sections of the Constitution to the satisfaction of the local Board. The DOJ responded to the complaints in a timely manner, requesting that local officials examine the matter and deal appropriately with any violators (LeFlore Papers 1946).

Even more devastating to African Americans in Mobile was that the state's white leaders were creating voting loopholes between the adoption and ratification of the Boswell Amendment. Milton Schnell, chairman of the Mobile Board of Registrars, colluded with Board members to preserve its quota system until the ratification of the Boswell Amendment. Schnell encouraged his staff to use this system regardless of the number of African American voters appearing at the polls. This approach, as expected, prevented most African Americans from registering. Only 14–15 African Americans a day were allowed to register. Once again, the NAACP filed affidavits with the DOJ offering proof that illiterate whites were being helped to complete the application process while qualified African Americans were intentionally denied (*Montgomery Advertiser* 1946). This time the NAACP denounced Schnell and McCovrey as racists and corrupted for ignoring and violating the United States Constitution (McLaurin n.d.).

Apart from these efforts, the commitment to voting rights drew the attention of new interest groups in Mobile. One of the most notable of these groups was the Negro Veterans Voters Association (NVVA). Like the NAACP, the NVVA labored for the full enfranchisement of African Americans (McLaurin 1972b). During the mid-1940s African Americans in Mobile began experiencing a heightened sense of injustice when black soldiers began returning from the battlefields of World War II. These veterans showed little inclination to accept the racial status quo they faced prior to their military service. Veteran James Jackson, Jr. maintained, with good humor and ready hands, that African Americans had carried their share of the burden in the war for the liberation of oppressed people:

> *Blacks fought in every theater, toiled as hard as White soldiers, and died. One in every ten men who answered the country's call was black. Black soldiers passed ammunition from sinking ships on the beaches of North Africa, Italy and France to the cacophony of chattering machine guns from stukas screaming low over our heads. We carved a piece of road out of the sheer sides of mountain peaks and through a steaming jungle fattened on monsoon rains. And when a convoy of the winged sons of Nippon came nosing out of the clouds [to] lay eggs on the road, one of us leaned onto a bucking 50-mm and shot one down. This was India and Burma. We did our part. Now, forever a part of the soil of Asia, of Europe, of African, and of all the oceans of the earth, we are tired of the dirt and the dangers and the loneliness and we want and dream of the peace, the security and the warmth of friendly smiles, the home feeling of belonging and being wanted; the amenities of the American democratic heritage in our hometowns down South. (LeFlore Papers, Undated, Box 10A, Series 8)*

Such expressions inspired the "New Negro" and many in the African American community sought changes through new and innovative forms of protest and new grass-roots organizations; thus, fueling the spirit of African American protest in Mobile. The NVVA was the recipient of this upsurge in black protest bourgeoning in the local community. The NVVA was championed by Mobilian Jessie Jacob Thomas.

Thomas was born in Whistler, Alabama on December 25, 1888. His educational experiences included studies in England and Africa where he learned architecture. Thomas designed the Thomas Building, one of the largest buildings on Davis Avenue where most of Mobile's African American businesses were located. The building had 26 rooms on two floors and included spaces for his office, a restaurant, beauty shop, T.V. shop and rooms for out-of-town visitors. He also supervised the construction of the Hillsdale Heights community, one of the largest housing projects for African Americans in Mobile (Davis-Horton 1991: 364).

Thomas quickly identified with the veterans returning from the war and insisted that African Americans initiate action against inequalities. His motto, "A voteless people is a hopeless people," led him into the heart of the political movement in Mobile. The naming of the veterans organization marks one of the truly fascinating stories of Mobile's African American history. According to legend, one day Thomas dreamed of three letters from NVVA. This vision came to him on several occasions but at the time he did not understand the reason. His search for meaning would end when he learned about the Boswell Amendment in the local newspaper. This anecdote reveals what Thomas considered a divine calling to fight black oppression. By the end of the 1940s the role that the NVVA played in the movement for African American enfranchisement overshadowed that of the NAACP. Thomas, a rising political star who gained national attention, temporarily rivaled LeFlore as Mobile's most influential African American leader (Davis-Horton 1991).

Many of the individuals that the NAACP sought to register in the 1946 Democratic Primary were veterans. However, instead of challenging the voting issue through the NAACP they reorganized under the leadership of Thomas. This group denounced the discriminatory practices of Mobile's Board of Registrars and, like the NAACP, called for African Americans to inundate the local Board with qualified applicants. Such steps taken by the NAACP and the fledgling NVVA led to an immediate jump in voter registration. While there were only 276 African American voters in January 1946, by the end of the year there were over 1,300 voters on the rolls (Mobile Press Register 1946d).

Despite the increase in voters, the real task for African Americans in Mobile remained the repeal of the Boswell Amendment. Local branches and leaders throughout Alabama began examining ways to block the final passage of the bill. Led mainly by their local NAACP, Birmingham and Montgomery debated the constitutionality of Boswell and recruited African Americans to challenge the system. In Mobile, the NAACP and the NVVA campaigned heavily against white conservatives who ran a campaign that portrayed African Americans in Alabama as subhuman and unfit to vote (McLaurin n.d.).

One notable opponent of the Boswell Amendment was Governor-Elect James E. Folsom who argued that the amendment was undemocratic and could lead to discrimination not only against Negro voters but to some white voters as well. Outspoken on the matter, Folsom emphasized that the impact of the Boswell Amendment would eventually lead to a small minority controlling state politics. Folsom, perhaps deliberately emulating the late President Franklin Delano Roosevelt, used fireside chats that were broadcast over the airwaves to inform Alabama voters on the deception of the Boswell Amendment (*Mobile Press Register* 1946b, 1946c).

Finally, eighty members of Alabama's clergy, speaking on behalf of the Protestant, Catholic and Jewish denominations, protested the Boswell Amendment. In Montgomery, a statement released by Richard Rives, the attorney for the ministers, maintained that local clergymen believed the amendment would place arbitrary powers in the hands of local registrars and that there was no objective way to interpret the proper understanding of the constitution (*Mobile Press Register* 1946a). Bishop Thomas J. Toolen of the Catholic Dioceses of Mobile called the amendment unethical, undemocratic and un-American. Rev. C.C. Daniel, Montgomery Superintendent for the Methodist Church, insisted that the Boswell Amendment would "set the state back for many years" (ibid.).

However, the proponents of African American disenfranchisement were just as active. McCorvey concluded that participation by members of the Democratic Party was crucial to the ratification of the amendment. McCorvey petitioned the Democratic Committee for money to mount what he hoped would be a last campaign to persuade white Alabamians to vote in favor of the amendment. By his own admission it was proper for him to lead a campaign to make the Alabama Democratic Party the "white man's party" (*Davis v. Schnell* 1949).

Thirty-five voted in favor of the committee spending $3,500 in a campaign to encourage Alabama voters to pass the amendment. Seven members voted against allocating the funds and one member failed to cast a vote. With the authorization of the funds, McCorvey began a massive effort to keep the political control of the state in the well-qualified hands of white Alabamians (*Davis v. Schnell* 1949).

Prior to the vote both proponents and opponents conceded that passage of the amendment would make it impossible for the African Americans to vote. McCorvey's campaign focused on convincing the voters of Alabama that only the Boswell Amendment stood between them and the rising tide of African American voters. His demagoguery undermined much of the progress made by the NAACP, the NVVA and Folsom.

Alabamians went to the voting booths early on November 6 and by the afternoon the outcome favored the proponents of the bill. With returns from 1,264 boxes of the state's 2,362 unofficially tabulated votes, the figures on the constitutional change were 56,780 for ratification of the amendment and 43,118 against it. Of these votes, Jefferson County, Alabama's largest and perhaps most racially divided county, favored the ratification 16,534 to 13,758. However, in other large counties where there was a mixture of African American and white leaders opposing this amendment the passage of Boswell did not fare as well. For example, with Richard Rives and others opposing the amendment, Montgomery, Alabama's third largest county, voted against ratification of the amendment. Similarly, in Mobile, with Catholic leadership and strong African American leadership from both the NAACP and NVVA, Mobile voters opposed the ratification of Boswell (*Davis v. Schnell* 1949).

The final count was 89,163 to 76,843 in favor of ratification. E.C. Boswell charged that in order to remove any doubt the local Boards should be given judicial status to carry out the will of the people. On November 15 Governor Sparks of Alabama formally announced the victory to the citizens of Alabama, emphasizing that plans should be made statewide to enforce the new law (*Mobile Press Register* 1946d).

Although devastating, it did not take long for LeFlore and Thomas, now co-members of several local organizations in Mobile, to agree that the ruling should be challenged before the state's highest court. Over the next year LeFlore gathered the names of all African Americans who had been denied access to voter registration through Boswell and urged them to file affidavits with the local NAACP. LeFlore's highly publicized efforts eventually led to one of the most divisive issues among African American leaders in Mobile (Kirkland 2012).

After LeFlore's successful efforts to build a case against the Mobile Board of Registrars the Mobile branch was instructed by the national branch of the NAACP to assist the Birmingham branch in contesting the case in Alabama. Stunned because he had fully expected the suit to originate in Mobile, LeFlore reluctantly acquiesced to the request of the national organization. Roy Wilkins, Secretary of the NAACP, believed Birmingham had the better chance of winning the case. Birmingham was also the logical choice.

The National NAACP had planned for several years to sue the Mobile and Birmingham Boards of Registrars for their voting laws through its "Operation Suffrage" program. The NAACP had sought to pilot the program in Birmingham since in fighting the Boswell Amendment there was a logical extension to the organization's earlier effort (Autry 1985; Lawson 1999). However, this rationale did not appease African Americans in Mobile. Moreover, to the disappointment of a growing number of African American leaders in the city, LeFlore continued to meet regularly with Mobile African Americans to keep them informed on the goals of the national branch and collect dues for the state's conferences of branches in support of the upcoming legal battle in Birmingham.

By early 1948 the Alabama branches were ready to take their case to the Alabama State Court. However, like the local NAACP, the NVVA and Thomas had gathered enough data and garnered enough support from the African American community in Mobile to make their own case against Boswell. Thus, prior to the NAACP filing suit, Hunter Davis and nine members of the NVVA filed their own lawsuit against the Board of Registrars of Mobile. LeFlore maintained:

> *It so happened that one of our board members, Mr. J. J. Thomas, who headed the Voters and Veterans League, had other thoughts about initiating the challenge against the Boswell Amendment and filed a suit against the Boswell Amendment within the thirty day period that we had decided that we would institute our court action. (McLaurin, n.d., Para 11)*

With both cases filed, the Court moved to hear the NVVA case on November 3, 1948. By this time significant strides were being made by blacks in other southern states. In Richmond, Virginia the efforts of an estimated fifty thousand African Americans led to Oliver Hill being elected to the city council; the first African American to do so since the late nineteenth century. Significant voting gains were also made in South Carolina where Judge Waring rebuked the state's Democratic Party efforts to limit African American participation and threatened to jail any party officers who failed to abide by his ruling. In that state, 35,000 black men and women lined up to vote in the Democratic Party Primary. In the summer of 1948 Palmer Weber Marshall, special counsel for the NAACP, believed that black leadership in the South was fighting for the ballot as never before and he encouraged the NAACP field staff to concentrate on its immediate efforts in that region (Sullivan 2009: 362–3).

The NVVA case, *Davis v. Schnell*, which later became the landmark case for voting rights in Alabama, argued that African Americans' constitutional right to vote had been violated by the Mobile Board through the illegal use of the Boswell Amendment. The Board of Registrars, however, based its argument on the premises that the legislature had not violated the 14th or 15th Amendments in adopting the Boswell Amendment; that the citizens of Alabama had not violated franchise rights by ratifying the Amendment and that the Board of Registrars had acted judiciously in registering black and white voters (*Davis v. Schnell* 1949). During the trial members of the Board of Registrars testified that although several applications for voter registration from the plaintiffs, including Hunter Davis, Julius B. Cook and Russell Gaskins, had been rejected they had been treated fairly.

The trial swung in favor of the NVVA when one Board member, E.J. Gonzales, refused to testify in favor of the defendants, maintaining that he could not join in the denials of the other members (McLaurin n.d.). Gonzales did testify on behalf of the plaintiffs. Gonzales, appointed to the Mobile Board of Registrars by Folsom to monitor the Board's treatment of African Americans, was a key witness for the defense. He testified that he had personally witnessed members of the Board using a double standard when registering black and white voters (*Davis v. Schnell* 1949).

The plaintiffs also used the testimony of Hunter Davis and Julius B. Cook. Both men testified that they were eligible and their right to vote was denied by the Mobile Board of Registrars (*Davis v. Schnell* 1949). Evidence revealed that both candidates met the residential and age requirements stipulated in Section 178 of the Constitution of Alabama. Moreover, they had been gainfully employed for the past 12 months and were US citizens of good character. The reason given for the denial of their ballots was failure to explain the US Constitution to the satisfaction of the Board (ibid.). Records used by the defense also revealed conclusively that the Board had a pattern of refusing to register African Americans.

From October 1947, the time when members of the current Board assumed office, to March 1, 1948, the filing date of the suit, 65 African Americans were registered and 57 were rejected because, as far as the Board was concerned, they could not "understand and explain" the constitution. These same records revealed that only 11 white voters were rejected and none as a result of the Boswell Amendment.

Finally, the records showed that since the incumbency of the Board over 2,800 whites and only 104 African Americans had been allowed to register. The total population of Mobile was 230,000. Sixty–four percent were white and 36 percent were African American (ibid.). Thus, the case designed by the NVVA turned out to be sounder than the NAACP or the Mobile Board of Registrars had originally believed. Perhaps the legitimacy of the NVVA's case was confirmed when the national conference finally came to its assistance.

On January 7, 1949 three members of the Mobile federal court ruled that the Boswell Amendment was unconstitutional because it had been used by the Mobile Board of Registrars to prevent Alabama citizens from registering due to their inability to read and comprehend the US Constitution. The court concluded that Boswell was a violation of the 14th and 15th Amendments. The three judge panel, consisting of Judge Julian McCord of the Fifth Circuit Court of Appeals and District Judges Clarence Mullins of Birmingham and John McDuffie of Mobile, ruled that "it clearly appears that this Amendment was intended to be, and is being used for the purpose of discriminating against applicants for the franchise on the basis of race and color" (ibid.)

Thus for the first time since the implementation of the Democratic Primary, the voter system, at least in theory, had to treat all voters in Alabama equally. Although the issue of race had been at the heart of African American disenfranchisement in Alabama prior to Boswell, this case allowed the issue to be debated at the judicial level. African American communities throughout the state began to experience a momentous upsurge in voter participation. According to one Birmingham writer, "States Righters have opposed mass registration and are decidedly against any law which would outlaw the poll tax. Regardless of these obstacles the Negro voters are on the increase, and there seems to be no limit to this increase" (*Gulf Informer* 1950, A1).

By any standard, the victory by the NVVA was most remarkable. Its reverberations were felt locally, regionally and nationally. The NVVA set a precedent in the South and permanently changed Alabama's voting laws. Although the fight was far from over, for all intents and purposes this ruling was a setback to white leadership (Feldman [1955] 1995). Another significance of this case was that it utilized the means of organization and litigation to attain justice without resorting to violence; which would mark many of the civil rights struggles in Alabama (and other states in the South) in subsequent years.

Thomas' ability to organize the African American community became the springboard for much of its success in Mobile. On January 10, 1949 the NVVA held a mass meeting at the Metropolitan A.M.E Church on Davis Avenue. Excited about the reversal of the Boswell Amendment, several hundred African American Mobilians attended. The tenor was jubilant but cautious. Leadership implored the attendees to go out the very next day to register, knowing that the Federal court was behind them. Civil rights leader Alex Herman declared that "The fighting has just begun. The other side isn't going to take this lying down" (*Mobile Press Register* 1949 A1).

However, with the intention of maintaining momentum, Thomas announced a southern campaign to raise $25,000 to fight future attempts to disenfranchise the African Americans. Other speakers stressed the importance of African Americans in Alabama not depending on outside help to gain their rights. This clarion call would prove to be the battle cry for African American leadership in Mobile throughout the remaining years of the civil rights movement. As expected, the abolition of the Boswell Amendment caused an immediate stir among the conservative southern white Democrats, popularly known as "Dixiecrats" and "Loyalists" who were committed to states' rights and the maintenance of segregation. These individuals believed that the federal government had overstepped its boundaries, usurped the rights of Alabama citizens and attempted to make African Americans and whites live together as one big family. Others believed that the government's attack against the state was cause for the "fruit of black sectionalism, prejudice and jealousy" (*Mobile Press Register* 1949). Shocking to many of these conservatives was the reality that they would have to compete more deliberately for the African American vote in order to effectively challenge the Republican Party, a move that had begun in the mid-1930s. (For additional discussion on the Dixiecrat movement, see Bernard 1974; Frederickson 2001.)

Similar to the African American community in Atlanta, Georgia, Mobile's African American community was being closely watched by southern legislators "looking for excuses for designing laws to keep Negroes from voting and try[ing] to prove that blacks will try and abuse their voting privileges by voting in blocs" (*Gulf Informer* 1949, A6). Although the number of African American voters in Mobile had not yet caught up with Atlanta's African American community, its increase influenced the outcome of local elections in 1950. Thus, by 1950 economic, political and ideological changes, wide-ranging and profound, were re-ordering southern society and eroding the foundations of racial domination. To deal with what most white conservatives understood as anti-white legislation, white legislators' leadership began examining ways to get around the abolishment of the Boswell Amendment. Dixiecrat Horace Wilkinson suggested that the Democratic Party become a private club, divorcing itself from any official state convention. This was unacceptable to most Democrats. However, what the committee did support was a new amendment to circumvent the African American vote (Fairclough 2001; Feldman [1955]1995).

When the court ruled that the Boswell Amendment was illegal it set forth additional guidelines to determine voter eligibility. Cohorts of the Boswell Amendment used this opportunity to create the "Boswell Junior Amendment." This time it was defeated by white moderates in Mobile. In response to angry protest from African American leadership in Mobile, State Senator Joseph Langan and several other white senators filibustered this amendment and it died in the Senate.

Joseph Langan was invaluable to civil rights progress in Mobile and became one of the most visible white advocates for civil rights in the state. Langan was instrumental in the re-organization of many of Alabama's state agencies, including industrial relations, finance and transportation—in addition to creating a merit system for government employees that allowed African American workers to gain access to public jobs. Langan also oversaw passage of local legislation that led to a merit system and voting machines for Mobile County (Dow 1993; Hoffman 1997).

In 1940 Langan served in the Alabama National Guard and was called to serve as a captain commanding the headquarters company of the 31st Division. While in the military he grew to know and respect African American soldiers. By his own admission he had fought side-by-side with blacks during World War II and admired how they had fought for a country that would not give them a job or let them drink from the same water fountain. Referring to freedom as the single most important blessing under the American system of government, Langan emphasized that all Americans had the inherent right and obligation to be involved in the government—specifically, the electoral process. To Langan, good government was related to voting. He believed that all Americans should have civil rights and supported efforts to abolish discriminatory laws (McLaurin 1972b; Fornof and Cook 1999).

Eventually, Langan joined hands with several other senators from Alabama to filibuster the Boswell Amendment in the Senate. These senators spent several days trying to defeat the Amendment, but simply wore out from fatigue (McLaurin n.d.). With the Boswell Junior Amendment, however, the outcome would be different. Langan maintained:

*And of course when this group then file to challenge the Boswell amendment, and it was declared unconstitutional, then at the next session of the legislature, legislation was introduced to try to meet the criteria that was set-up in the court's decision as to why the Boswell amendment was unconstitutional. Well, this again was directly aimed at keeping black people from voting in Alabama. So, I finally discussed this matter with the governor who felt that something should be done to defeat this legislation or not even allow the constitutional amendment to be presented to the people. And—because of its repressive nature. And finally, there were four or five senators that did agree out of the total senate that we should try to block it. So we did put on a filibuster for a number of days speaking against this constitutional amendment. And as it was drawing close of the session of the legislature, we filibustered night and day until the final twelve o'clock midnight of the final day of the session. Even though Senator Allen and some others in presiding in the chair tried to throw the rule book out of the window, we were able to finally, under the rules of the senate by the small group of five senators, even though, they castigated us and made all kind of defamatory remarks about us and everything from a racial standpoint. We did filibuster because we felt that it was injustice for a person who had fought to protect this country not to be allowed to cast a vote in selecting the officials for our government. (McLaurin 1972b, Para 15)*

Efforts to find holes in the Boswell Amendment were made continuously by local Boards around the state. As chairman of the Board of Registrars in Birmingham, H.A. Thompson controlled voter registration in the city. First appointed in 1947, Thompson, who was called "Mr. Gus," was a 70-year-old man described by the *Birmingham News* as a "strong Dixiecrat plumper." He served as chairman until 1955 and during that time he fought to prevent what he called the "mass registration of all persons over the age of 21 years, regardless of the qualifications now required under the laws of the State of Alabama" (Eskew 1997: 87). In his courthouse office by eight every morning, Thompson opposed poll tax reform and all other democratic measures designed to enlarge the voting pool in Birmingham, something that he feared "would result in a social and economic calamity in Alabama" (ibid.).

In Mobile, the Board attempted to limit the African American vote by slowing down the registration process. On one occasion, for example, Estella Hicks, a local schoolteacher stood in line "all day" before being turned away (McLaurin n.d., Para 12). However, with the progress already in motion, the attempts to slow down the African American vote and desegregation were unsuccessful. LeFlore recalled in an interview with McLaurin the comparable progress in social and racial matters in Mobile at the time:

*But as I sit here and realize that we were able to get our library system desegregated merely by filing a petition, pointing out at the same time we filed the petition we were ready to go to court. We were able to get our terminal restaurant facilities desegregated, because we filed petitions with the federal authorities ... We were able to get our city buses desegregated by filing a suit. (Ibid.: Para 22)*

## Conclusion

By the early 1950s, Mobile's African American community had set the stage for civil rights progress in the state. Not only had it challenged the future of Jim Crow by organizing a bus boycott in 1942, its African American leadership had challenged and helped abolish Alabama's all-white Democratic Primary and the Boswell Amendment. These actions made it possible for the African American community to legally fight for future political enfranchisement. As a result, the Mobile African American community increased its voter participation and raised the level of its political awareness. Moreover, these events drew national attention and became the political model for the enfranchisement of African Americans throughout the state. Compelling, though, was the fact that the Mobile African American community's battle for voting rights was accomplished in an era of racial upheaval. Not only had whites vehemently rejected African Americans' civil rights, the acts of unbridled violence that it willed against African Americans in the state—acts that would come to symbolize the modern civil rights movement in Alabama—never materialized in Mobile. This was no small feat for African Americans in any southern state, especially those who lived in "the heart of Dixie." Thereafter, Martin Luther King, Jr., the movement's most salient civil rights leader, would rise to national prominence. King would make his mark in Montgomery, Alabama, just over 150 miles north of Mobile. Alabama would also have numerous other outstanding and courageous African Americans to move the struggle for civil rights forward. However, what African Americans in Mobile achieved politically in the 1940s connected them indelibly to political gains made by African Americans in Alabama throughout the civil rights era and beyond.

To the extent the civil rights movement rested upon collective action, a socio-political activism, particularly through its electoral process, had a direct impact on legislation. Simply, without actively participating in the voting process a group stands little chance of translating their preferences into public policy. Evidently, no group has been able to gain middle-class status without the help of the national government adopting legislation to assist them and that it has been through the electoral process that such legislation is influenced (Smith et al. 1987). Likewise, blacks in Mobile relied heavily on the electoral process to change their social status. During the modern movement Mobile blacks influenced local and regional legislation in hopes of procuring political and social equality.

However, the battle in Mobile and around the nation continues to be a struggle for the African American community. The Voting Rights Act of 1965 was an extension of the 15th Amendment. It insisted that states and local governments refrain from using discriminatory practices designed to prevent African American citizens from voting. However, despite federal legislative efforts to rectify the situation by re-authorizing the landmark Voting Rights Act for another 25 years, African Americans (and other minorities) continue to face obstacles at voting booths. Conservative political parties and activists continue to target historically disenfranchised voters by employing modern, sophisticated, subtle and technologically oriented tactics—including, but not limited to, voter caging, voter purging, lying flyers (publicizing bogus election rules and wrong election dates), deceptive Robocalls, menacing billboards, poll watcher networks, early voting rule manipulations and difficult voter registration requirements (Serwer 2012). Of these, the most controversial technique is the voter ID law. Twelve states passed legislation in 2011 to require or request a photo ID to vote. Five of them—Minnesota, Missouri, Montana, New Hampshire and North Carolina—had Democratic governors who vetoed the legislation. The remaining seven were Alabama, Kansas, Rhode Island, South Carolina, Texas, Tennessee and Wisconsin. In June 2012, Attorney General Eric Holder, the first African American to serve in this position in the nation's history, said: "The past two years have brought nearly two dozen new state laws and executive orders, from more than a dozen states, that could make it significantly harder for eligible voters to cast ballots in 2012" (Martin 2012: Para 11).

And another 13 states are planning to enact similar laws. Prior to the recent US Supreme Court ruling in *Shelby County v. Holder*, some states were required to obtain Federal preclearance prior to enacting any new election laws. But the Supreme Court ruling on June 25, 2013 in the *Shelby County v. Holder* case waived this requirement, at least until its formula can be deemed as constitutional. This decision meant that states like Texas that have passed photo identification requirements but were waiting for Federal preclearance may now immediately take effect. Many believe the voter ID laws are largely the GOP tactics to exclude Democratic-leaning voters, especially when one sees the forms of identification that these laws consider valid (e.g., a concealed carry license).

The justification given to enacting voter ID laws was to prevent voter fraud. However, in many instances there appears to be no concrete evidence of fraud at the levels claimed by the proponents of law. For example, in Georgia, Secretary of State Cathy Cox has stated that she could not recall one documented case of voter fraud relating to the impersonation of a registered voter at the polls during the 10-year period she was in the office. South Carolina State Attorney General, David Wilson, attempted to justify the new voter ID law by claiming that over 900 "dead voters" might have voted in recent elections, but managed to identify only six "individuals" to support his exaggerated claim. Therefore, policy makers should redirect their efforts to secure reliable data on the nature and extent of voter fraud by region instead of weighing on their political ideologies (conservative vs. liberal) or subjective fears and opinions. Additionally, they should consider alternative and effective ways of preventing it while ensuring the voter turnout is unaffected. The one-size-fits-all policy of voter ID laws does not seem to be the right measure.

# References

Autry, Dorothy. 1985. "The NAACP in Alabama: 1913–1952." Ph.D. dissertation, University of Notre Dame.

Bernard, William D. 1974. *Dixiecrats and Democrats: Alabama Politics, 1942–1950.* Tuscaloosa, AL: The University of Alabama Press.

Bracey, John H., Jr. and August Meier, eds. 1991. National Association for the Advancement of Colored People. 1991. *Papers of the NAACP: Part 12. Selected Branch Files, 1913–1939, Series A: The South.* Bethesda, MD: University Publications of America.

*Davis v. Schnell*, Civil Action No. 758, 81 F. Supp. 872 (S.D. Ala. 1949). Retrieved January 12, 2012: https://www.courtlistener.com/alsd/89Dp/davis-v-schnell/.

Davis-Horton, Paulette. 1991. *Avenue … The Davis Avenue Story.* Mobile, AL: Horton, Inc.

Dow, Patsy B. 1993. "Joseph N. Langan: Mobile's Racial Diplomat." Master's Thesis, Department of History, University of South Alabama.

Egerton, John. 1995. *Speak Now Against the Day: The Generation Before the Civil Rights Movement in the South.* Chapel Hill: The University of North Carolina Press.

Eskew, Glenn T. 1997. *But for Birmingham: The Local and National Movements in the Civil Rights Struggle.* Chapel Hill: The University of North Carolina Press.

Fairclough, Adam. 2001. *Better Day Coming: Blacks and Equality, 1890–2000.* New York: Penguin Books.

Feldman, Glenn. [1955] 1995. *From Demagogue to Dixiecrat: Horace Wilkinson and the Politics of Race.* Lanham, MD: University Press of America.

Fornof, John and Davy Cook. 1999. *A Quiet Revolution: The Story of John LeFlore.* Documentary. Mobile, AL: WEIQ, Public Television Services.

Foster, Vera Chandler. 1949. "Boswellianism: A Technique n the Restriction of Negro Voting." *Phylon* 10: 26–37.

Frederickson, Kari. 2001. *The Dixiecrat Revolt and the End of the Solid South, 1932–1968*. Chapel Hill: The University of North Carolina Press.

Grafton, Carl and Anne Permaloff. 1985. *Big Mules and Branchheads: James E. Folsom and Political Power in Alabama*. Athens: University of Georgia Press.

*Gulf Informer*. 1949. "Colored Votes Significant in Two Elections: Mobile, Atlanta Watched By Designing Foe," September 14.

*Gulf Informer*. 1950. "More Potential Negro Voters in Alabama." June 17.

Hoffman, Roy. 1997. "Pushing the Limits Joe Langan's Mobile," *The Mobile Register*. September, A–4.

Jackson, Emory O. 1945. "NAACP letter to the Alabama Public Service Commission," *Birmingham World*. December 1.

Kirkland, Scotty E. 2012. "Mobile and the Boswell Amendment," *Alabama Review* 65(3): 205–49.

Lawson, Stephen F. 1999. *Black Ballots: Voting Rights in the South, 1944–1969*. Lanham, MD: Lexington Books.

LeFlore Papers, Box 2, May 16, 1944. Folder 6. NAACP files, Mobile branch, correspondence, "An Emergency Appeal to the Citizens of Mobile." University of South Alabama Archives, Mobile, Alabama.

———, Box 8, May 15 and October 2, 1945. Folders 11–12. Personal correspondence, John L. LeFlore to Thurgood Marshall. University of South Alabama Archives, Mobile, Alabama.

———, Box 8, November 24, 1945. Folders 11–12. Personal correspondence, Harold H. Buckles to John L. LeFlore. University of South Alabama Archives, Mobile, Alabama.

———, Box 8, January 5, 1946. Folders 13–16. Personal correspondence, John L. LeFlore to Tom G. Clark. University of South Alabama Archives, Mobile, Alabama.

———, Box 8, January 29, 1946. Folders 13–16. Personal correspondence, John L. LeFlore to L. Caudle. University of South Alabama Archives, Mobile, Alabama.

———, Box 8, January 31, 1946. Folders 13–16. Personal correspondence, John L. LeFlore to Kenneth Smith. University of South Alabama Archives, Mobile, Alabama.

———, Box 3, April 3, 1946. Folder 2. NAACP files, Mobile branch, John L. LeFlore Affidavit. University of South Alabama Archives, Mobile, Alabama.

———, Box 8, January 5, 1948. Folder 17. Personal correspondence, John L. LeFlore to Thurgood Marshall. University of South Alabama Archives, Mobile, Alabama.

Long, Michael G. 2012. *I Must Resist: Bayard Rustin's Life in Letters*. San Francisco, CA: City Lights Books.

Martin, Gary. 2012. "Texas bracing for legal battle against feds over Voter ID law," *Houston Chronicle*. Retrieved July 23, 2012: http://blog.chron.com/txpotomac/2012/06/texas-bracing-for-legal-battle-against-feds-over-voter-id-law/.

McLaurin, Melton. 1970. "Second interview with John L. LeFlore." *McLaurin Oral History Project*. Retrieved August 8, 2012: http://www.southalabama.edu/archives/html/manuscript/oralhist/oralhist1b.htm.

———. n.d. "Third interview with John L. LeFlore and Wiley Bolden." *McLaurin Oral History Project*. Retrieved August 8, 2012: http://www.southalabama.edu/archives/html/manuscript/oralhist/oralhist1d.htm.

———. 1972a. "Fifth Interview with John L. LeFlore, October 9, 1972." *McLaurin Oral History Project*. Retrieved August 8, 2012: (http://www.southalabama.edu/archives/html/manuscript/oralhist/oralhist1f.htm).

———. 1972b. "Joseph Langan Interview, October 12, 1972." *McLaurin Oral History Project*. Retrieved August 8, 2012: http://www.southalabama.edu/archives/html/manuscript/oralhist/oralhist3.htm.

———. 1973. "Mobile Blacks and World War II: The Development of a Political Consciousness." in *Gulf Coast Politics in the Twentieth Century*, eds. Ted Carageorge and Thomas Jasper Gilliam. Pensacola, FL: Historic Pensacola Preservation Board, pp. 47–56.

*Mobile Press Register*. 1946a. "State Clergymen Flay Vote Plan." November 1.

———. 1946b. "Boswell Proposal Imposes New Rule on Qualifications." November 3.

———. 1946c. "Folsom Will Hit Vote Amendment." November 13.

———. 1946d. "Sparks Proclaims Boswell Now Official Law." November 15.

———. 1949. "Colored Assembly Urged to Attempt To Register Here." November 10.

———. 1990. "Black/White Mobile." Special issue, p. 3.

*Montgomery Advertiser*. 1946. "Let's Face It." February.

Serwer, Adam. 2012. "10 Dirty Ways to Swing an Election," *Mother Jones*. Retrieved January 10, 2013: http://www.motherjones.com/politics/2012/11/election-dirty-tricks.

Smith, J. Owens, Mitchell F. Rice and Woodrow Jones, Jr. 1987. *Blacks and American Government: Politics, Policy and Social Change*. Dubuque, IA: Kendall/Hunt Publishing.

Sullivan, Patricia. 2009. *Lift Every Voice: The NAACP and the Making of the Civil Rights Movement*. New York: The New Press.

Thomason, Michael. 2001. *Mobile: The New History of Alabama's First City*. Tuscaloosa, Alabama: The University of Alabama Press.

Thornton, J. Mills, III. 2002. *Dividing Lines: Municipal Politics and the Struggle for Civil Rights in Montgomery, Birmingham, and Selma*. Tuscaloosa, Alabama: The University of Alabama Press.

US Supreme Court. April 3, 1944. *Smith v. Allwright-Page 321 US 664*. Retrieved January 21, 2012: http://supreme.justia.com/cases/federal/us/321/649/case.html.

Verney, Kevern. 2013. "Every Man Should Try: John L. LeFlore and the National Association for the Advancement of Colored People in Alabama, 1919–1956," *Alabama Review* 66(3): 186–210.

# The African American Church as an Enclave and Ethnic Resource: The Role of the Church in Economic Development

## Marci Bounds Littlefield

## Introduction

The connection between religious beliefs and practices, and economic behavior has a long and rich history within the sociological literature. Historically, the Black church is the primary institution through which African Americans engage in self-help activities as it serves as a resource for addressing community concerns. Evidence of this history can be found in the works of W.E.B. Du Bois as he conducted the first sociological study on the church in the United States (Du Bois 1903). At the turn of the twentieth century he carried out empirical studies of Black communities throughout this nation and in both urban and rural settings, inquiring into subjects including, but not limited to, differences between urban and rural churches and large and small congregations, differences between denominations, charitable contributions of churches and differences in preaching styles (Du Bois 1903). E. Franklin Frazier was also one of the first to engage in the sociological inquiry of the Black church. He argues that the church has four major economic functions: 1) the church owns real estate and makes economic investments in the community whether this includes the church building or other facilities, 2) the church establishes mutual aid societies that evolve into insurance companies, 3) the church is instrumental in the creation of organized black fraternal organizations and 4) the church helps to organize and build schools, pay teachers and provide scholarships (Frazier 1964). Although Du Bois and Franklin are influential historical figures in this field the preponderance of recognition for the origin and development of this field is provided to White scholars.

In his classic study on the connection between religion, group experiences and entrepreneurship, Weber (1958) contends that the Protestant doctrine, the entrepreneurial behavior of Protestants, played a major role in the global expansion of modern capitalism. Relatedly, Simmel (1997) and Kraybill and Nolt (1995) suggest that the western world's adamant embrace of modern capitalism is due to its adherence to religious doctrine and philosophy as a sustaining force for business activity and competition. The focus on economic activities is particularly strong among the minority groups facing resistance to their participation in the state, such as the Poles in Russia and Eastern Prussia, Huguenots in France during the reign of Louis XIV, Nonconformists and Quakers in England and Jewish people throughout much of history (Butler 2005; Weber 1958). While religion's role in economic behavior and the formation of business enterprises has been examined for many groups, it has not been documented in any detailed manner among African Americans since the works of Du Bois and Franklin.

The dearth of literature on the role of religion in the economic lives of African Americans is surprising. With a history of oppression and inequality extending from slavery to today, African Americans are, arguably, the most marginalized group within the US. Seventy-five percent of African Americans have some level of church affiliation; thus, one can conclude that the church remains largest recipient of African Americans' volunteer time and financial contributions (Hill 1994). The continued marginality of African Americans within this society, despite strong involvement in religious activities, raises the question of whether the link between religion and economic behavior documented by previous scholars still applies to the experiences of African Americans today. This chapter examines the extent to which African American churches facilitate business development and how African American churches act as a vital economic organization, an enclave and an ethnic resource in the relationship to business development.

# Background

## Business Development and Marginalized Groups

Small businesses are the means by which millions of workers enter the economic and social mainstreams of American society. Many immigrant groups have used business ownership as a way to overcome social and economic restrictions to create wealth for their communities (Butler 2005). Business ownership is especially effective in ethnic communities because ethnic enclaves allow groups to circumvent discrimination to create economic independence, success and community development—all commonly viewed as a model for the American dream (ibid.).

Despite the success of these groups, numerous assessments of self-employment trends among African Americans indicate a lack of business development when compared to other ethnic minority groups (Bates 1997; Light and Rosenstein 1995). Scholars cite a lack of financial and social capital as a major contributing factors to low levels of self-employment and business success among African Americans (Bates 1997; Aronson 1991; Horton 1988; Fratoe 1988). Overall, the experiences of individual African American business owners differs from other marginalized racial groups who use ethnic enclaves to overcome adverse societal conditions through business development (Bonacich and Modell 1980; Butler 2005; Light and Rosenstein 1995; Portes and Manning 1986). Historically, African Americans have benefited from the efforts of the African American church to offset adverse racial and economic conditions and serve as an enclave of economic opportunity.

## The African American Church

The African American church has historically been involved in multiple community service activities including, but not limited to, the anti-slavery movement, organizing insurrections, providing loans to small business, supporting institutions of higher education, financing banks and insurance companies and fighting for civil and voting rights (Lincoln and Mamiya 1990; Billingsley 1999; Butler 2005). Congregational studies suggest that African American churches continue to be actively engaged in providing social services to its members (Littlefield 2010; Billingsley 1999; Chaves and Tsitsos 2001; Tsitsos 2003). Some scholars argue that African American congregations have higher levels of certain types of activities when compared to other congregations (Littlefield 2010; Chaves and Tsitsos 2001; Tsitsos 2003). Congregations usually offer services which address basic human and community needs. African American congregations are actively involved in providing these types of services by offering programs such as education, mentoring, substance abuse programs and job training or assistance programs. (Billingsley 1999; Chaves and Tsitsos 2001; Hill 1994). Additional research documents the role of the church in providing health services (Billingsley and Caldwell 1994) and community development efforts (Billingsley 1999; Chaves and Higgins 1992).

Despite the existing research on churches and their role in the community, limited attention has focused on understanding how religious beliefs and practices translate into business development and behavior. Previous research findings suggest that religion promotes the ethos of thrift, hard work and self-help while providing a historical connection between religion and economic behavior in the lives of African Americans. The provision of social capital through the African American church is an important means of understanding the significant contributions of this institution to the business development of its members.

Social capital studies explore the extent and means through which social relationships allow individuals to gain access to cultural, social and economic resources (Coleman1988; Portes 1998; Sherkat and Ellison 1999). These types of resources are important sources of power and produce values and norms, which influence behavior. Thus, social capital is a way to understand the resources to which different groups have access to by virtue of membership. Literature assessing how social capital is embedded in religious institutions is less common. Faith-based organizations have historically been a vehicle by which groups have responded to structural and cultural marginality by providing a forum to address group-specific needs (Bartkowski and Regis 2003; Sherkat and Ellison 1999).

Understanding the role that religious institutions have in creating economic development opportunities and in influencing economic behavior is important because of the unaddressed needs and continued marginalization of some in the African American community. This project adds to the existing literature by attempting to understand the role that social institutions like the church play in the business process and economic development for African Americans.

# Methods

## Sample and Procedure

This qualitative study was conducted over a two-year period. The sample consists of African American churches located within Sunnyside, a large urban area in the southern region of the United States.[1] Churches whose membership was 75 percent African American were labeled as African American churches for the purposes of this project. Subjects were contacted via telephone at their church and invited to participate in a face-to-face interview. All of the individuals that participated in the face-to-face interviews were in leadership positions (e.g., pastor, senior minister, or head administrator). During the interview, questionnaires were completed which included demographic questions and institutional priorities.

There are 87 African American churches in Sunnyside. I conducted 57 formal interviews which yielded a 67 percent response rate. The typical church in this study was Baptist, its

---

1    The name of the city, all churches and participants are pseudonyms.

building was owned and included a staff of one to four paid workers. Sixty-seven percent of the pastors in this study had a history of business ownership and 76 percent held college or professional degrees.

## Measures

Business or entrepreneurial activities were operationalized as how churches participate in the process of initiating and supporting individual business endeavors. Using the emergent theme process, definitions of being entrepreneurial were identified and categorized. The entrepreneurial process was considered participation in at least two of the following areas of business assistance: encouragement, technical assistance, office materials, financial resources and providing encouragement. These categories were ranked in their level of importance with encouragement being the least and financial resources the most active form of entrepreneurial support. Participation in two of the four areas of business assistance was considered entrepreneurial.

## Entrepreneurial Models

Each church was categorized and assessed according to their level of entrepreneurial support as Tuskegee, active or non-active churches. Tuskegee churches provided three to four forms of business assistance, active churches provided at least two forms of business assistance and non-active churches did not provide any business assistance. Business support was organized into categories: 1) encouragement (teaching and preaching about self-employment, advertising business information in their church and/or encouraging self-employment); 2) technical assistance (informational and educational forms of business support, including legal consultation and loan assistance); 3) office support (office structure, office materials and incubator related services) and 4) financial assistance (start-up costs, general maintenance fee, interest-free loans and other financial needs). The following charts are a visual explanation of these categories.

Table 19.1 illustrates the entrepreneurial models which distinguish between the different levels of business support and the way in which this participation promotes self-help. Tuskegee churches believe that business development creates opportunities and is the route for upward mobility. This group is committed to business ownership and this is an important part of their agenda. Active congregations take an assertive role in self-employment, which includes basic networking, posting business information on a bulletin board and/or offering classes or other forms of technical advice. Inactive churches did not contribute to business development.

**Table 19.1    Business Support Activities**

| Type of Support | Types of Business Support Activities |
| --- | --- |
| Encouragement | Teaching or Preaching, and Advertising |
| Technical Assistance | Informational, Educational, Legal and Loans |
| Office Support | Space, Telephone, Fax Machines, Office Materials |
| Financial Support | Start-Up Costs, General Maintenance Fees, Loans |

# Results

Table 19.2 depicts the congregations in this study. The next section uses direct quotations to explain the business activities of the churches in this study.

**Table 19.2    Church Characteristics by Category**

| Entrepreneurial Category | Church Characteristics | Community and Business Support, Business Involvement and Community Activities |
| --- | --- | --- |
| Inactive (16) | Less than 500 Members<br>Pastor High School Diploma<br>Less than 10 Years | None, Education Scholarships |
| Active (24) | Over 500 Members<br>Pastor Has at Least College Degree<br>Older than 20 Years | Business Support: Encouragement, Technical Assistance, Office and Financial (Two of Four Areas)<br>Community Support:<br>Job Referrals<br>Educational/scholarship<br>Learning Center<br>Bill Assistance<br>Food/Clothing/Shelter<br>Legal Assistance<br>Nursing/Immunization<br>Juvenile Services |
| Tuskegee (17) | Less than 300 Members<br>Pastor Has as Least College Degree<br>Less than 10 Years Old | Business Support: Encouragement, Technical Assistance, Office and Financial (Three of Four Areas)<br>Community Support<br>Job Referrals<br>Educational Scholarship<br>Food/Clothing/Shelter<br>Bill Assistance<br>Nursing/Immunization<br>Down Payment Assistance<br>Business Classes<br>Business Loans/In-Kind/Referral<br>Investment Clubs |

## Tuskegee Churches

Most of the churches expressed an interest in business development; however, their degree of commitment was measured by their specialized business activities. These activities ranged from inspirational messages encouraging self-help to providing incubator-related services which aid in the facilitation of business development. Tuskegee churches exhibited the highest commitment to business development and promoted the notion that business ownership and support are central to the churches' agenda. This is evident in a statement by a Tuskegee pastor:

> Yes, business development is a priority in our church. It is my belief that you do not come to help people until we can be self-sufficient and if we promote business in the church then our members will make the church grow. I teach it and preach it. We take

*what we get and aggressively work with it. We are entrepreneurs for Christ. (Eastside Baptist).*

This pastor is convinced of the benefits of self-employment and went on to further talk about one of the church's business initiatives:

*We have a fish fry every Friday and we make twenty to fifty thousand dollars a year. It helps us to do what we do. It is my belief that we don't come to help people until we can be self-sufficient. Jesus didn't say we just need the word of God, we need bread and if we promote business in the church then the members make the church grow. (Eastside Baptist).*

This Tuskegee pastor then discusses ways in which the church provides resources for business development and how business development is encouraged in his congregation:

*One business needed a trailer, we helped and he [then] employed others in the church. The credit union needed help from beginning to end. We have seminars with different real estate people and insurance people. I encourage it and preach it and several members have businesses and are employing people in the church. (Second Samuel).*

## Promoting business development

Many Tuskegee pastors understand the benefits of promoting business development. In fact, most of these pastors express similar ideas concerning their commitment to business development. Several examples are below:

- Yes I talk about starting a business over the pulpit. I believe God is moving us to start our own business instead of relying on the government. I push it, I try to find resources, I hook them up with other people, and I promote it whole heartily. (Emmanuel Baptist)
- We push business development because people do not have the skills, so you have to do something dynamic like starting your own business. Without skills a burden is placed on them, so we have to form businesses so people do not have to rely on traditional structures. We push business development so people can make it. And we are trying to help people who have ideas to bring them into fruition. (Mt Calvary)
- When you have your own business then you have control of your life, and you don't know when you will be downsized working for someone else. Having a business allows you to have financial freedom and you can be freed up to do God's business. When you don't have money you are hindered, it stops you from serving God. We promote it here. (Bethel)
- Yes it is a priority. I promote it. I mention information from the pulpit and we have cards and advertisement in the hallways. The Bible shows us to render what is God's first. God doesn't intend for you to be in debt, so God encourages you to do things for yourself and not be dependent on others. (Greater Union)
- We offer financial planning God's way on Sunday. We believe in direct investing. We have backed bookstores, trophies businesses, card businesses, this is important to the community. If people are thinking of starting their own business, we encourage them and give them the needed information to help them. (Mt Sinai)

- It's all about building and rebuilding. We are in a low-income and no-income community so our needs outweigh our finances. We work with banks to help people get financed. I've put my names on loans for people. The banks look at the credit references of the trustees and we let the bank come out and see what the community is doing. Every good pastor should be a businessman. Soul winning is the beginning point but not the ending point; we are concerned about the whole person. (Faith Temple)

Implied in these statements is a belief in self-help that I label "community capitalism." Community capitalism is rooted in the churches' beliefs about self-help which promotes self-sufficiency and autonomy, but is also connected to the greater good of the church and "God's Kingdom." Therefore, as the lives of individual members are sustained and prosper through business development, the church also benefits since these members give money back to the church. As one Tuskegee pastor explained: "In the talent parable, Jesus was speaking of resources and he literally spoke of coins. Those who multiplied the coins given by Jesus were 'blessed' or rewarded. Those who did not were frowned upon" (Eastside Baptist).

Therefore, the talent parable given by this group means they believe God gives all of us something and that he, in return, expects us to prosper. Self-employment was used as an example of prosperity and wealth building. This group prioritized self-employment as a form of self-help as described in the talent parable. Thus having financial freedom through self-employment frees up one's time "to do God's business." The following quotes link self-help, self-employment and community capitalism:

- When you own your own business you have control over your life. It allows you to have financial freedom to do God's business. You determine your net worth when you work for yourself. (Eastside Baptist)
- I believe God is moving us to start our own business instead of relying on the government to help us. It is time to start our own. (Bethel United Methodist)
- Our doctrine promotes salvation, and liberation; liberate yourself from working for someone else. Our pastor promotes economic empowerment. (New Hope Temple)

The belief in not relying on government assistance was a common theme among Tuskegee churches. Instead, they were interested in creating a culture promoting the principles of self-help while providing resources for people to act on those ideas. Mt. Calvary represented the best example of understanding the promotion of business development in churches because it offers a business incubator for local entrepreneurs.

> We have an incubator where people not just members can use our church as their office. They can use paper, our phones as their business number and we house them until they get on their feet. We also support our businesses owners in our church. So far we have a temporary employment service, a legal services, marketing services, business management services and accounting services all in our incubator. (Pastor Mt Calvary)

He then explains in detail the services offered to those interested in business development including networking, business-plan writing, marketing, idea conceptualization and start-up costs. Most importantly, he teaches that the church operates like a business: "Everything is corporately structured; we combined business training with economic empowerment. Our mission is to provide community and economic development opportunities that produce leaders of high moral character committed to building family and community" (Mt. Calvary).

Self-employment represents a viable option for members of Mt. Calvary who are not college educated. Some of the long-range goals of Tuskegee churches include opening a credit union, providing on-site marketing sales, personal finance classes, youth entrepreneurship training and internships and investment clubs.

Although Mt Calvary represents the most entrepreneurial church in this study, it accurately captured the culture created through business development. The idea that there is a connection between business enterprise and community building clearly supports the notion that an entrepreneurial culture can be developed through these practices. These churches regularly engage in economic development activities ranging from business classes centered on starting a business to discussions of broad topics promoting business development. This group has created a culture conducive for business development and their religious tenets confirm this commitment. Weber (1958) suggested the connection between religious ideas, economic behavior and the existence of Tuskegee churches further verifies this connection.

The Tuskegee churches are the most entrepreneurial examples in this study and, as a group, they have the fewest number of members. These churches explained their commitment to self-employment as a direct result of their size. Their small size gave the ministers more personal interactions with members and allowed them to better recognize the needs of their members. They argue that larger churches are more bureaucratic and unable to provide "hands on" services to their members as they do:

> The smaller churches have a feel for family and improvement. You find that within the small congregations you know them more. With big churches it has to push through other committees and smaller churches can help right away. We know our members more than big churches and we have a greater feel for what people need and want. Yes, we have taken up love offerings if they need a financial loan and it is interest free but you have to be a member. Unless you are proposing a big program that would make a lot of money, the big churches would not help you. The spirit is manifested in the smaller churches and we are better able to care for our members because we do not have a large congregation. We are family oriented and we all work together. (New Hope)

Trust is also a crucial factor in explaining their level of involvement in business development as it offers an additional means of support for entrepreneurs. Church members are motivated to enter into self-employment because they have a support system that offers financial resources, informational networks and a Christian ideology that supports this agenda:

- People are encouraged to start their own business because there is less fear of failure; we trust each other. (Wesley)
- We take care of each other. We have even taken up a collection for struggling business owners. (Mt. Zion)

Overall these pastors espouse a strong self-help and Protestant ethic value system while promoting entrepreneurship through leadership, sermons, interactions with the congregation and the allocation of business support (i.e., loans, supplies, etc.). Tuskegee pastors reported encouraging business development and frequently associated their influence with the entrepreneurial behavior of their congregations. Wealth is seen as a vehicle for community development and business activities are endorsed because people believe financial freedom is what God desires for their lives. Even the Tuskegee churches with fewer resources create opportunities because of the promise that they see implied in aiding business development; business development creates opportunities and is perceived as the route for upward mobility. This entrepreneurial climate offers more than resources: it gives people hope and a sense of personal efficacy. People who are part of these churches internalize this entrepreneurial spirit and adopt it as part of their religious and daily behavior.

## Active Churches

At first glance, active churches resemble Tuskegee churches since they also promote business development. However, there are crucial differences between active and Tuskegee churches. Active churches were more likely to have larger congregations and resources. Active churches also had a more comprehensive agenda and business development was not a priority over other social services. While active churches have more resources to support business development, they participated in fewer areas of business support than did the Tuskegee churches. When asked, this group proclaimed their commitment to business development in theory. But, in practice they were less committed to actually providing financial support or technical assistance which are two areas of crucial business importance. Rather, active churches were more traditional in their ideology and business development was not seen as being the only method of economic uplift. These churches did not have formal mechanisms in place to facilitate business support. For active churches, business support was more theoretical.

Although active churches supported the idea of business development, it was not their main priority. Comments from members of some of these churches illustrate this point:

- Yes I encourage people to be in business for yourself and I do this at men's meetings and my wife does this at the ladies' events. We have a number of business owners in our church that we patronize; we have barbers, beauticians, people who sew ... we also have a strong outreach ministry it is called WE CARE, our 501.C3, and we solicit outside donations. But winning souls is my main focus. God will prosper you, but if people want to start a business and if God called them to that then yes, we will help then but this is not our focus. (Full Gospel)
- Our church environment is conducive to entrepreneurship; businesses are well supported by making members aware of businesses in our church directory. We provide advertisement and we encourage it at other meeting and people have access to our copy machine but it is not a priority in our church. (Olivet)

Overall, the pastor's influence and level of vision offered to the ministry help us to understand why churches were classified Tuskegee or active. Historically, in African American churches the pastor has a vital role in shaping the agenda of the church and this held true for the Sunnyside churches. The following active church comment on the role of the pastor is illustrative: "We haven't done anything more because our Pastor has not prioritized it on his goals and objectives and without his full backing the ministry never got off the ground" (Joy Tabernacle).

In essence, the pastor's vision determines the level of commitment to business ownership and support. While the larger active churches have more resources and offer a comprehensive self-help agenda, these churches were more likely to have a community development corporation, credit unions, housing units and day care centers and provide other community services.

Some of the active churches included in this study have economic development corporations, credit unions and rotating credit associations and offer classes and incubators. Representatives of these churches spoke of the value of resources in the entrepreneurial process and how this helps people with businesses while creating an entrepreneurial environment. Active churches take a proactive role in promoting self-employment. This includes offering basic networking skills training, the posting of one's business information in a bulletin or offering classes on business etiquette. These churches are usually larger, have more resources and articulate an extensive community-oriented agenda.

## Inactive Churches

Inactive churches are primarily focused on religious activities and offer only limited support for participation in economic activities. While they may provide scholarships to member students, they are most committed to developing and implementing religious functions. The following pastors comment on their objectives vis-à-vis business development:

- No it is not a priority, saving souls is and reaching out to the community. (Community of Faith)
- No the church is my main focus, winning souls. You can go to heaven poor with deliverance from sins; God will prosper you. (The Arc)
- No that is not my job to do that. If people want to have a business that is okay, but my job is to make sure people get saved. (New Zion)

None of the inactive churches provided active support to the entrepreneurial process and this fits within their overall mission since they identified their commitment to "saving souls" as their primary objective. These churches were labeled "Jesus centered" and emphasized "preparation for heaven" as their main priority. Again, these churches make a distinction between doing Godly-centered activities and "worldly" activities. Worldly activities were anything that was not focused on going to heaven and was perceived as being against God's order in the church.

## Discussion

Understanding the way African American churches continue to respond to limited economic opportunities for their members is important in light of the history of race in America. Historically, churches have responded to discrimination and limited opportunities by creating social networks and resources for community empowerment. In this chapter, understanding the way in which African American churches respond as enclaves of opportunities and sources of social support continues to be important for African Americans is vitally important. In many ways, this project helps to explain how the African American church culture fuels entrepreneurial behavior. African American congregations typically offer basic social support services. However, few current studies consider the ways the church contributes to the individual entrepreneurial process by facilitating self-help.

Although this sample was composed of different denominations, Tuskegee and active churches both expressed dual missions as they were concerned with both prophetic and priestly functions. Tuskegee and active churches were prophetic churches in that they were also committed to activities that promoted personal and community development. The pastors in both active and Tuskegee churches connected their beliefs to business support. These themes were communicated to the congregation and are important because they connect the religious tenets of Christianity to the ideas of self-help and business development while creating a business culture within the church. The factors that make the church environment conducive to self-employment include the teachings of the pastor or the senior minister, the resources of the organization, the ideology of the church and the trusting environment the church offers.

Most Sunnyside churches expressed self-help ideas. The exceptions are among the inactive churches which are primarily concerned with priestly functions. Self-help is a common aspiration of the church and has historically been part of its mission, whether churches are interested in exercising self-autonomy to receive higher education or start community development programs. Teaching others to participate in their own development is a common theme, rooted in the Protestant ethic and business ownership is a natural extension of these types of self-help attitudes. Potentially, this project suggests that African American churches exhibit self-help attitudes, again, similar to the Protestant ethic, and there is a connection between values and economic behavior.

This value system suggests a belief in giving to the poor and promoting spiritual, community and economic development. According to this group, self-help and business development is the way God is moving African Americans to take control over their lives. Table 19.3 is a description of the types of business offered by Tuskegee and active congregations.

**Table 19.3    Types of Business Supported by Sunnyside Churches**

| Business Type | No. of Businesses Supported |
| --- | --- |
| Bookstore | 10 |
| Housing | 8 |
| Daycare | 7 |
| Restaurants | 5 |
| Schools | 4 |
| Community Development Corporation | 4 |
| Bible College | 2 |
| Fashion | 2 |
| Landscaping | 2 |
| Events Marketing | 2 |
| Rent Homes | 2 |
| Parking Lots | 2 |
| Housing Development | 2 |

Overall, these congregations are concerned with their members' economic lives, but this manifests itself in different ways. Tuskegee churches not only provided help in self-employment, they also provided bill assistance, job referral and placement services and other forms of help. Almost every church articulated their role as being an agent of support for the African American community. The type of support and the form of self-employment depends on the orientation of the pastor. If the pastor articulated ideas of self-help then, in most cases, the church promoted self-employment in an active and measurable way. If the pastor was not in favor of self-employment or did not see it as a part of the churches' agenda then the churches' participation in the provision of business support was minimal. The size of the church was important because smaller churches were less bureaucratic and had an intimate relationship with their congregants. This relationship allowed greater insight into the personal needs of the congregation and the possibilities of non-traditional forms of help. These churches articulated a strong self-help ideology which promoted the need for its member to "have your own."

The concept of an informal incubator is important in understanding the findings presented in this study because it shows the ways in which minority groups work to create businesses. Specifically, the African American church acts as an informal incubator because many churches provide housing, furniture, telephone, education, technical advice, loans, legal advice and networks. The major difference between informal and formal incubators and the church is that, within the church, people are encouraged to start a business, which is not typical of other business incubators since they assume that people already want to start a business. Therefore, people are, literally, taken from the conceptual stage of desiring to own a business through the process of actually helping them build and maintain one. For formal incubators, already having a business is a prerequisite, but the church offers its members an opportunity to start their own business and create their own opportunities. In some instances the church creates an entrepreneurial community where the members are supported and can operate in an environment of trust. Membership has its privileges and being a member of a Tuskegee church offers its members one or more of the following benefit(s): access to resources, psychological and moral support and opportunities to develop new skills. These benefits increase the overall success rate of the business by reducing the cost of going into business and staying in business.

The church, as an organization, offers similar benefits to the African American community as the enclave offered to immigrant groups. Although the enclave refers to a physical space where immigrants reside, the church offers a number of benefits that are similar to those received by members of ethnic enclaves. Enclaves are a place where immigrant groups obtain affordable housing, find employment and get connected to networks. Enclaves also symbolize and sustain ethnic identity. African American churches provide affordable housing to the elderly, help members with employment opportunities, educational opportunities and business development support and perpetuate a religious identity. The church is an ethnic resource for African Americans because it has an ethnic culture, structural and relational relationships, social capital and multiplex networks that connect the entire group. These resources are crucial for the small business owner. Although all ethnic groups have ethnic resources, the African American church has the potential to exercise these resources in a way that could benefit the business owner as well as the church community.

Generally, Sunnyside churches are involved in entrepreneurial activities that include community programs and business ownership. Most of the literature on business development treats the whole phenomenon as a resource issue, but some churches participate in the entrepreneurial process despite limited resources. This suggest that self-help is viable, even with limited funds, and worth pursuing. Churches can provide a supportive business environment without providing tangible forms of self-help if they promote the ideology of self-employment. Through messages and other forms of pastoral support, people are motivated to pursue self-employment through the messages and behaviors of African American churches, particularly those highlighted in this study.

# Conclusion

This research identifies the way churches contribute to business development activities, serve as an ethnic resource and be a source of social support similar to the networks found in ethnic enclaves. Active and Tuskegee churches support the hypothesis that the value system of the church explains their level of entrepreneurial behavior. This value system describes their entrepreneurial spirit that is part of the subculture of the church. At the core of this value system is a need to achieve, commitment to hard work and a desire to improve the lives of African Americans. This religious asceticism creates churches that in turn promote self-employment as a method of survival and an option for financial freedom coupled with resources. This entrepreneurial climate offers more than resources because it gives people hope and a sense of personal efficacy. People who are part of these churches internalize this entrepreneurial spirit and they adopt it as part of their religious behavior.

The church has historically served as a conduit for self-help for African Americans. Continued limited opportunities necessitate that the African American church continue to facilitate self-help efforts for its members who are marginalized in society. Many churches reported that their community development and self-employment efforts were a necessary and direct response to discrimination and lack of opportunities for the members of their churches. This suggests that pastoral encouragement proved to be an essential factor in encouraging business development. It is well documented that African churches participate in what I label "community entrepreneurship" by forming schools, credit unions and affordable housing units to name a few. However, the role of the African American church in promoting self-employment is less common and contributes to the literature by connecting religious beliefs to tangible economic behaviors and presents a clear commitment to a self-help ideology.

This project was the initial stage in identifying the incidence of African American churches' involvement in the business development of its members. Churches that have visionary pastors, many with business-related histories, and who have experience with self-employment are more likely to actively promote business ownership. This research is limited because, while it describes participation in self-employment, the strength of that participation is not measured. Further study would include measuring the number of businesses each church reports helping, the level and length of participation in the process of entrepreneurial support, evidence supporting the church's responsibility in initiating these enterprises and the success of these enterprises.

# References

Aronson, Robert. 1991. *Self-Employment: A Labor Market Perspective*. Ithaca, NY: IRL Press.

Barnes, Sandra.2004. "Priestly and Prophetic Influences on Black Church Social Services," *Social Problems* 51(2): 202–21.

Barktowski, John P., and Helen A. Regis. 2003. *Charitable Choice: Religion, Race and Poverty in the Post-Welfare Era*. New York: New York University Press.

Bates, Timothy. 1997. *Race, Self-Employment and Upward Mobility: An Illusive American Dream*. Baltimore, MD: The Johns Hopkins University Press.

Billingsley, Andrew. 1999. *Mighty Like a River: The Black Church and Social Reform*. New York: Oxford University Press.

———— and Cleopatra Howard Caldwell. 1994. "The Social Relevance of the Contemporary Black Church," *National Journal of Sociology* 8(3): 403–27.

Bonacich, Edna, and John Modell. 1980. *The Economic Basis of Ethnic Solidarity: Small Business in the Japanese American Community*. Berkeley: University of California Press.

Butler, John Sibley. 2005. *Entrepreneurship and Self-Help Among Black Americans: A Reconsideration of Race and Economics*, 2nd edn. Albany, NY: State University of New York Press.

Chaves, Mark and Lynn M. Higgins. 1992. "Comparing the Community Involvement of Black and White Congregations," *Journal for the Scientific Study of Religion* 31(4): 425–40.

———, and William Tsitsos. 2001. "Congregations and Social Services: What They Do, How They Do It, and With Whom?" *Nonprofit and Voluntary Sector Quarterly* 30: 660–68.

Coleman, John A. 1988. "Social Capital in the Creation of Human Capital," *American Journal of Sociology* 94: 95–120.

Du Bois, W.E.B. [1903] 2007. *The Souls of Black Folk*. Reprint: New York: Cosimos.

Fratoe, Frank A. 1988. "Social Capital of Black Business Owners," *The Review of Black Political Economy* 16(4): 33–50.

Frazier, E. Franklin. 1963. *The Negro Church in America*. New York : Schocken Books.

Hill, Robert B. 1994. "The Role of the Church in Community and Economic Development." *National Journal of Sociology* 8(1): 149–59.

Horton, Hayward Derrick. 1988. "Occupational Differentiation and Black Entrepreneurship: A Sociodemographic Analysis," *National Journal of Sociology* 2(2): 187–201.

Kraybill, Donald B. and Steven M. Nolt. 1995. *Amish Enterprise: From Plows to Profits*. Baltimore, MD: The Johns Hopkins University Press.

Light, Ivan and Carolyn Rosenstein. 1995. "Expanding the interaction Theory of Entrepreneurship," in *The Economic Sociology of Immigration: Essays on Networks, Ethnicity and Entrepreneurship*, ed. Alejandro Portes. New York: Russell Sage Foundation, pp. 166–212.

Lincoln, C. Eric and Lawrence H. Mamiya. 1990. *The Black Church in the African American Experience*. Durham, NC: Duke University Press.

Littlefield, Marci B. 2010. "Social Services, Faith-Based Organizations, and the Poor," *Nonprofit and Voluntary Sector Quarterly* 39: 1014–26.

Portes, Alejandro. 1998. "Social Capital: Its Origins and Applications in Modern Sociology," *Annual Review of Sociology* 24: 1–24.

——— and Robert D. Manning. 1986. *Competitive Ethnic Relations*. Orlando, FL: Academic Press.

Simmel, Georg. 1997. *Essays on Religion*, trans. Horst Jurgen Helle and Ludwig Nieder. New Haven, CT: Yale University Press.

Sherkat, Darren and Christopher G. Ellison. 1999. "Recent Developments and Current Controversies in the Sociology of Religion," *Annual Review of Sociology* 25: 363–94.

Tsitsos, William. 2003. "Race Differences in Congregational Social Service Activity," *Journal for the Scientific Study of Religion* 42: 205–15.

Weber, Max. 1958. *The Protestant Ethic and the Spirit of Capitalism*, trans. Talcott Parsons. New York: Charles Scribner's Sons.

# Not Televised but on Display: Exhibiting and Remembering Vestiges of the Black Freedom Movement

## Derrick R. Brooms

## Introduction

The Black Power Movement of the 1960s and 1970s was one of the most significant developments in the African American experience. Exploding across the United States, Black Power exhibited resistance and creativity, innovation and anger and posited itself as a regal force to redefine race relations in the second half of the twentieth century and beyond. Yet, for all of its accomplishments, Black Power has been excluded from mainstream memory and primarily has been neglected in the cultural landscape. This stands in stark contrast to the modern Civil Rights Movement which is celebrated and heavily memorialized throughout our cultural fabric. This creates a glaring paradox where, deeply embedded within the civil rights memories, are the resulting multiple movements that spawned in the aftermath—such as the Black Power Movement and the Red Power Movement to name a few. Quite frequently, these movements are strategically and intentionally disassociated from both civil rights work and civil rights memory, thus circulating through American memory in forms that are under continuous negotiation and debate. The goal of this chapter is twofold. First, I examine how the Black Freedom Movement is narrated and represented. Second, I examine the ways in which institutions such as museums reinterpret past historical events, thereby creating institutionalized collective memory.

In this study, I use Black Power as a prism to analyze the challenges and demands of exploring and interpreting contemporary history through representations and memory. Additionally, I argue that the past matters. Remembrance is always a form of selective forgetting and memories of the Black Power era are dwarfed by those of the Civil Rights Movement. Moreover, it is quite evident that mainstream ideologies are embedded within the dominant narrative of the Civil Rights Movement which distorts and suppresses as much as it reveals (see Hall 2005). Schwartz (1996) argues that representations of the past can be mobilized to serve partisan purposes, meaning they can be commercialized for the sake of tourism; they can shape a nation's sense of identity, build hegemony, or serve to shore up the political interests of the state; and they can influence the ways that people understand their world. This research explores the many facets of the memory of the modern black freedom struggle of the late 1960s and early 1970s. Memory is used here to refer to the process by which people recall, lay claim to, understand and represent the past (Bodnar 1992). Further, as Confino (1997) notes, memory has come to denote the representation of the past and the making of it into a shared cultural knowledge by successive generations in "vehicles of memory" such as books, films, museums, commemorations, etc.

Until recently, few events of the Civil Rights Movement have helped shape the collective memory of the period. Certain events are denoted as "key events" including among others the *Brown vs. Board of Education* decision of 1954, the sit-ins of the early 1960s and the March on Washington in 1963 (Dwyer 2000; Hall 2005; Lawson and Payne 2006). Not only does this interpretation reduce the entire Civil Rights Movement to a few key events, these events provide for an easy interpretation between good and evil, while allowing many Americans to distance themselves from the nuanced ways in which racism and discrimination permeated throughout both the South and North. Black Power has received even less attention within the cultural landscape and American memory, to the extent that it is part of our collective social amnesia.

In recent years, museums dedicated to memorializing the Civil Rights era have been established in several southern cities. These sites are places where the meaning of civil rights is currently undergoing active negotiation. These museums share the common theme of defining the struggle of African Americans for human rights. Most importantly, the struggle of African Americans for human rights is defined as it is seen through African American eyes and shows the continued concern with the search for roots (Duffy 2001: 14). As Dwyer (2000) notes, these sites, including museum exhibitions, are important in ensuring that the struggles and stories of the Civil Rights era will be remembered. However, objects in the built environment serve as elements in a continuing struggle to define the contemporary significance of the era and, depending on how the movement is framed, there is as much remembering as there is forgetting. It also shows who will be included and what legacies will be retold. For instance, the National Civil Rights Museum in Memphis, Tennessee, displays social movements that were ignited by the Civil Rights Movement, such as the Red Power Movement, Black Power Movement, Women's Movement, and Gay and Lesbian Movement, thus allowing visitors to see the national impact and importance of the Civil Rights Movement. Additionally, these connections show that the legacy of the Civil Rights Movement lives on today.

As a major turning point in American race relations, Fuller (2006) contends that the movement is constantly used as a reference point for judging the state of contemporary race relations. Similarly, Gray (1997) has argued that representations of the Civil Rights era convey contemporary political and cultural hopes; in particular, the belief that America has transcended racism (ibid.: 351). This allows for a mainstream perspective that the Civil Rights era is over, because its soldiers succeeded in dismantling racist structures and in guaranteeing equality before the law. This view diminishes the role of the Black Power era in contributing to the change brought about in the Civil Rights era. However, the fight for civil rights continues and, therefore, memories of the era, which necessarily extend beyond 1968, must be kept alive so as to avoid willful social forgetting and collective amnesia across regional location and generations. Inasmuch as the Civil Rights era is heralded for its triumphs, it is celebrated in our cultural landscape at the expense of Black Power and all of its accomplishments.[1]

---

1    A "Civil Rights Bill" was passed in Michigan during the 2006 elections; the bill prohibits the use of race in hiring practices and educational initiatives. The bill was controversial because it was supported by the Ku Klux Klan and dubbed "Civil Rights Initiative"; the bill was proposed under the false pretense that it would provide equality.

# Methodology

The settings for this research project are Black-centered museums in the United States. The first level of narrowing down the list of museums to analyze was purely existential. Having created a list of over one hundred Black-centered museums, the focus was narrowed to museums of history and culture. The second level of narrowing down the list of museums to analyze was geographic and relied on what was accessible to the researcher. Data for this study were part of a larger project whereby museum exhibits were reviewed over a seven-year period, from 2006 until 2013. The research conducted for this project is based on the reviews and analyses of 15 museum sites, with specific attention given to a commemorative exhibit. The commemorative museum exhibit used in this study was on extended display for a year. Through preliminary research, it became clear that multiple windows into the world of museum exhibiting exist. Accordingly, several methodologies are employed in conducting this research, including interpretative methodology and content analysis of the exhibit, the museum, and a variety of different texts. Additionally, I use a proposal for the cultural landscape in Chicago as a key moment in the contest over Black Power memory.

## Ethnographic Methods

The primary method of inquiry used in this research was content analysis. This method included examining museum collections, analyzing exhibits and engaging in other museum activities where appropriate and applicable (such as tours, presentations and lectures). These observations set the stage for accessing a primary window of investigating the ways in which collective memories are institutionalized.

Content analysis provided access to the first window for investigating racial representations in museums as exhibited in temporary as well as permanent displays. Ethnographies, which "stand in" as written textual re-presentations of other cultures and group identities, have recently been subjected to critique for their pretense to "realism" (Marcus and Fischer 1986). In the current study, visual representations and narrations of the Black Power era in museums and the cultural landscape were subjected to the same type of critique. In interpreting exhibits, methods were employed within the field of cultural studies that explore issues such as signifying practices, negotiating standards of balance and objectivity, informational content, and representations of the alternate narrative. These cultural studies concepts explain a variety of approaches to representation that interconnect the disciplines of anthropology, sociology, museum studies, ethnic studies and art historical models of representation. Using cultural studies techniques, issues of race, culture, identity and memory were investigated.

## Research Sites

I examine exhibition practices within museums and the research findings presented here focus on exhibitions at five of the 15 locations reviewed. Each of these sites was chosen because they housed an exhibit that focused on the Black Power era during the fieldwork period for this project. The research sites include the Black Holocaust Museum (Milwaukee, WI), the Northwest African American Museum (Seattle, WA), the African American Museum of Iowa (Cedar Rapids, IA), the Du Sable Museum of African American History and Culture (Chicago, IL), and the National Civil Rights Museum (Memphis, TN). The Black Holocaust Museum was founded in 1988 as a communal institution. The intended purpose of the museum was to share the history, tragedy, suffering and torment of the "peculiar institution" of slavery and its aftermath following the Civil War and up to the Civil Rights Movement. According to James Cameron, the museum's founder, the museum was devoted to preserving the history of lynching in the United States and the struggle of Black people for equality. Due to financial constraints, the museum closed its doors in August 2008; however, a virtual version of the museum opened in 2012. The Northwest African American Museum opened in 2008 and focuses on the histories, arts and cultures of people of African descent. The museum's mission is to present and preserve the connections between the Pacific Northwest and people of African descent, and to celebrate Black experiences in the United States. The African American Museum of Iowa opened in 2003 with a stated mission to preserve, exhibit and teach the African American heritage of Iowa. In Chicago, Margaret and Charles Burroughs founded the Ebony Museum of Negro History and Art in 1961 in the front room of their home. In 1968, the museum was renamed to the DuSable Museum in honor of Jean Baptiste Point DuSable, a Haitian fur trader and the first non-Native American permanent settler in Chicago. The purpose of the museum is to improve public understanding of Black history, art, culture and contributions to the nation and the world. Noted as one of the premier heritage and cultural museums in the United States, the National Civil Rights Museum was founded in 1991 and conjoins the site of the Lorraine Motel in Memphis where Dr. Martin Luther King, Jr. was assassinated in 1968. The main goal of the museum is to bolster public knowledge in the lessons of the Civil Rights Movement and its worldwide influence.

## Collective and Collected Memory

Olick and Levy (1997) use a case study of official representations of the Holocaust in the Federal Republic of Germany to address the ways that collective memory constrains political claim making. In contrast to the commonly held views that the past is either durable or malleable, they characterize collective memory in political culture as an ongoing process of negotiation through time. Additionally, other researchers have broadly noted the ways in which individuals reinterpret past historical events or figures using presently constructed definitions (Ducharme and Fine 1995; Schwartz 1996, 1997). In this investigation, I note the link between the production of social memory within the frames of remembrance and collective memory that, therefore, situate memory as indubitably a social phenomenon (Irwin-Zarecka 1994).

Recollection of the past is an active and constructive process, not a simple matter of retrieving information. To remember is to place a part of the past "in the service of conceptions and needs of the present" (Schwartz 1996: 374). Underlying this explanation of collective memory is the active past that forms our identities. Specifically, history is the remembered past to which we no longer have an "organic" relation, while collective memory is based on the relevance of the past to the present. Group memberships provide the materials for memory and prod the individual into recalling particular events and forgetting others (Olick 1999). According to Halbwachs ([1925] 1992), memories become generalized "imagos" over time and such imagos require a social context for their preservation. Memories, in this sense, are as much the products of the symbols and narratives available publicly, and of the social means for storing and transmitting them, as they are the possessions of individuals.

The goal of this chapter is not so much to elaborate on the concept of collective memory as it is to apply this concept to the analysis of museum work. I use ethnographic data collected at five black-centered museums to explore the ways that museum exhibits help create institutional collective memories. Additionally, I examine how these constructions are played out within the cultural landscape through street names. I argue that museums' exhibiting practices: 1) are racial projects that allow for African American authenticity and autonomy, and 2) empower ethnic groups by providing a lens through which they can (re) create themselves with a positive racial self-identity. More specifically, I argue that black-centered museums, through their visual representations and narratives of African American life during the Black Power Era, create an institutionalized collective memory of identity and triumph that is broadened with each additional story told.

## Findings: Defining and Narrating Black Power and Freedom

In the museums examined for this study, the Black Power era was defined as a key period in the African American experience. The Black Power era embodies a bridge that connects Black desires of freedom from previous centuries to the current time. In a word, the Black Power era was "revolutionary" in myriad social, cultural and political ways. According to Joseph (2009), the Black Power era (1954–75) remains a controversial and understudied period in American history. These years parallel the golden age of modern civil rights activism and found kinship in ideas of anti-colonialism and Third World liberation movements. Black Power emerged within the political struggles that marked the post-World War II world. During the latter half of the modern civil rights era, "Black Power" became a rallying cry, as blacks expressed strong nationalist and pan-Africanist sentiments centered on self-identity and self-determination (Hamilton and Carmichael 1992). In general, Black Power incorporated a myriad of ideas including group solidarity, self-respect and the guarantee of life, liberty and the pursuit of a good life for all Americans, especially Blacks. This period is also defined by the assertive actions of Black people in determining their own leadership, consumer patterns and activity, and the development of a positive self-image.

Given this multifaceted perspective, much of what was called Black power was viewed as a militant extension of race politics and Black separatism. This is especially so given how this ideology was incorporated by different factions across Black communities and how it was perceived by white America. Black Power has its roots in a nationalist program represented by Martin Delaney in the nineteenth century, and Marcus Garvey, Malcolm X and the Nation of Islam continued this philosophy throughout the twentieth century. The Black Power slogan was popularized by Stokeley Carmichael via his grass-roots organizing activities of the mid-1960s. It was incorporated into the rhetoric of the Black Panther Party (most notably in their 10-Point Program) and later used when the Black Power movement evolved from confrontations in the streets of America to college campuses with the establishment of Black Studies programs and into electoral politics as well (Dawson 1996).

## Politicizing the Present

As Morris (1999) notes, the impact of the Civil Rights Movement on race relations and the nation's social fabric has been monumental. This pivotal movement has had significant influence on social movements in many countries. The intent here is not to provide a detailed account of the modern Civil Rights Movement, as such accounts are available in the vast literature that has emerged over the last thirty years (see Morris 1984; Garrow 1986; Robnett 1997). Having previously stated its prominence, the purpose here is to present an analysis of how the Black Freedom Era has been (re)negotiated in the cultural landscape and museum exhibitions, while also examining the different historic moments within the period that are selected for remembering.

The Black Freedom Movement challenged the United States to live up to its stated ideals of racial equality, citizenship and democracy. It dared America to become a nation with equal justice for all. Activists and participants of the movement struggled to end discrimination and segregation and to gain equal access to voting rights, education and public facilities. Museum exhibits focusing on the Black Freedom Era attempt to capture these struggles through the location of the displays, artifacts, voices and people of the movement. However, when studying any museum exhibition, the first thing we need to know is the relationship between that exhibition and its political and economic setting (Potter and Leone 1992). Stories of the past are structured by contemporary relationships among groups directly affected. Within the past few decades, two key developments of Black Freedom history and memory occurred in Chicago. First was the proposal to rename a section of a street, West Monroe, to Fred Hampton Way and the second was the DuSable Museum's commemorative exhibit, "A Right Given but Denied," which was on display as a traveling exhibit in 2006. Each of these cases work to bring the racial past into the present as they challenge how the struggle is remembered and denote the attempts to institutionalize these memories.

## Renegotiating the Cultural Landscape

In March 2006, Alderwoman Madeline Haithcock surprised her fellow politicians when she proposed to rename a portion of Monroe Street on Chicago's Westside to "Chairman Fred Hampton Way" to honor the slain "hero." Hampton founded the Chicago chapter of the Black Panther Party in November 1968 and immediately established a community service program that provided free breakfast for schoolchildren and a medical clinic that did not charge patients for treatment. Hampton also taught political education classes and initiated a community control-of-police project. As articulated by J. Edgar Hoover, then director of the Federal Bureau of Investigation, the activities of the Black Panthers in Chicago were viewed as incendiary and eventually led to an all-out assault on the organization by the Chicago police. In 1969, the Black Panther Party headquarters on West Monroe Street was raided three times and over a hundred members were arrested. In December 1969, police raided the Panther headquarters—they later claimed that the Panthers had opened fire and a shoot-out took place—where Hampton and fellow Black Panther leader Mark Clark were gunned down. While conflicting accounts (and recounts) emerged, perceptions of the incident were divided along racial lines. Supporters of the Black Panther Party, especially within Black communities, continue to hail Hampton as a hero, while the mainstream has vilified him as a "cop killer." The proposed street name infuriated Fraternal Order of Police president Mark Donahue who called it a "dark day" in the city's history "when we honor someone who would advocate killing policemen." Additionally, some of the families of police officers killed in the line of duty mobilized in opposition.[2] Through newspaper editorials and speeches at local government meetings, outspoken critics were successful in halting the renaming of West Monroe Street.

---

2    The debates that the "Fred Hampton Way" sparked were covered within the local media; see Fran Speilman, "Street Name: 'Embarrassment' or fair tribute," *Chicago Sun Times*, March 1, 2006. The uproar caused by the proposal motivated an influential alderman to end honorary street designations in Chicago. Mayor Richard Daley's support of this measure is evidenced in his response, "Everybody will want a street sign." By identifying "every other citizen" as equally deserving, Daley strips Hampton from historical significance and assigns him ordinary status. Clearly, Hampton's reputational legacy is called into question and his importance is denigrated.

Commemorating Fred Hampton not only highlights tensions within the political landscape, it also sheds light on the significance of interpreting and remembering past moments for present generations. Many of the Black activists promoting the renaming of the street supported this measure because it was based on both Hampton's legacy as a social activist and as a memorial to his (unjust) death at the hands of the police (see Wilkins and Clark 1973).[3] In contrast, police officials and others bemoaned the proposal because of, from their understanding, Hampton's insistence on, if needed, racial violence (i.e., his support of blacks arming themselves in self-defense and the Black Panther Party's surveillance of the police). The Fred Hampton street-renaming controversy is the latest in a long line of struggles over and for the use of memory (and individual legacies) in contemporary representations (such as Black Freedom memory). With this muddled history, the proposal to rename West Monroe Street fits into a growing commemorative pattern in the United States, where the politics of memory often conflict with mainstream national narratives (see Alderman 2006).

The challenges brought forth by the Hampton street-renaming proposal is a microcosm of both civil rights and Black Power history in American public memory and brings attention to challenges wrought by museums in representing the past. The Hampton proposal is indicative of the problematic nature of weaving African Americans into the cultural fabric of this nation. Additionally, reactions to the Hampton proposal point out how historical events and individuals are remembered, what those memories mean, how they matter and how they are politicized within the current landscape. For instance, Dwyer (2006) notes that the numerous forms of civil rights commemoration (streets, schools, museums, etc.) create a multi-layered environment that, through its symbolic power and the large number of visitors, serves as a forum in the continuing struggle to define the contemporary significance of the Civil Rights Movement. Memorials often open new chapters of struggle associated with the meaning and significance of the past. The arrival of the movement's memorial legacy on the cultural landscape offers insight into that legacy's victories and shortcomings, especially since memorials are elements of the built environment that help (un)fix and represent social identities (ibid.: 6). In institutionalizing collective memory, museums keep alive those pasts which may have present (and/or future) functions that are associated with the mechanisms of memory: place, narrative and interpretation. To these points, what is to be said of Black Power history and its silencing within the cultural landscape and, by extension, American memory?

The Black Freedom Movement is remembered predominantly through a master narrative and, until recently, few events of the movement have helped shape collective memory of the period. Certain events of the period are denoted as "key" events: the *Brown vs. Board of Education* decision of 1954, the Montgomery bus boycott of 1955, the Little Rock school integration crisis in 1957, the sit-ins of the early 1960s, the March on Washington in 1963 and the Alabama campaigns of 1963 (Birmingham) and 1965 (Selma). Not only does this interpretation reduce the entire Black Freedom Movement to a few key events, but these events provide for an easy interpretation between good and evil, thus, enabling many Americans to distance themselves from the ugliness of bigotry. The master narrative is not a multi-layered approach to understanding the era, especially since the Black Power

---

3    The historical record of [white] police brutality against Black men in Chicago, IL has come under fervent review in recent political circles. Much of this fury has stemmed from a special prosecutors' report ("The Chicago Torture Report") that concluded Chicago police officers tortured dozens of black suspects over the course of two decades. Another report comes from a 1993 film, "The End of the Nightstick: Confronting Police Brutality in Chicago," which investigates charges of institutional racism, violence and cover-up. Similarly, in 1999, U.S. Rep. Danny K. Davis (D-Chicago) asked then-President Bill Clinton to appoint a federal task force to investigate incidents of police brutality and misconduct.

and Civil Rights movements both shared the same time period. The major differences, of course, were how each was defined and accepted (or not, in the case of Black Power) by mainstream society, and the images used to communicate rhetoric, values and demands. For instance, images of the two movements stand in stark contrast to one another. Consider the following scenarios: a sagacious and non-threatening Martin Luther King versus an angry and threatening Malcolm X; a reserved and humble Rosa Parks versus a demanding and seemingly lawless Angela Davis, and a peaceful and nonviolent march versus gun-toting and militant Black Panther protestors.

## Recontextualizing the Black Freedom Movement

The DuSable Museum's "A Right Given But Denied" exhibit and the National Civil Rights Museum's section entitled "Organizations (1910–1940)" both merit attention for their remapping of Civil Rights memory. Both exhibits explore the circumstances that ignited the Black Freedom Movement during the mid-twentieth century. Additionally, they both explore events prior to and during the traditional framing of the Civil Rights Movement, including developing strategies for change following the Civil War, the forms of Black protest at the dawn of the modern movement, highlights of the Chicago movement, and how the movement continues today. In doing so, we can see how the Black Power Movement, its activists, organizations and culture, overlapped the Civil Rights Movement.

The "A Right Given But Denied" exhibit opens with two images of Dr. Martin Luther King Jr.; the first is a cast bronze bust of the civil rights leader, while the second is a reproduction of a photograph titled "In Memory of Dr. King." In contrast to the master-narrative, the exhibit attempts to provide a historic context for the Black Freedom Movement by chronicling the African American fight for freedom throughout the American experience. In achieving this goal, the exhibit uses the Declaration of Independence to frame the legacy of injustice that African Americans have faced. The Declaration proclaims that "all men are created equal" and pronounces such lofty goals as "freedom, justice, and equality." This line of rhetoric stands in stark contrast to the historic legacy of legal and extra-legal measures used to deny African American freedom. To further emphasize this point, replications of the Emancipation Proclamation, in addition to the 13th, 14th and 15th Amendments, are also displayed. These amendments were meant to affirm African American equality by also declaring slavery illegal, African American citizenship guaranteed, and suffrage a right for all U.S. citizens regardless of race, color, or previous condition of servitude. The Emancipation Proclamation was a political ploy used by President Abraham Lincoln to "declare" African American freedom during the Civil War. The Proclamation only freed blacks within Confederate states and, since these states seceded from the Union and established their own government/constitution, did not impact enslaved Africans in the northern states. As a political ploy, that allowed Lincoln's army to recruit African Americans, the Proclamation has been hailed for its "symbolic freedom" of Blacks.

A textual reference within the exhibit's "Slavery and the Right to Freedom" section notes that early African American experience did not reflect America's founding principles of life, liberty and justice for all. As the text notes, African Americans were sold as property and their movement throughout the country was severely restricted. The text is followed by four images. The first is a picture of 50–60 half-naked enslaved Africans; they are posed for the picture, standing, sitting and squatting, and looking directly at the camera. The second image is a replica of an auction advertisement for the sale of enslaved Africans and the third image is a replica bill of sale, listing several enslaved Africans among the property of an estate. The final image is a picture of enslaved Africans picking cotton. These four images are used to depict the hardships of African American life during slavery, which is an important rhetorical strategy in displaying enslavement experiences in many Black-centered museums (Brooms 2011). Continuing with the theme of hardship and the fight to freedom is the section on Jim Crow. The text explains that during the Jim Crow era, African American inferiority was reinforced through laws and constitutional provisions by separating blacks and whites in public spaces and preventing African American males from working. Also noted is the "separate but equal" precedent that was established in the 1896 *Plessy vs. Ferguson* case. Jim Crow, and the state-sanctioned mandates that preceded it, is an important antecedent to the Civil Rights Movement, as it provided the context in which the movement took shape. Morris (1999) argues that blacks in the South were controlled politically, primarily, because their disenfranchisement barred them from participating in the political process. As a result, their constitutional rights were violated because they could not serve as judges nor participate as jurors. Economically, blacks were kept at the bottom of the economic social order because they lacked even minimal control in that institution.

The exhibit provides further historical details by displaying a 1939 picture of the Pullman Porters and a brief mention of A. Phillip Randolph's proposal for a March on Washington Movement before turning attention to events that fit within the traditional Civil Rights era time-frame. Pictures of Thurgood Marshall, the Montgomery bus boycotts, and student sit-ins highlight this section. Marshall served as the head of the NAACP Legal Defense Fund, argued the *Brown vs. Board of Education* case of Topeka, Kansas, and served as the first African American judge of the Supreme Court. Marshall's inclusion emphasizes his role within the movement and his legacy in Civil Rights memory as a champion for justice and equality. A picture of Rosa Parks anchors the Montgomery bus boycotts and Parks's refusal to give up her seat has turned into a symbolic act of defiance and civil disobedience. Similarly, the exhibit's pictures of student sit-ins illustrate the conscientious and potentially dangerous decisions of many young Americans to attempt to dismantle segregationist laws. The two displayed pictures of student sit-ins offer polarizing visuals of activists versus aggressors. The first picture is of two African American students being dragged in the street by police officers, while the second picture displays a mixed-race group of student protestors staging a sit-in in front of the Wieboldt Store on South State Street in downtown Chicago in response to police violence. On the one hand, the museum visitor gets a glimpse of the brutality imposed upon activists and, on the other hand, visitors see the steadfast use of nonviolent, peaceful protest in action that crossed racial lines. According to Morris (1999), sit-ins were especially important to the modern Civil Rights Movement because these protests became a mass movement themselves, which spread throughout the South and mobilized an important base. The sit-ins also had a lasting impact as they led to demonstrations to end racial segregation at pools, churches and other businesses and institutions. Additionally, these protests led to the establishment of the Student Non-violent Coordinating Committee (SNCC), a social movement organization of students, and provided a forum for white college students to participate in the Civil Rights Movement.

The 1963 March on Washington and the Civil Rights Act of 1964 are highlighted within the exhibit, as they are considered key triumphs of the Civil Rights Movement within the national narrative. A picture of the marchers at the ground level is displayed and it allows visitors to see the multiple ways that people participated in the march and how they asserted their identity. For instance, male marchers wore signs that read "I Am A Man." These visuals denounce the American apartheid system in which blacks were forced into second-class citizenship status that disallowed black males from assuming full manhood. The symbolism carried in the "We Demand Marchers" image is quite powerful. The photographer has captured an image of men and women carrying a host of "We Demand" signs insisting on ending police brutality, while also requesting decent jobs and passage of voting rights legislation. All of the signs petitioned for these changes to occur immediately, as each ended with "NOW!" Museumgoers view a familiar aerial photo of the March on Washington showing the crowd stretching past the Washington Monument. It is estimated that over 250,000 people were in attendance. The audience turn-out is important in establishing the March as a resounding success. Again, in confirming its laudatory achievements, a picture of the meeting with President Kennedy, Dr. King, and the organizers of the March is displayed. Additional leaders in the photograph include A. Phillip Randolph, Roy Wilkins and Whitney Young. The meeting verifies governmental approval of the March, which was a key political victory for the organizers. However, what is missing from the collection of pictures is the role of women in the March and the tightrope walk that the presidential cabinet enforced upon the speakers. The sanctioning, and required revisions, of John Lewis's speech garnered much attention for its imposition of freedom of speech and staunch rejection of governmental criticism in a public forum (see Fairclough 1997). Furthermore, the leadership, engagement and support of women in the Black Freedom Movement are critical elements that still remain underscored in remembering the movement (Blumberg 1990; Crawford et al. 1990; Collier-Thomas and Franklin 2001; Olson 2001; Holsaert et al. 2012). These omissions are important as they reveal a, still, patriarchal viewing and collective memory of the era.

The exhibit concludes with a video trilogy on the deaths of Medgar Evers, Emmett Till, and the Birmingham Four. The 1955 killing of Emmett Till was a brutal affair and served as a painstaking reminder of the brutality of white supremacist ideology. Till's mother and the Black press generated national publicity by allowing an open casket funeral, to fully display the grotesque injustice of his death.[4] Because of the widespread attention of the lynching, the brutality and raw racism of the Jim Crow regime were displayed on a national stage where it was debated and denounced (Morris 1999). African Americans were further enraged when the murderers were acquitted of the charges. The video fits into a recent thrust to resurrect the life of Emmett Till and renegotiate the centrality of his death to the modern Civil Rights Movement. His killing inspired blacks throughout the North and South to engage in dismantling Jim Crow. Hudson-Weems (1998) argues that Till was *the* catalyst of the Civil Rights Movement and his exclusion from Civil Rights history neglects the importance of Till to the lives of many indelibly affected by it. Till's death was one of many brutal killings in which blacks were the targets of racial violence.

Similarly, Evers's death in 1963 enraged Civil Rights activists and sympathizers throughout the nation. Evers was shot in the back in the front yard of his home after returning from an NAACP meeting. In fact, he was murdered just hours after President John F. Kennedy's speech on national television in support of civil rights (see Vollers 1995; Birnbaum and Taylor 2000). The title of the video dedicated to Medgar Evers quipped, "Medgar you did not die in vain." The Birmingham Four video pays homage to the September 15, 1963 murders of four young African American girls attending Sunday school at the Sixteenth Baptist Church in Birmingham, Alabama. Denise McNair, Cynthia Wesley, Carole Robertson and Addie Mae Collins, aged 11–14, were killed while 20 others were injured, when a bomb exploded at the church, which was also a center for civil rights meetings. The bombing occurred just 18 days after the March on Washington and several days after the courts had ordered the desegregation of Birmingham's schools. Clearly, the message of the videos denotes that slain Civil Rights activists serve as both motivation and purpose for others who participate in the cause afterward.

---

4    Emmett Till's body was found in Mississippi's Tallahatchie River weighted down by a seventy-five pound cotton gin fan that was tied around his neck with barbed wire. His body was barely recognizable; one eye was gouged out and his head was crushed.

# Conclusion

In the past 20 years, there has been an explosion of museums dedicated to preserving and interpreting the African American experience in America. This explosion is due to increased interest in memorial work where incorporating cultural history and social movement history in the memorial landscape has been spawned through new museum sites, expanded museum collections and changes to the civic infrastructure (i.e., proposals to (re)name streets, schools and community centers). Much of this work has benefited from significant contributions from the public and private sectors. More importantly, the contest over historical memories extends into the present day. Much of this is a result of continued national and international diversity efforts to not only exhibit the African American experience, but to institutionalize it by establishing several key sites, including an African American museum on the National Mall in Washington, DC that has now become a realization and is set to open in 2015.[5]

The historical legacy of Black Power is that it established a world with people of African descent at its center and gave birth to the founding of Black Studies programs and departments, Afrocentricity, Kwanzaa, Black student unions on college campuses and other Black-centered programs (Joseph 2006, 2007). Other groups have followed these examples as women, Latinos and GLBTs now promote their own political agendas rather than acquiescing to notions of assimilation. Black Power spanned across multiple continents and offered new words, images and political frameworks that impacted and influenced a wide spectrum of American and global communities. Before contemporary discussions of multiculturalism and diversity entered America's national lexicon, Black Power promoted new definitions of citizenship, identity and democracy that, although racially specific, inspired a variety of multiracial groups in their efforts to shape a new world.

Museums are sites of a contention to define and use history because Black Power era history and memory are still contested subjects in modern America. In many museums, this era is dwarfed by the national Civil Rights narrative and becomes posited as an asterisk. The national Civil Rights narrative suggests that the social movement ended in 1968, when laws had been passed and, seemingly, many of the institutional needs of Black communities had been met. This narrative constrains Black Power participants and events onto a cultural "sideline," as if their efforts are relatively less significant than participants in more mainstream organizations and institutions. Exploring the Black Power era presents a compelling counter-narrative to the lauded "successes" of the previous decades. Narratives and representations of government infiltration, sabotage, cooptation, harassment and exploitation of Black institutions and organizations, coupled with racially motivated violence against Blacks, are not memories that provide for an easy digestion of the contradictions of American democracy, equality and freedom; the great "triumphs" of the Civil Rights movement. In fact, the Black Power era unmasks many of the failures of what is traditionally referred to as the "Civil Rights Movement." The narratives and contests of the Black Power era are needed now more than ever for fuller and richer representations of contemporary American history. As Lubar (1997) asserts, exhibits and representations should not be limited to reminiscence or commemoration. They should add perspective by aspiring to a greater critical distance and by putting the artifacts and story in context. This would aid in our understanding the legacy of the past, as our memories of the era can also play a critical role in shaping our personal, group and political identities.

---

5    Ruffins (1998) notes that the idea of an African American museum on the Mall in Washington, DC surfaced over a ten-year period between 1984 and 1994. One of the main questions that the advisory committee had to consider was the presentation of slavery, which has been interpreted as a holocaust in many African American circles.

The differences in museum presentations of the Civil Rights Movement and the Black Power era demonstrate that memory is not knowledge *of* the past—it is knowledge *from* the past. As such, it is thought to advance and validate identities, fuel grievances and give meaning and narrative coherence to individuals and collectivities (Margalit 2002:14). Unlike the distant past, exhibiting the recent past is wrought with challenges and demands of living memories (see Irwin-Zarecka 1994; Zelizer 1995; Schwartz 1997). For instance, in exploring the distant past, curators often avoid many of the contested aspects of historical interpretation because of the public's lack of a direct or personal connection to that history (Brooms 2011). As illustrated by the discussions of the Fred Hampton Boulevard proposal and the range of exhibits on the Civil Rights Movement and the Black Power Era, the recent past forces both curators and visitors into an uncomfortable, and often unacknowledged, confrontation over the meaning, ownership, complexity and interpretation of the recent past (see Yeingst and Bunch 1997). The museum, therefore, is a site where the struggle over interpretation of history is fought out in the exhibit representations.

## Acknowledgements

This research was partially supported by an Intramural Research Incentive Grant from the Office of the Executive Vice President for Research and Innovation at the University of Louisville, grant number 50851. The opinions and conclusions expressed herein are solely those of the author and should not be construed as representing the opinions or policy of any unit of the University.

## References

Alderman, Derek, H. 2006. "Street Names as Memorial Arenas: The Reputational Politics of Commemorating Martin Luther King Jr. in a Georgia County." in *The Civil Rights Movement in American Memory*, eds. Renee C. Romano and Leigh Raiford. Athens, GA: University of Georgia Press, pp. 67–95.

Birnbaum, Jonathan and Clarence Taylor, eds. 2000. *Civil Rights Since 1787: A Reader on the Black Struggle*. New York: New York University Press.

Blumberg, Rhoda Lois. 1990. "Women in the Civil Rights Movement: Reform or Revolution?" *Dialectical Anthropology* 15(2–3): 133–9.

Bodnar, John. 1992. *Remaking America: Public Memory, Commemoration, and Patriotism in the Twentieth Century*. Princeton, NJ: Princeton University Press.

Brooms, Derrick R. 2011. "Lest We Forget: Exhibiting (and Remembering) Slavery in African American Museums." *Journal of African American Studies* 15: 508–23.

Collier-Thomas, Bettye and V.P. Franklin. 2001. *Sisters of the Struggle: African-American Women in the Civil Rights-Black Power Movement*. New York: New York University Press.

Confino, Alon. 1997. "Collective Memory and Cultural History: Problems and Method." *American Historical Review* 102(5): 1386–403.

Crawford, Vickie, Jacqueline Rouse and Barbara Woods, eds. 1990. *Women in the Civil Rights Movement: Trailblazers and Torchbearers*. New York: Carlson.

Dawson, Michael C. 1996. "Black Power in 1996 and the Demonization of African Americans." *Political Science and Politics* 29(3):456–61.

Ducharme, Lori J. and Gary Allen Fine. 1995. "The Construction of Demonization of Nonpersonhood: Constructing the Traitorous Reputation of Benedict Arnold." *Social Forces* 73: 1309–31.

Duffy, Terrence M. 2001. "Museums of 'Human Suffering' and the Struggle for Human Rights." *Museum International* 209(53,1): 10–16.

Dwyer, Owen J. 2000. "Interpreting the Civil Rights Movement: Place, Memory, and Conflict." *Professional Geographer* 52(4): 660–71.

———. 2006. "Interpreting the Civil Rights Movement: Contradiction, Confirmation, and the Cultural Landscape." in *The Civil Rights Movement in American Memory*, eds. Renee C. Romano and Leigh Raiford. Athens, GA: University of Georgia Press, pp. 5–27.

Fairclough, Adam. 1997. "Civil Rights and the Lincoln Memorial: The Censored Speeches of Robert R. Moton (1922) and John Lewis (1993)." *The Journal of Negro History* 82(4): 408–16.

Fuller, Jennifer. 2006 "Debating the Present through the Past: Representations of the Civil Rights Movement in the 1990s." in *The Civil Rights Movement in American Memory*, eds. Renee C. Romano and Leigh Raiford. Athens, GA: University of Georgia Press, pp. 167–96.

Garrow, David. 1986. *Bearing the Cross: Martin Luther King, Jr., and the Southern Christian Leadership Conference*. New York: Morrow.

Gray, Herman. 1997. "Remembering Civil Rights: Television, Memory and the 1960s." in *The Revolution Wasn't Televised: Sixties Television and Social Conflict*, eds. Lynn Spigel and Michael Curtin. New York: Routledge Press, pp. 349–58.

Halbwachs, Maurice. [1925] 1992. "The Reconstruction of the Past." in *On Collective Memory*, trans. Lewis S. Coser. Chicago, IL: University Of Chicago Press.

Hall, Jacquelyn Dowd. 2005. "The Long Civil Rights Movement and the Political Uses of the Past." *Journal of American History* 3: 1233–63.

Hamilton, Charles V. and Stokely Carmichael. 1992. *Black Power: The Politics of Liberation*. New York: Vintage.

Holsaert, Faith S., Martha Prescod, Norman Noonan, Judy Richardson, Betty Garman Robinson, Jean Smith Young and Dorothy M. Zellner, eds. 2012. *Hands on the Freedom Plow: Personal Accounts by Women in SNCC*. Champaign: University of Illinois Press.

Hudson-Weems, Clenora. 1998. "Resurrecting Emmett Till: The Catalyst of the Modern Civil Rights Movement." *Journal of Black Studies* 29(2): 179–88.

Irwin-Zarecka, Iwona. 1994. *Frames of Remembrance: The Dynamics of Collective Memory*. New Brunswick, NJ: Transaction Publishers.

Joseph, Peniel E. 2006. *The Black Power Movement: Rethinking the Civil Rights-Black Power Era*. New York: Routledge Press.

———. 2007. *Waiting 'til the Midnight Hour: A Narrative History of Black Power in America*. New York: Holt.

———. 2009. "The Black Power Movement, Democracy, and America in the King Years." *The American Historical Review* 114(4): 1001–16.

Lawson, Steven F. and Charles Payne. 2006. *Debating the Civil Rights Movement, 1945–1968 (Debating Twentieth-Century America)*. New York: Rowman & Littlefield Publishers.

Lubar, Steven. 1997. "Exhibiting Memories." in *Exhibiting Dilemmas: Issues of Representation at the Smithsonian*, eds. Amy Henderson and Adrienne L. Kaeppler. Washington, DC: Smithsonian Institution Press, pp. 15–27.

Marcus, George E. and Michael M.J. Fischer. 1986. *Anthropology as Cultural Critique: An Experimental Moment in the Human Sciences*. Chicago, IL: University of Chicago Press.

Margalit, Avishai. 2002. *The Ethics of Memory*. Cambridge, MA: Harvard University Press.

Morris, Aldon. 1999. "A Retrospective on the Civil Rights Movement: Political and Intellectual Landmarks." *Annual Review of Sociology* 25: 517–39.

Morris, Aldon. 1984. *The Origins of the Civil Rights Movement: Black Communities Organizing for Change.* New York: Free Press.

Olick, Jeffrey K. 1999. "Collective Memory: The Two Cultures." *Sociological Theory* 17(3): 333–48.

———— and David Levy. 1997. "Collective Memory and Cultural Constraint: Holocaust Myth and Rationality in German Politics." *American Sociological Review* 62: 921–36.

Olson, Lynne. 2001. *Freedom's Daughters: The Unsung Heroines of the Civil Rights Movement from 1830 to 1970.* New York: Scribner.

Potter Jr., Parker B. and Mark P. Leone. 1992. "Establishing the Roots of Historical Consciousness in Modern Annapolis, Maryland." in *Museums and Communities: The Politics of Public Culture*, eds. Ivan Karp and Steven D. Lavine. Washington, DC: Smithsonian Institutional Press, pp. 476–505.

Robnett, Belinda. 1997. *How Long? How Long?: African American Women in the Struggle for Civil Rights.* New York: Oxford University Press.

Ruffins, Fath Davis. 1998. "Culture Wars Won and Lost, Part II: The National African-American Museum Project." *Radical History Review* 70: 78–101.

Schwartz, Barry. 1997. "Collective Memory and History: How Abraham Lincoln became a Symbol of Racial Equality." *Sociological Quarterly* 38: 469–96.

————. 1996. "Memory As a Cultural System: Abraham Lincoln in World War II." *American Sociological Review* 61: 908–27.

Vollers, Maryanne. 1995. *Ghosts of Mississippi: The Murder of Medgar Evers, the Trials of Byron de la Beckwith, and the Haunting of the New South.* Boston, MA: Little Brown.

Wilkins, Roy and Ramsey Clark. 1973. *Commission of Inquiry into the Black Panthers and the Police.* New York: Metropolitan Applied Research Center.

Yeingst, William and Lonnie G. Bunch. 1997. "Curating the Recent Past: The Woolworth Lunch Counter, Greensboro, North Carolina." in *Exhibiting Dilemmas: Issues of Representation at the Smithsonian*, eds. Amy Henderson and Adrienne L. Kaeppler. Washington, DC: Smithsonian Institution Press, pp. 143–55.

Zelizer, Barbara. 1995. "Reading the Past Against the Grain: The Shape of Memory Studies." *Critical Studies in Mass Communication* 12: 214–35.

# Index